Roee Rosen

THE BLIND MERCHANT

Sternberg Press

SCHOOL OF THE MUSEUM OF FINE ARTS
AT TUFTS UNIVERSITY

Foreword

The book you have just opened consists of three elements: the complete text of Shakespeare's *The Merchant of Venice*, a supplementary text by Roee Rosen responding to the play, and 145 drawings by the artist. In the book, each double spread includes a drawing on the right side and, on the left, the Shakespearean text alongside Rosen's parasitical text. Rosen's ongoing annotation adopts Shylock's vantage point, and also provides a prologue to the play: before becoming a usurer, Shylock was a Venetian glass merchant until falling victim to a pogrom-like attack, during which his wife was raped and murdered and his eyes were gouged out. Thus, all the drawings depicting scenes in which Shylock is present are blind drawings, line drawings that were executed with closed eyes.

In this early work dating from 1989–1991, now being printed and distributed as a book for the first time, we find Rosen developing some of his interests and sensibilities in a seminal form. Here, long before his cross-gender projects such as *Live and Die as Eva Braun* (1997), where the viewer assumes the persona of Hitler's lover, and more than a decade before he completed the oeuvre of Belgian-Jewish pornographic surrealist painter and novelist Justine Frank (2003), Rosen was already hyperfictionalizing well-established narratives. And not only that, but here we find a Rosen compelled by commentary. What later in his work will become a gallery of female commentators (Anne Kastorp, Joanna Führer-Ha'sfari, and Rosa Chabanova), here appears as the story of a Jewish man, *the* Jewish man—Shylock. Running in parallel to Shakespeare's story, his narrative is a parasitic one, engulfing and hanging from the verses of the original play. The three elements of Shakespeare's complete text of *The Merchant of Venice*, Rosen's supplementary text written around the body of the play, and the 145 drawings together comprise a polyphonic piece in which each element echoes and intertwines with the others. Although the Shakespearean text is reproduced with no alterations, Rosen's text and drawings assume expositional liberties beyond, say, those of Talmudic annotations. One such example would be the Prologue, narrating a prehistory for its protagonist, Shylock. There is no equivalent prologue in Shakespeare, and Rosen's text is juxtaposed with a monologue from *The Jew of Malta* by Christopher Marlowe, in which Barabas recalls his own history (it is, of course, Marlowe who writes this self-incrimination of the repulsive other, the Jewish usurer). The drama of composites results from the dynamics of the relations between the three elements (Text A, Text B, Drawings). There is no attempt, though, to formally blur the autonomy of each element.

Following the prologue, *The Blind Merchant* moves directly into the first act of *The Merchant of Venice*, annotated by the parasite text and illuminated by the drawings. But the story of Shylock's forced conversion is also the story of the increasing tensions, contradictions, struggles, and ultimate incompatibility between the play and the superimposed, foreign voice. On two occasions, those foreign elements choose to "depart" altogether from the original play, and follow their own will. In the second scene of the second act, it is Tubal, Shylock's friend and a marginal character in the play, who becomes a focal point, although Shakespeare has yet to mention him. Tubal is of importance for Rosen partly because he is the only other Jew in the play (Jessica, Shylock's daughter, converts to Christianity) and the only one who does not desert him. In the middle of the third act, the drawings rebel against the authority of the play and take a visit to the zoo, an epiphanic menagerie located at the heart of the book. Another departure occurs toward the end where, in the fifth act, the happy romantic resolutions are neglected in favor of Shylock's hallucinated party.

The parasite text feeds upon the play, and locates itself according to its own taste; it is the text of a foreigner (Rosen's mother tongue being Hebrew). There are two places in the book where use is made of the Hebrew language—inside the drawings. What is being written in those instances is as important as the fact that the projected reader of the book is one who is not familiar with the language, and would be excluded from, and deprived of, a certain perfection, a certain belonging. This friction between the different voices in the book culminates at the end of the play, after Shylock's famous exit in the fourth act. The fifth act is the romantic resolution, but the foreign elements, the parasitical text and the drawings, ignore the finality of Shylock's exit and concentrate exclusively on him.

When Shylock is not on the stage, the drawings are mostly watercolors, with frequent use of other materials, executed, of course, with open eyes. The drawings, being the stage, offer a recognizable cast: Louise Brooks, for instance, "plays" Nerissa, Dirk Bogarde plays Bassanio, and Edward Said appears in a double role, as both the Prince of Morocco and the Prince of Aragon. Shylock himself is an attempt at a blind self-portrait by Rosen, and a gallery of close friends is cast for some of the other characters; for example, his then-wife Emma plays Portia. There are also indications of "set designs" for the different scenes (the "male" Venice pictures are vertical, the "female" Belmont scenes horizontal; slight changes of frame and insertions of other visual devices identify locations). But the gradual deviance of the story resonates in the stage perception, and its "rules" become less and less restrictive as the play proceeds. The final drawings, those of the fifth act, are a blind sequence based on Goya's famous *The Sleep of Reason Produces Monsters* from *Los Caprichos*, a series that ends with the sleeper waking up.

With all its diversions and entanglements, Rosen's *The Blind Merchant* seems to be true to Shakespeare's *The Merchant of Venice* insofar as it follows the basic logic of a play, as a form in search of another form. In the case of a theater play, it is the written text in search of a stage performance, while in the book the written text is juxtaposed with text and image that run parallel and against it in search of another voice that is performed within the book rather than on stage. The cameos and the themes tell of the time when this work was composed and written. This was the time when avant-garde's originality was questioned, when the subaltern were asked to speak, when humor was masochistic once more, when seeing could not but be dialectic, and *Rosencrantz and Guildenstern Are Dead* was released as a film in theaters. That moment, just before Bill Clinton and Silicon Valley took over our imagination, our knowledge, our relationships, and our time, new formations for putting together text and image and archiving them were called for. In the late '80s, before the hyperlink and WYSIWYG, two Jewish thinkers suddenly returned from the other side of the twentieth century—Aby Warburg and Walter Benjamin. The *Atlas* and the *Arcades* were experienced as legends for the new uncharted maps of relations between text and image, fragment and archive, which were about to change completely. The future to come, which is now our all-too-familiar present of perpetually de-historicizing time and space, had to be tackled through archaic and devastated tools of minor histories. In every double spread of *The Blind Merchant*, we can see these tensions contemplated and activated. Rosen's way of working with and against Shakespeare's play through text and image not only gives testimony to that moment, but confronts its demands through the book form.

As mentioned before, we can see in this early work of drawing and text many of the characteristics of Rosen's later work. The device he developed with his blind drawings seems to follow him in his later work. Those familiar with Rosen's painterly talents would argue that *The Blind Merchant* is the odd one out, having nothing to do with the lush stylistic technique of his aquarelles and canvases. But if we refer to some his videos, we find that a similar logic is applied in *The Confessions* (2008), for example, where a kind of blind drawing is taking shape in the form of a surrogate delivery of text by women who do not understand its meaning. These are confessions of the artist told in the first person by three illegal foreign workers residing in Israel, and they deliver the monologues in Hebrew, a language they do not speak, by reading a transliteration of the text in Latin letters from a teleprompter. Auto-puppeteering and ventriloquism have companioned him since.

This underlying logic of a system which contradicts itself has been central for Rosen. In *The Blind Merchant*, it embodies the mode of operation of a sort of mechanical Turk, that chess whiz mentioned at the beginning of Benjamin's theses on the concept of history. This is not the melancholic angel of history flying with his head turned backwards, but the dwarf of theology residing inside the magnificent machine of history. To put it differently, we can finish with a quote from Rosen's adopted forefather, Franz Kafka, who wrote in his diary on November 18, 1917: "There is a goal, but no way; what we call the way is only wavering."

—Joshua Simon

ROEE ROSEN

THE BLINND MERCHANT

1989 -1991

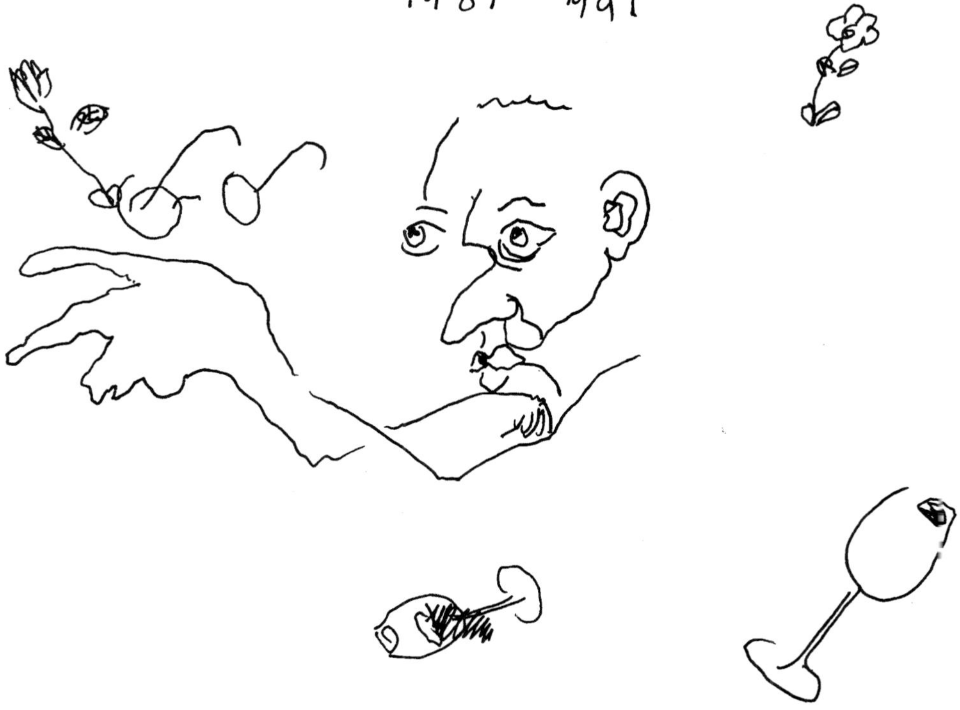

PROLOGUE

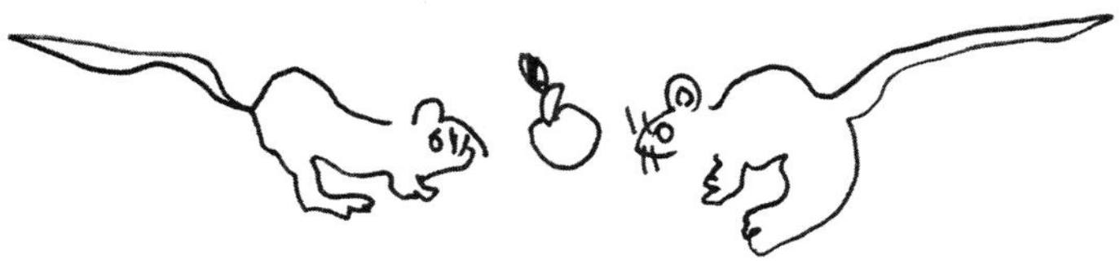

I

And it is him in the picture, Shylock,

and his wife, Leah, and their daughter,

Jessica, just after they have first arrived

in the city, in the house, his house,

and he began trading in glassware,

very optimistic about glass,
    As for myself,
very much taken with
    I walk abroad 'a nights
transparencies,
    And kill sick people
reflections and crystal glitter.
    groaning under walls.

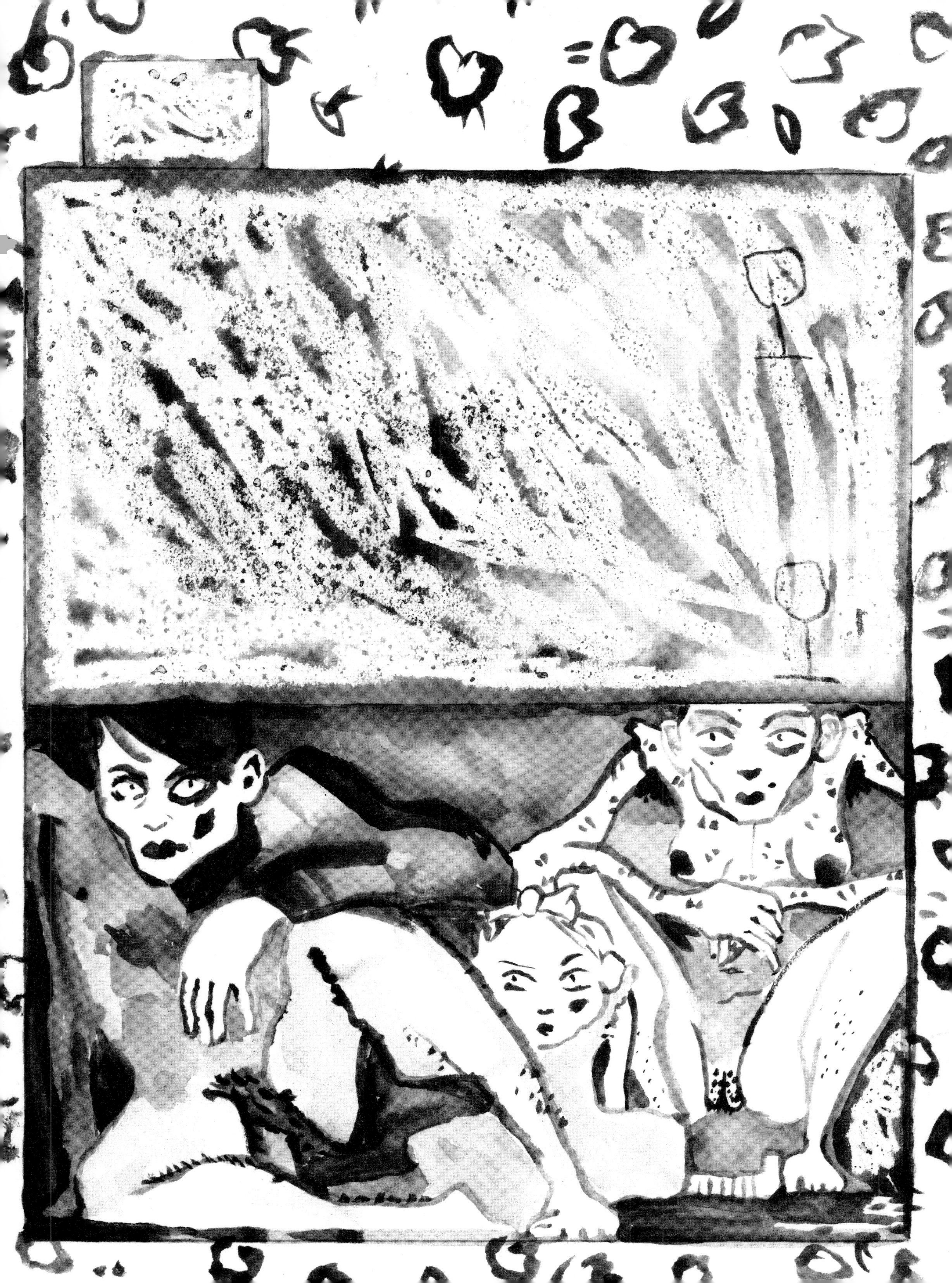

II

And the glass business began to blossom.

Sometimes I go about and poison wells,

And still they did not look

And now and then, to cherish Christian thieves,

to the side, but

I am content to lose some of my crowns

looked to the side all the time.

That I may, walking in my gallery,

And asparagus instead of lettuce,

See 'em go pinioned along by my door.

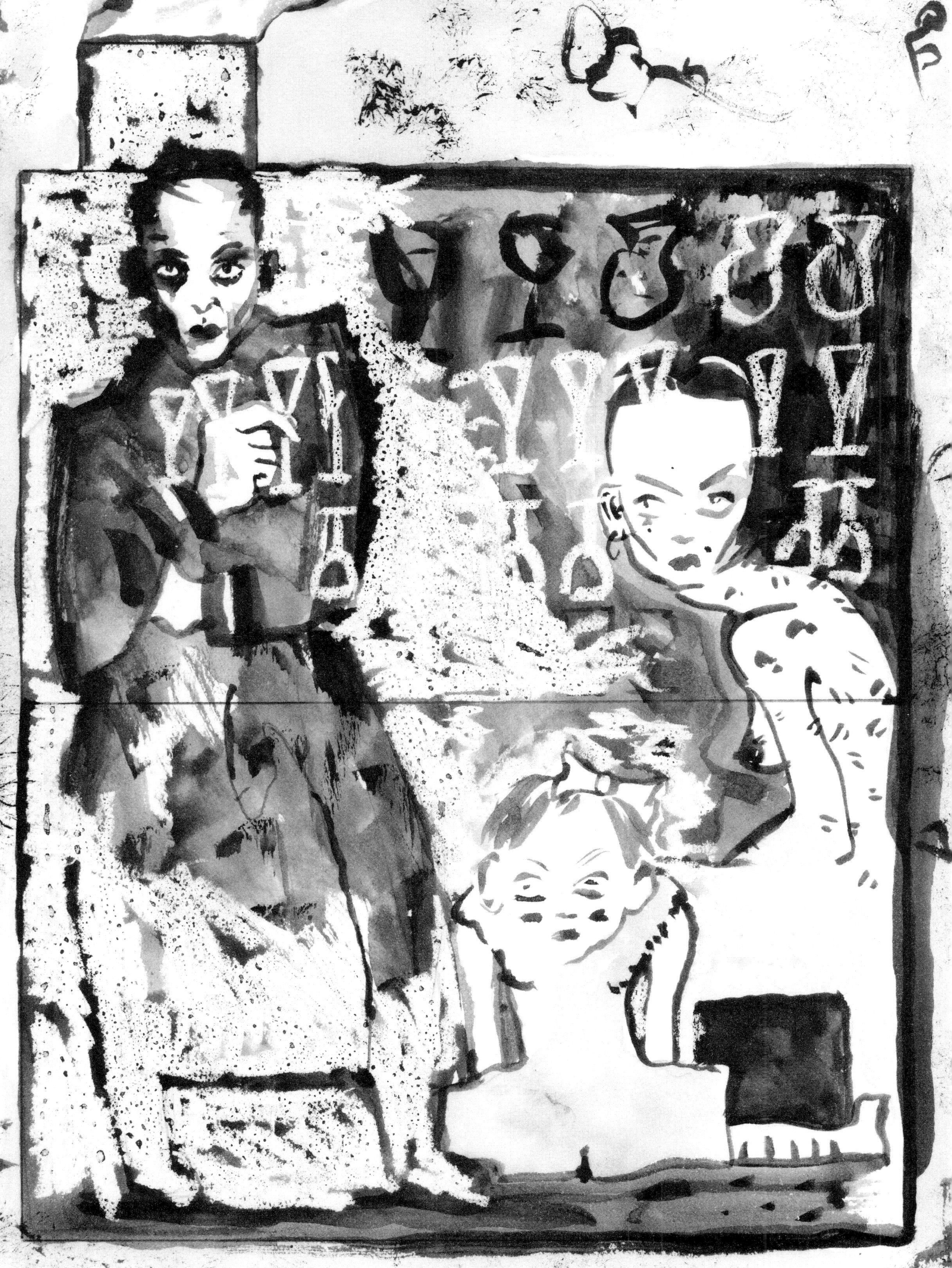

III

and he bought for the child, for Jessica,

Being young, I studied physic and began

he bought a soft doll, not only pretty

To practice first upon the Italian.

to look at, but also very pleasant to touch,

There I enriched the priests with burials

and its smell, the excellent smell of linen,

And always kept the sexton's arms in ure

and for his wife, who cared so much for music,

With digging graves and ringing dead men's knells.

for Leah he purchased a private cellist.

(And once in a while he would sense a dangerous

memory, and would say to himself:

"My parents! My parents!" and he would try to weep,

or he would say to himself: "God! God!" and,

again, try to weep. And once in a while

he would think from right to left),

and he was stroking the glass all the time,

and washing, washing his hands all the time.

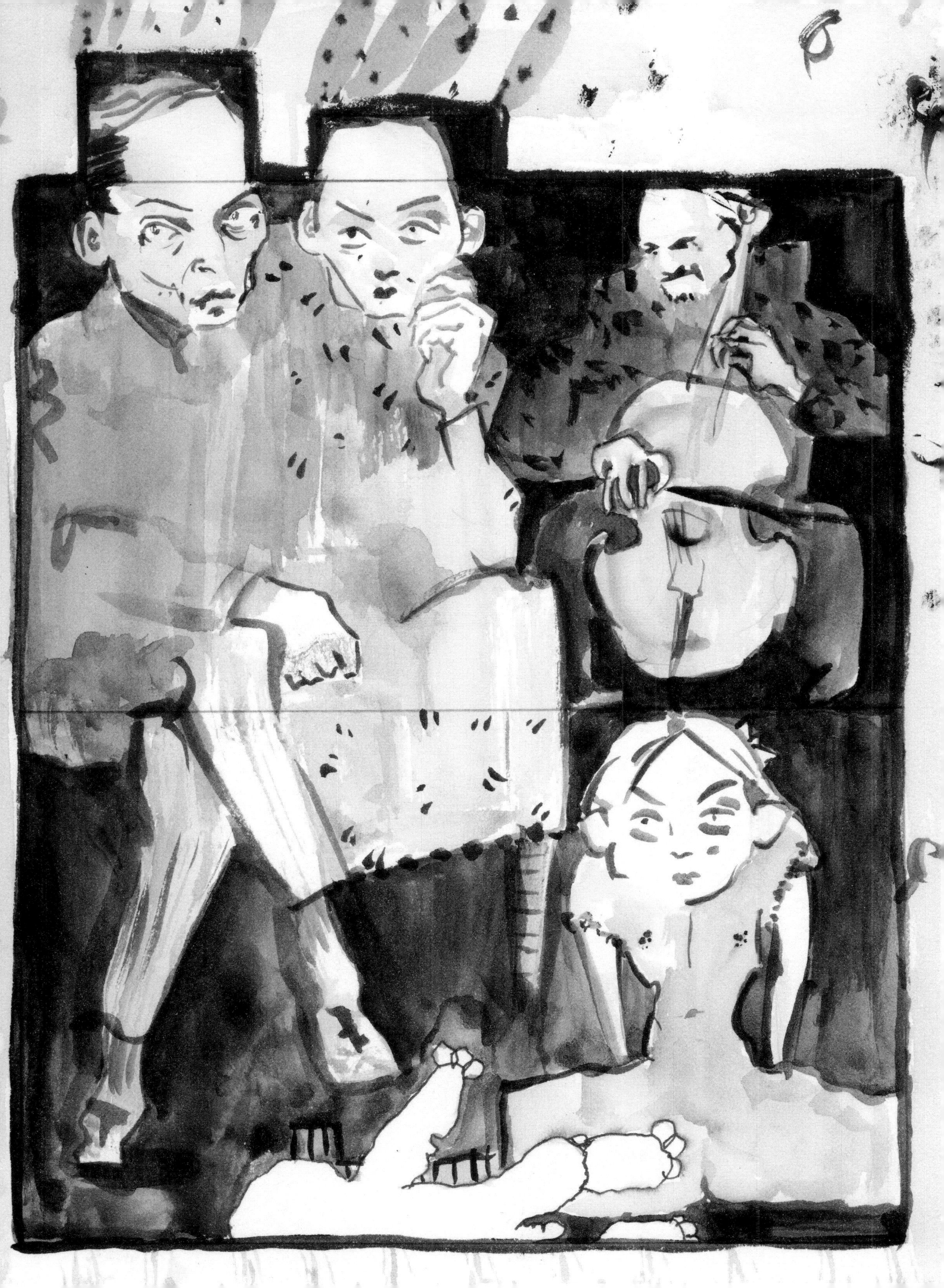

IV

And after that I was an engineer,
And they wore very expensive smiles, but
And in the wars 'twixt France and Germany,
maybe stolen (the smiles), as he knew
Under pretense of helping Charles the Fifth,
that they would come one evening
Slew friend and enemy with my stratagems.

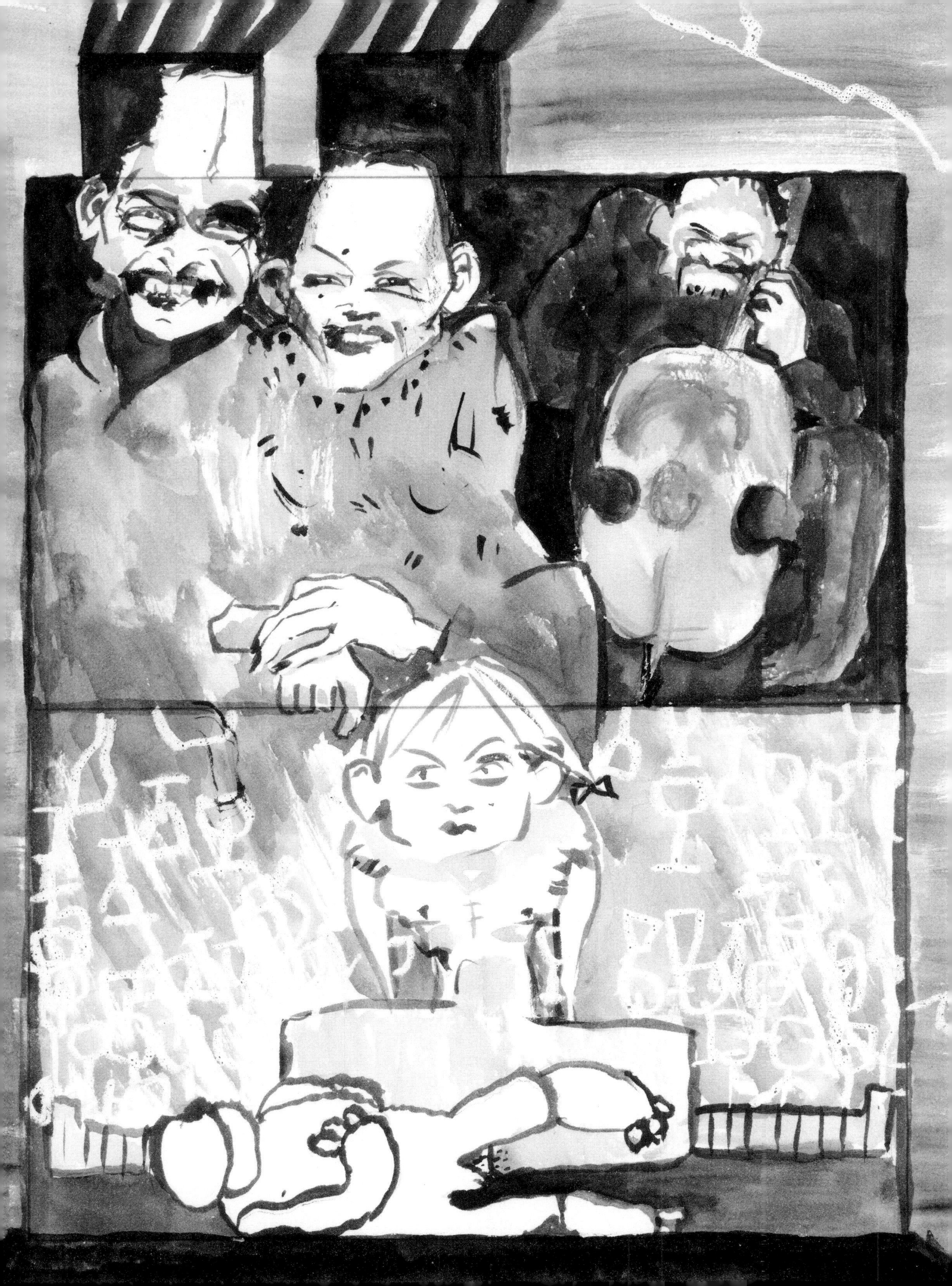

V

Ding,
and they would come,
dong,
they would come and
bell.

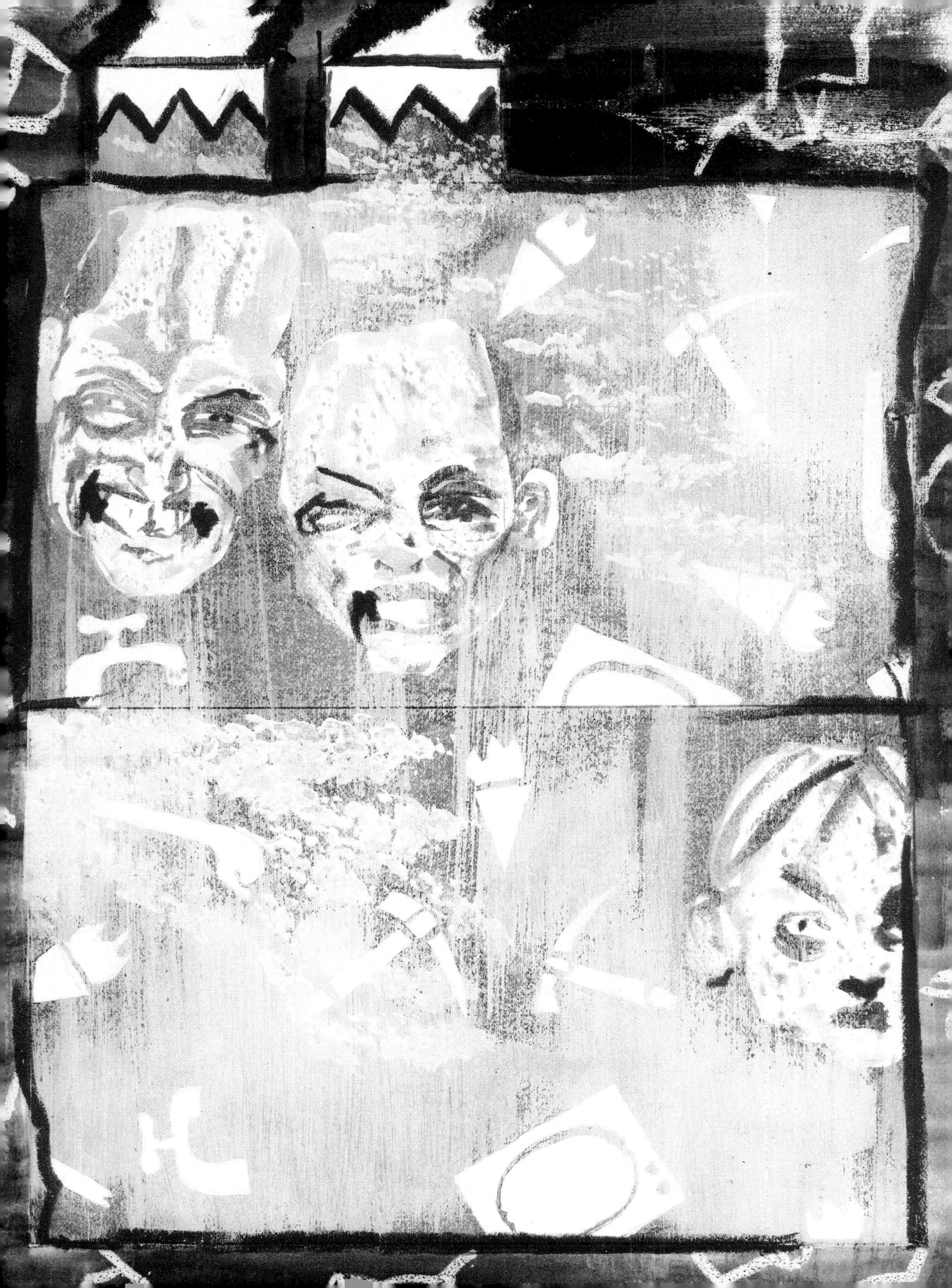

VI

and they came very strong

Tell me where is fancy bred,

and they sang funny funny

Or in the heart or in the head?

and they gouged his eyes

How begot, how nourished?

and to his wife did deeds

Reply, reply.

swift and mighty

It is engender'd in the eyes,

and burned her dead

With gazing fed; and fancy dies

in the same position

In the cradle, where it lies.

in which

Let us all ring fancy's knell;

in which

I'll begin it—Ding, dong, bell.

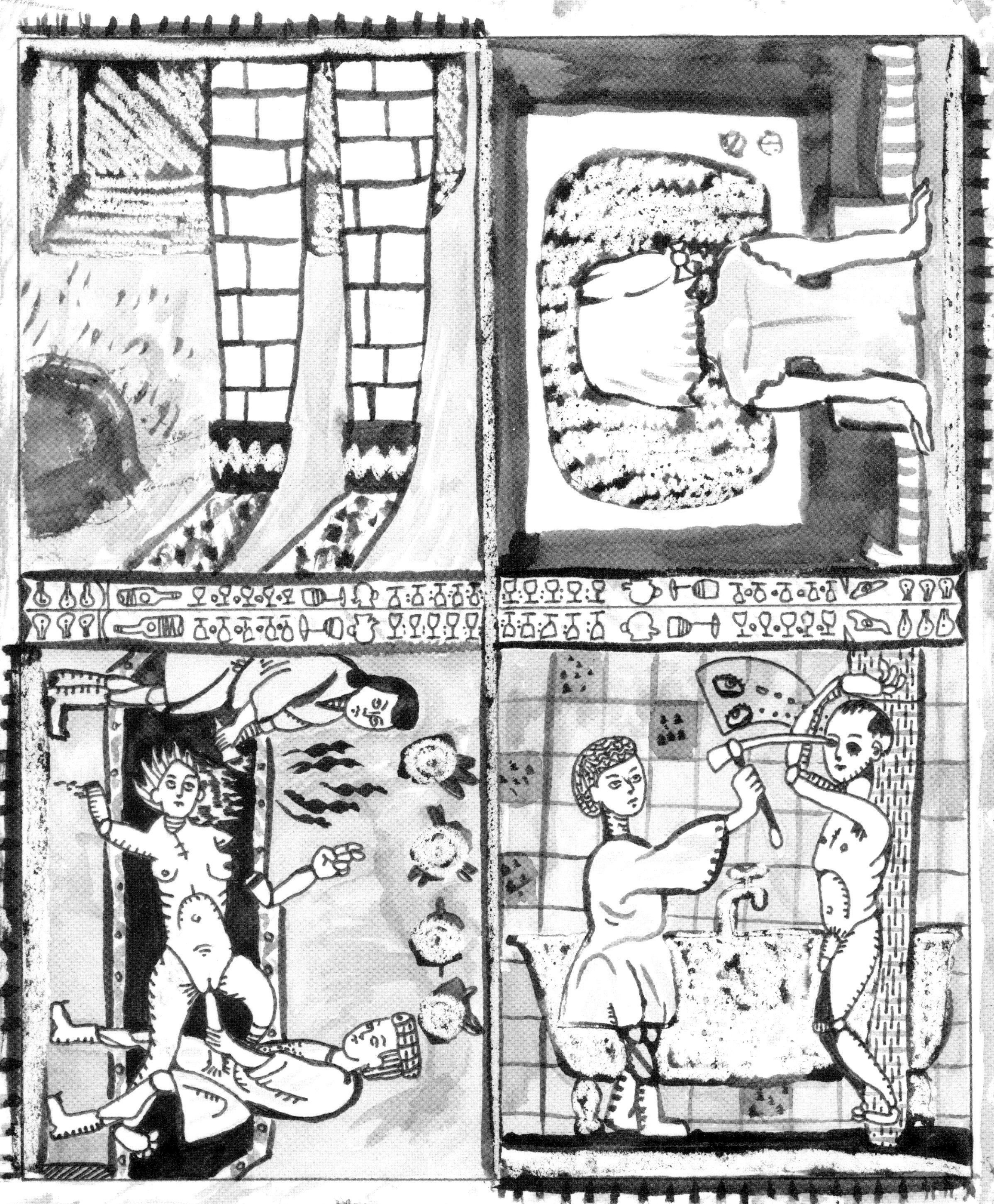

VII

But Jessica. They did not harm Jessica.

Hello daughter. It's Father. Mother went.
    Then after that I was an usurer,
Everything's fine. The glass that's hidden
    And with extorting, cozening, forfeiting,
in the depot is intact. I smell
    And tricks belonging unto brokery,
transparencies and reflections and glitter.
    I filled the jails with bankrouts in a year,
I smell good things coming.
    And with young orphans planted hospitals,
Father smells and loves everything.

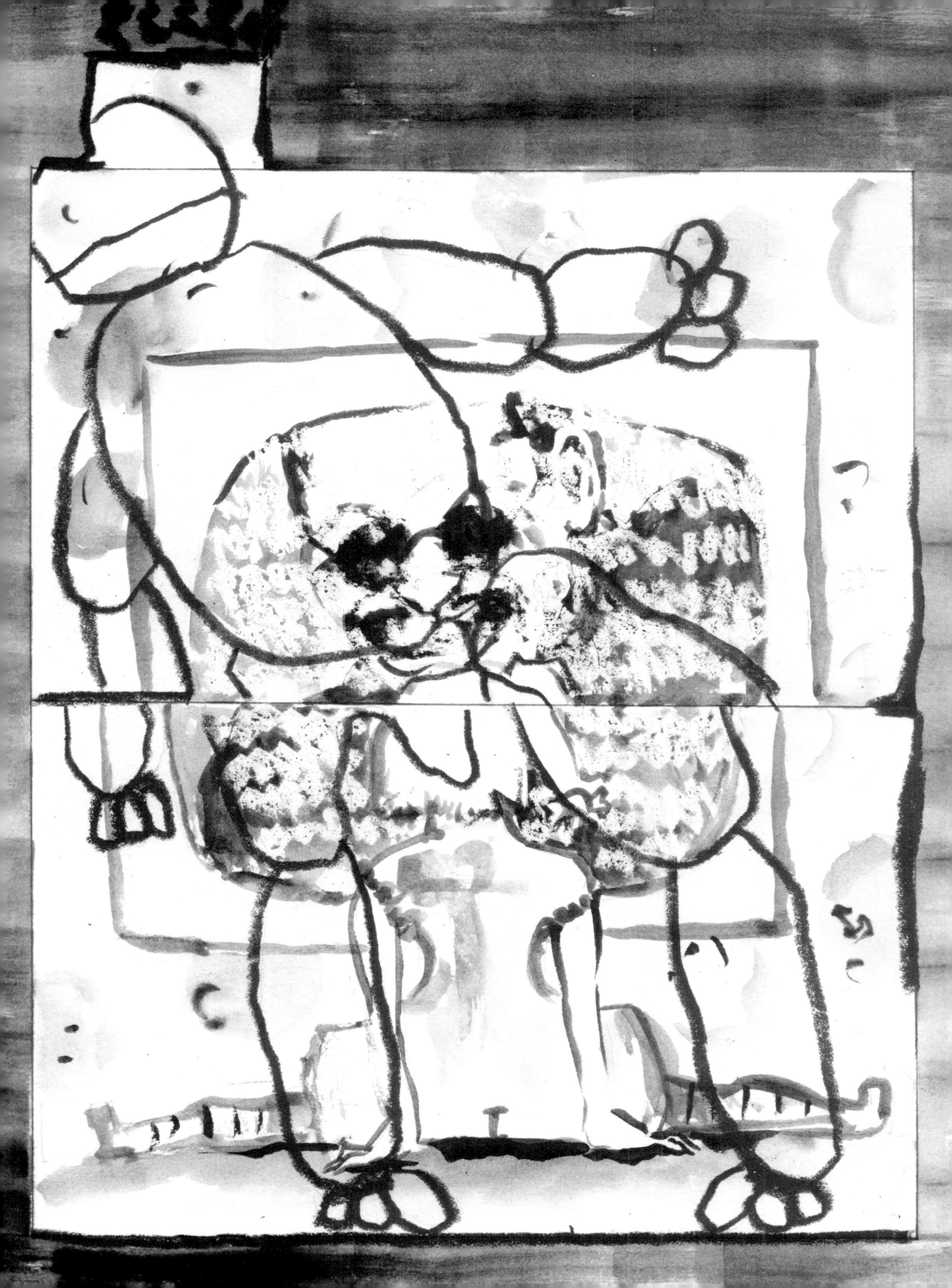

VIII

A blind man is clumsy with glass.

And every moon made,

And the clown-servant would put the glass

some or other mad,

splinters in his soup.

And now and then

And when more glass would break, Shylock

one hang himself for grief,

would spank the child and then he would weep fiercely

Pinning upon his breast

and beg forgiveness. And the child would

a long great scroll,

thrust pins in

How I with interest

the doll and cause him

tormented him.

severe pains in parts,

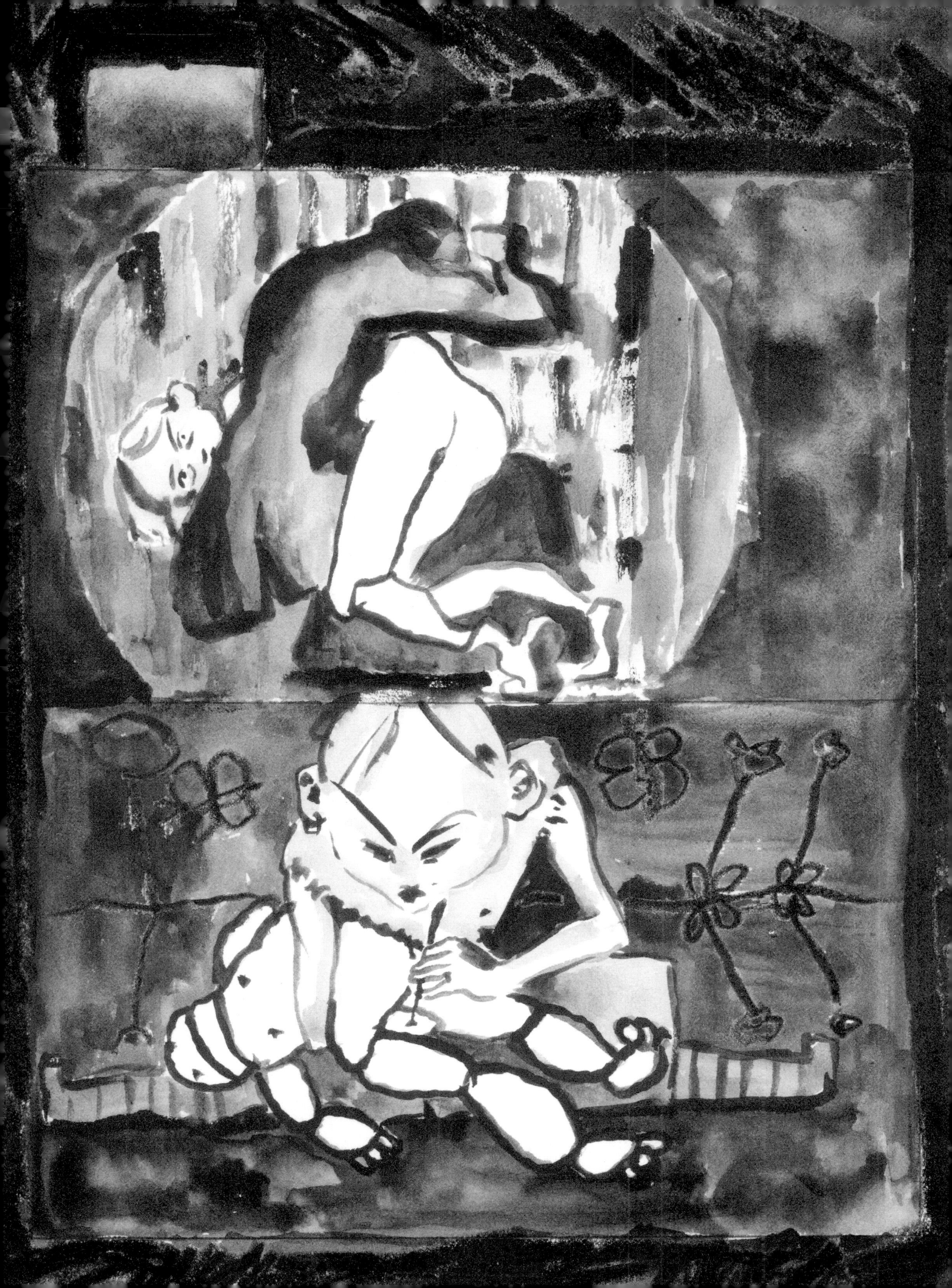

IX

and then he was forbidden glass.

But mark

And the clown-servant taught the child.

how I am blessed

And his beloved mother wrinkled and shrank

for plaguing them:

and died hard and sour. In a different place

I have

altogether. Everything is fine.

as much coin

Everything is fine altogether.

as will buy the town.

I smell.

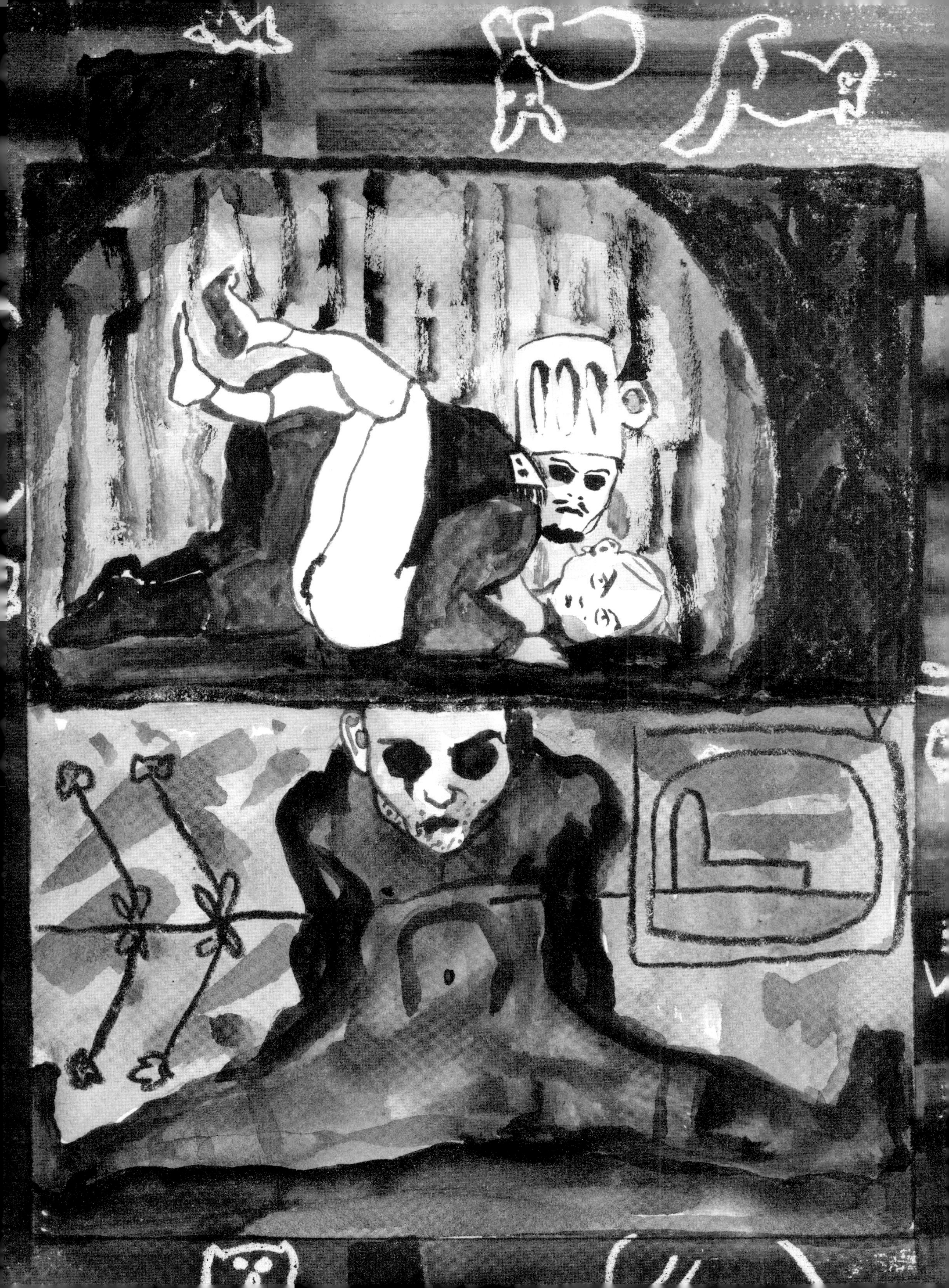

X

Now it is spring.

But tell me now, how hast thou spent thy time?

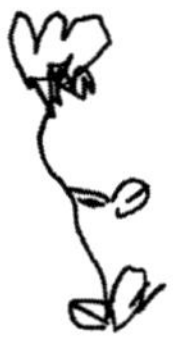

FIRST ACT

SMELL

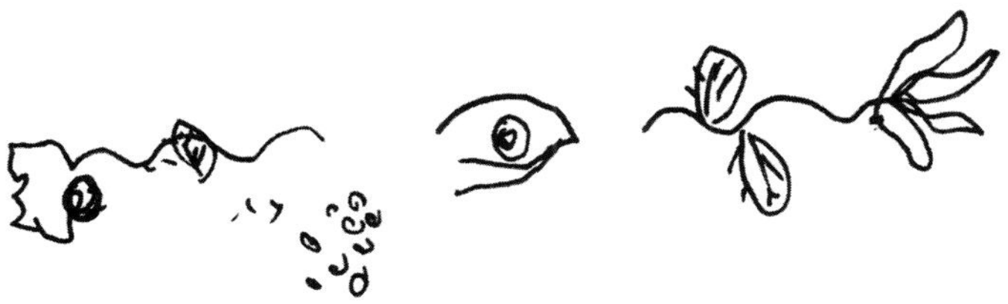

Scene I—Venice. A Street.

Enter Antonio, Salarino, and Salanio.

ANTONIO
In sooth, I know not why I am so sad:
It wearies me; you say it wearies you;
But how I caught it, found it, or came by it,
What stuff 'tis made of, whereof it is born,
I am to learn;
And such a want-wit sadness makes of me,
That I have much ado to know myself.

Very mysterious, this.
It is spring now, and Antonio is young and healthy and a very successful glass merchant and his friends are with him, and yet he is sad. It is mysterious and mysterious. We can actually see, see the sadness like a picture; it is a beautiful sadness. It is sort of big and strong (and gentle and hazy).

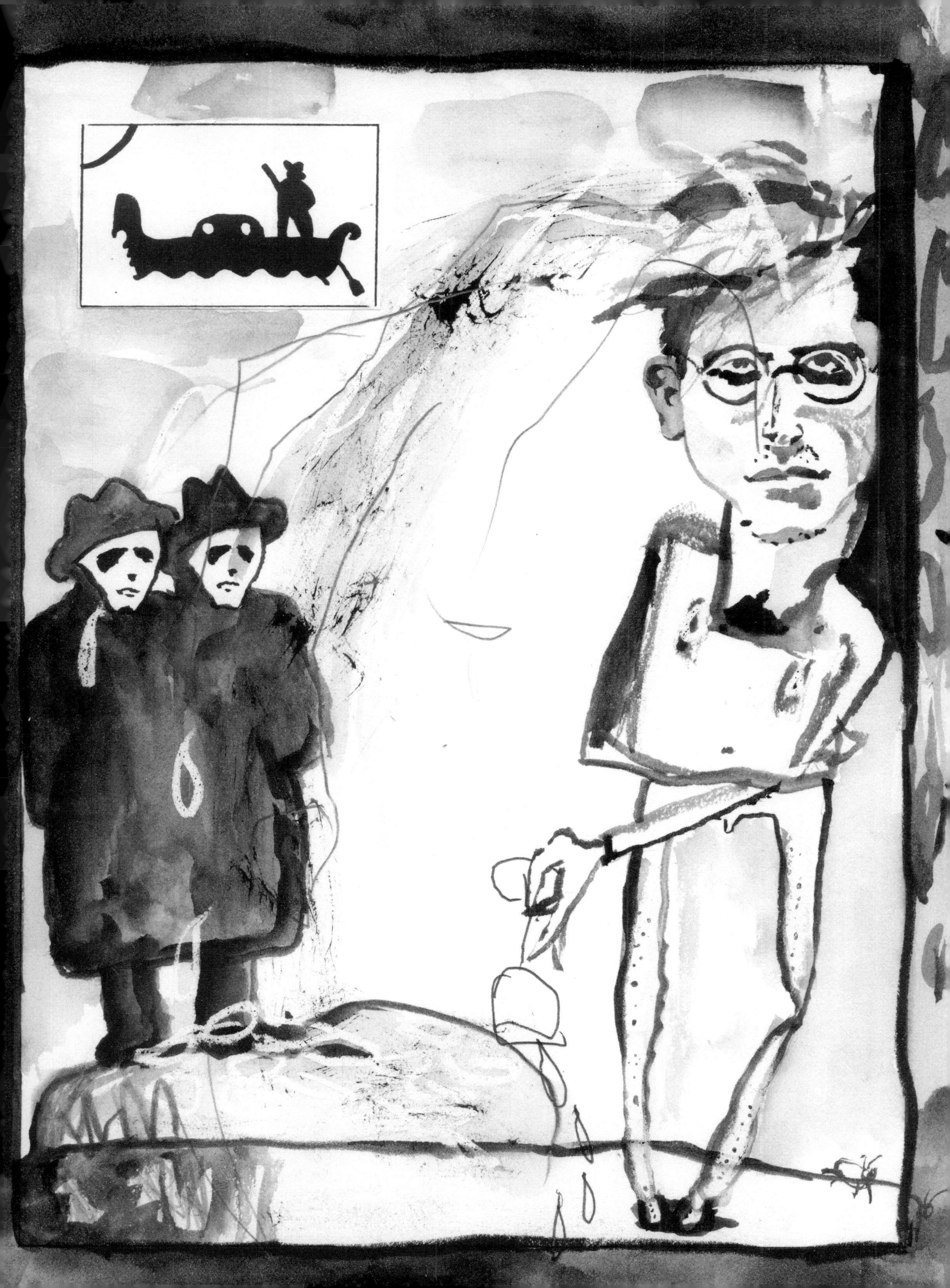

SALARINO
Your mind is tossing on the ocean;
There, where your argosies with portly sail,—
Like signiors and rich burghers on the flood,
Or, as it were, the pageants of the sea,—
Do overpeer the petty traffickers,
That curtsy to them, do them reverence,
As they fly by them with their woven wings.

SALANIO
Believe me, sir, had I such venture forth,
The better part of my affections would
Be with my hopes abroad. I should be still
Plucking the grass to know where sits the wind;
Peering in maps for ports, and piers, and roads;
And every object that might make me fear
Misfortune to my ventures, out of doubt
Would make me sad.

SALARINO
My wind, cooling my broth,
Would blow me to an ague, when I thought
What harm a wind too great might do at sea.
I should not see the sandy hour-glass run
But I should think of shallows and of flats,
And see my wealthy Andrew dock'd in sand
Vailing her high-top lower than her ribs
To kiss her burial. Should I go to church
And see the holy edifice of stone,
And not bethink me straight of dangerous rocks,
Which touching but my gentle vessel's side
Would scatter all her spices on the stream,
Enrobe the roaring waters with my silks;
And, in a word, but even now worth this,
And now worth nothing? Shall I have the thought
To think on this, and shall I lack the thought
That such a thing bechanc'd would make me sad?
But tell not me: I know Antonio
Is sad to think upon his merchandise.

ANTONIO
Believe me, no: I thank my fortune for it,
My ventures are not in one bottom trusted,
Nor to one place; nor is my whole estate
Upon the fortune of this present year:
Therefore, my merchandise makes me not sad.

Antonio suspects, perhaps rightly, that Salerio and Solanio are trying, not intentionally perhaps, to confuse the alluring sadness with something else, smaller and stiffer, and yet, this sadness here, it is a sadness worthy of its name, surely not one that relies on estates. Sadness, sadness here. You cannot bargain with it. Antonio shivers,

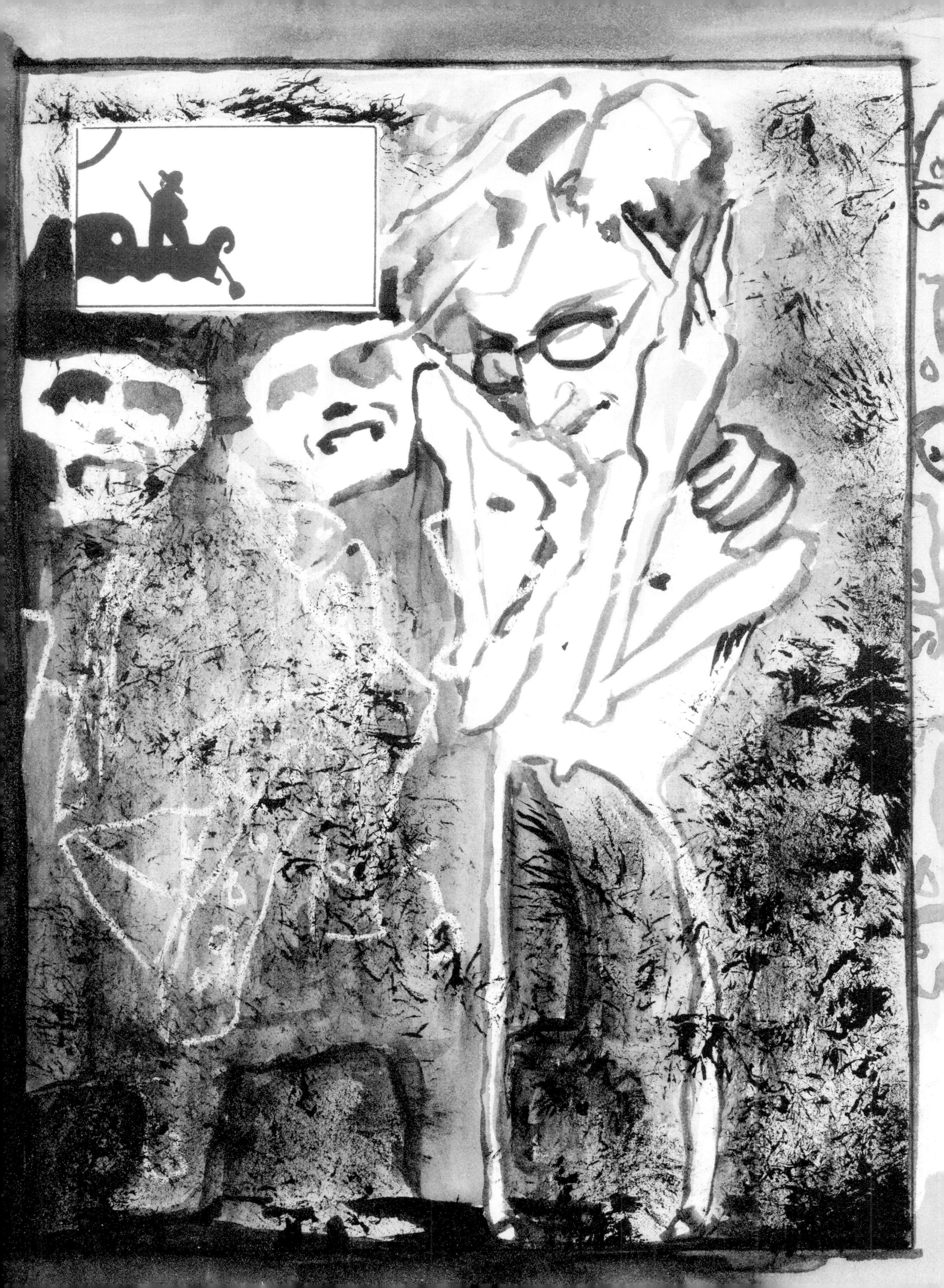

SALARINO
Why, then you are in love.

ANTONIO
Fie, fie!

SALARINO
Not in love neither? Then let's say you are sad,
Because you are not merry: and 'twere as easy
For you to laugh and leap, and say you are merry,
Because you are not sad. Now, by two-headed Janus,
Nature hath fram'd strange fellows in her time:
Some that will evermore peep through their eyes
And laugh like parrots at a bag-piper,
And other of such vinegar aspect
That they'll not show their teeth in way of smile,
Though Nestor swear the jest be laughable.

really shivers when Salerio and Solanio insinuate his sadness stems from carnal matters.
Big, poor sadness.
Fragile sadness, surrounded by enemies.

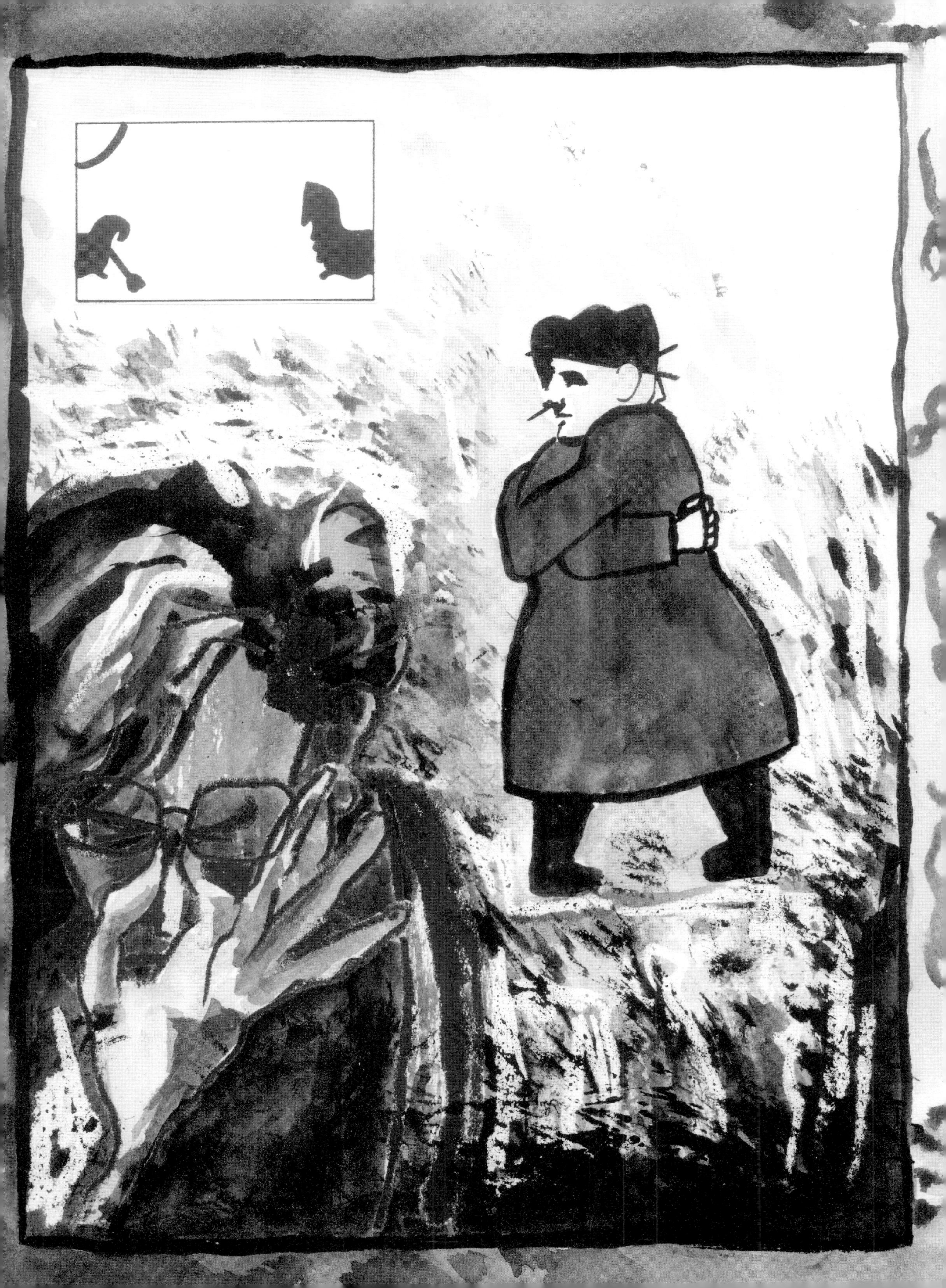

Enter Bassanio, Lorenzo, and Gratiano.

SALANIO
Here comes Bassanio, your most noble kinsman,
Gratiano, and Lorenzo. Fare ye well:
We leave you now with better company.

SALARINO
I would have stay'd till I had made you merry,
If worthier friends had not prevented me.

ANTONIO
Your worth is very dear in my regard.
I take it, your own business calls on you,
And you embrace the occasion to depart.

SALARINO
Good morrow, my good lords.

BASSANIO
Good signiors both, when shall we laugh? say when?
You grow exceeding strange: must it be so?

SALARINO
We'll make our leisures to attend on yours.

Exeunt Salarino and Salanio.

LORENZO
My Lord Bassanio, since you have found Antonio,
We too will leave you; but, at dinner-time,
I pray you, have in mind where we must meet.

BASSANIO
I will not fail you.

And when all those people are compacted into the street, we may fear even more for the sadness, but somehow it arouses the sadness still more, it strengthens and grows. And we realize that the sadness is related in some mysterious way to Bassanio, and that all the noise and people around are only a form of delay, and the delay is related to the sadness.

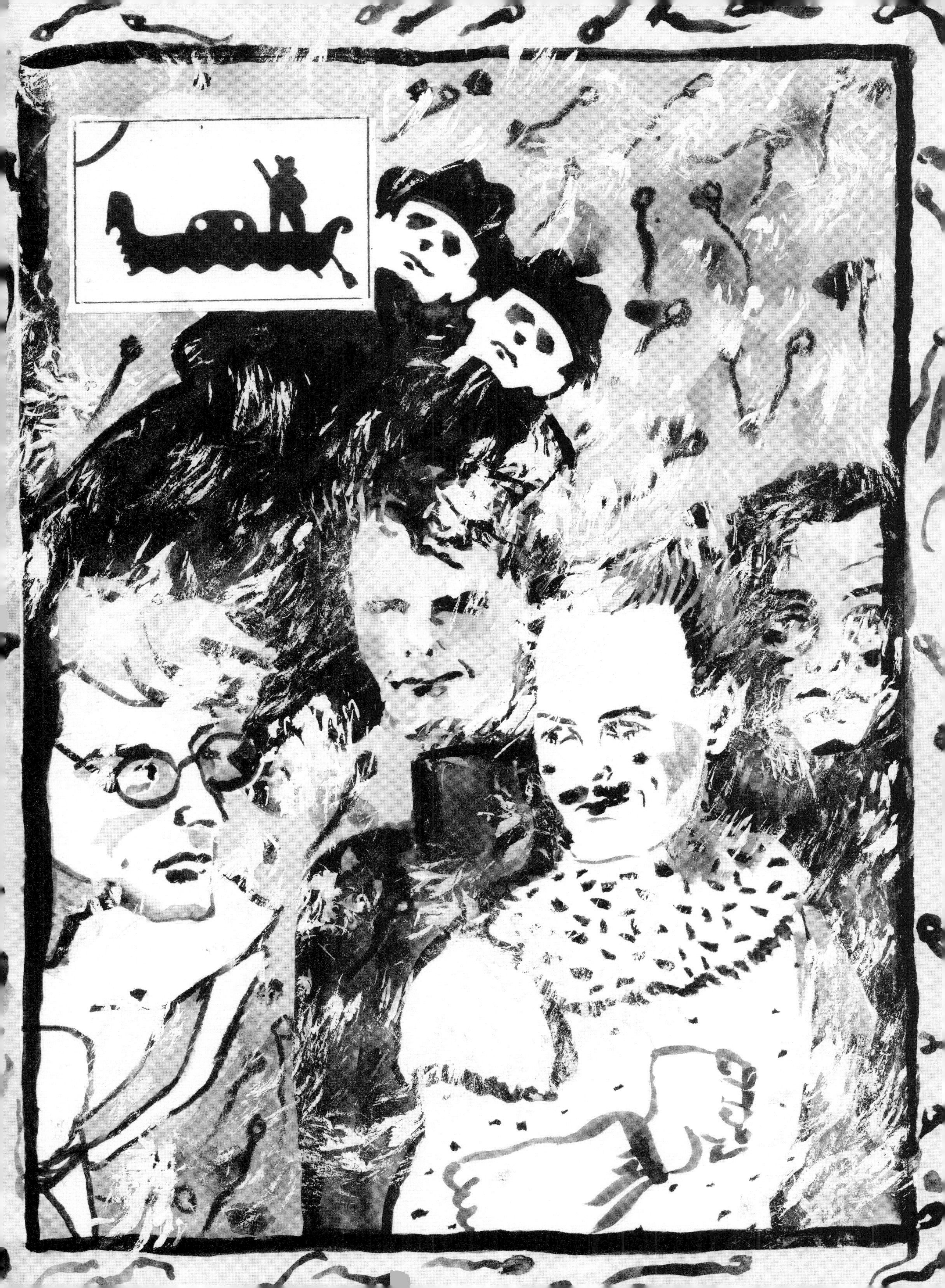

GRATIANO
You look not well, Signior Antonio;
You have too much respect upon the world:
They lose it that do buy it with much care:
Believe me, you are marvellously chang'd.

ANTONIO
I hold the world but as the world, Gratiano;
A stage where every man must play a part,
And mine a sad one.

GRATIANO
Let me play the fool:
With mirth and laughter let old wrinkles come,
And let my liver rather heat with wine
Than my heart cool with mortifying groans.
Why should a man, whose blood is warm within,
Sit like his grandsire cut in alabaster?
Sleep when he wakes, and creep into the jaundice
By being peevish? I tell thee what, Antonio—
I love thee, and it is my love that speaks—
There are a sort of men whose visages
Do cream and mantle like a standing pond,
And do a wilful stillness entertain,
With purpose to be dress'd in an opinion
Of wisdom, gravity, profound conceit;
As who should say, 'I am Sir Oracle,
And when I ope my lips let no dog bark!'
O, my Antonio, I do know of these,
That therefore only are reputed wise
For saying nothing; when, I am very sure,
If they should speak, would almost damn those ears
Which, hearing them, would call their brothers fools.
I'll tell thee more of this another time:
But fish not, with this melancholy bait,
For this fool-gudgeon, this opinion.
Come, good Lorenzo. Fare ye well awhile:
I'll end my exhortation after dinner.

"I am being sustained," says Antonio to himself and to the sadness, and feels a tickle in the thin veins of his eyes. Gratiano's stage-blather does not bother him. On the contrary, it is a price of sorts, and Antonio, Antonio loves to pay.

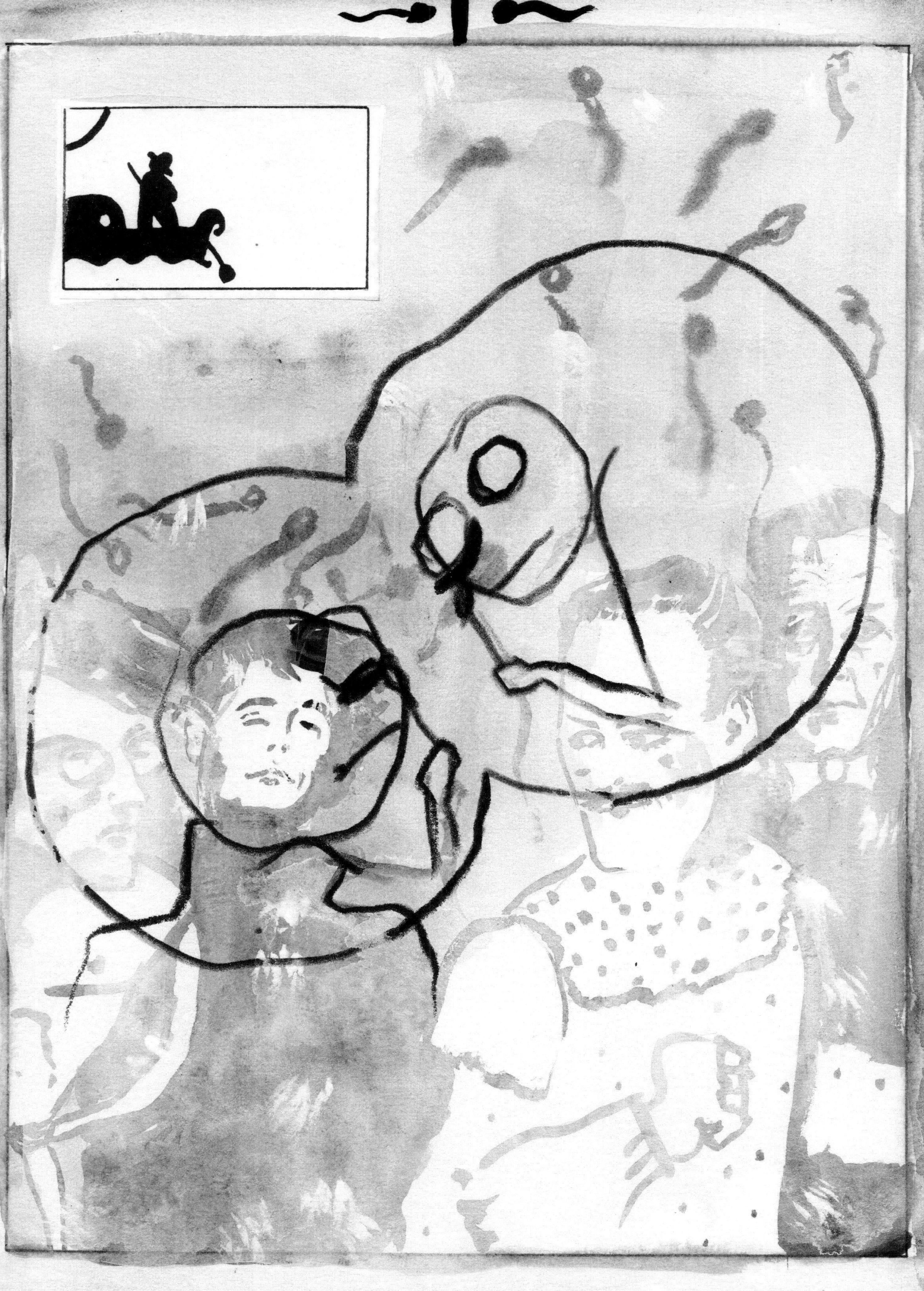

LORENZO
Well, we will leave you then till dinner-time.
I must be one of these same dumb-wise men,
For Gratiano never lets me speak.

GRATIANO
Well, keep me company but two years moe,
Thou shalt not know the sound of thine own tongue.

ANTONIO
Farewell: I'll grow a talker for this gear.

GRATIANO
Thanks, i' faith; for silence is only commendable
In a neat's tongue dried and a maid not vendible.

Exeunt Gratiano and Lorenzo.

ANTONIO
Is that anything now?

BASSANIO
Gratiano speaks an infinite deal of nothing, more than any man in all Venice. His reasons are as two grains of wheat hid in two bushels of chaff: you shall seek all day ere you find them, and, when you have them, they are not worth the search.

ANTONIO
Well, tell me now, what lady is the same
To whom you swore a secret pilgrimage,
That you to-day promis'd to tell me of?

BASSANIO
'Tis not unknown to you, Antonio,
How much I have disabled mine estate,
By something showing a more swelling port
Than my faint means would grant continuance:
Nor do I now make moan to be abridg'd
From such a noble rate; but my chief care
Is, to come fairly off from the great debts
Wherein my time, something too prodigal,
Hath left me gag'd. To you, Antonio,
I owe the most, in money and in love;
And from your love I have a warranty
To unburthen all my plots and purposes
How to get clear of all the debts I owe.

And when Gratiano and Lorenzo exit, Antonio says to himself, "I am being sustained some more," and to the sadness he says, "It's getting closer, something is coming," he says to the sadness, and the sadness is content.

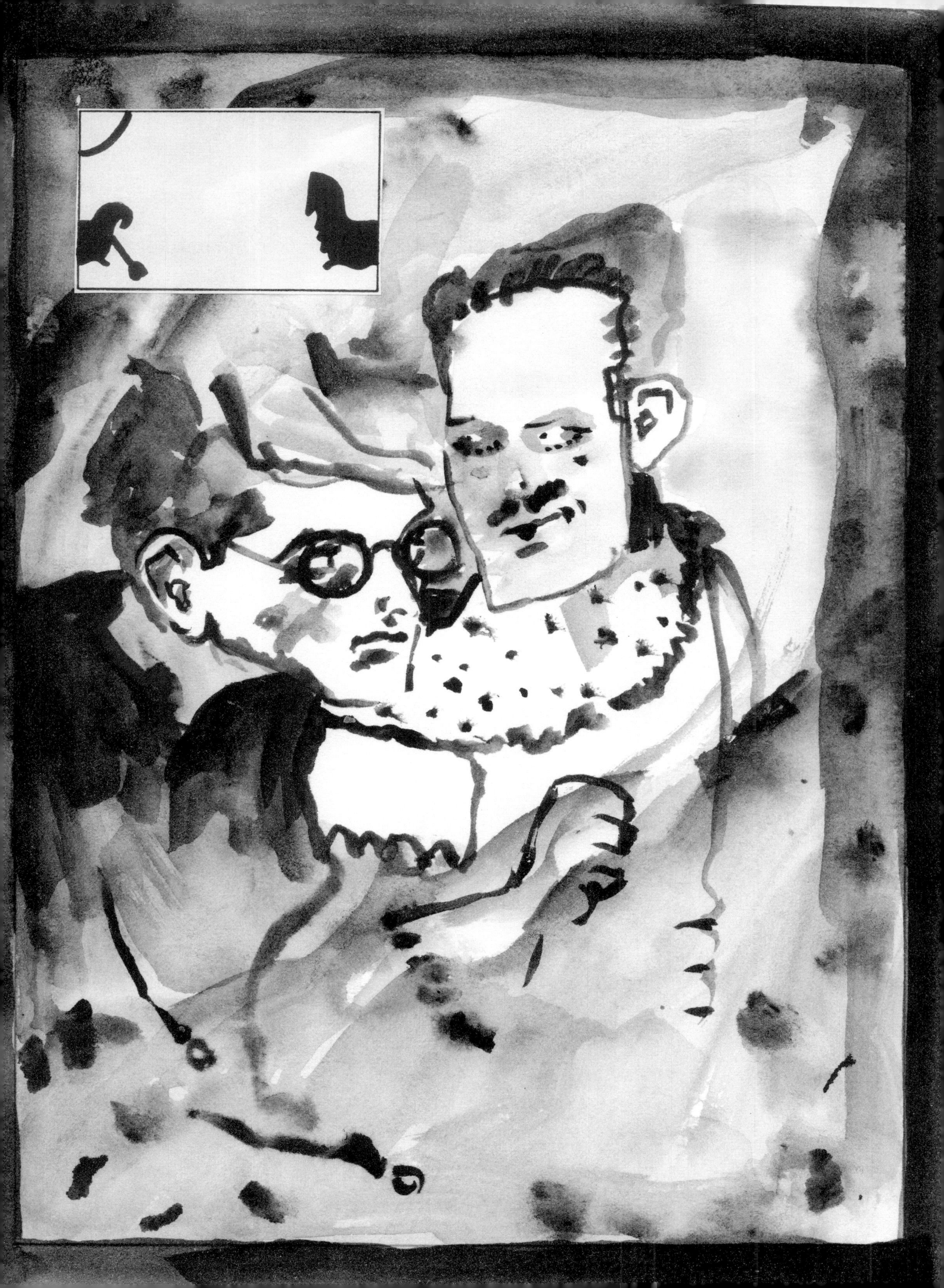

ANTONIO
I pray you, good Bassanio, let me know it;
And if it stand, as you yourself still do,
Within the eye of honour, be assur'd,
My purse, my person, my extremest means,
Lie all unlock'd to your occasions.

BASSANIO
In my school-days, when I had lost one shaft,
I shot his fellow of the self-same flight
The self-same way with more advised watch,
To find the other forth, and by adventuring both,
I oft found both. I urge this childhood proof,
Because what follows is pure innocence.
I owe you much, and, like a wilful youth,
That which I owe is lost; but if you please
To shoot another arrow that self way
Which you did shoot the first, I do not doubt,
As I will watch the aim, or to find both,
Or bring your latter hazard back again,
And thankfully rest debtor for the first.

ANTONIO
You know me well, and herein spend but time
To wind about my love with circumstance;
And out of doubt you do me now more wrong
In making question of my uttermost
Than if you had made waste of all I have:
Then do but say to me what I should do
That in your knowledge may by me be done,
And I am prest unto it: therefore speak.

And as Bassanio delays the matter some more, as Bassanio titillates him gently with fables, Antonio says to himself, "I am being sustained, sustained!" and to the sadness he says, "We are being tortured!"—and the sadness is happy.

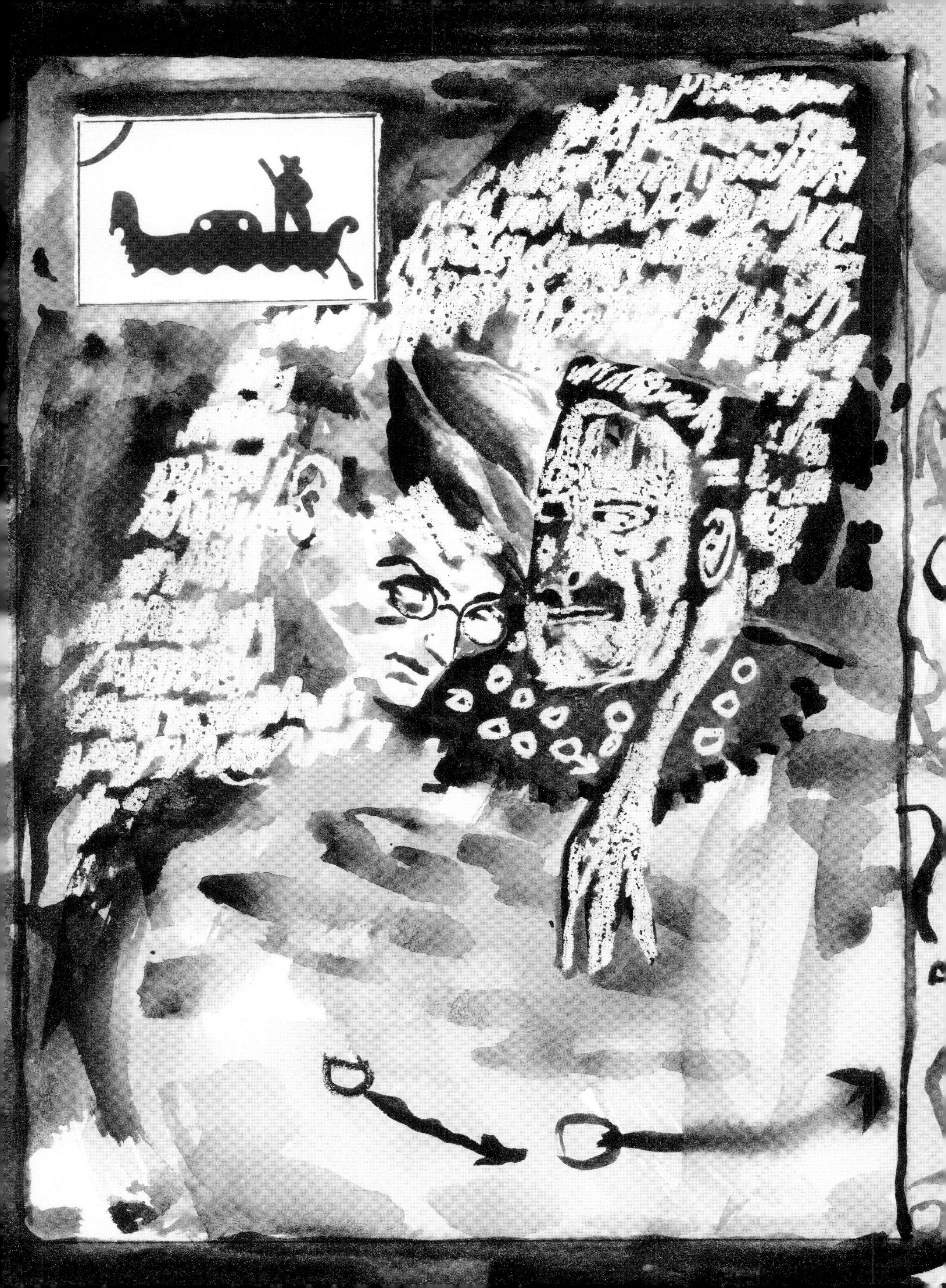

BASSANIO
In Belmont is a lady richly left,
And she is fair, and, fairer than that word,
Of wondrous virtues: sometimes from her eyes
I did receive fair speechless messages:
Her name is Portia; nothing undervalu'd
To Cato's daughter, Brutus' Portia:
Nor is the wide world ignorant of her worth,
For the four winds blow in from every coast
Renowned suitors; and her sunny locks
Hang on her temples like a golden fleece;
Which makes her seat of Belmont Colchos' strond,
And many Jasons come in quest of her.
O my Antonio! had I but the means
To hold a rival place with one of them,
I have a mind presages me such thrift,
That I should questionless be fortunate.

**We can already see.
We can already see.
We can already see barely. But see.
And the sadness is decomposed in the image of a sweet tear. The sadness is decomposed and composed and decomposed.**

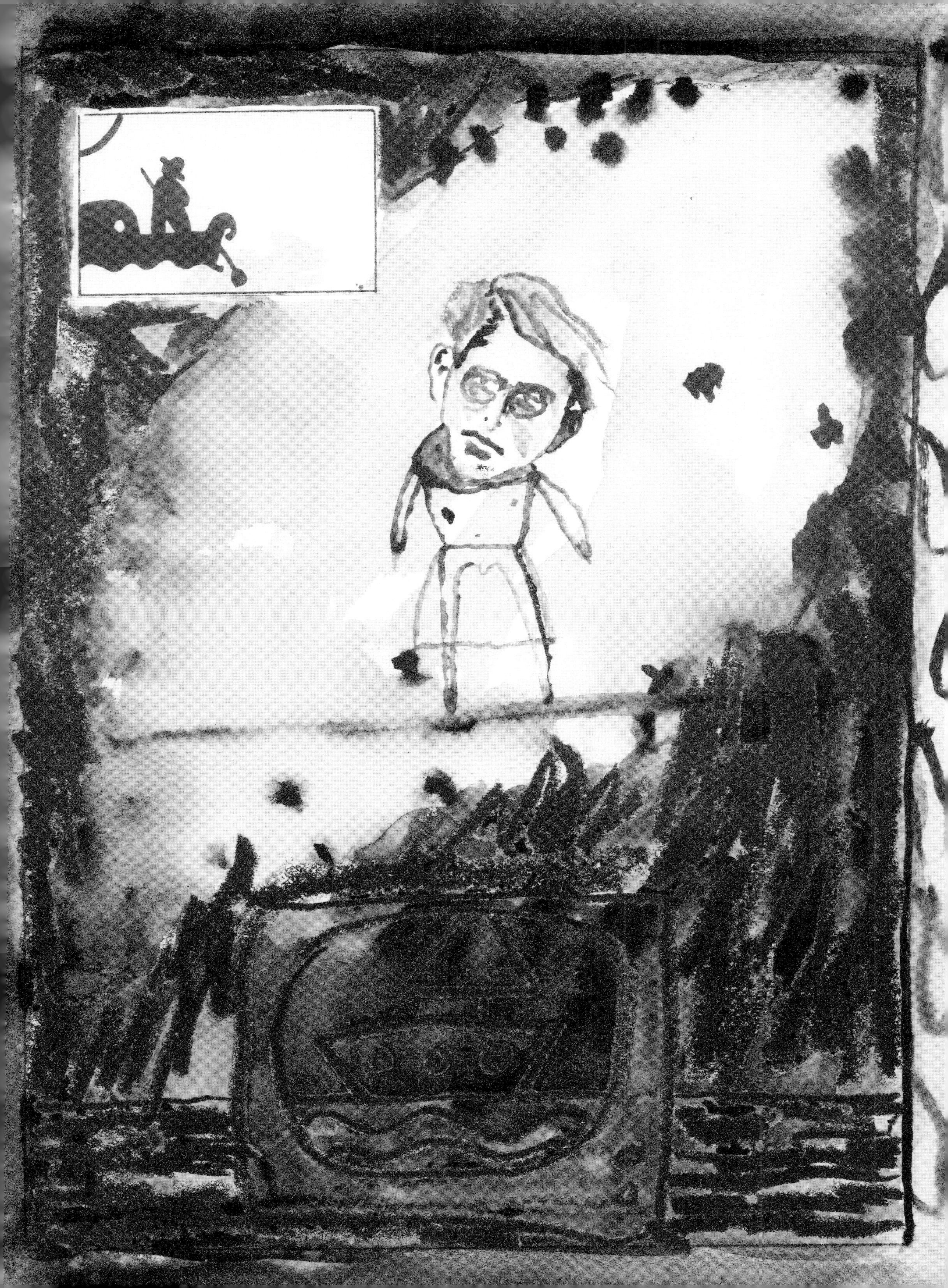

ANTONIO
Thou knowest that all my fortunes are at sea;
Neither have I money, nor commodity
To raise a present sum: therefore go forth;
Try what my credit can in Venice do:
That shall be rack'd, even to the uttermost,
To furnish thee to Belmont, to fair Portia.
Go, presently inquire, and so will I,
Where money is, and I no question make
To have it of my trust or for my sake.

As Antonio loves to pay.

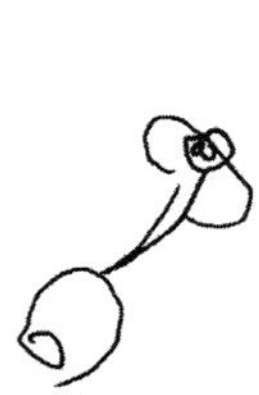

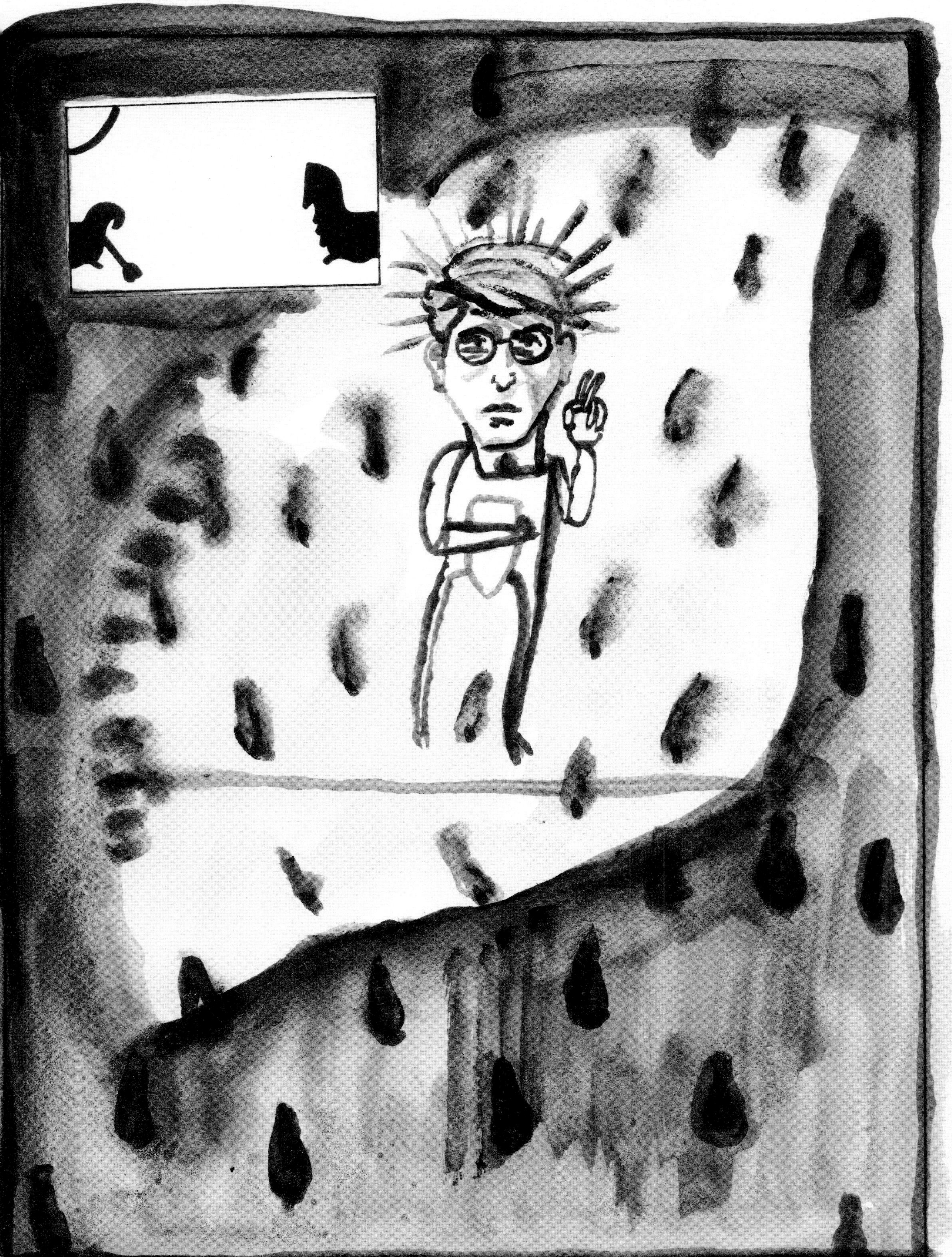

Scene II—Belmont. A Room in Portia's House.

Enter Portia and Nerissa.

PORTIA
By my troth, Nerissa, my little body is aweary of this great world.

"My little body is aweary," says Portia—
and we wonder, why say "little," for
instance?
Is it modesty here, or a kind of royal
pampering, demanding sympathy? And
why say "my body"? Antonio, one may
think, is weary in a more general, or
more spiritual, manner, and here—
a weary body?
We wonder, but anyhow we smell a
different smell, thicker and sticky and
different.

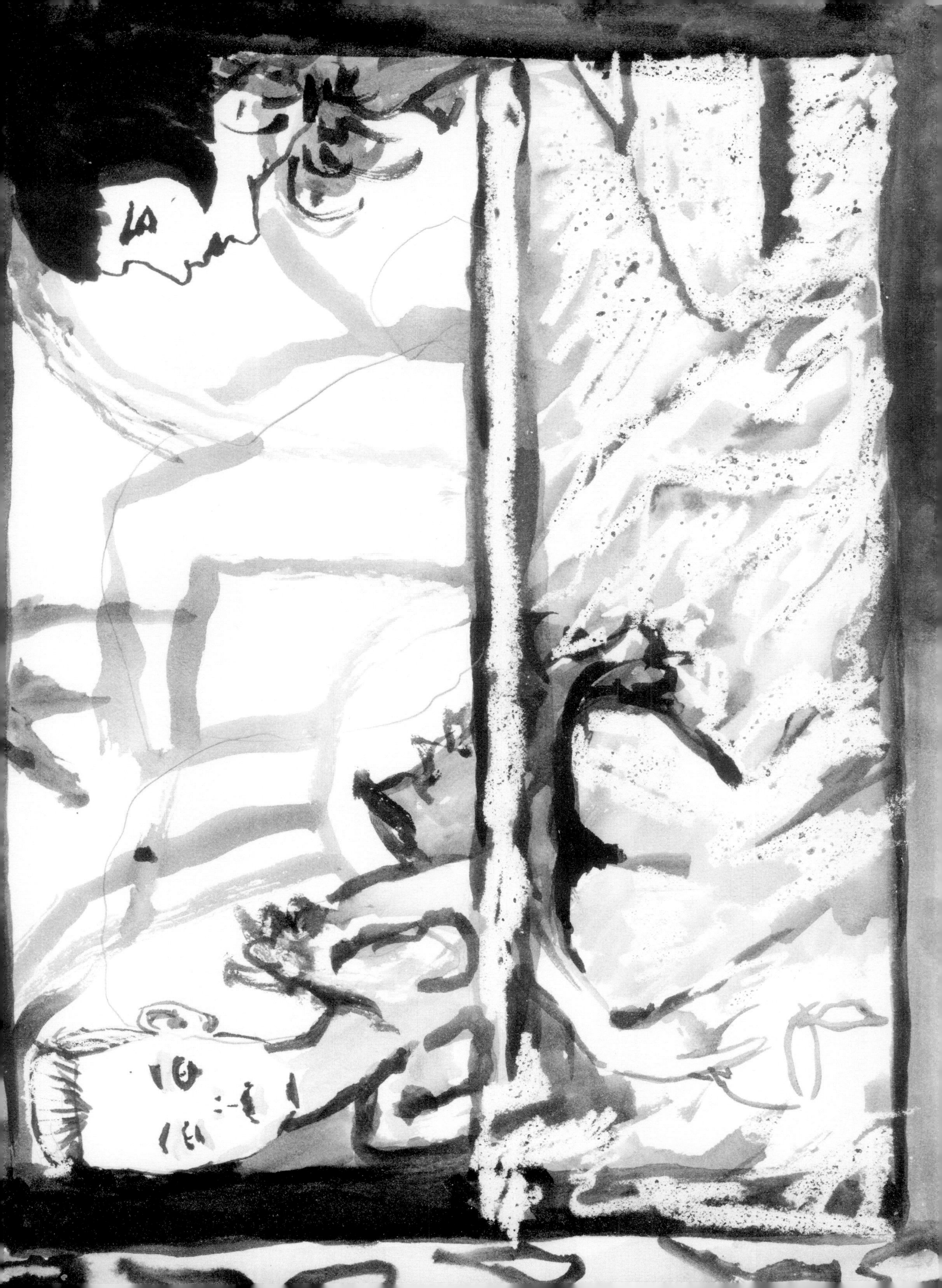

NERISSA
You would be, sweet madam, if your miseries were in the same abundance as your good fortunes are: and yet, for aught I see, they are as sick that surfeit with too much as they that starve with nothing. It is no mean happiness therefore, to be seated in the mean: superfluity comes sooner by white hairs, but competency lives longer.

PORTIA
Good sentences and well pronounced.

NERISSA
They would be better if well followed.

Nerissa says, "They would be better if well followed," and we may ask—is this a reproach? And we may ask—what is the origin of the reproach? Is it the bitter servant's reproach, the haughtiness of hard life? Or maybe the reproach itself is the required service?

And maybe it is not a reproach after all, but rather a code, a code of private jokes, somehow related to the thick smell. The thick smell stands still.

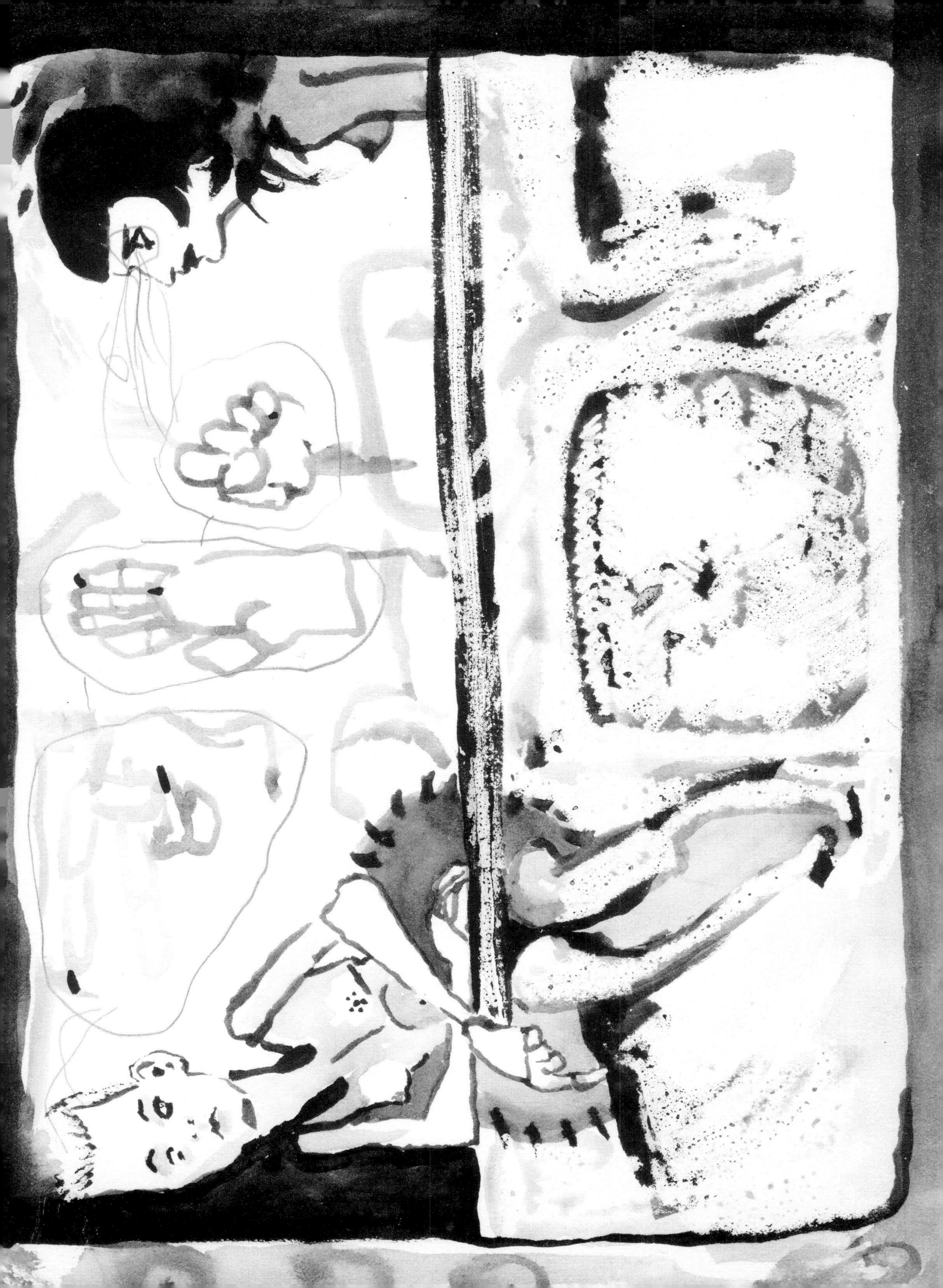

PORTIA

If to do were as easy as to know what were good to do, chapels had been churches, and poor men's cottages princes' palaces. It is a good divine that follows his own instructions: I can easier teach twenty what were good to be done, than be one of the twenty to follow mine own teaching. The brain may devise laws for the blood, but a hot temper leaps o'er a cold decree: such a hare is madness the youth, to skip o'er the meshes of good counsel the cripple. But this reasoning is not in the fashion to choose me a husband. O me, the word 'choose!' I may neither choose whom I would nor refuse whom I dislike; so is the will of a living daughter curbed by the will of a dead father. Is it not hard, Nerissa, that I cannot choose one nor refuse none?

NERISSA

Your father was ever virtuous, and holy men at their death have good inspirations; therefore, the lottery that he hath devised in these three chests of gold, silver, and lead, whereof who chooses his meaning chooses you, will, no doubt, never be chosen by any rightly but one who you shall rightly love. But what warmth is there in your affection towards any of these princely suitors that are already come?

PORTIA

I pray thee, over-name them, and as thou namest them, I will describe them; and, according to my description, level at my affection.

"It is not hard..." says Portia, but by now, by now we already start to realize, perhaps, that it is indeed a kind of joke, or rather, a whole comedy. As if something, we sense, was written in advance, and Portia and Nerissa, they know, while they are reciting, they know everything in advance, here indeed is a tasteless joke,

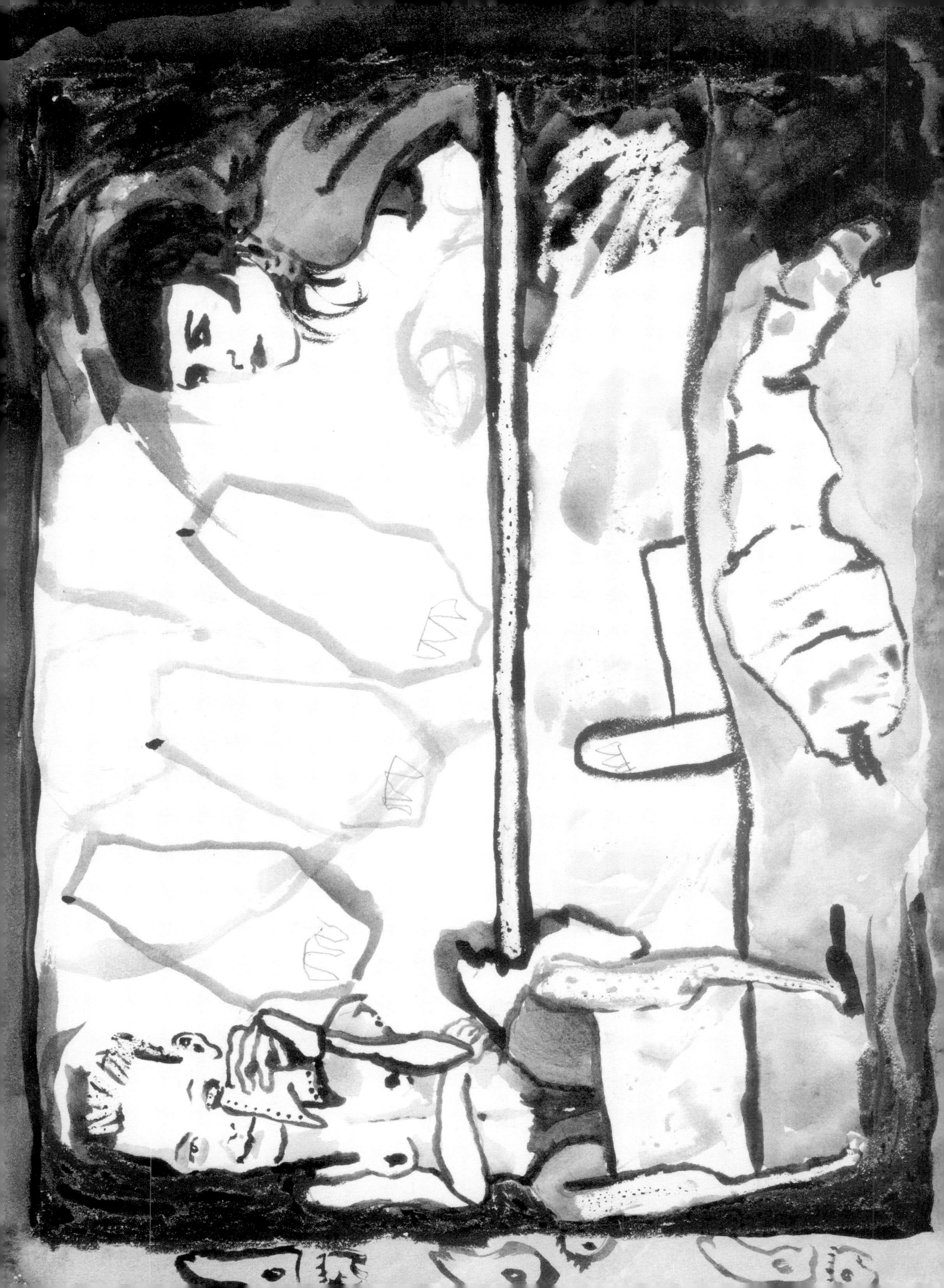

NERISSA
First, there is the Neapolitan prince.

PORTIA
Ay, that's a colt indeed, for he doth nothing but talk of his horse; and he makes it a great appropriation to his own good parts that he can shoe him himself. I am much afeard my lady his mother played false with a smith.

NERISSA
Then is there the County Palatine.

PORTIA
He doth nothing but frown, as who should say, 'An you will not have me, choose.' He hears merry tales, and smiles not: I fear he will prove the weeping philosopher when he grows old, being so full of unmannerly sadness in his youth. I had rather be married to a death's-head with a bone in his mouth than to either of these. God defend me from these two!

NERISSA
How say you by the French lord, Monsieur Le Bon?

PORTIA
God made him, and therefore let him pass for a man. In truth, I know it is a sin to be a mocker; but, he! why, he hath a horse better than the Neapolitan's, a better bad habit of frowning than the Count Palatine; he is every man in no man; if a throstle sing, he falls straight a-capering; he will fence with his own shadow: if I should marry him, I should marry twenty husbands. If he would despise me, I would forgive him, for if he love me to madness, I shall never requite him.

and yet a funny sort of joke, or rather, a ceremony that, as it was written in advance, nothing about it is a real threat, a sort of a joke that, as it was written in advance, is a terrible joke, a chilly comedy, related to the thick smell, and both belong to death.

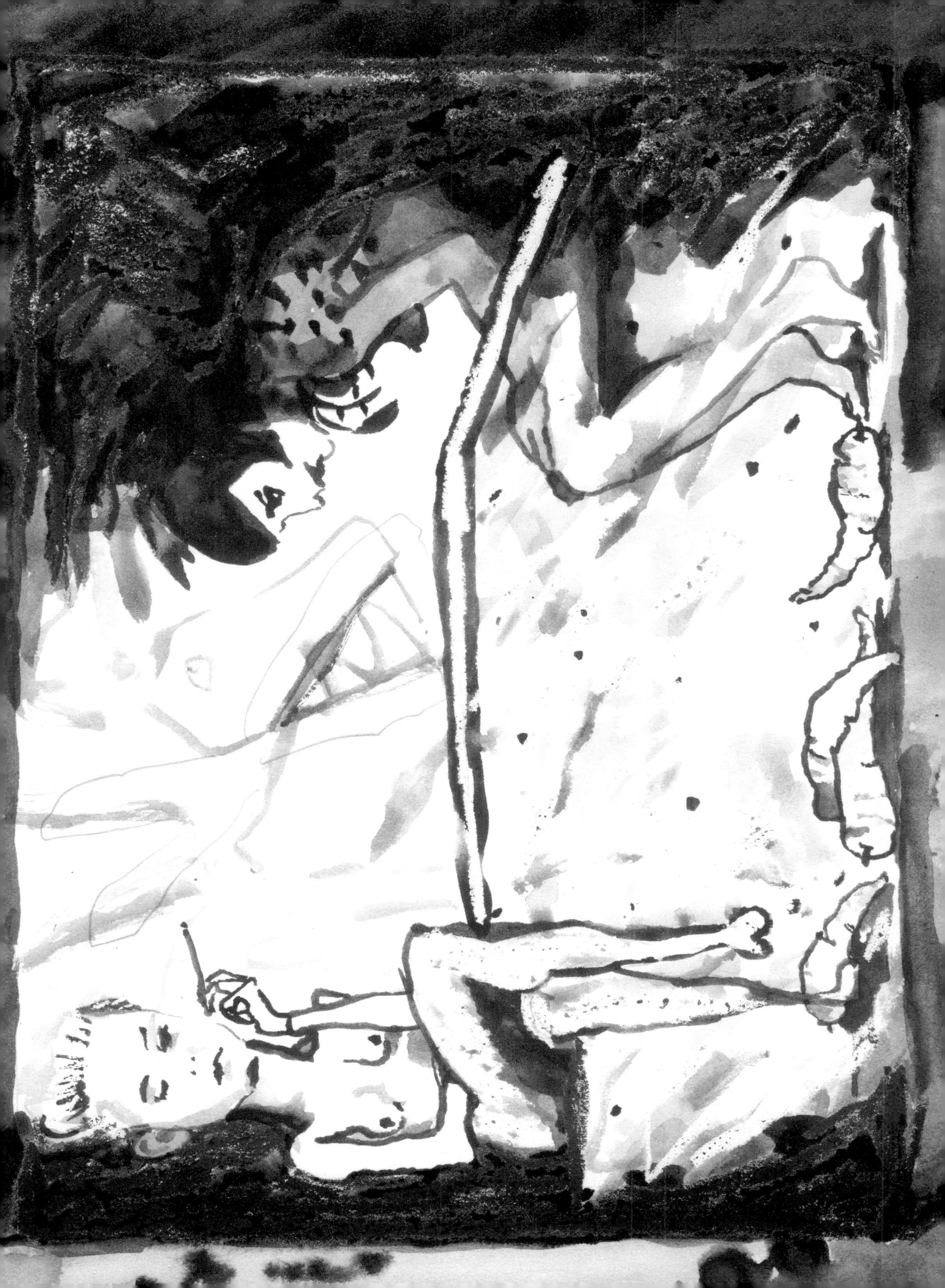

NERISSA
What say you, then, to Falconbridge, the young baron of England?

PORTIA
You know I say nothing to him, for he understands not me, nor I him: he hath neither Latin, French, nor Italian; and you will come into the court and swear that I have a poor pennyworth in the English. He is a proper man's picture, but, alas! who can converse with a dumb-show? How oddly he is suited! I think he bought his doublet in Italy, his round hose in France, his bonnet in Germany, and his behaviour every where.

NERISSA
What think you of the Scottish lord, his neighbour?

PORTIA
That he hath a neighbourly charity in him, for he borrowed a box of the ear of the Englishman, and swore he would pay him again when he was able: I think the Frenchman became his surety and sealed under for another.

NERISSA
How like you the young German, the Duke of Saxony's nephew?

PORTIA
Very vilely in the morning, when he is sober, and most vilely in the afternoon, when he is drunk: when he is best, he is a little worse than a man, and when he is worst, he is little better than a beast. An the worst fall that ever fell, I hope I shall make shift to go without him.

NERISSA
If he should offer to choose, and choose the right casket, you should refuse to perform your father's will, if you should refuse to accept him.

PORTIA
Therefore, for fear of the worst, I pray thee, set a deep glass of Rhenish wine on the contrary casket, for, if the devil be within and that temptation without, I know he will choose it. I will do anything, Nerissa, ere I will be married to a sponge.

NERISSA
You need not fear, lady, the having any of these lords: they have acquainted me with their determinations; which is, indeed, to return to their home and to trouble you with no more suit, unless you may be won by some other sort than your father's imposition depending on the caskets.

PORTIA
If I live to be as old as Sibylla, I will die as chaste as Diana, unless I be obtained by the manner of my father's will. I am glad this parcel of wooers are so reasonable, for there is not one among them but I dote on his very absence, and I pray God grant them a fair departure.

Portia's body may be weary, but her tongue is quick and flexible. Nerissa throws her names like flies, and she catches them with her tongue, and rolls and suspends them upon the palate.

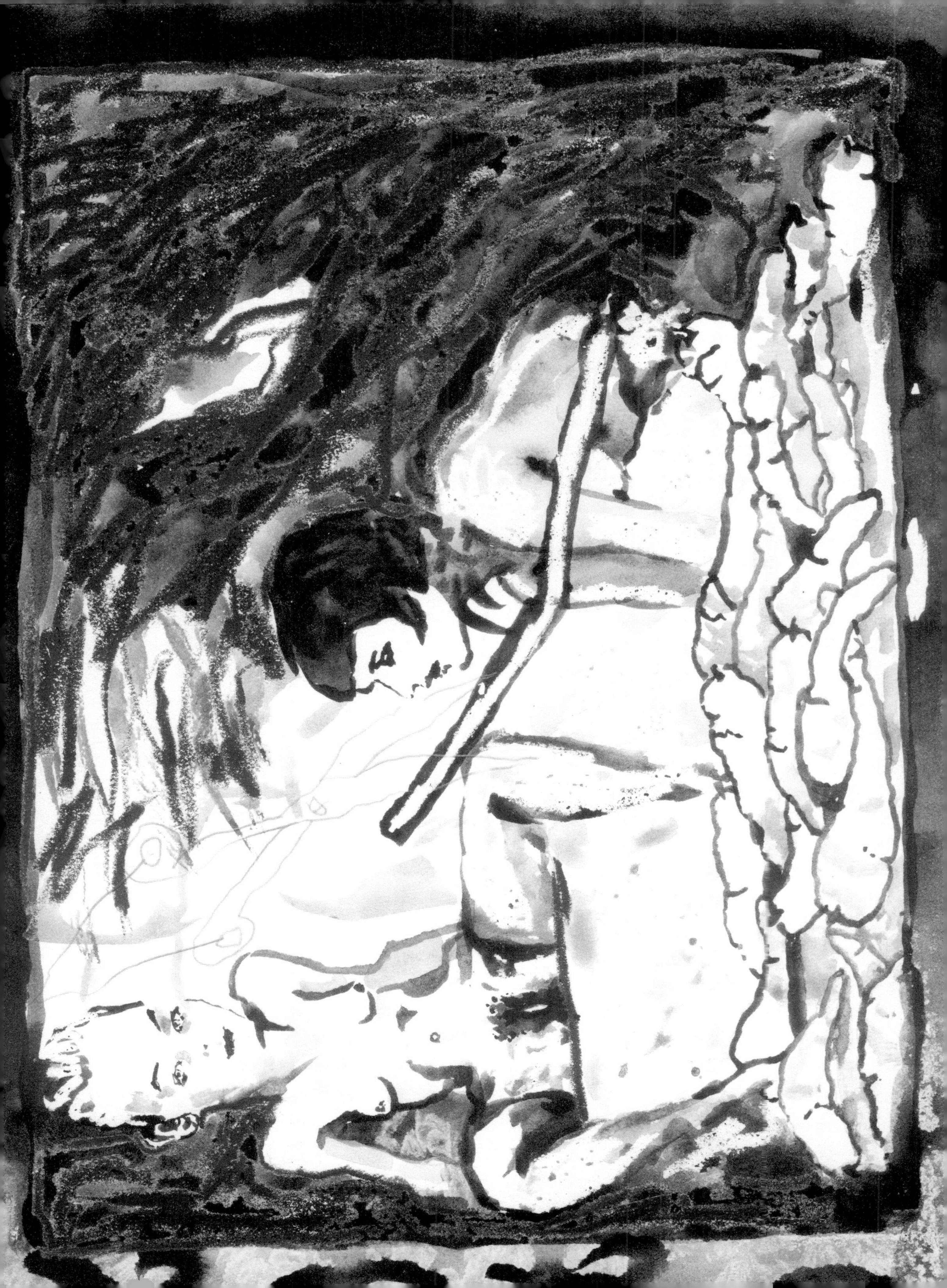

I.II.6

NERISSA
Do you not remember, lady, in your father's time, a Venetian, a scholar and a soldier, that came hither in the company of the Marquis of Montferrat?

PORTIA
Yes, yes: it was Bassanio; as I think, he was so called.

NERISSA
True, madam: he, of all the men that ever my foolish eyes looked upon, was the best deserving a fair lady.

PORTIA
I remember him well, and I remember him worthy of thy praise.

Enter a Servant.

How now! what news?

SERVANT
The four strangers seek for you, madam, to take their leave; and there is a forerunner come from a fifth, the Prince of Morocco, who brings word the prince his master will be here to-night.

PORTIA
If I could bid the fifth welcome with so good heart as I can bid the other four farewell, I should be glad of his approach: if he have the condition of a saint and the complexion of a devil, I had rather he should shrive me than wive me. Come, Nerissa. Sirrah, go before.
Whiles we shut the gate upon one wooer, another knocks at the door.

Exeunt.

And the name of Bassanio being mentioned, it is also a part of the joke, we understand, for here is a conviction, Portia's and Nerissa's and ours, that Bassanio will be coupled with Portia, and the anticipation of what is to come is an anticipation of what has already come to be, and the whole is a joke, sensual and sober (and we feel sorry, already we are sorry, and Portia may be as well, sorry for the Prince of Morocco, that perhaps he as well understands in advance the feeble role he has been given), and we love the splendid smell.

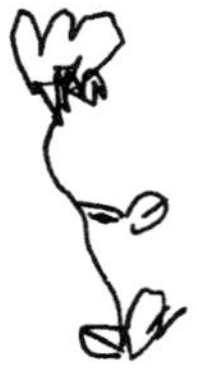

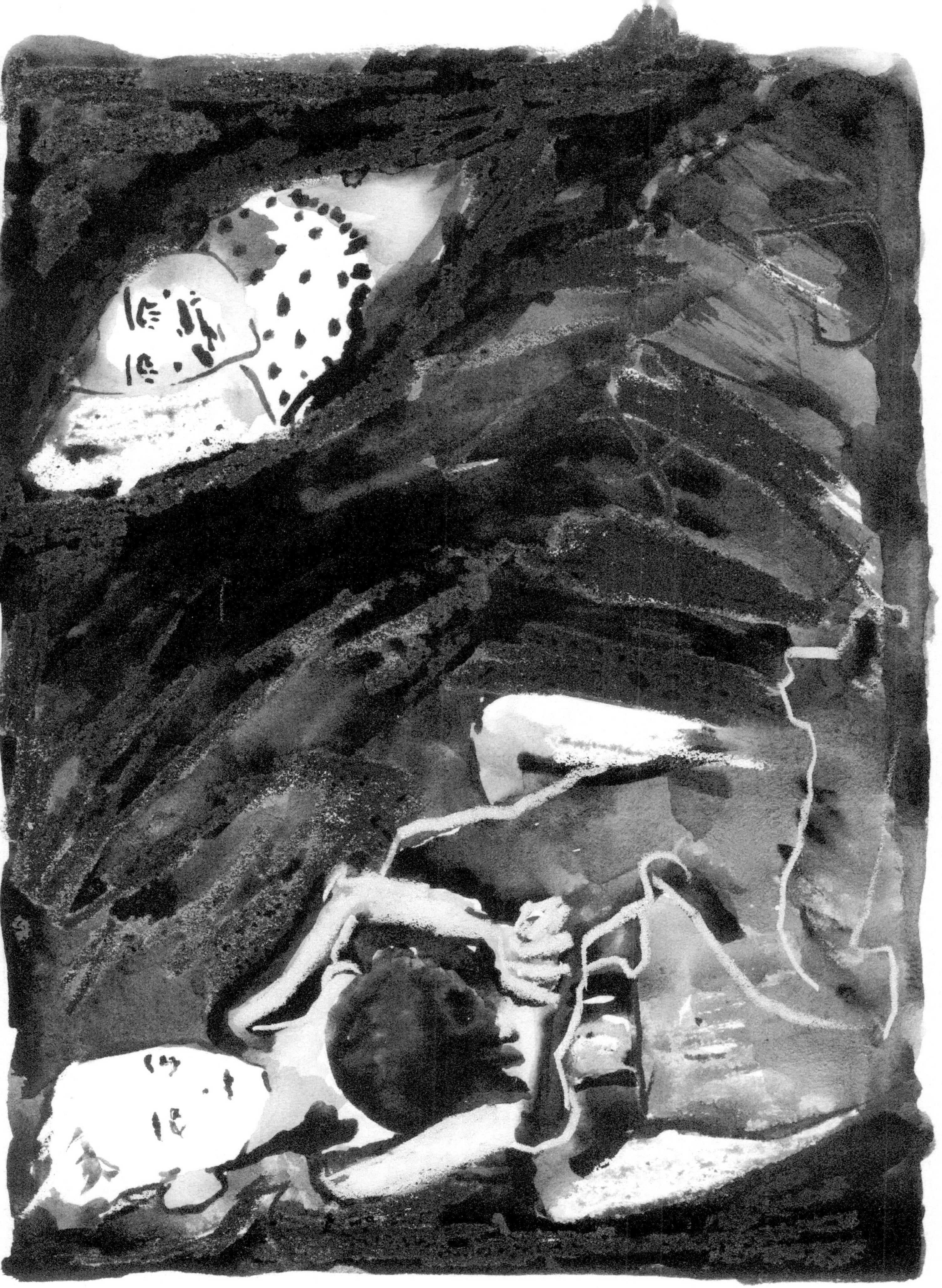

Scene III—Venice. A Public Place.

Enter Bassanio and Shylock.

SHYLOCK
Three thousand ducats; well?

BASSANIO
Ay, sir, for three months.

SHYLOCK
For three months; well?

BASSANIO
For the which, as I told you, Antonio shall be bound.

SHYLOCK
Antonio shall become bound; well?

BASSANIO
May you stead me? Will you pleasure me? Shall I know your answer?

Since his eyes were gouged, this is the first time he has been approached by Bassanio, and it wakens a small delight that rattles in his belly. He knows the delight. He knows that it is a tiny and dirty delight, and yet a delight. Definitely.

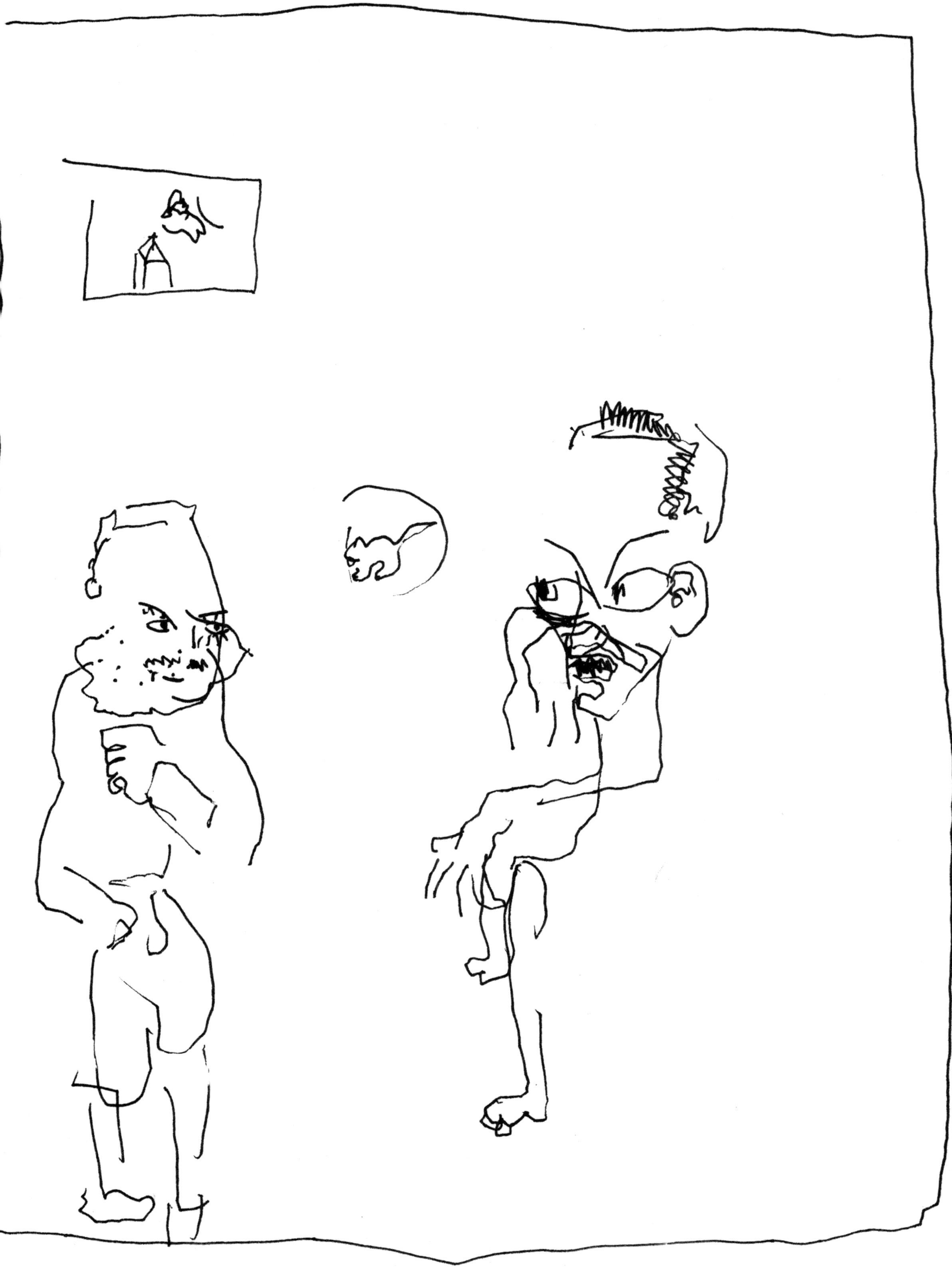

SHYLOCK
Three thousand ducats, for three months,
and Antonio bound.

BASSANIO
Your answer to that.

SHYLOCK
Antonio is a good man.

BASSANIO
Have you heard any imputation to the contrary?

In the middle of the delight, the blind merchant twice envisions his dead wife and, dimly, a crown.

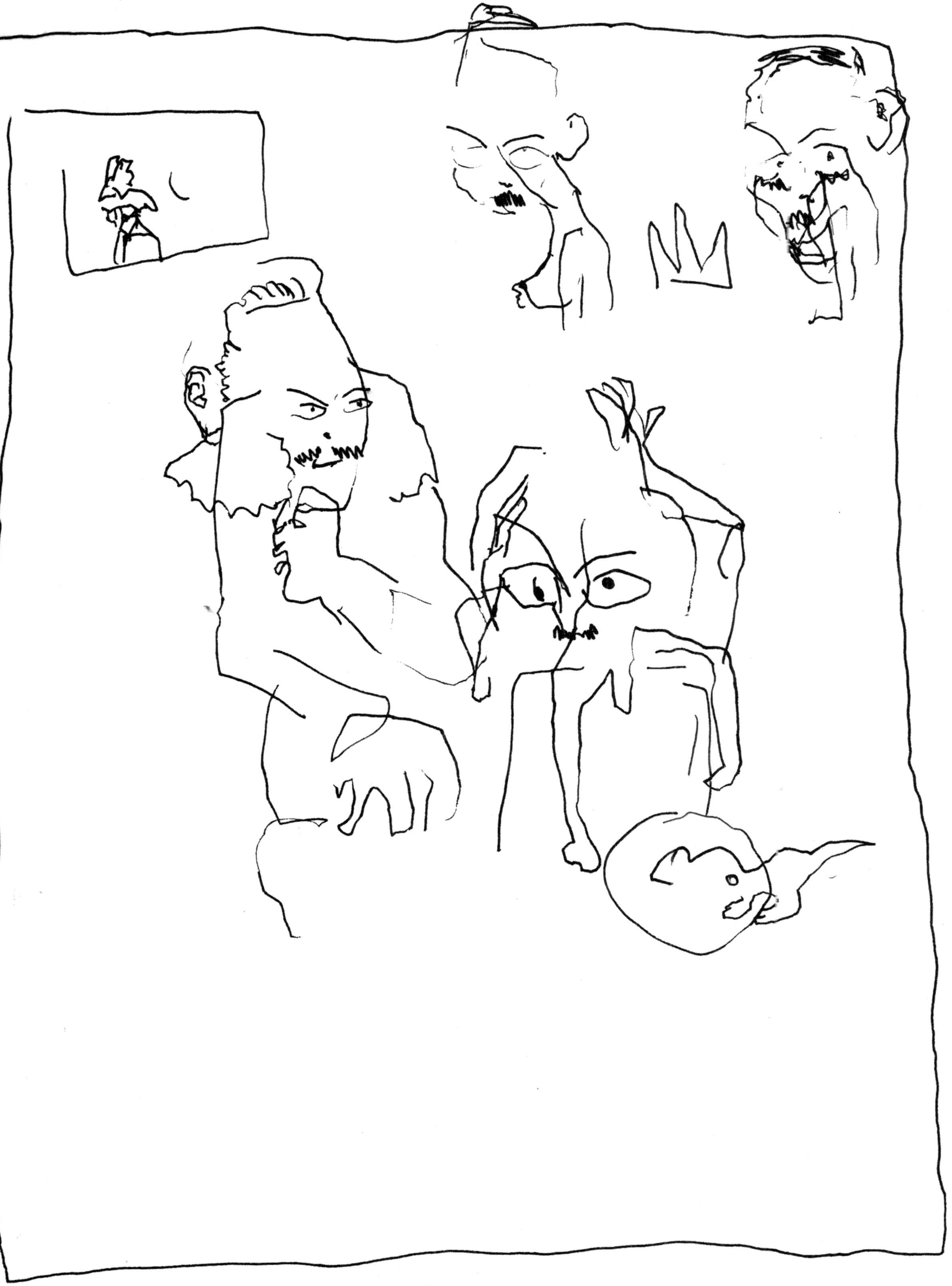

SHYLOCK

Ho, no, no, no, no: my meaning in saying he is a good man is to have you understand me that he is sufficient. Yet his means are in supposition: he hath an argosy bound to Tripolis, another to the Indies; I understand moreover upon the Rialto, he hath a third at Mexico, a fourth for England, and other ventures he hath, squandered abroad. But ships are but boards, sailors but men: there be land-rats and water-rats, land-thieves, and water-thieves,—I mean pirates,—and then there is the peril of waters, winds, and rocks. The man is, notwithstanding, sufficient. Three thousand ducats; I think, I may take his bond.

He tries to regulate the vision for the benefit of the dirty delight, to erase Leah and enlarge the crown. And his tongue rolls. It rolls as colorful as a colorful carpet.

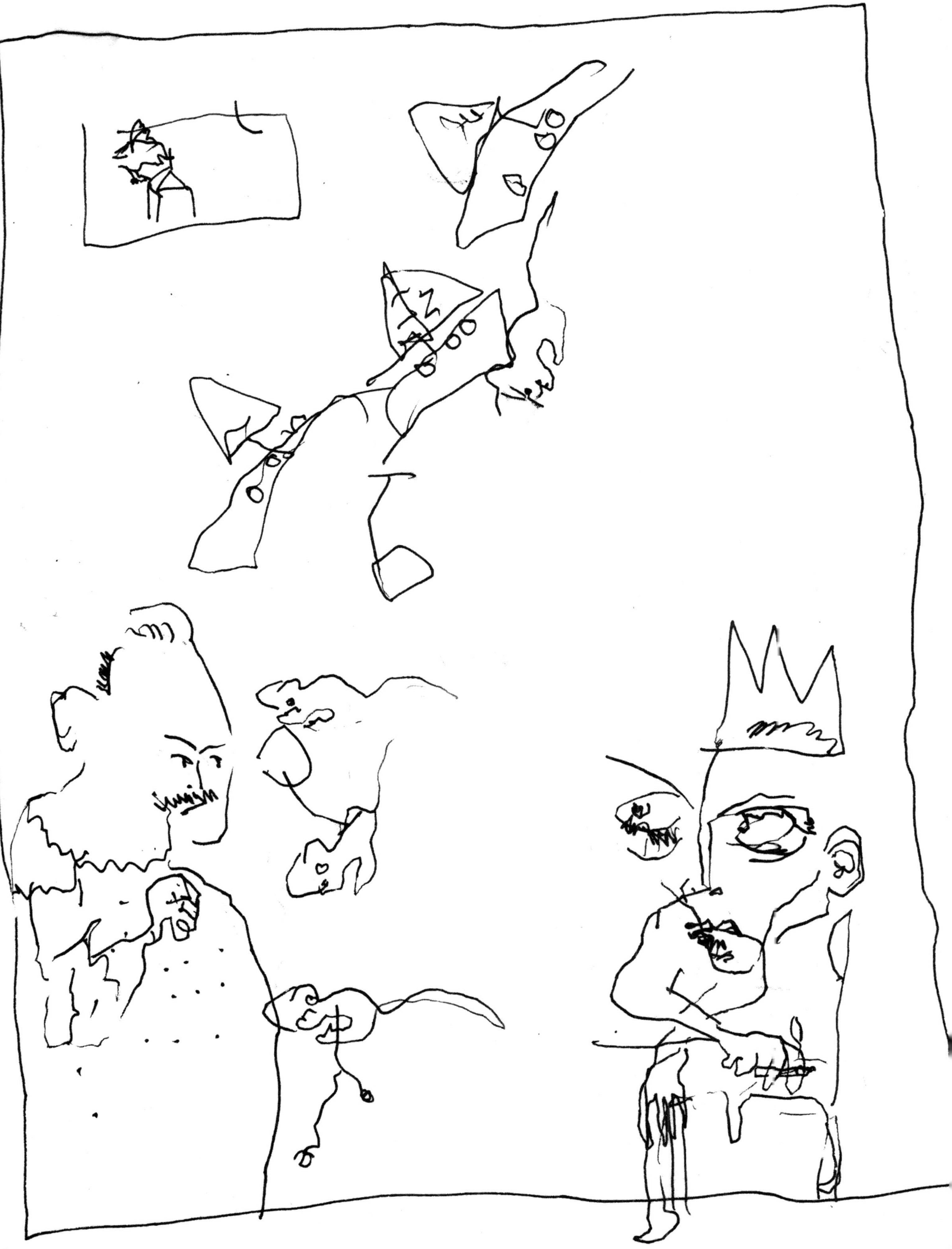

BASSANIO
Be assured you may.

SHYLOCK
I will be assured I may; and, that I may be assured, I will bethink me. May I speak with Antonio?

BASSANIO
If it please you to dine with us.

SHYLOCK
Yes, to smell pork: to eat of the habitation which your prophet the Nazarite conjured the devil into. I will buy with you, sell with you, talk with you, walk with you, and so following; but I will not eat with you, drink with you, nor pray with you. What news on the Rialto? Who is he comes here?

I smell sweet I smell (he thinks in the middle of the delight) as I speak sweet I sweet smell and I.

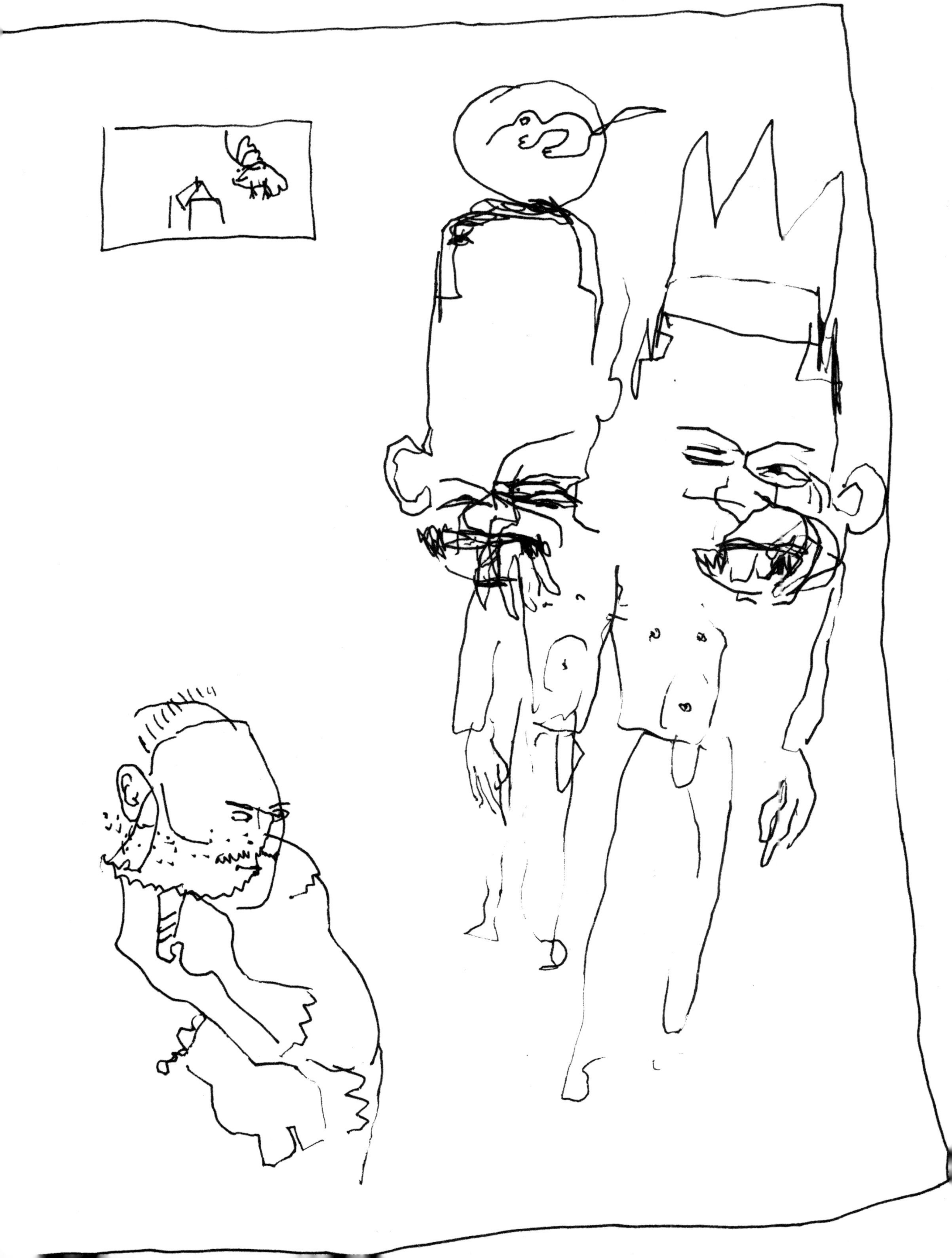

Enter Antonio.

BASSANIO
This is Signior Antonio.

SHYLOCK
[*Aside.*] How like a fawning publican he looks!
I hate him for he is a Christian;
But more for that in low simplicity
He lends out money gratis, and brings down
The rate of usance here with us in Venice.
If I can catch him once upon the hip,
I will feed fat the ancient grudge I bear him.
He hates our sacred nation, and he rails,
Even there where merchants most do congregate,
On me, my bargains, and my well-won thrift,
Which he calls interest. Cursed be my tribe,
If I forgive him!

BASSANIO
Shylock, do you hear?

And Antonio. Indeed. It is the first time since—but his tongue rolls from within him. But within him the slimy vision expands and contracts like a heart.

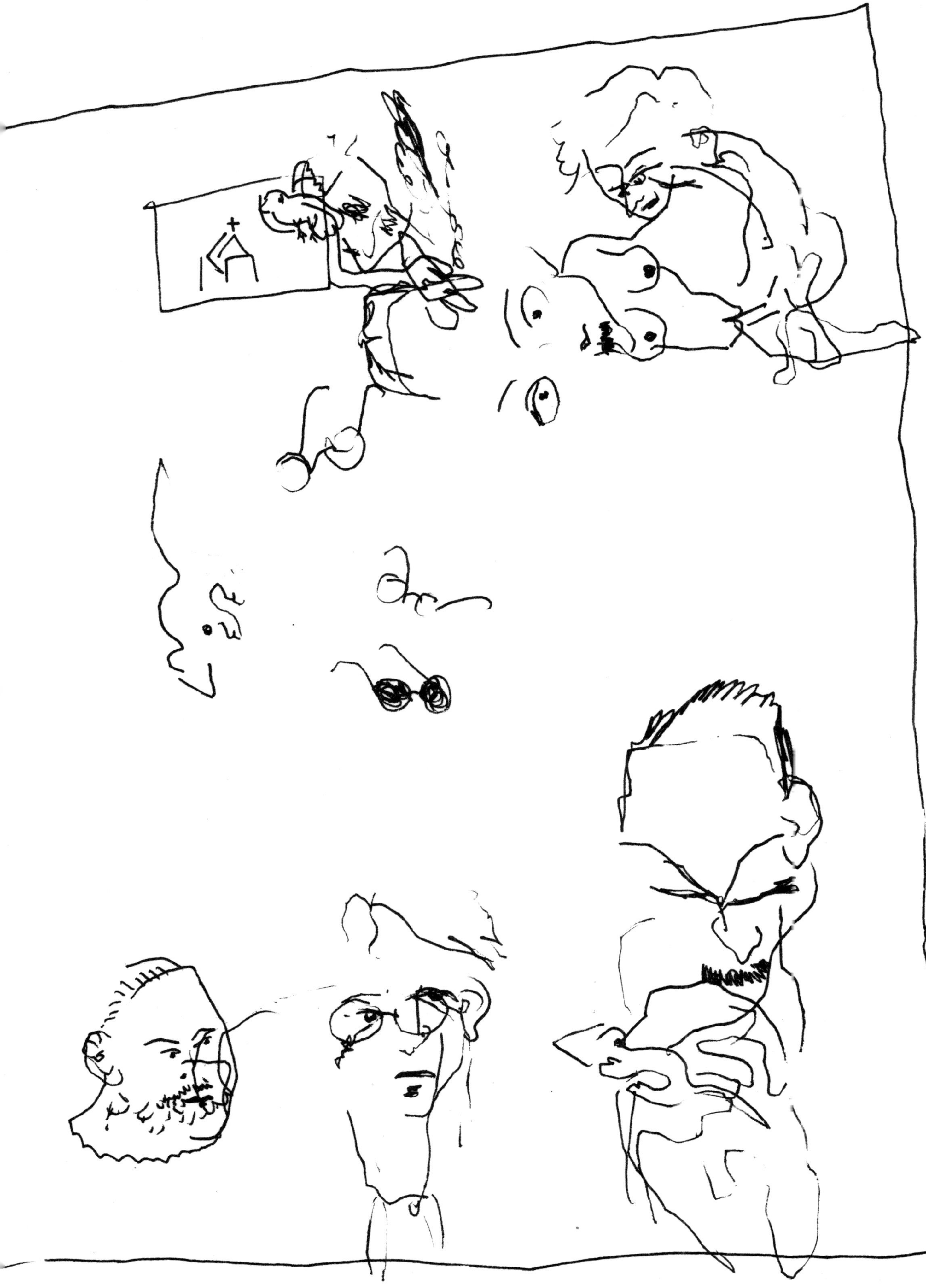

I.III.6

Shylock, do you hear?

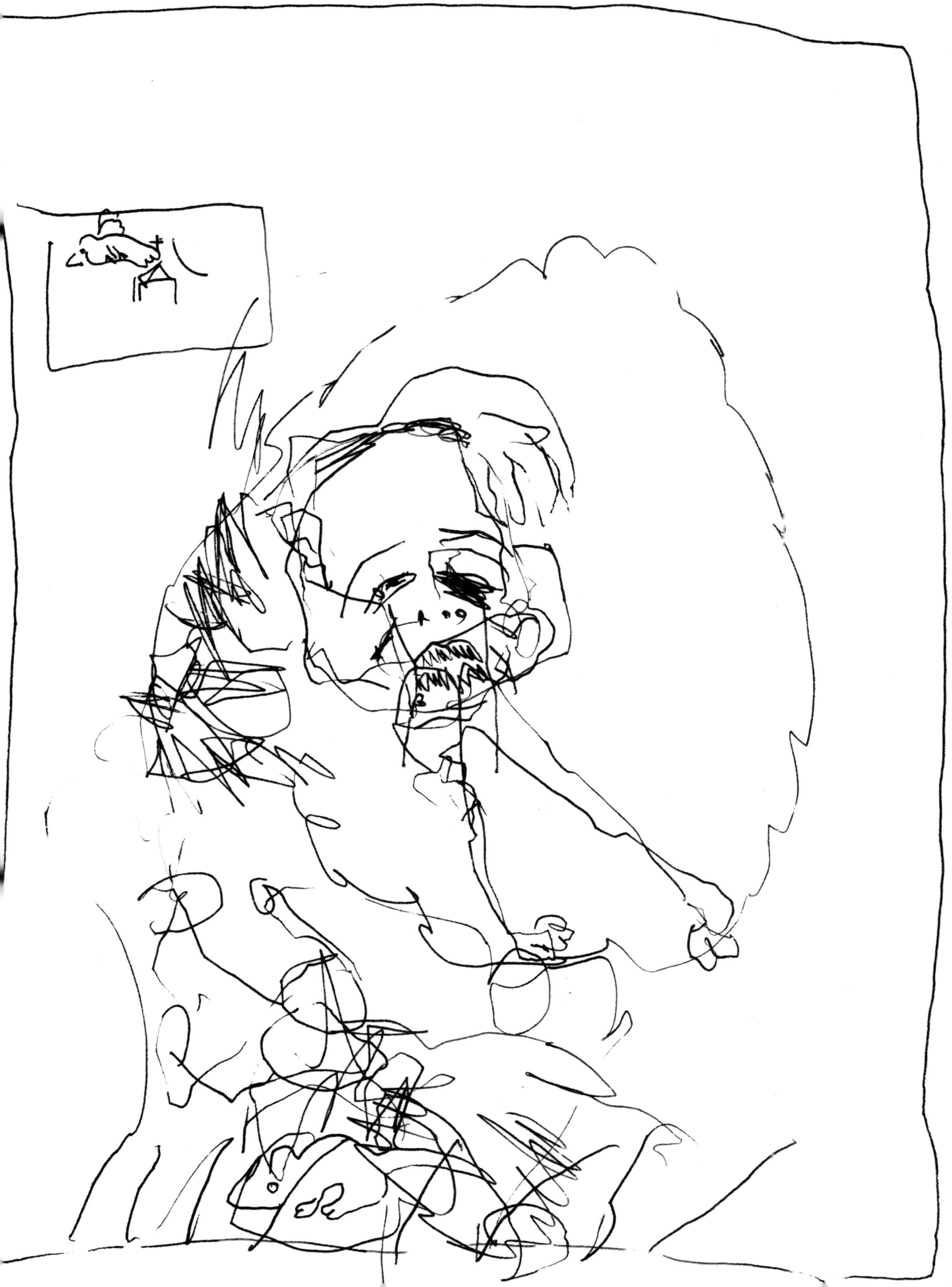

I.III.7

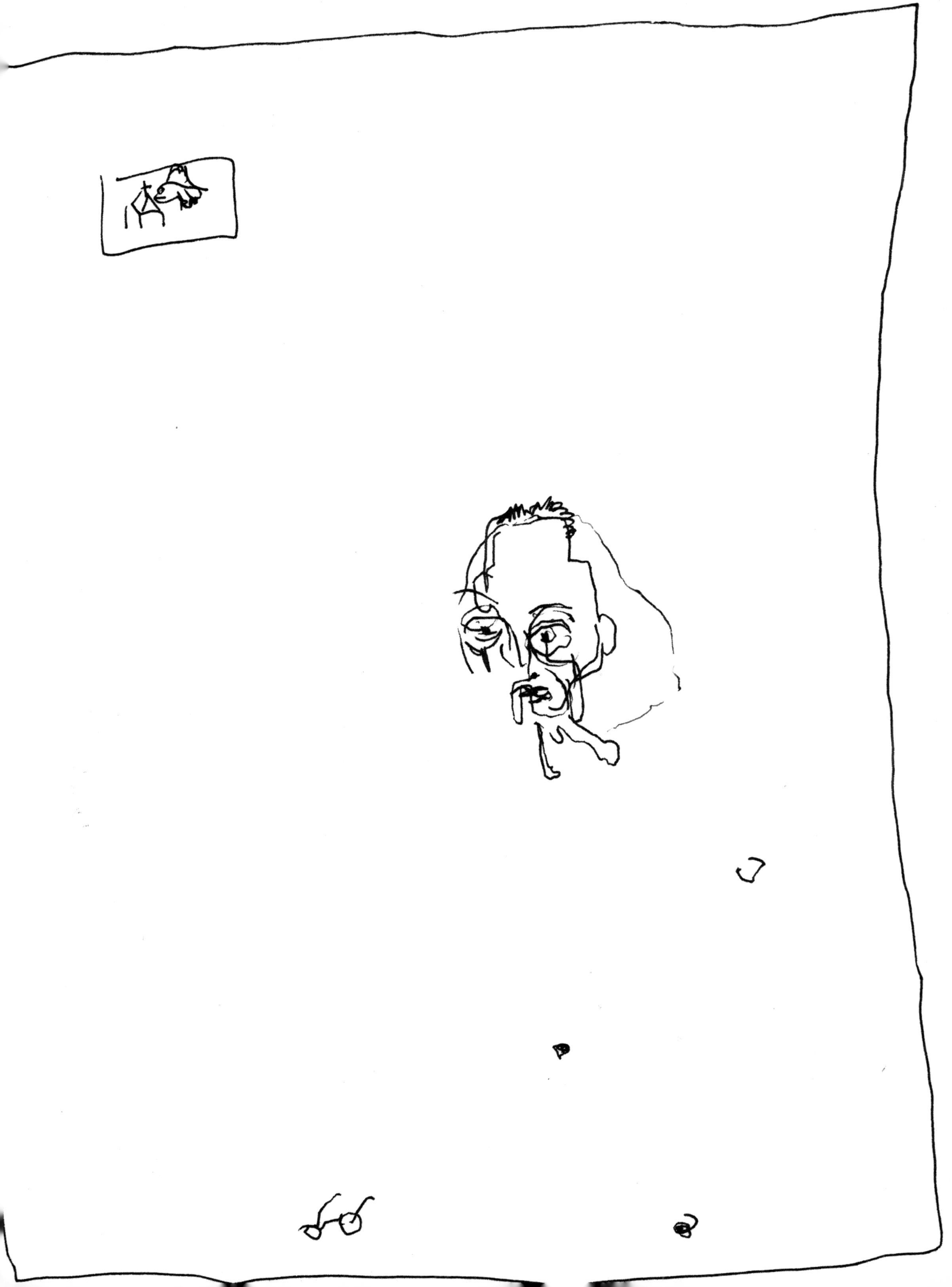

SHYLOCK
I am debating of my present store,
And, by the near guess of my memory,
I cannot instantly raise up the gross
Of full three thousand ducats. What of that?
Tubal, a wealthy Hebrew of my tribe,
Will furnish me. But soft! how many months
Do you desire? [*To Antonio.*] Rest you fair, good signior;
Your worship was the last man in our mouths.

ANTONIO
Shylock, albeit I neither lend nor borrow
By taking nor by giving of excess,
Yet, to supply the ripe wants of my friend,
I'll break a custom. [*To Bassanio.*] Is he yet possess'd
How much ye would?

SHYLOCK
Ay, ay, three thousand ducats.

ANTONIO
And for three months.

SHYLOCK
I had forgot; three months; you told me so.
Well then, your bond; and let me see. But hear you;
Methought you said you neither lend nor borrow
Upon advantage.

ANTONIO
I do never use it.

Fragile delight.
Hard and bitter its short life.
Shylock pumps, pumps it with power, but the delight and the power are one, and the delight, maybe, pumps him with the power, and he

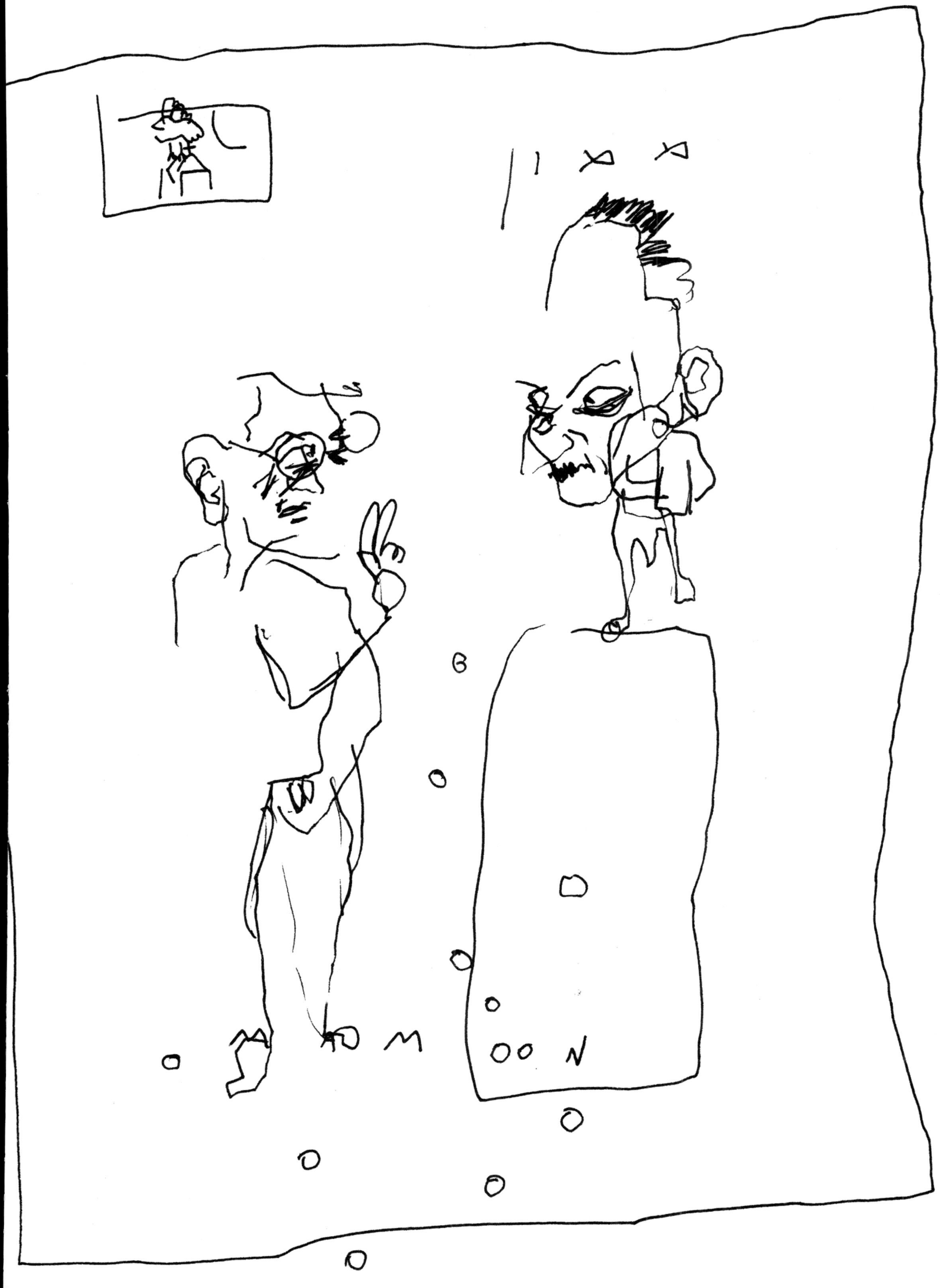

SHYLOCK
When Jacob graz'd his uncle Laban's sheep,—
This Jacob from our holy Abram was,
As his wise mother wrought in his behalf,
The third possessor: ay, he was the third,—

ANTONIO
And what of him? did he take interest?

SHYLOCK
No; not take interest; not, as you would say,
Directly interest: mark what Jacob did.
When Laban and himself were compromis'd,
That all the eanlings that were streak'd and pied
Should fall as Jacob's hire, the ewes, being rank,
In end of autumn turned to the rams;
And, when the work of generation was
Between these woolly breeders in the act,
The skilful shepherd peel'd me certain wands,
And, in the doing of the deed of kind,
He stuck them up before the fulsome ewes,
Who, then conceiving, did in eaning time
Fall parti-colour'd lambs, and those were Jacob's.
This was a way to thrive, and he was blest:
And thrift is blessing, if men steal it not.

dirties the power with the delight, and beyond the friction of power with delight waits the vision, and beyond it groan other entities—the terrible imagination, and the clean hatred, and it is almost unknown to Shylock whence Shylock draws the Bible and torments himself with self-deprecation,

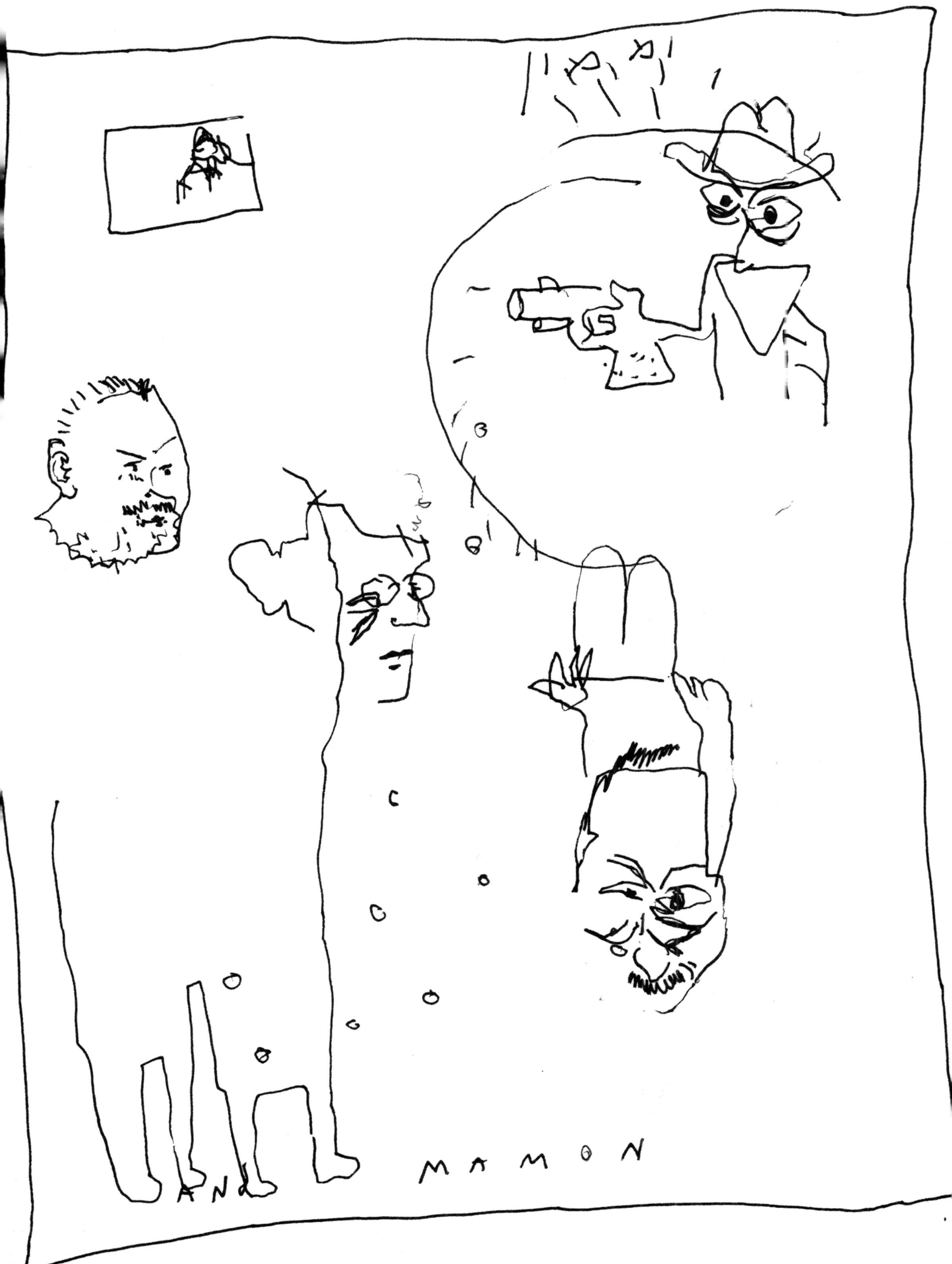
AND
MAMON

ANTONIO
This was a venture, sir, that Jacob serv'd for;
A thing not in his power to bring to pass,
But sway'd and fashion'd by the hand of heaven.
Was this inserted to make interest good?
Or is your gold and silver ewes and rams?

SHYLOCK
I cannot tell; I make it breed as fast: But note me, signior.

ANTONIO
Mark you this, Bassanio,
The devil can cite Scripture for his purpose.
An evil soul, producing holy witness,
Is like a villain with a smiling cheek,
A goodly apple rotten at the heart.
O, what a goodly outside falsehood hath!

SHYLOCK
Three thousand ducats; 'tis a good round sum.
Three months from twelve, then let me see the rate.

ANTONIO
Well, Shylock, shall we be beholding to you?

and now he is already almost maybe blind with confusing powers, and his tongue, oi, and his tongue,

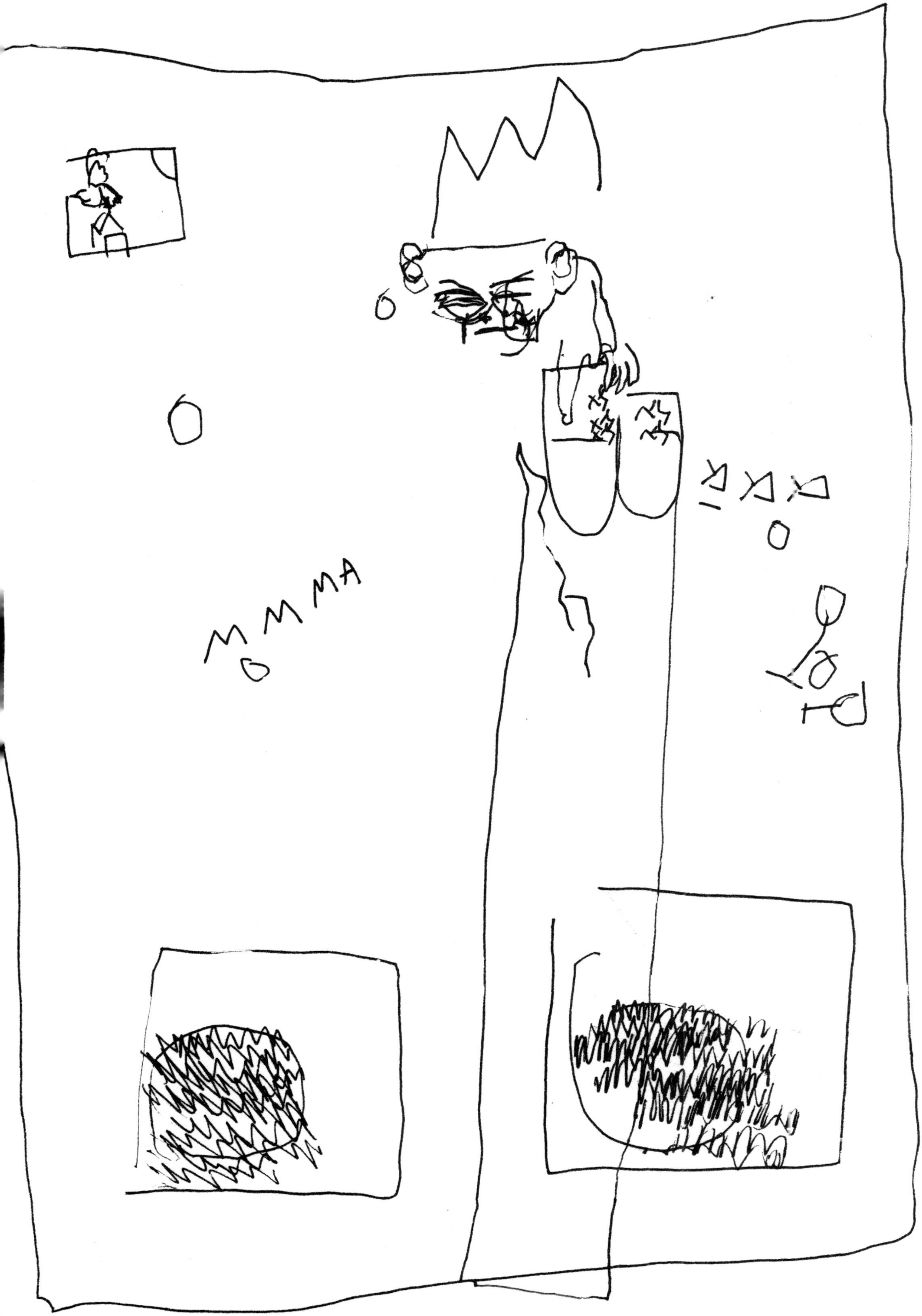
MMMA

SHYLOCK
Signior Antonio, many a time and oft
In the Rialto you have rated me
About my moneys and my usances:
Still have I borne it with a patient shrug,
For sufferance is the badge of all our tribe.
You call me misbeliever, cut-throat dog,
And spet upon my Jewish gaberdine,
And all for use of that which is mine own.
Well then, it now appears you need my help:
Go to then; you come to me, and you say,
'Shylock, we would have moneys:' you say so;
You, that did void your rheum upon my beard,
And foot me as you spurn a stranger cur
Over your threshold: moneys is your suit.
What should I say to you? Should I not say,
'Hath a dog money? Is it possible
A cur can lend three thousand ducats?' or
Shall I bend low, and in a bondman's key,
With bated breath, and whispering humbleness,
Say this:—
'Fair sir, you spet on me on Wednesday last;
You spurn'd me such a day; another time
You call'd me dog; and for these courtesies
I'll lend you thus much moneys?'

and his tongue is released, its safety-catch springs open, and his tongue meddles with the delight (already almost unrecognizable as such) with tears and sweat.
His rolling tongue is the delight and also a whip that flogs the delight. And as it was released, the order was disordered and remained only whip.

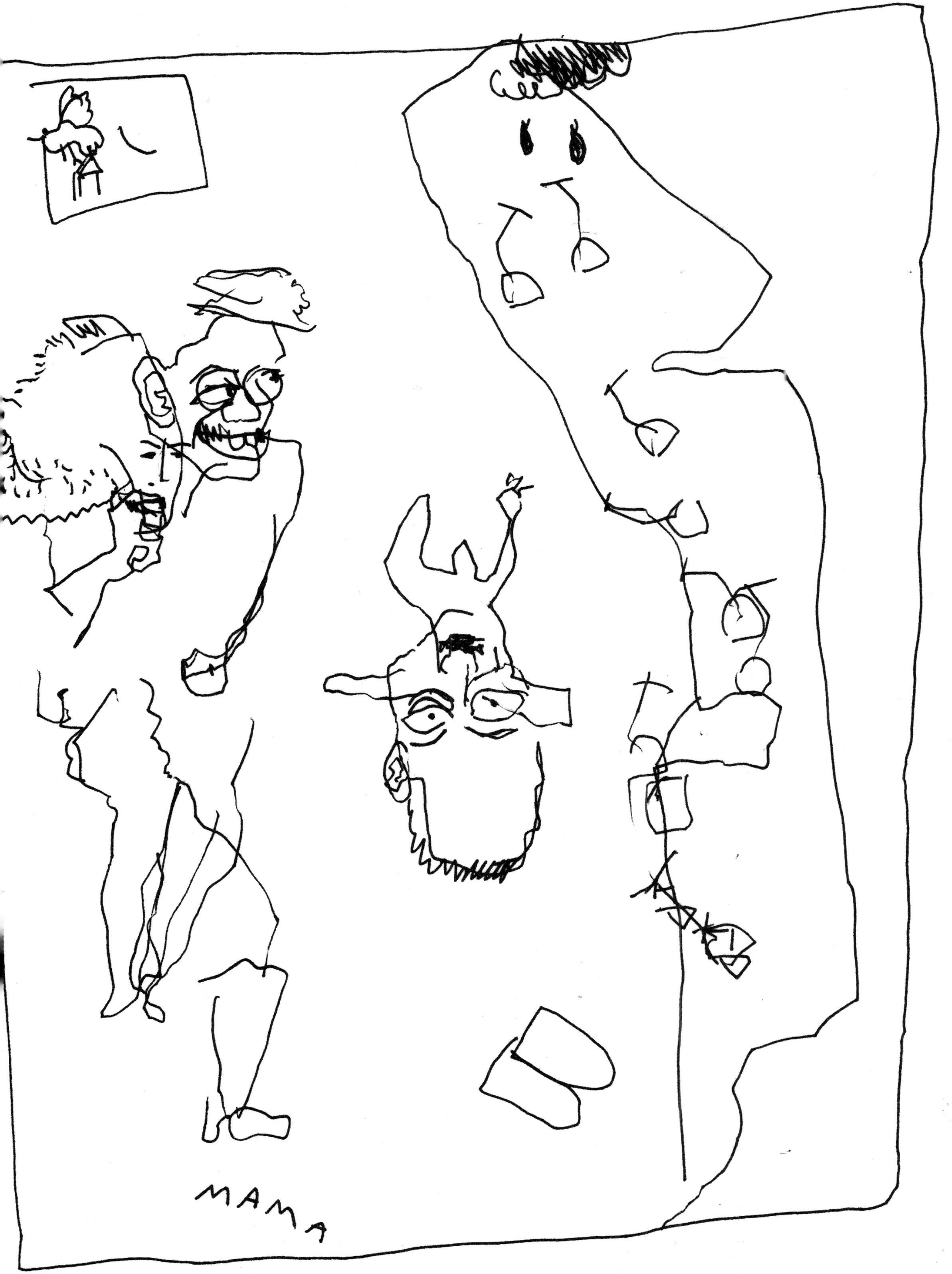
MAMA

ANTONIO
I am as like to call thee so again,
To spet on thee again, to spurn thee too.
If thou wilt lend this money, lend it not
As to thy friends,—for when did friendship take
A breed for barren metal of his friend?—
But lend it rather to thine enemy;
Who if he break, thou mayst with better face
Exact the penalty.

SHYLOCK
Why, look you, how you storm!
I would be friends with you, and have your love,
Forget the shames that you have stain'd me with,
Supply your present wants, and take no doit
Of usance for my moneys, and you'll not hear me:
This is kind I offer.

ANTONIO
This were kindness.

The rise after the fall is a complicated maneuver for Shylock, as the fall left him even smaller, and thin, and sweaty. Nor does Antonio's Christian chatter bother him, but the need to restrain himself and represent himself and achieve a handsome revenge—and the labor of the rise, and the dissatisfaction of the rise, and here,

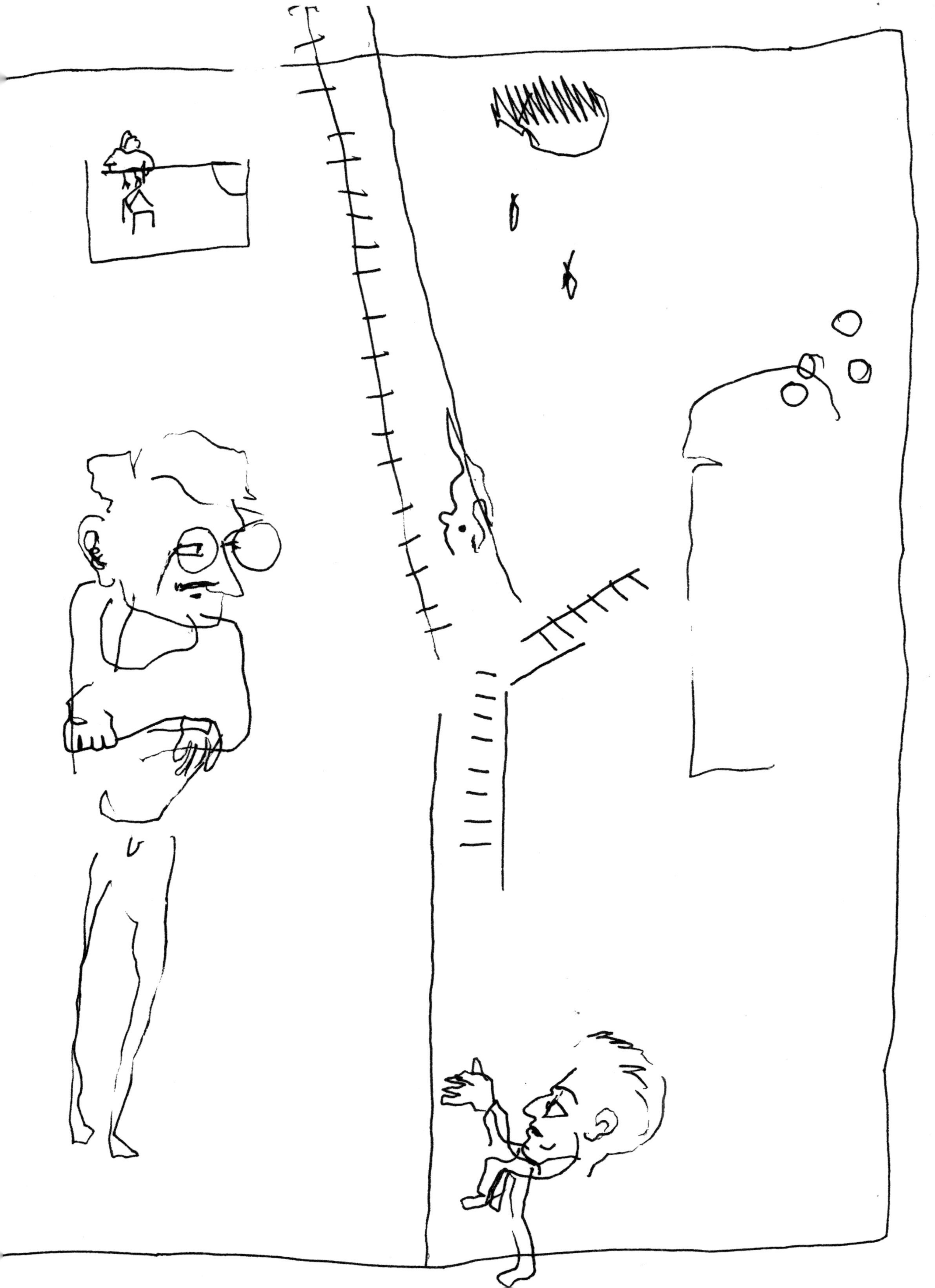

SHYLOCK
This kindness will I show.
Go with me to a notary, seal me there
Your single bond; and, in a merry sport,
If you repay me not on such a day,
In such a place, such sum or sums as are
Express'd in the condition, let the forfeit
Be nominated for an equal pound
Of your fair flesh, to be cut off and taken
In what part of your body pleaseth me.

here it occurs to Shylock there is a third way, just so naturally, just so like a small, simple delight, and the third way is his way, just so natural, like a small, dirty delight, and the third way

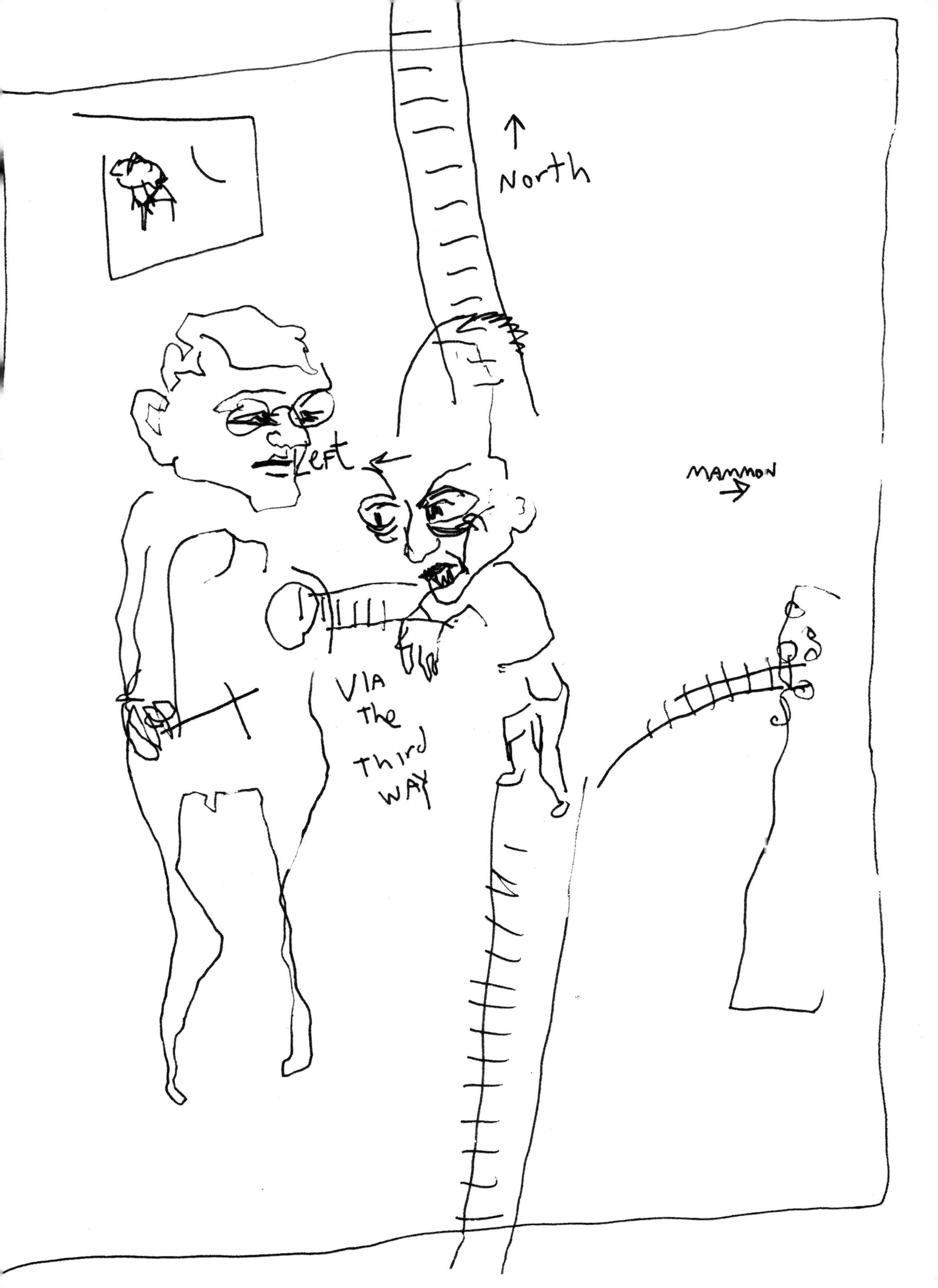
North
Left
MAMMON
VIA the Third WAY

ANTONIO
Content, i' faith: I'll seal to such a bond,
And say there is much kindness in the Jew.

BASSANIO
You shall not seal to such a bond for me:
I'll rather dwell in my necessity.

ANTONIO
Why, fear not, man; I will not forfeit it:
Within these two months, that's a month before
This bond expires, I do expect return
Of thrice three times the value of this bond.

already spreads ahead, like a red, moist carpet, and Shylock secretes a small Shylock-impression which has entrenched itself within the Christian pound-of-flesh, and as he has seeded something terrible enough and natural enough of himself

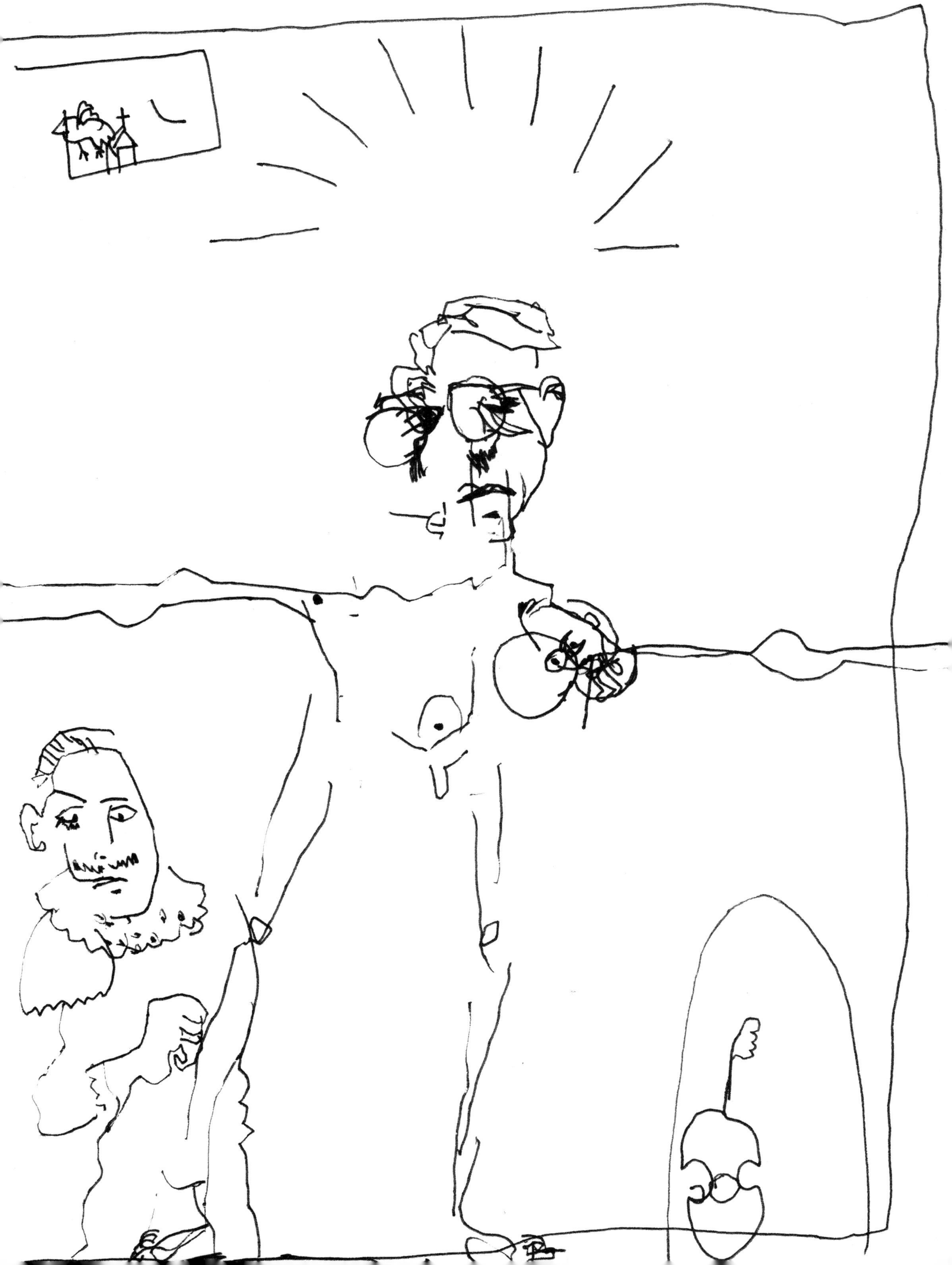

SHYLOCK
O father Abram! what these Christians are,
Whose own hard dealing teaches them suspect
The thoughts of others. Pray you, tell me this;
If he should break his day, what should I gain
By the exaction of the forfeiture?
A pound of man's flesh, taken from a man,
Is not so estimable, profitable neither,
As flesh of muttons, beefs, or goats. I say,
To buy his favour, I extend this friendship:
If he will take it, so; if not, adieu;
And, for my love, I pray you wrong me not.

ANTONIO
Yes, Shylock, I will seal unto this bond.

SHYLOCK
Then meet me forthwith at the notary's;
Give him direction for this merry bond,
And I will go and purse the ducats straight,
See to my house, left in the fearful guard
Of an unthrifty knave, and presently
I will be with you.

Exit Shylock.

Shylock exits, and with him all the rest of Shylock's precious baggage—a cloud of black tears and mice and dead mother and dead Leah and the three ways and the ladder and the dirty vision and the dirty delight and black glasses and glass splinters and dimly a crown and sacred commandments and a foreign snake tongue and an over-developed sense of smell—this is Shylock's precious baggage, and more.

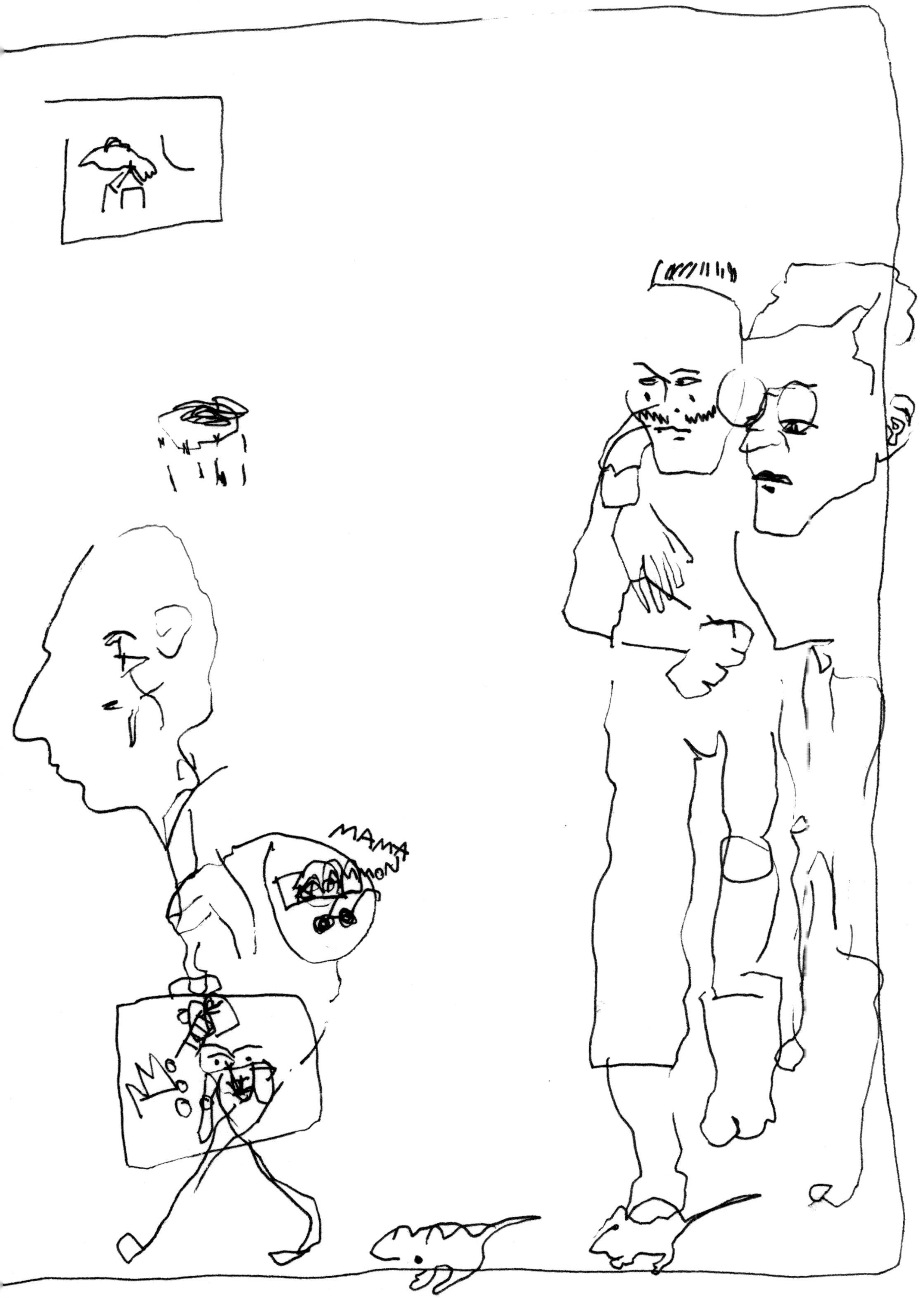
MAMA

I.III.16

ANTONIO
Hie thee, gentle Jew.
This Hebrew will turn Christian: he grows kind.

BASSANIO
I like not fair terms and a villain's mind.

ANTONIO
Come on: in this there can be no dismay;
My ships come home a month before the day.

Exeunt.

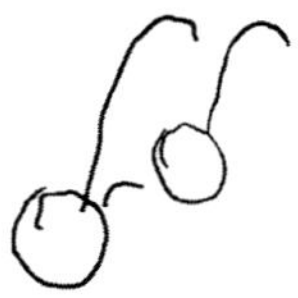

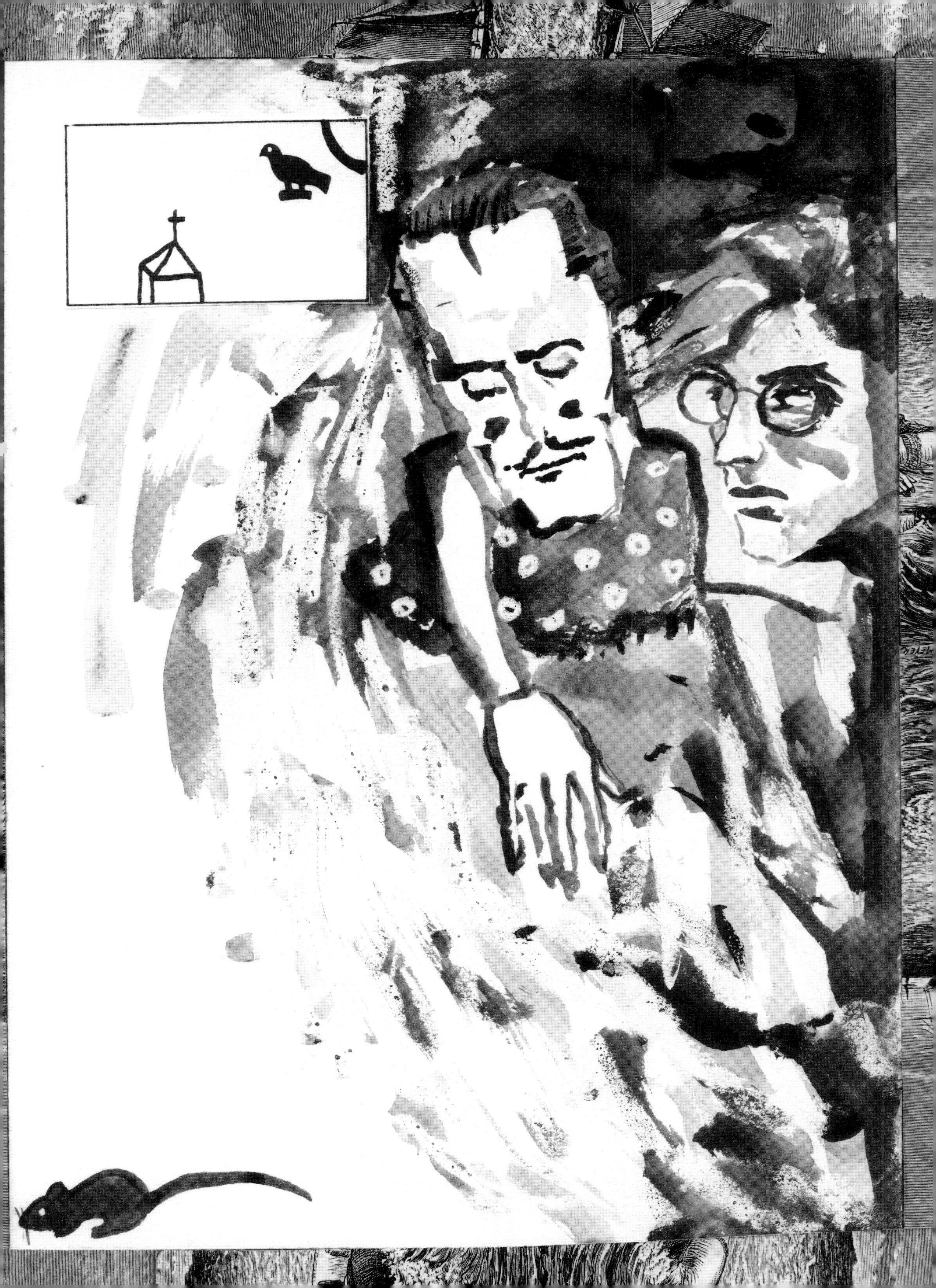

SECOND ACT

SPOTS

Scene I—Belmont. A Room in Portia's House.

Flourish of Cornets. Enter the Prince of Morocco, and his Followers; Portia, Nerissa, and Others of her Train.

MOROCCO
Mislike me not for my complexion,
The shadow'd livery of the burnish'd sun,
To whom I am a neighbour and near bred.
Bring me the fairest creature northward born,
Where Phœbus' fire scarce thaws the icicles,
And let us make incision for your love,
To prove whose blood is reddest, his or mine.
I tell thee, lady, this aspect of mine
Hath fear'd the valiant: by my love, I swear
The best regarded virgins of our clime
Have lov'd it too: I would not change this hue,
Except to steal your thoughts, my gentle queen.

PORTIA
In terms of choice I am not solely led
By nice direction of a maiden's eyes;
Besides, the lottery of my destiny
Bars me the right of voluntary choosing:
But if my father had not scanted me
And hedg'd me by his wit, to yield myself
His wife who wins me by that means I told you,
Yourself, renowned prince, then stood as fair
As any comer I have look'd on yet
For my affection.

MOROCCO
Even for that I thank you:
Therefore, I pray you, lead me to the caskets
To try my fortune. By this scimitar,—
That slew the Sophy, and a Persian prince
That won three fields of Sultan Solyman,—
I would outstare the sternest eyes that look,
Outbrave the heart most daring on the earth,
Pluck the young sucking cubs from the she-bear,
Yea, mock the lion when he roars for prey,
To win thee, lady. But, alas the while!
If Hercules and Lichas play at dice
Which is the better man, the greater throw
May turn by fortune from the weaker hand:
So is Alcides beaten by his page;
And so may I, blind fortune leading me,
Miss that which one unworthier may attain,
And die with grieving.

PORTIA
You must take your chance;
And either not attempt to choose at all,
Or swear before you choose, if you choose wrong,
Never to speak to lady afterward
In way of marriage: therefore be advis'd.

MOROCCO
Nor will not: come, bring me unto my chance.

PORTIA
First, forward to the temple: after dinner
Your hazard shall be made.

MOROCCO
Good fortune then!
To make me blest or cursed'st among men!

Cornets, and exeunt.

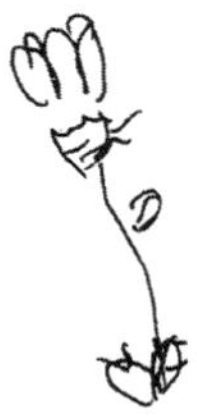

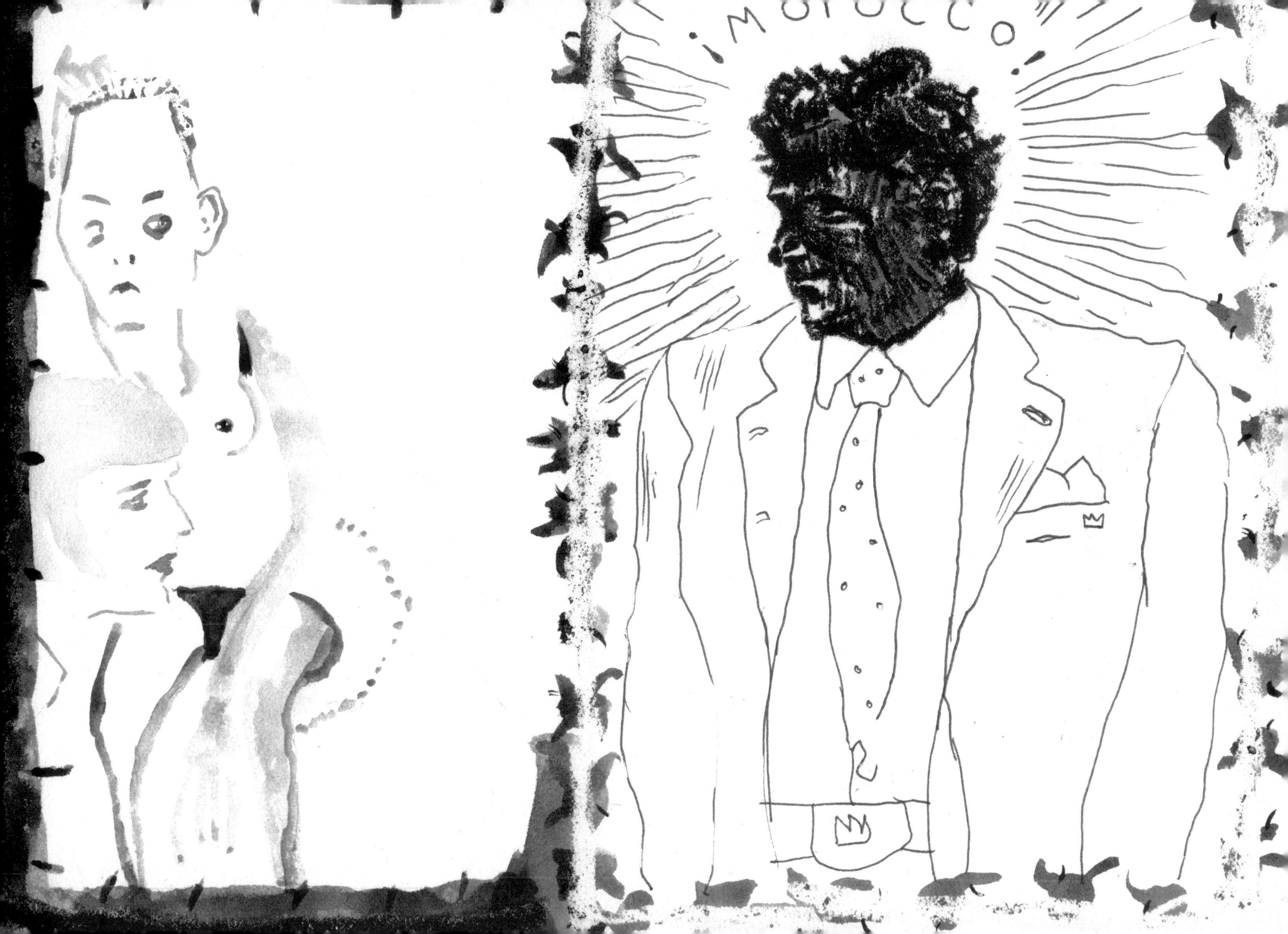

Scene II—Venice. A Street.

Enter Launcelot Gobbo.

LAUNCELOT

Certainly my conscience will serve me to run from this Jew my master. The fiend is at mine elbow, and tempts me, saying to me, 'Gobbo, Launcelot Gobbo, good Launcelot,' or 'good Gobbo,' or 'good Launcelot Gobbo, use your legs, take the start, run away.' My conscience says, 'No; take heed, honest Launcelot; take heed, honest Gobbo;' or, as aforesaid, 'honest Launcelot Gobbo; do not run; scorn running with thy heels.' Well, the most courageous fiend bids me pack: '*Via!*' says the fiend; 'away!' says the fiend; 'for the heavens, rouse up a brave mind,' says the fiend, 'and run.' Well, my conscience, hanging about the neck of my heart, says very wisely to me, 'My honest friend Launcelot, being an honest man's son,'—or rather an honest woman's son;—for, indeed, my father did something smack, something grow to, he had a kind of taste;—well, my conscience says, 'Launcelot, budge not.' 'Budge,' says the fiend. 'Budge not,' says my conscience. 'Conscience,' say I, 'you counsel well;' 'fiend,' say I, 'you counsel well:' to be ruled by my conscience, I should stay with the Jew my master, who, God bless the mark! is a kind of devil; and, to run away from the Jew, I should be ruled by the fiend, who, saving your reverence, is the devil himself. Certainly, the Jew is the very devil incarnal; and, in my conscience, my conscience is but a kind of hard conscience, to offer to counsel me to stay with the Jew. The fiend gives the more friendly counsel: I will run, fiend; my heels are at your commandment; I will run.

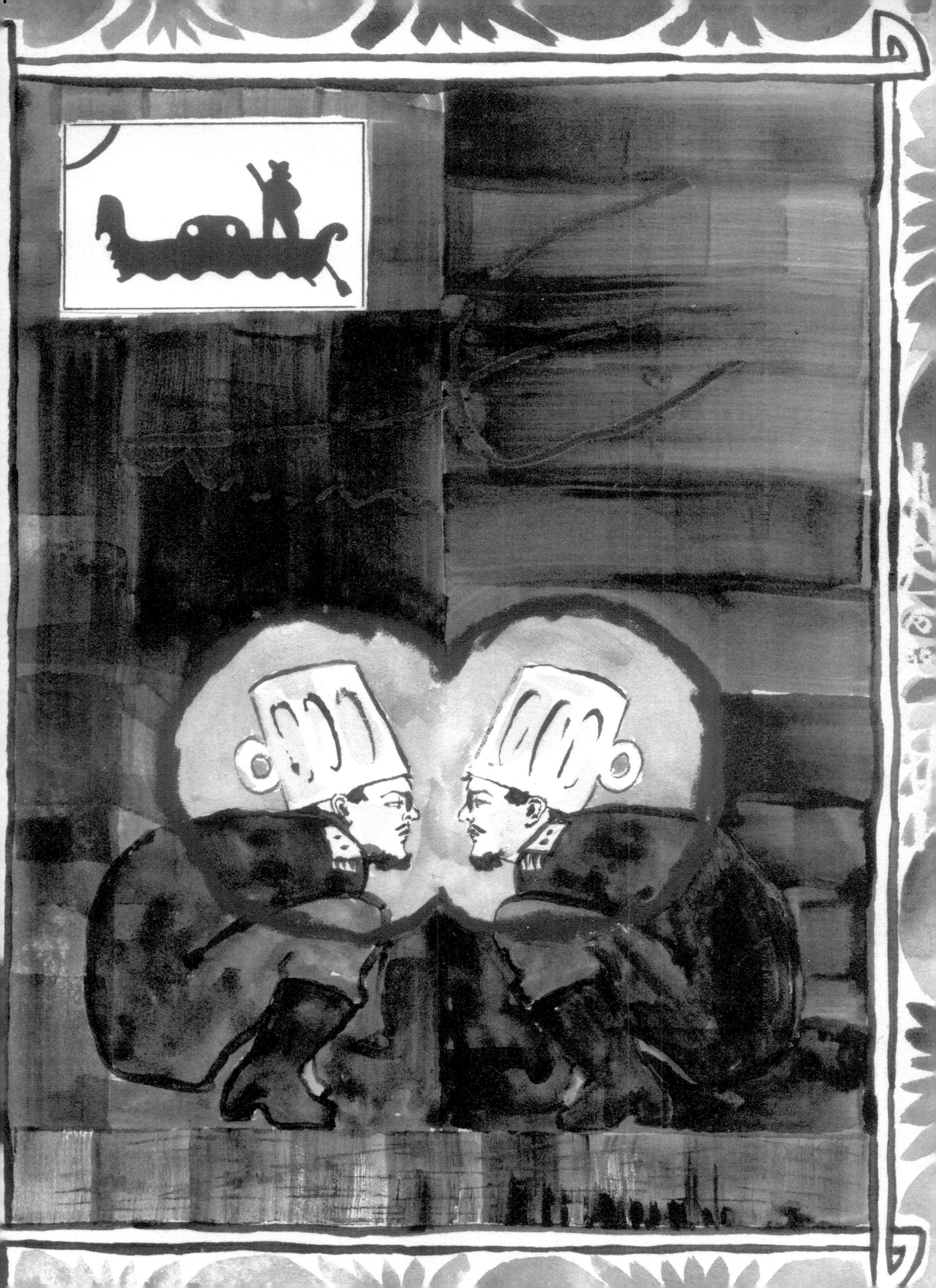

Enter Old Gobbo, with a basket.

GOBBO

Master young man, you; I pray you, which is the way to Master Jew's?

LAUNCELOT

[*Aside.*] O heavens! this is my truebegotten father, who, being more than sandblind, high-gravel blind, knows me not: I will try confusions with him.

GOBBO

Master young gentleman, I pray you, which is the way to Master Jew's?

LAUNCELOT

Turn up on your right hand at the next turning, but, at the next turning of all, on your left; marry, at the very next turning, turn of no hand, but turn down indirectly to the Jew's house.

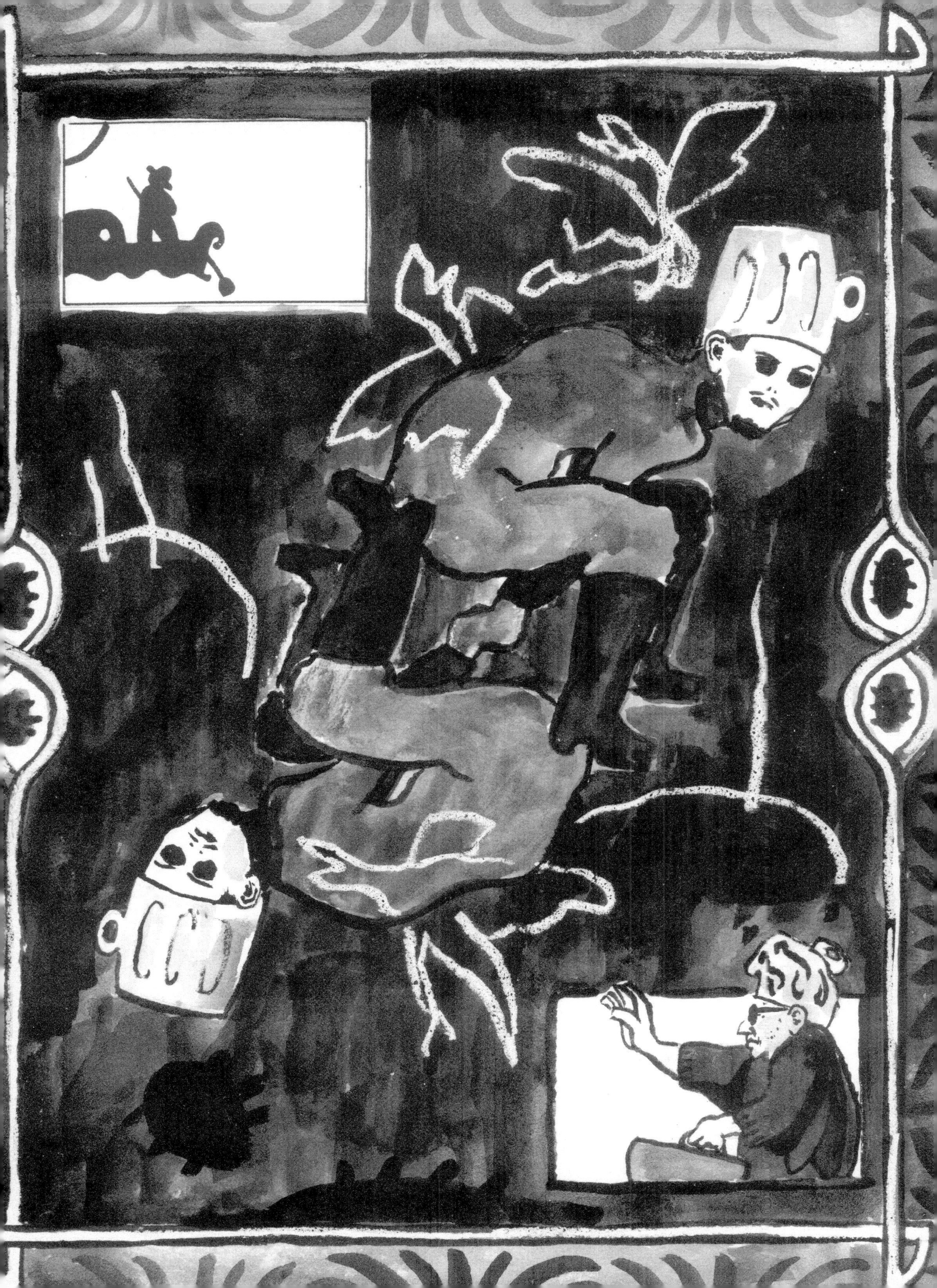

GOBBO

By God's sonties, 'twill be a hard way to hit. Can you tell me whether one Launcelot, that dwells with him, dwell with him or no?

LAUNCELOT

Talk you of young Master Launcelot? [*Aside.*] Mark me now; now will I raise the waters. Talk you of young Master Launcelot?

GOBBO

No master, sir, but a poor man's son: his father, though I say it, is an honest, exceeding poor man, and, God be thanked, well to live.

LAUNCELOT

Well, let his father be what a' will, we talk of young Master Launcelot.

GOBBO

Your worship's friend, and Launcelot, sir.

LAUNCELOT

But I pray you, ergo, old man, ergo, I beseech you, talk you of young Master Launcelot?

GOBBO

Of Launcelot, an't please your mastership.

LAUNCELOT

Ergo, Master Launcelot. Talk not of Master Launcelot, father; for the young gentleman,—according to Fates and Destinies and such odd sayings, the Sisters Three and such branches of learning,—is, indeed, deceased; or, as you would say in plain terms, gone to heaven.

GOBBO

Marry, God forbid! the boy was the very staff of my age, my very prop.

LAUNCELOT

[*Aside.*] Do I look like a cudgel or a hovel-post, a staff or a prop? Do you know me, father?

GOBBO

Alack the day! I know you not, young gentleman: but I pray you, tell me, is my boy,—God rest his soul!—alive or dead?

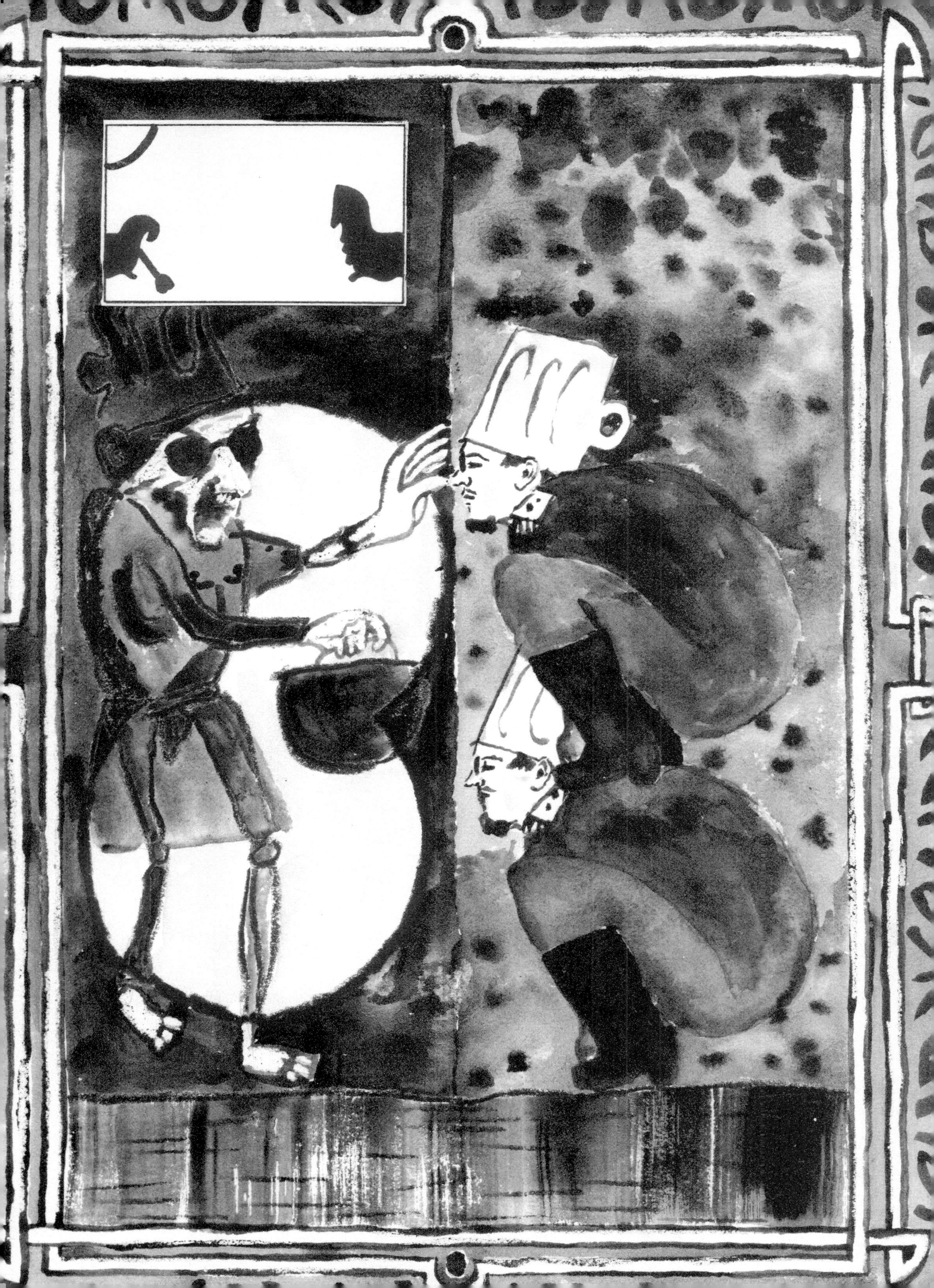

LAUNCELOT
Do you not know me, father?

GOBBO
Alack, sir, I am sand-blind; I know you not.

LAUNCELOT
Nay, indeed, if you had your eyes, you might fail of the knowing me: it is a wise father that knows his own child. Well, old man, I will tell you news of your son. Give me your blessing; truth will come to light; murder cannot be hid long; a man's son may, but, in the end, truth will out.

GOBBO
Pray you, sir, stand up. I am sure you are not Launcelot, my boy.

LAUNCELOT
Pray you, let's have no more fooling about it, but give me your blessing: I am Launcelot, your boy that was, your son that is, your child that shall be.

GOBBO
I cannot think you are my son.

LAUNCELOT
I know not what I shall think of that; but I am Launcelot, the Jew's man, and I am sure Margery your wife is my mother.

Forgive me, but I would like

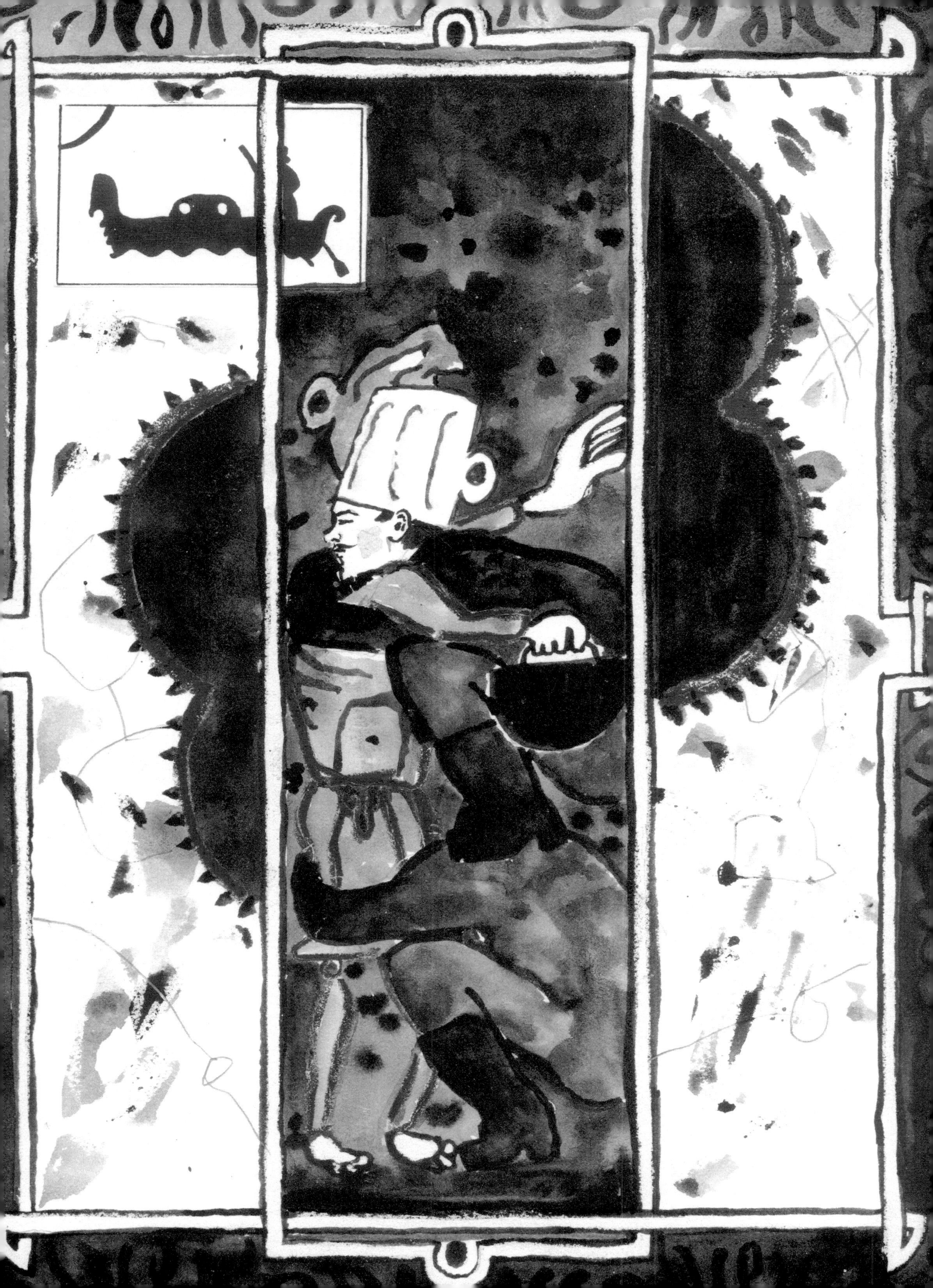

GOBBO

Her name is Margery, indeed: I'll be sworn, if thou be Launcelot, thou art mine own flesh and blood. Lord worshipped might he be! what a beard hast thou got! thou hast got more hair on thy chin than Dobbin my thill-horse has on his tail.

LAUNCELOT

It should seem then that Dobbin's tail grows backward: I am sure he had more hair on his tail than I have on my face, when I last saw him.

GOBBO

Lord! how art thou changed. How dost thou and thy master agree? I have brought him a present. How 'gree you now?

LAUNCELOT

Well, well: but, for mine own part, as I have set up my rest to run away, so I will not rest till I have run some ground. My master's a very Jew: give him a present! give him a halter: I am farnished in his service; you may tell every finger I have with my ribs. Father, I am glad you are come: give me your present to one Master Bassanio, who, indeed, gives rare new liveries. If I serve not him, I will run as far as God has any ground. O rare fortune! here comes the man: to him, father; for I am a Jew, if I serve the Jew any longer.

Forgive me, please, but I would like to speak of something else,

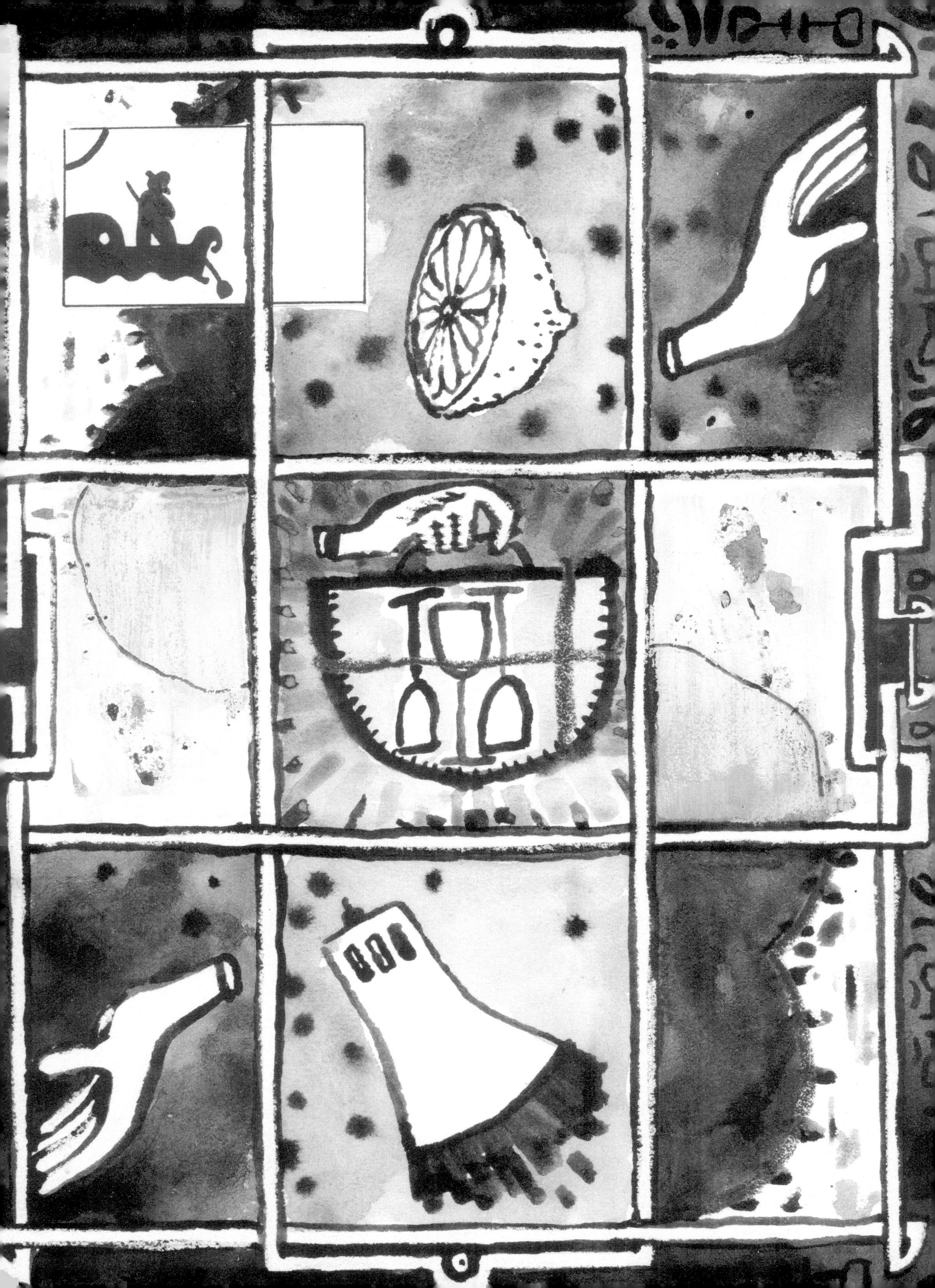

Enter Bassanio, with Leonardo, and other Followers.

BASSANIO
You may do so; but let it be so hasted that supper be ready at the very furthest by five of the clock. See these letters delivered; put the liveries to making; and desire Gratiano to come anon to my lodging.

Exit a Servant.

LAUNCELOT
To him, father.

GOBBO
God bless your worship!

BASSANIO
Gramercy! wouldst thou aught with me?

GOBBO
Here's my son, sir, a poor boy,—

LAUNCELOT
Not a poor boy, sir, but the rich Jew's man; that would, sir,—as my father shall specify,—

GOBBO
He hath a great infection, sir, as one would say, to serve—

LAUNCELOT
Indeed, the short and the long is, I serve the Jew, and have a desire, as my father shall specify,—

GOBBO
His master and he, saving your worship's reverence, are scarce cater-cousins,—

LAUNCELOT
To be brief, the very truth is that the Jew having done me wrong, doth cause me,—as my father, being, I hope, an old man, shall frutify unto you,—

GOBBO
I have here a dish of doves that I would bestow upon your worship, and my suit is,—

LAUNCELOT
In very brief, the suit is impertinent to myself, as your worship shall know by this honest old man; and, though I say it, though old man, yet poor man, my father.

BASSANIO
One speak for both. What would you?

LAUNCELOT
Serve you, sir.

GOBBO
That is the very defect of the matter, sir.

to speak of Tubal, through smooth, nursing affection. Do stare at his younger age, his superb smile, projecting oxygen abundance and sound physique.
Tubal the dreamer. He sees a loaf of black bread, grainy, warm, waiting, crusty outside, fragrant within. Wholesome, correct joy, the gratifying expectation of a believer.
The healthy fantasy: HO Tubal, thanks a lot, order is, hallo hallo, outside outside, inside inside, friendship, spirit, very pretty well.

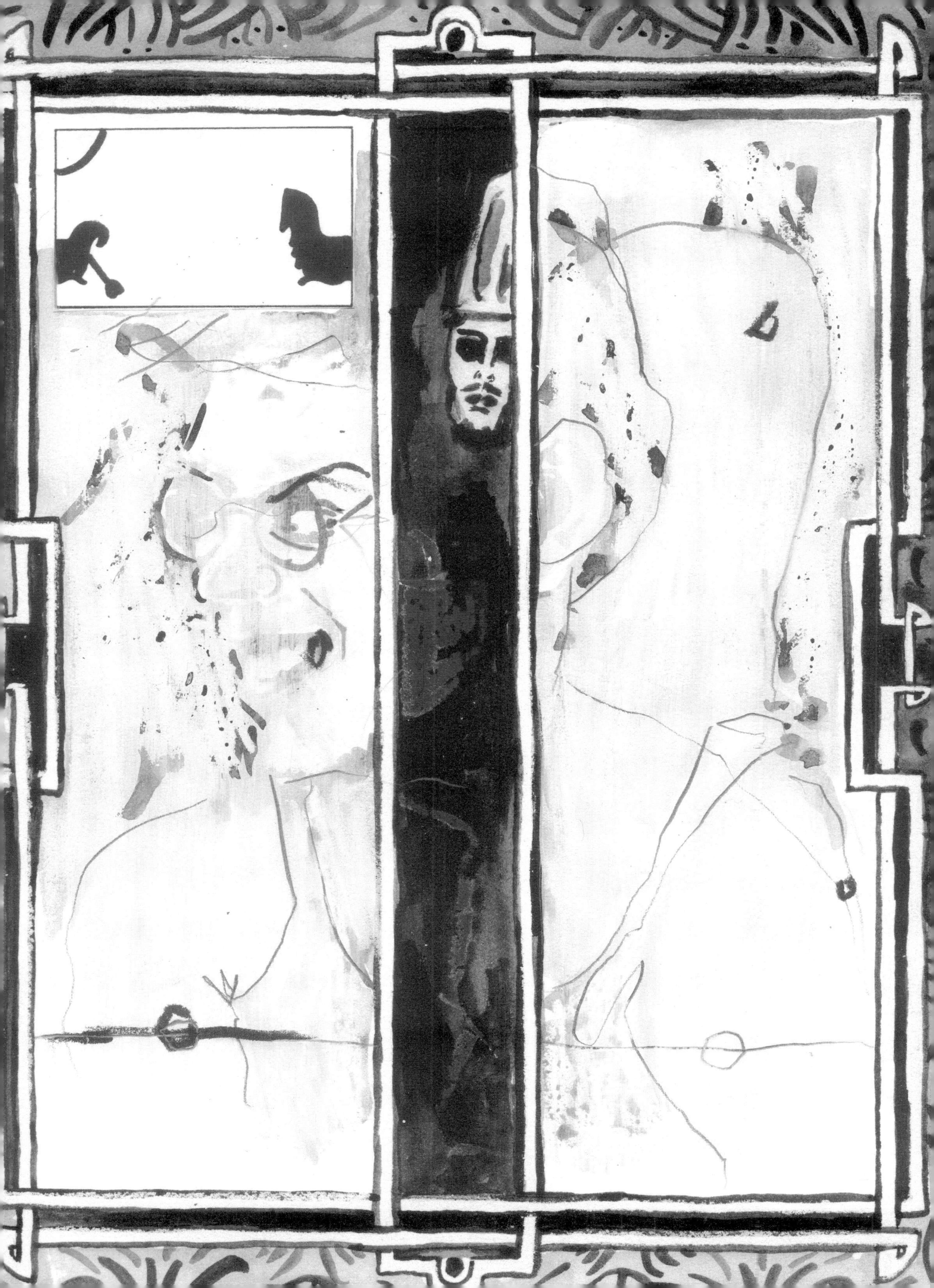

BASSANIO
I know thee well; thou hast obtain'd thy suit:
Shylock thy master spoke with me this day,
And hath preferr'd thee, if it be preferment
To leave a rich Jew's service, to become
The follower of so poor a gentleman.

LAUNCELOT
The old proverb is very well parted between my master Shylock and you, sir: you have the grace of God, sir, and he hath enough.

BASSANIO
Thou speak'st it well. Go, father, with thy son.
Take leave of thy old master, and inquire
My lodging out. [*To his followers.*] Give him a livery
More guarded than his fellows': see it done.

LAUNCELOT
Father, in. I cannot get a service, no; I have ne'er a tongue in my head. Well, [*Looking on his palm.*] if any man in Italy have a fairer table which doth offer to swear upon a book, I shall have good fortune. Go to; here's a simple line of life: here's a small trifle of wives: alas! fifteen wives is nothing: a 'leven widows and nine maids is a simple coming-in for one man; and then to 'scape drowning thrice, and to be in peril of my life with the edge of a feather-bed; here are simple 'scapes. Well, if Fortune be a woman, she's a good wench for this gear. Father, come; I'll take my leave of the Jew in the twinkling of an eye.

Exeunt Launcelot and Old Gobbo.

I wish you could love Tubal as I do.
He has so much energy. He has such a big good-morning. His teeth are all in excellent shape, and he does not stink at all, this good friend of Shylock's (what is good, true, a true friend of Shylock's (truth, what is truth (in fact the only, the only friend (and not just a friend, a loving friend (the only Shylock-lover in this hostile territory of spots forgive me nevermind))))).
And he dreams of bread. Suppertime. The bread rests on a table and is surrounded by what it takes. Below the table, a floor. Above the bread, two smiling children, chubby cherubim. And above them, a visage of a wife. Wife is calm and content. Wife is admired and smiling. And around the table and the bread and the floor and Tubal are white walls, dumbly defining a house. And in the middle of each wall, a window. The windows smile a curtained smile. Outside the smile stretches politely the outside. Tubal leaves the house to the outside and returns from the outside to the house, leaves the house to the outside (labor and wander and long) and returns from the outside to the house (which is a house), HO Tubal, thanks a lot, order is, hallo hallo, early autumn outside, and sweet and wet within, friendship, spirit, civil stretches, very pretty pretty well.

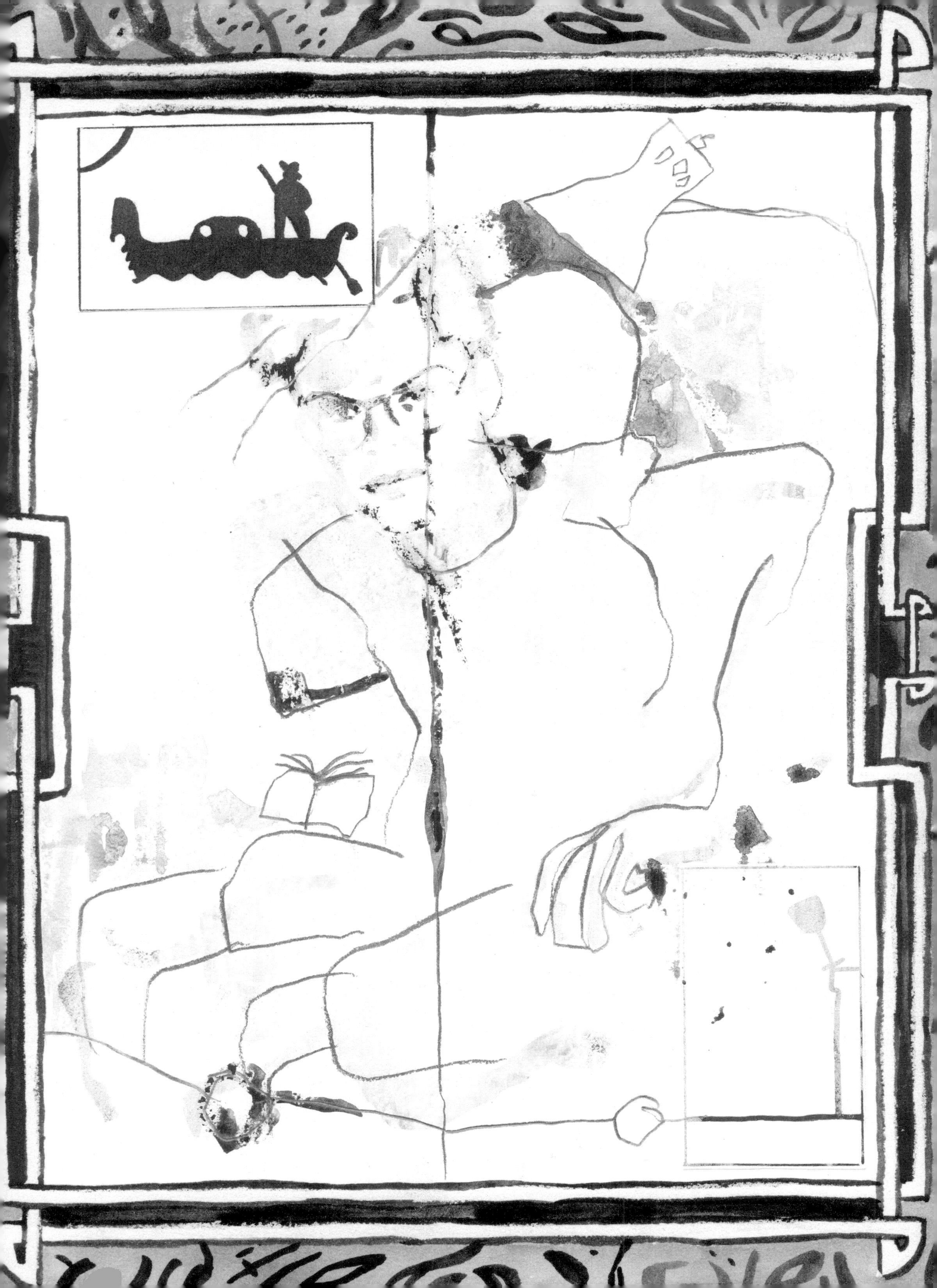

Tubal feels the need. His order-in-the-dream is something to speak about. He wants to be the orator of his fantasy. Peep at his good eagerness. All his body quivers with intention. It is the matter of poetry. He says: I am Tubal and you are Shylock. (It is not a bad beginning. Every song needs an attentive ear—but) he says it like an actor. And he is no actor. Tubal thinks he is *really* Tubal. And as he says what he says, language ossifies a little. Language has its own opinions. And as it ossifies, a small doubt-slot widens within the picture. Yet, still. He has so much wind. His muscles young his hair thick. He digs his nails into the language. He says: Shylock, Shylock is not me. True, language, for both of us, is foreign. And it is one language that speaks for both. But I know it is more complex. I know nothing is not altogether unforeign or ununforeign. I know nothing. True, Shylock lost, but he is a different foreigner to language than I. Shylock, he fights language. He tries to swindle her, to ground her by wild, stupendous tongue-attacks, by blindly spitting himself at her. Not me. I know modesty. Foreign and I respect each other. (Tubal hears, now he hears, the mocking sneer of language. He knows he has no control. But still, he has wind). He says: I say what is right. Mark me now. I keep my eyes open. I am thankful when it is due. Black fruits in Africa. A kind king in Denmark. Serious flesh in Germany. Thanks a lot. Order is called for, and I say: Hallo, order. The house in the house, and the outside outside. There is a need to take pains for order. Pains are called for. If language is the house, and if it is foreign, then it has simply to be one's foreign house. Outspoken silence. One speaks for both, says Tubal to himself, and in a funk they both watch how the clumsy fear bursts forth from within the doubt-slot. LO Tubal, thanks a lot, order is perhaps, early autumn outside and soggy slag within, bread and word and pretty sorry, maybe pretty pretty still.

BASSANIO
I pray thee, good Leonardo, think on this:
These things being bought, and orderly bestow'd,
Return in haste, for I do feast to-night
My best-esteem'd acquaintance: hie thee, go.

LEONARDO
My best endeavours shall be done herein.

Enter Gratiano.

GRATIANO
Where is your master?

LEONARDO
Yonder, sir, he walks.

Exit.

GRATIANO
Signior Bassanio!—

BASSANIO
Gratiano!

GRATIANO
I have a suit to you.

BASSANIO
You have obtain'd it.

GRATIANO
You must not deny me: I must go with you to Belmont.

BASSANIO
Why, then you must. But hear thee, Gratiano;
Thou art too wild, too rude and bold of voice;
Parts that become thee happily enough,
And in such eyes as ours appear not faults;
But where thou art not known, why, there they show
Something too liberal. Pray thee, take pain
To allay with some cold drops of modesty
Thy skipping spirit, lest, through thy wild behaviour,
I be misconstru'd in the place I go to,
And lose my hopes.

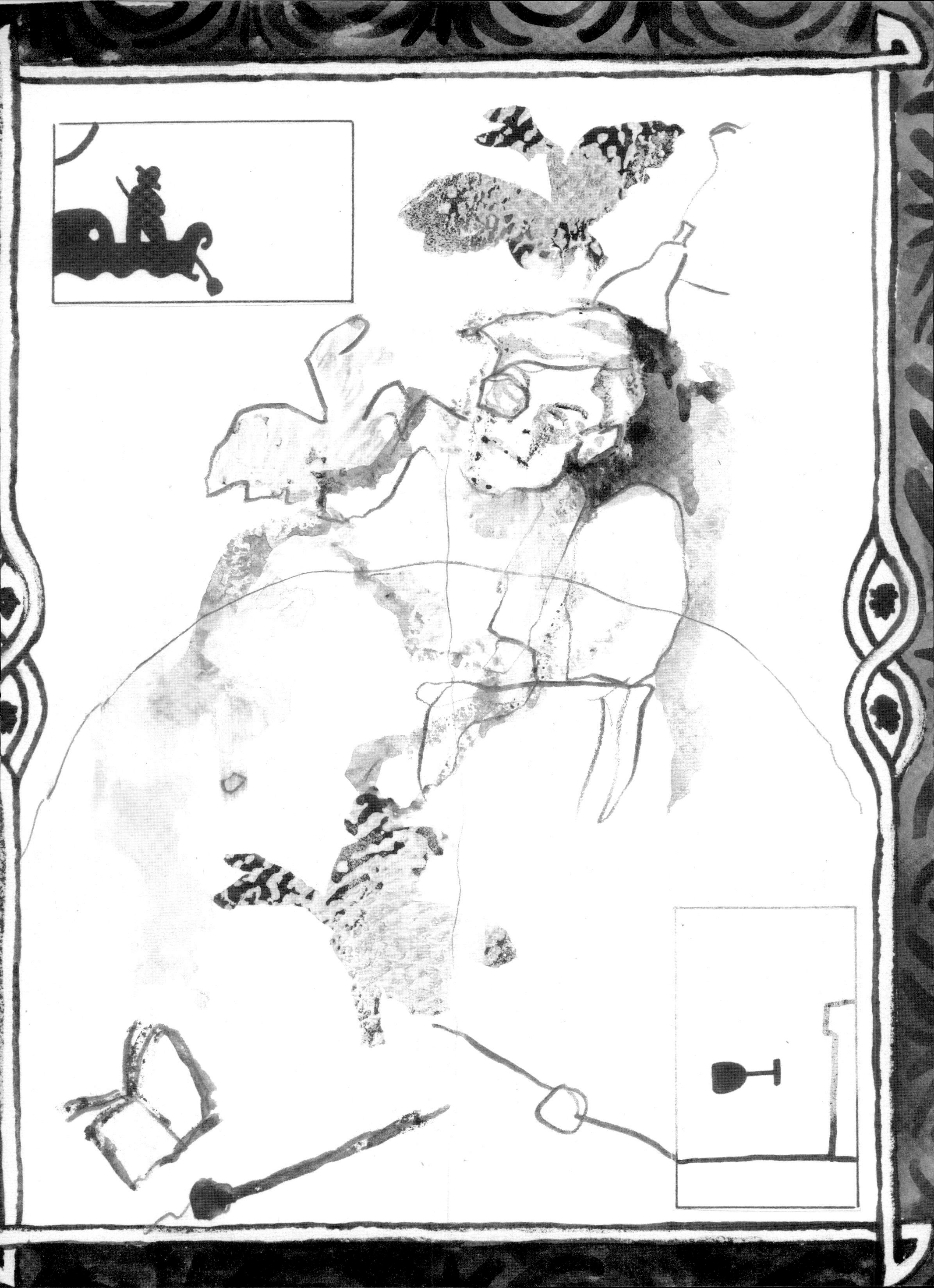

It should raise waters. Listen to the gloomy. Listen how language. Stare at the Tubal travesty and his fight with the foreign tongue. He says: I have a plan and Shylock has no eyes. But had. Had, once, big, convincing eyes he had and charm and head and glass. And the child was as healthy as my will-be. Has had. Should should. The more I ask for less more, the more less I get. Now it should raise waters, this question of language. He knows it needs not be asked constantly (blessed-forgetting-Amen). Fortunes were dealt favoring Tubal and he insists on approving. But the question of language points at the collision. The collision is there for good. There are things you cannot come to terms with. Real things with no terms. Tiny, hidden obstacles. How I care not for music. His eyes that seemed to be forever. He remembers how Leah's body was forgotten. And her language was so clear and refined and and even maybe almost natural. And so the order turns into a dark film, covering for good. The more I want it to take place the more or less it does. Maybe it is a different birth. The collision, thinks Tubal the thinker, is a despair that may still breed hope. The hope, deduces Tubal the hoper, is, according to his terms, miserly and clenched. Ergo, he is forced to love it. The collision consumes his love. Ergo, it is his only territory. Thanks a lot. Weary, he should end here. Travel tomorrow. But now, he wants to have a name for his collision. He wants, at least, to call it by name. He wants to make it nominal.

But only one word comes to his lips.

GRATIANO
Signior Bassanio, hear me:
If I do not put on a sober habit,
Talk with respect, and swear but now and then,
Wear prayer-books in my pocket, look demurely,
Nay more, while grace is saying, hood mine eyes
Thus with my hat, and sigh, and say 'amen;'
Use all the observance of civility,
Like one well studied in a sad ostent
To please his grandam, never trust me more.

BASSANIO
well, we shall see your bearing.

GRATIANO
Nay, but I bar to-night; you shall not gauge me
By what we do to-night.

BASSANIO
No, that were pity:
I would entreat you rather to put on
Your boldest suit of mirth, for we have friends
That purpose merriment. But fare you well:
I have some business.

GRATIANO
And I must to Lorenzo and the rest;
But we will visit you at supper-time.

Exeunt.

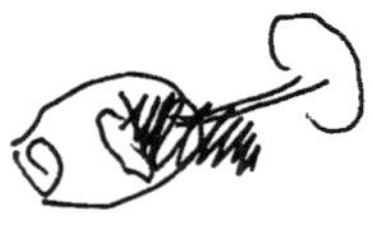

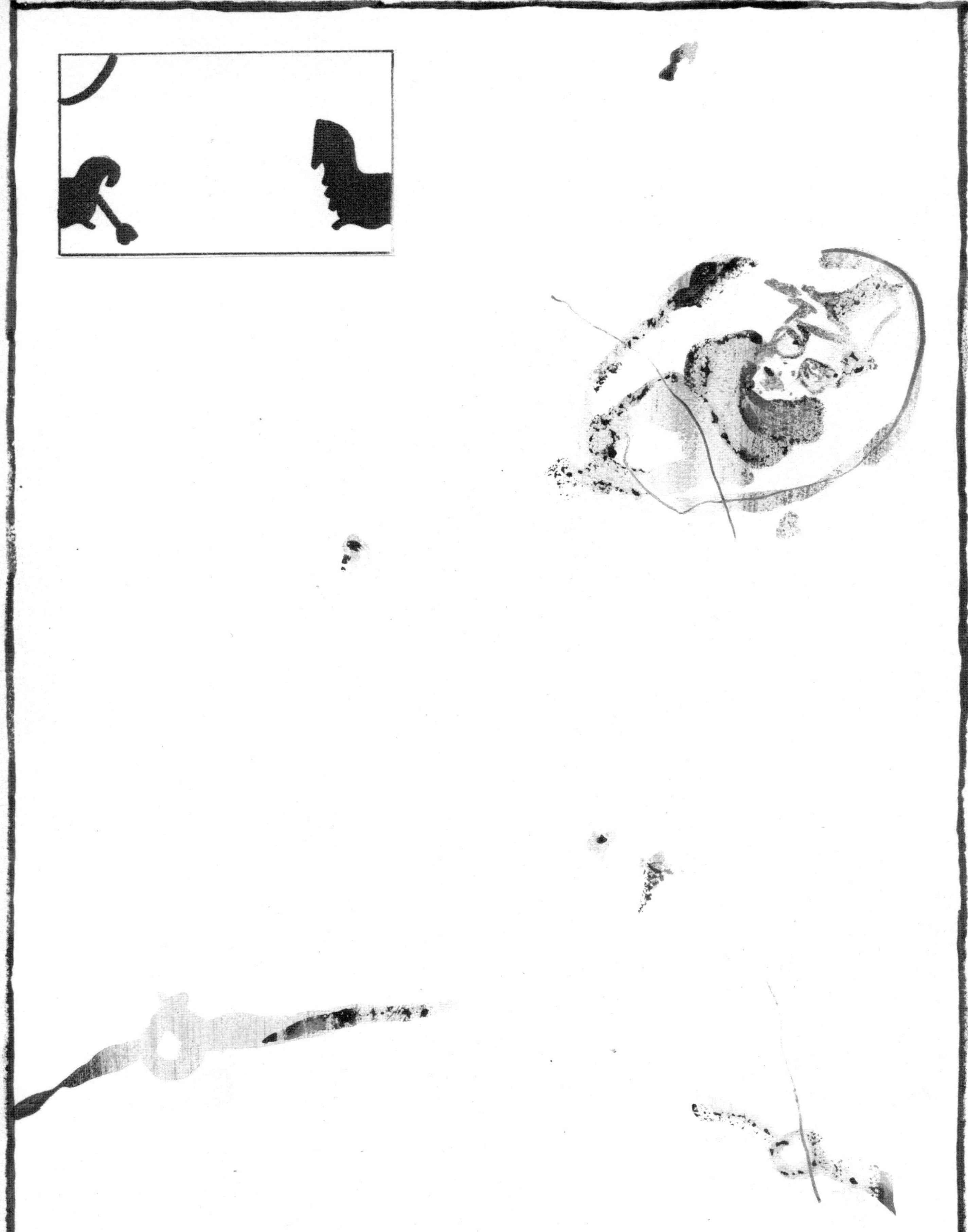

Scene III—The Same. A Room in Shylock's House.

Enter Jessica and Launcelot.

JESSICA
I am sorry thou wilt leave my father so:
Our house is hell, and thou, a merry devil,
Didst rob it of some taste of tediousness.
But fare thee well; there is a ducat for thee:
And, Launcelot, soon at supper shalt thou see
Lorenzo, who is thy new master's guest:
Give him this letter; do it secretly;
And so farewell: I would not have my father
See me in talk with thee.

LAUNCELOT
Adieu! tears exhibit my tongue. Most beautiful pagan, most sweet Jew! If a Christian did not play the knave and get thee, I am much deceived. But, adieu! these foolish drops do somewhat drown my manly spirit: adieu!

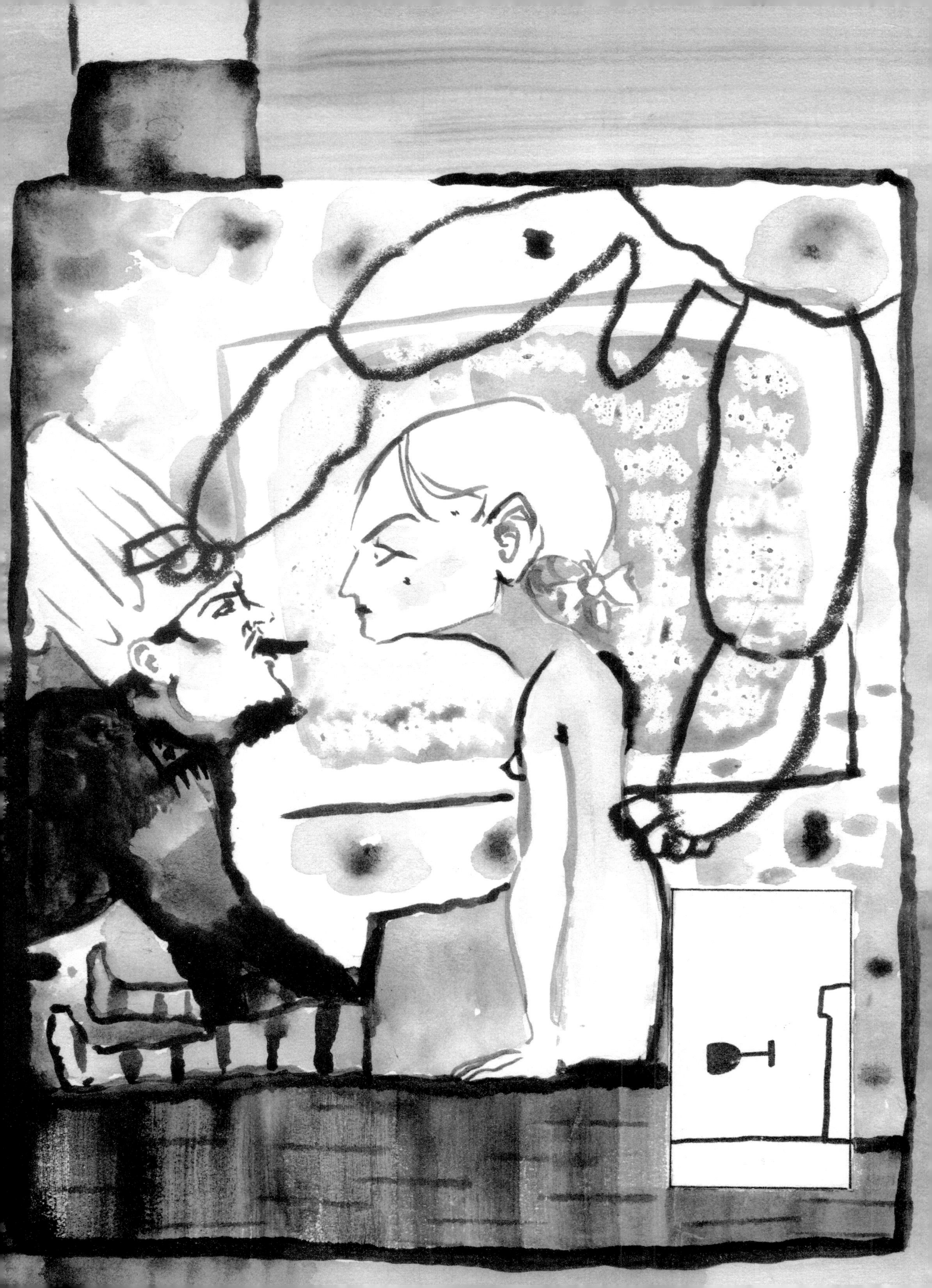

II.III.2

JESSICA

Farewell, good Launcelot.

Exit Launcelot.

Alack, what heinous sin is it in me
To be asham'd to be my father's child!
But though I am a daughter to his blood,
I am not to his manners. O Lorenzo!
If thou keep promise, I shall end this strife,
Become a Christian, and thy loving wife.

Exit.

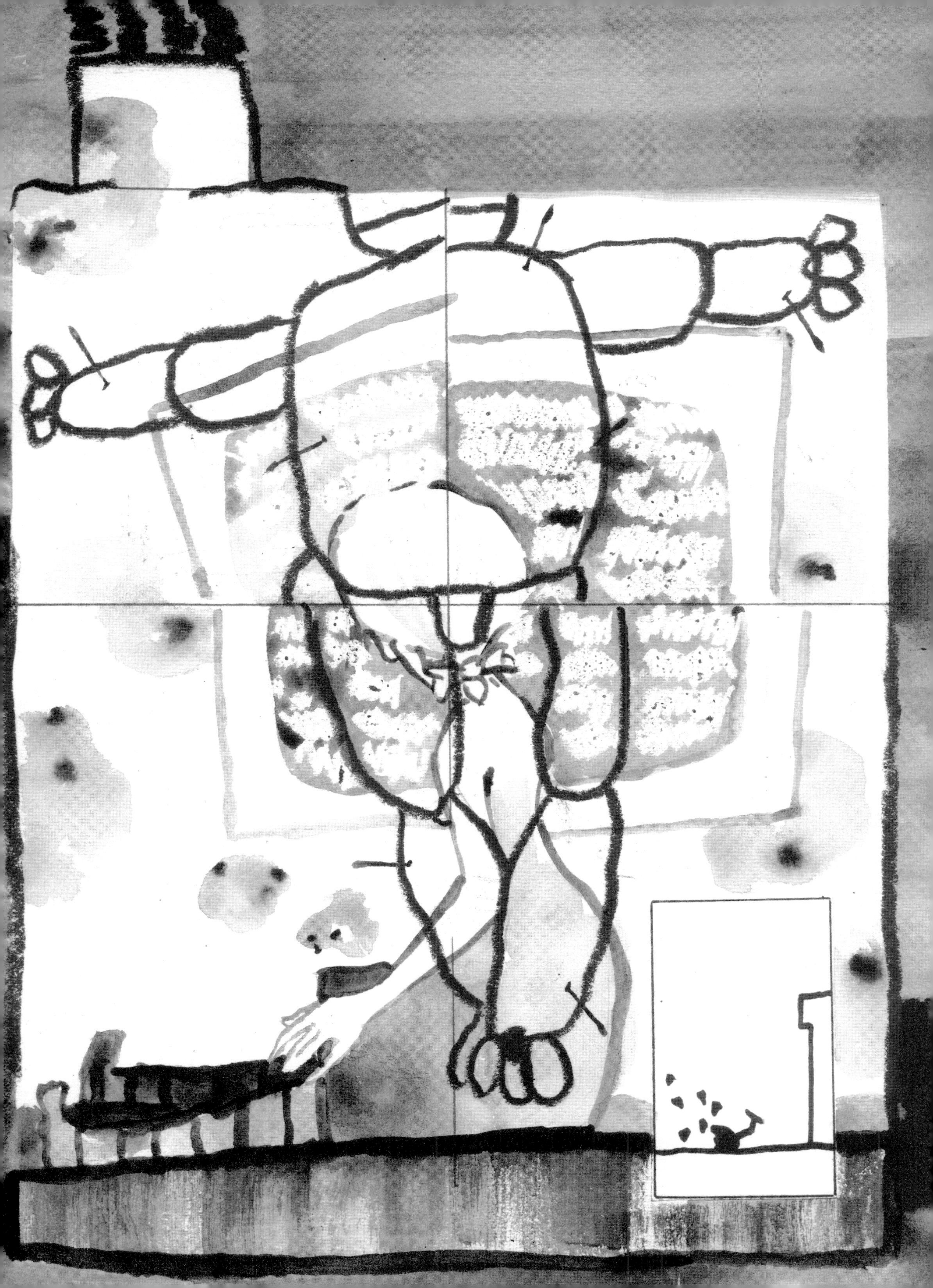

Scene IV—The Same. A Street.

Enter Gratiano, Lorenzo, Salarino, and Salanio.

LORENZO
Nay, we will slink away in supper-time,
Disguise us at my lodging, and return
All in an hour.

GRATIANO
We have not made good preparation.

SALARINO
We have not spoke us yet of torch-bearers.

SALANIO
'Tis vile, unless it may be quaintly order'd,
And better, in my mind, not undertook.

LORENZO
'Tis now but four o'clock: we have two hours
To furnish us.

Enter Launcelot, with a letter.

Friend Launcelot, what's the news?

LAUNCELOT
An it shall please you to break up this, it shall seem to signify.

LORENZO
I know the hand: in faith, 'tis a fair hand;
And whiter than the paper it writ on
Is the fair hand that writ.

GRATIANO
Love news, in faith.

LAUNCELOT
By your leave, sir.

LORENZO
Whither goest thou?

LAUNCELOT
Marry, sir, to bid my old master, the Jew, to sup to-night with my new master, the Christian.

LORENZO
Hold here, take this: tell gentle Jessica
I will not fail her; speak it privately.

Exit Launcelot.

Go, gentlemen,
Will you prepare you for this masque to-night?
I am provided of a torch-bearer.

SALARINO
Ay, marry, I'll be gone about it straight.

SALANIO
And so will I.

LORENZO
Meet me and Gratiano
At Gratiano's lodging some hour hence.

Look at Lorenzo,
peculiar and *charmant*!
When he was only thirteen,
he already had
three Scandinavian aunts!

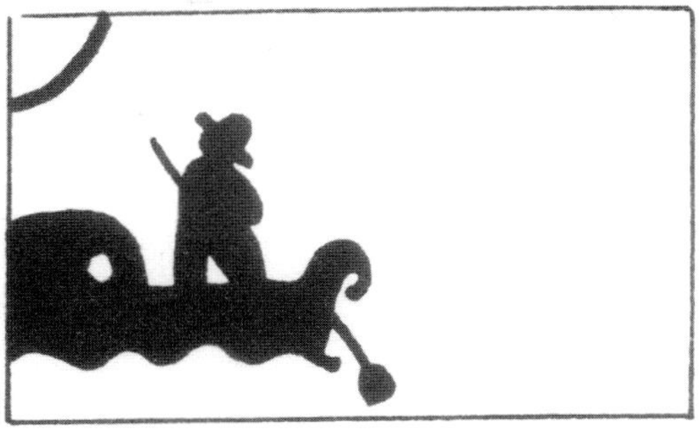

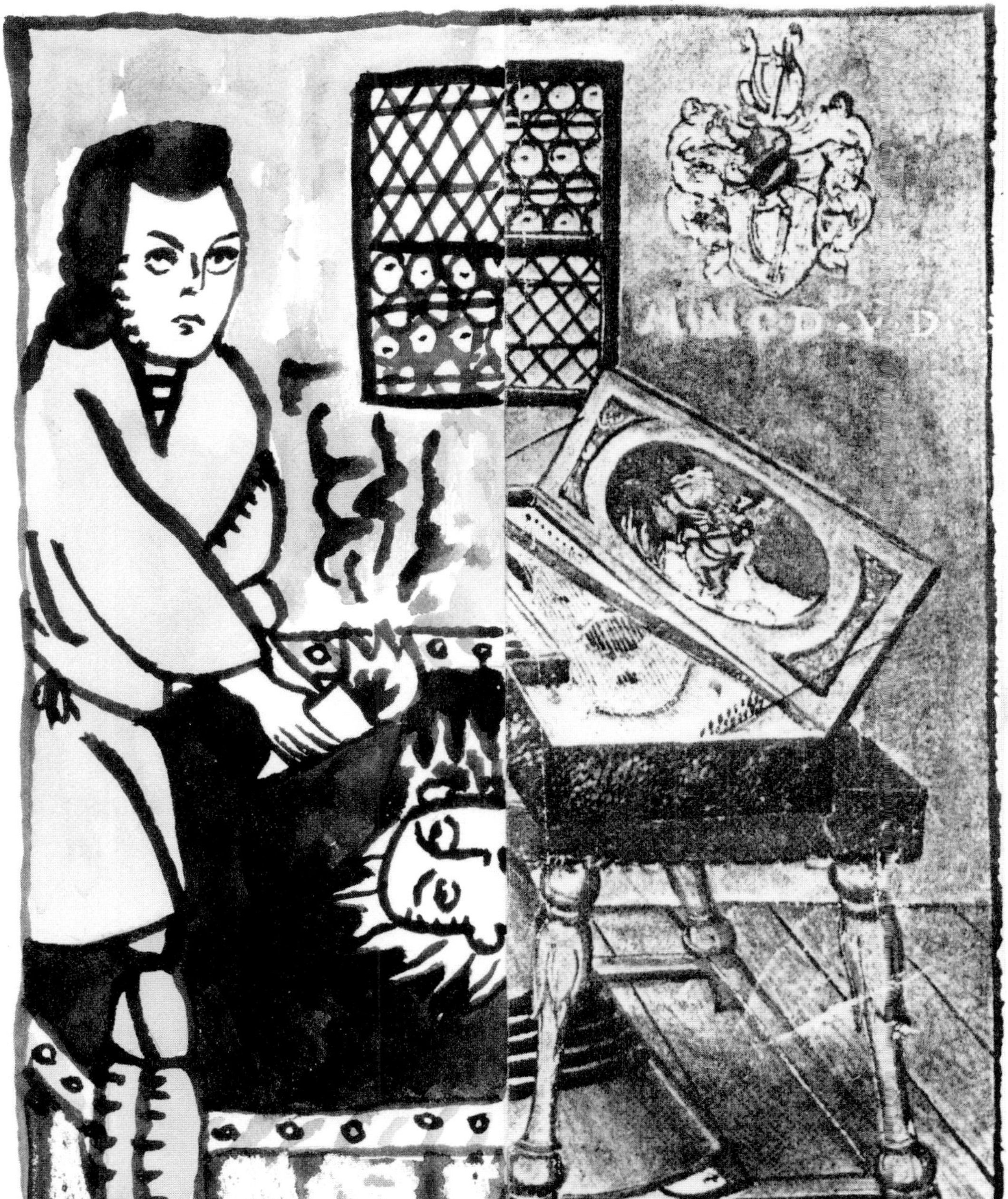

II.IV.2

SALARINO
'Tis good we do so.

Exeunt Salarino and Salanio.

GRATIANO
Was not that letter from fair Jessica?

LORENZO
I must needs tell thee all. She hath directed
How I shall take her from her father's house;
What gold and jewels she is furnish'd with;
What page's suit she hath in readiness.
If e'er the Jew her father come to heaven,
It will be for his gentle daughter's sake;
And never dare misfortune cross her foot,
Unless she do it under this excuse,
That she is issue to a faithless Jew.
Come, go with me: peruse this as thou goest.
Fair Jessica shall be my torch-bearer.

Exeunt.

He licked cherry confiture from the navel of Helma, the aging countess! With his amazing nostrils he sniffed death drawing near from her perfumed belly. With his sharp eyes he observed her wrinkles, and absorbed the sweet and red, and the nervous spasms of orgasm and fear. Her dependency amused him! Lily had the muscles of a porter and a Greek torso! She whipped, and he spanked! Afterwards he would accompany her at the piano. She had a deep, deep alto! It ended with an unpleasant scandal.
Ingrid was toffee pink all over. She taught him the wonders of the rectum in depth. He would cite her Theognis and annotate!
He, he deserted a wealthy widow in favor of a little Turk!
Every day he proved the existence or the non-existence of different things, every day in a different way!
He had a parrot that whistled Couperin.
He fried it in butter and capers.
He never lost his sense of humor, and never smiled!
Home was never an issue, but now it is time for something more homely and stable. Something that would involve, so to speak, a rigorous investment from the metaphysical sphere, alongside tits.
And he found something special and charming.
Lorenzo can hardly wait!

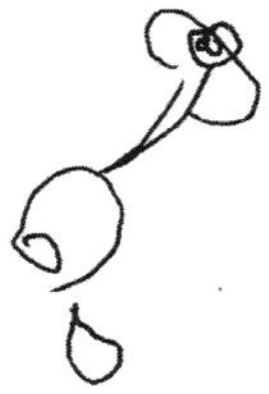

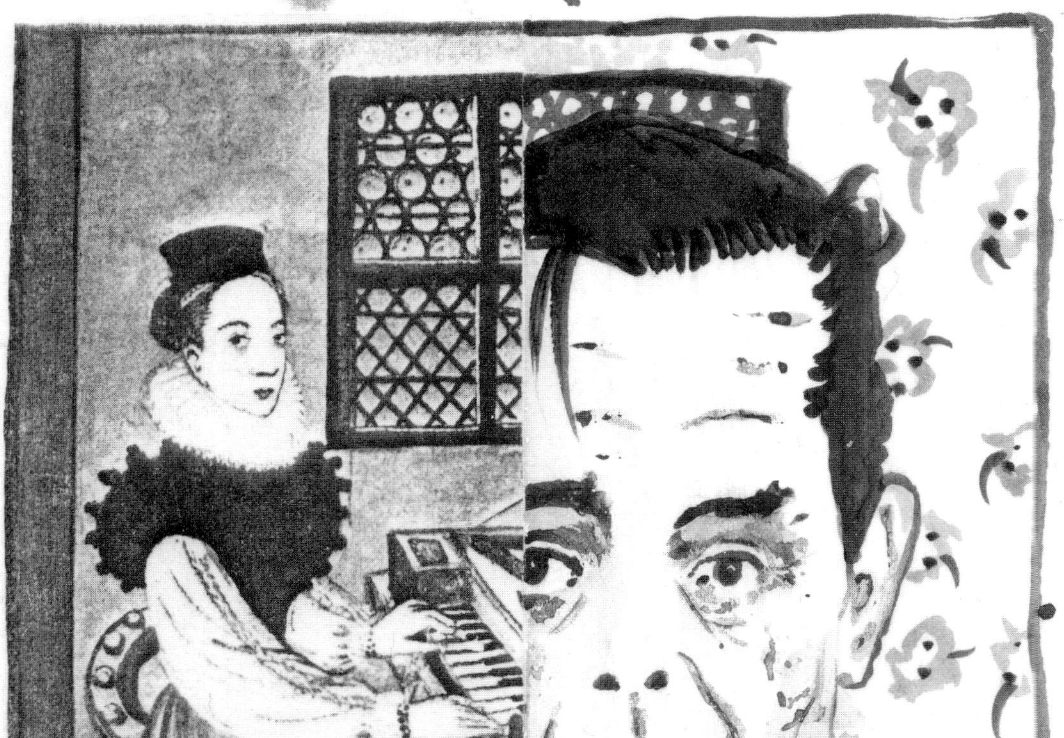

Scene V—The Same. Before Shylock's House.

Enter Shylock and Launcelot.

SHYLOCK
Well, thou shalt see, thy eyes shall be thy judge,
The difference of old Shylock and Bassanio:—
What, Jessica!—thou shalt not gormandize,
As thou hast done with me;—What, Jessica!—
And sleep and snore, and rend apparel out
Why, Jessica, I say!

Shylock's response upon being informed that his servant has deserted him starts with the fine sentence: "Thou shalt see, thy eyes shall be thy judge," an approach that, the speaker being blind, enfolds not only thin irony (shalt *see*, thy *eyes*), but also a potential for the instant evocation of regret, perhaps even pity. The continuation is an exemplary performance of subtle verbal manipulation. While crying for his beloved daughter, while preparing for the hard exit to the outer outside, Shylock has the inspiration to approach the clown with oozing, venomous, intimidating insinuations, paternal reproach, and an ornamented lyricism. It will be a mistake to assume, though, that Shylock has not been hurt by the desertion. Desertion, even when the deserter is merely a slothful, gluttonous, fornicating clown-servant, desertion means pain, means betrayal, fear and horror. But Shylock, for him being deserted is almost a professional affair. He was trained at being deserted. The desertion ache is mingled with, and made mild by, a sort of pride of sportsmanship, derived from the ability to demonstrate a skilled coordination, to recover flexibly from the panic, sponge in the pain and mold it.

There is a need to unify life, as is done by the orchestra conductor, who listens to all the rebellious instruments and shapes their shouts into a single reasonable tune.

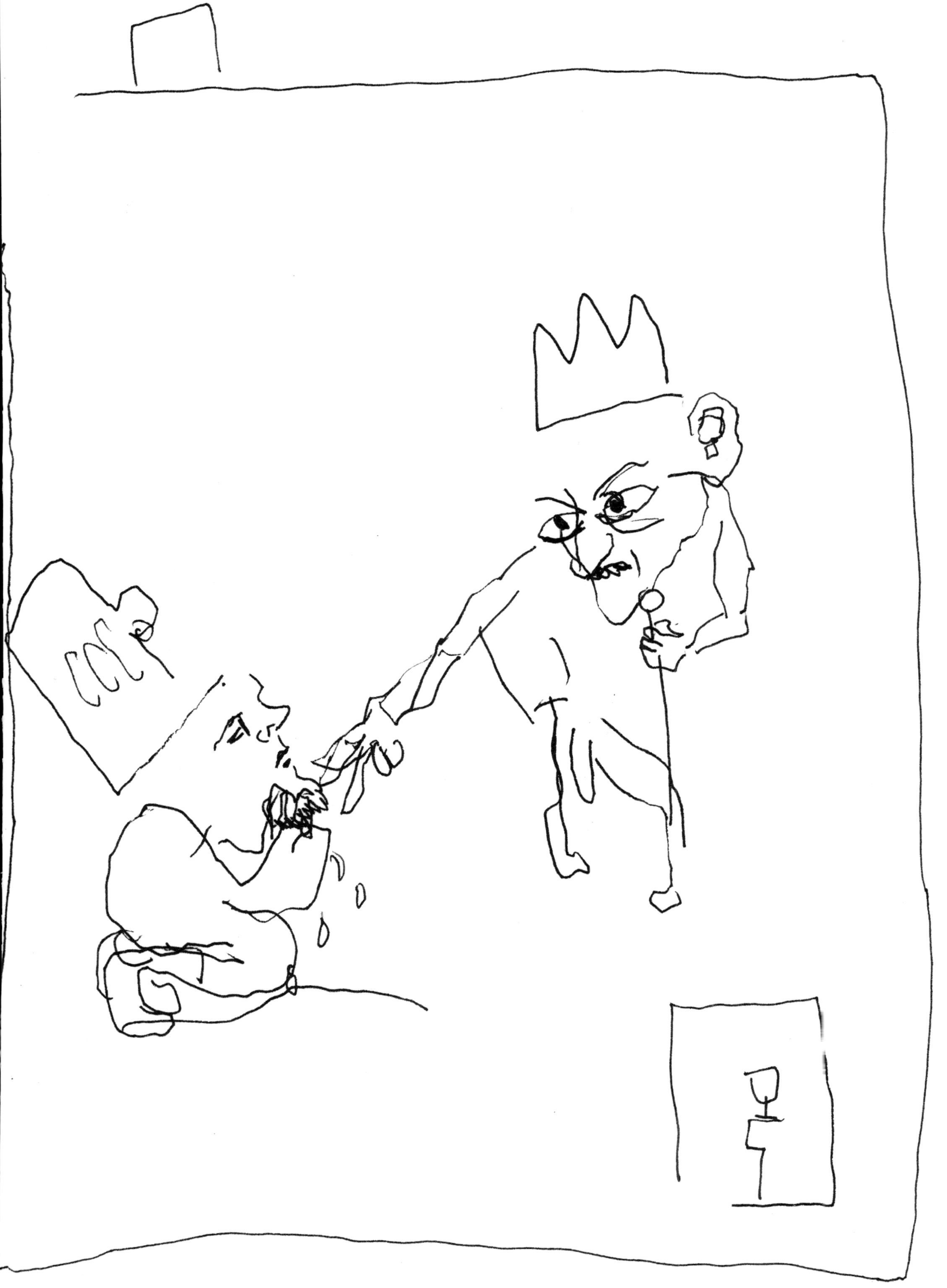

LAUNCELOT
Why, Jessica!

Launcelot, imitating Shylock's cry, seems to be saying: Pff, metaphor! Pff, orchestra, conductor, instruments! Here, there is no written score to consult. Here, it is comical. Here it is me, and I fart. Pff, pff! Twice pff! Shylock is stunned, he is temporarily numb—but it will be a mistake to assume that his brief shock has been caused by the clown's crudeness. He is indeed surprised, but we could have expected him to respond with slashing verbal fury. Even when he would not conduct, he would believe he does, and even if he would not believe, he would pretend to. Sportsmanship and survival are somewhat mixed in his case. No. Something worse causes him dismay. He says to himself: I still do not know precisely what it is. But it feels irreversible and sober. Like decay. It feels like a skin rash, skin disease. My skin feels it, and I do too. Like blisters or

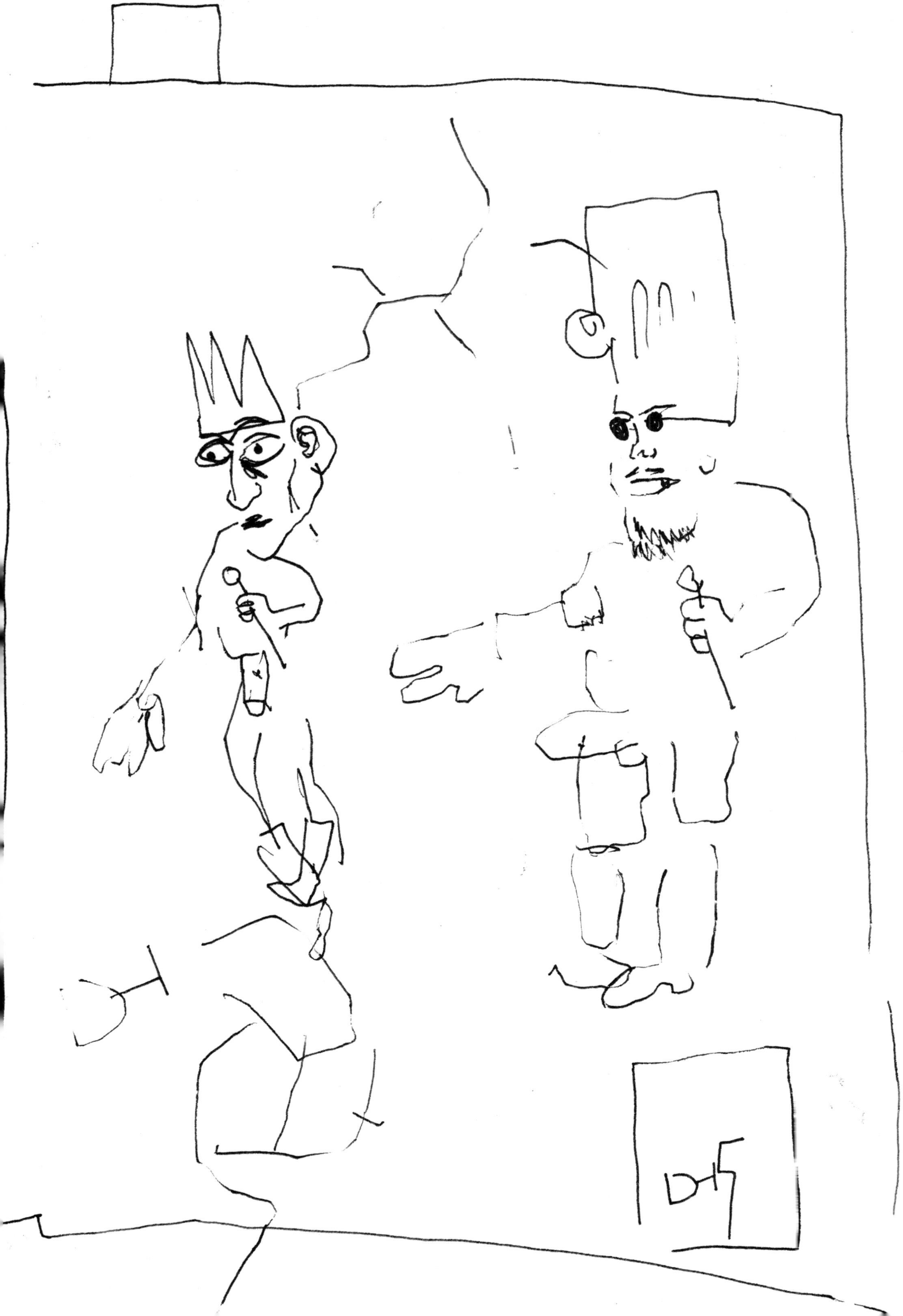

or spots.
There is some new stench here. Shylock feels a funny tickle inside the tips of his fingers. He looks at them and sees nothing and says to himself—but of course I do not, after all, I am blind. He is blind, but in a way, he does not want to look, quite the opposite, he wishes he had sight so that he could close his eyes, willingly stop seeing, and smell. Touch and smell. Smell the lost smell, the sweet, personal saltiness of Leah's armpits, touch the hair there, soft and private. Willingly to be disjointed. The way you desire. In the good darkness.
And then, as you glide down.

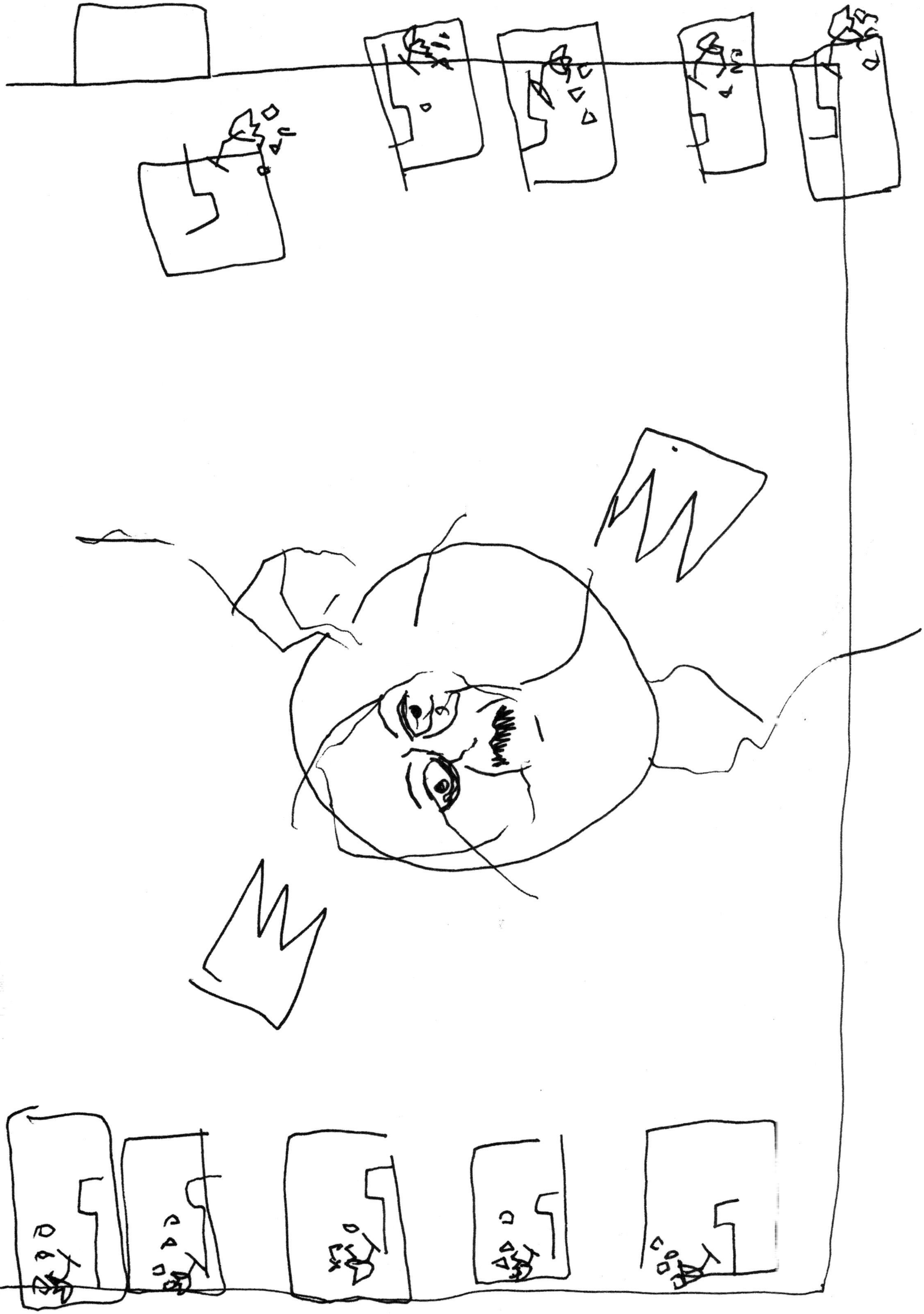

SHYLOCK
Who bids thee call? I do not bid thee call.

LAUNCELOT
Your worship was wont to tell me that
I could do nothing without bidding.

Those longings make him shorter. And exposed. He feels as if he has been a long time in a hot bath. There is so much pettiness to attend to, and no steam.
And as the longings soften him from above, the new enemy stench attacks him from behind. We are certainly no orchestra, but maybe still, at least, some decent pity. Solo violin.
Give me a small violin.
Being a practical man, Shylock cries for his beloved daughter.
Pff.

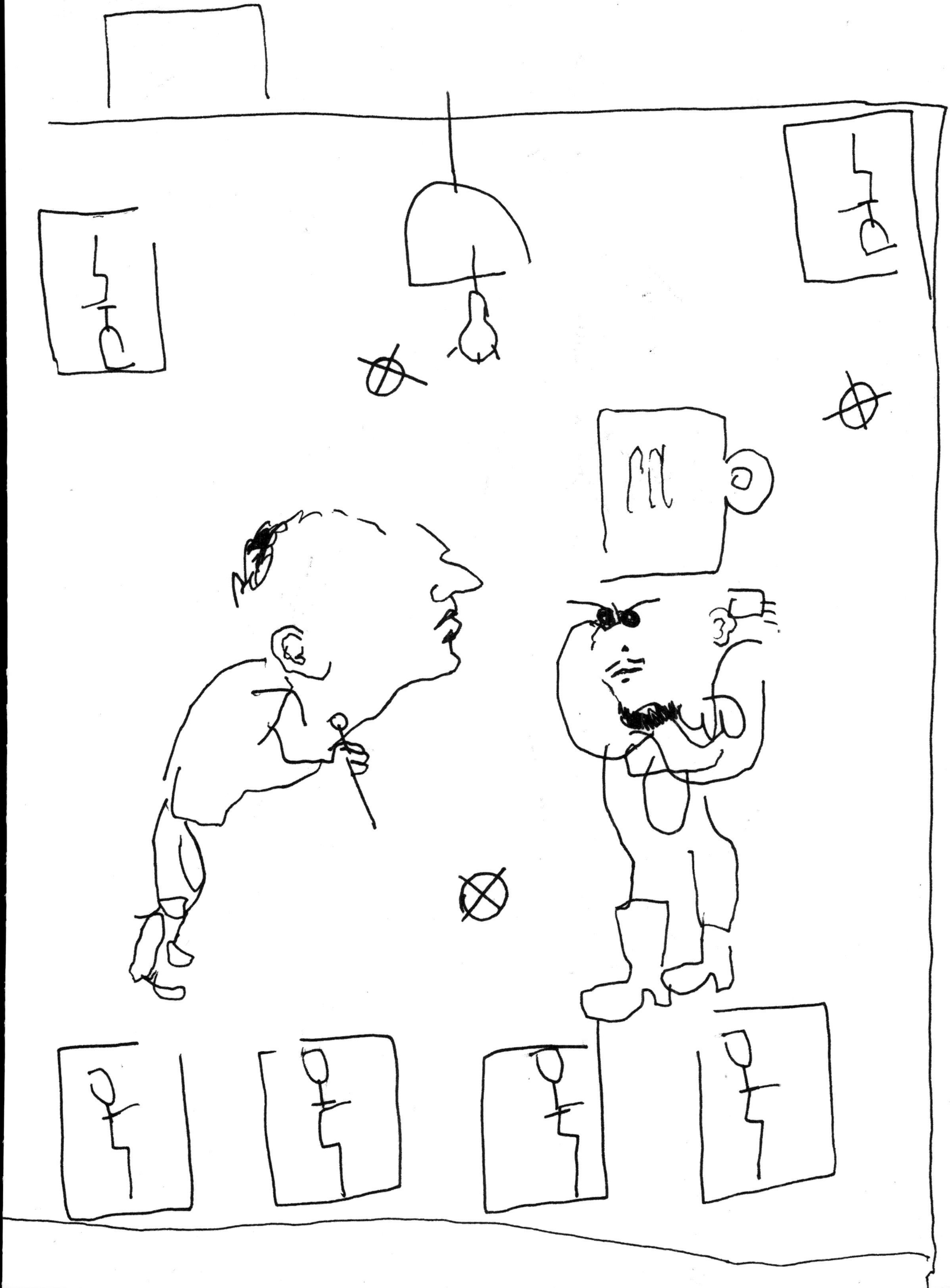

Enter Jessica.

JESSICA
Call you? What is your will?

SHYLOCK
I am bid forth to supper, Jessica:
There are my keys. But wherefore should I go?
I am not bid for love; they flatter me:
But yet I'll go in hate, to feed upon
The prodigal Christian. Jessica, my girl,
Look to my house. I am right loath to go
There is some ill a-brewing towards my rest,
For I did dream of money-bags to-night.

Pff, practical, pff, beloved. A risky and slimy matter, longings. Take from a man some armpit perfume that gave him some wanted sensation. Attack him on the other frontier. Soon he feels the need. The subject of his longings being unattainable (in this case, dead), he substitutes the longing with a longing for the longing, an amusing and wretched move, and from there, because of the hunger, the way is short to another conversion, say, for a sewerage. And there you have comedy. The bird, played by the flute.

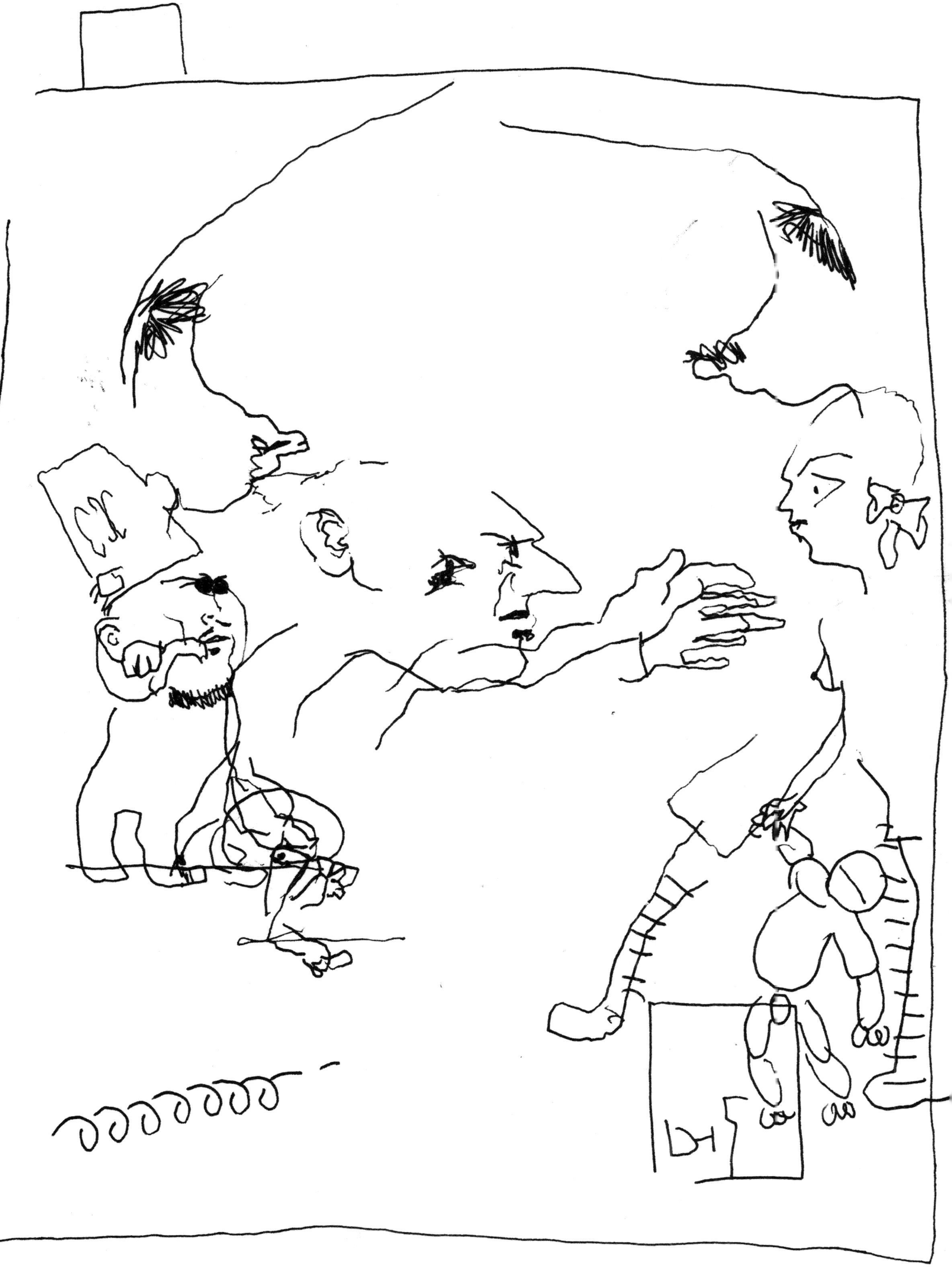

LAUNCELOT
I beseech you, sir, go: my young master doth expect your reproach.

SHYLOCK
So do I his.

LAUNCELOT
And they have conspired together: I will not say you shall see a masque; but if you do, then it was not for nothing that my nose fell a-bleeding on Black-Monday last, at six o'clock i' the morning, falling out that year on Ash-Wednesday was four year in the afternoon.

And as he speaks to his daughter with an excited haste, as he tells her, "I am not bid for love," as he calls her "my girl" and asks her to look after his house, we see that he is a defeated animal. Does
he know the defeat and only pretends
to deny?
Does he not understand?
Does he not see?
The nauseating tickle of the new smell floods all of his screen like spots, and the sly longings draw him towards the risky, ring-shaped trap of pestering memories and self-hatred. He is a defeated animal. Somebody says: You are a disgusting, old, blind animal. You were wrong to begin with, but now you are not even what you were. You have no claim. So choke on memories in the ring dungeon. The bait was pulled out from under your nose, and you lift off.

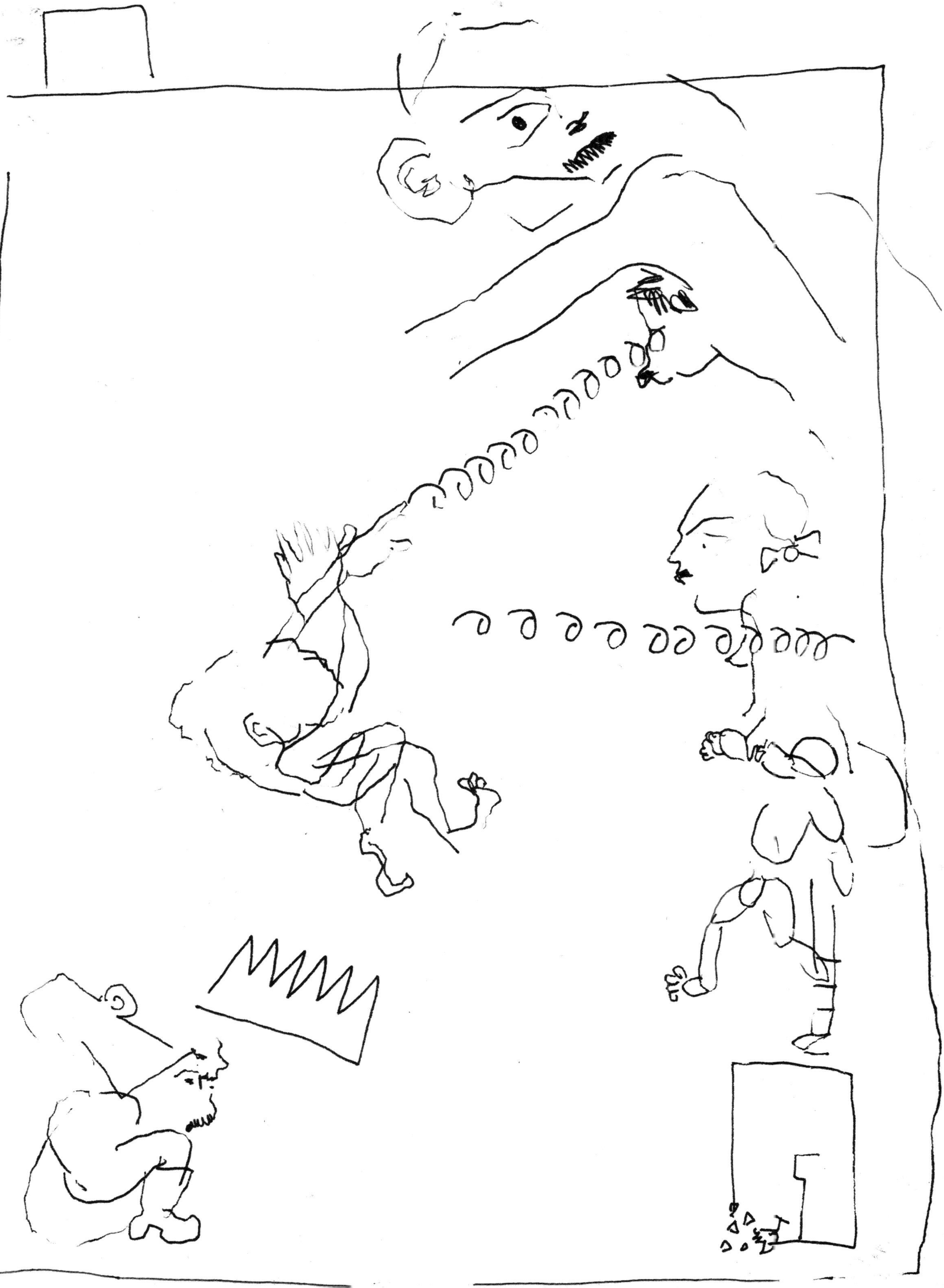

SHYLOCK
What! are there masques? Hear you me, Jessica:
Lock up my doors; and when you hear the drum,
And the vile squealing of the wry-neck'd fife,
Clamber not you up to the casements then,
Nor thrust your head into the public street
To gaze on Christian fools with varnish'd faces,
But stop my house's ears, I mean my casements;
Let not the sound of shallow foppery enter
My sober house. By Jacob's staff I swear
I have no mind of feasting forth to-night;

And as he warns his daughter not to do what she will happily, spitefully do, Shylock experiences the little moment of loathing himself. It is a moment the size of a ring, and its shape, a ring shape. The ring itself was a gift from Leah, and it serves as a reminder of the dream's bulk and the enormous dimensions of the past, and how repulsive it was, even then, to be *he—he*, a parasite on the body of his wife, *he* silencing her, drooling on her thighs, with venomous insinuations born from nothing. The will to hug these of all memories, that is what Shylock means when he says "my sober house." The ring. The ring must

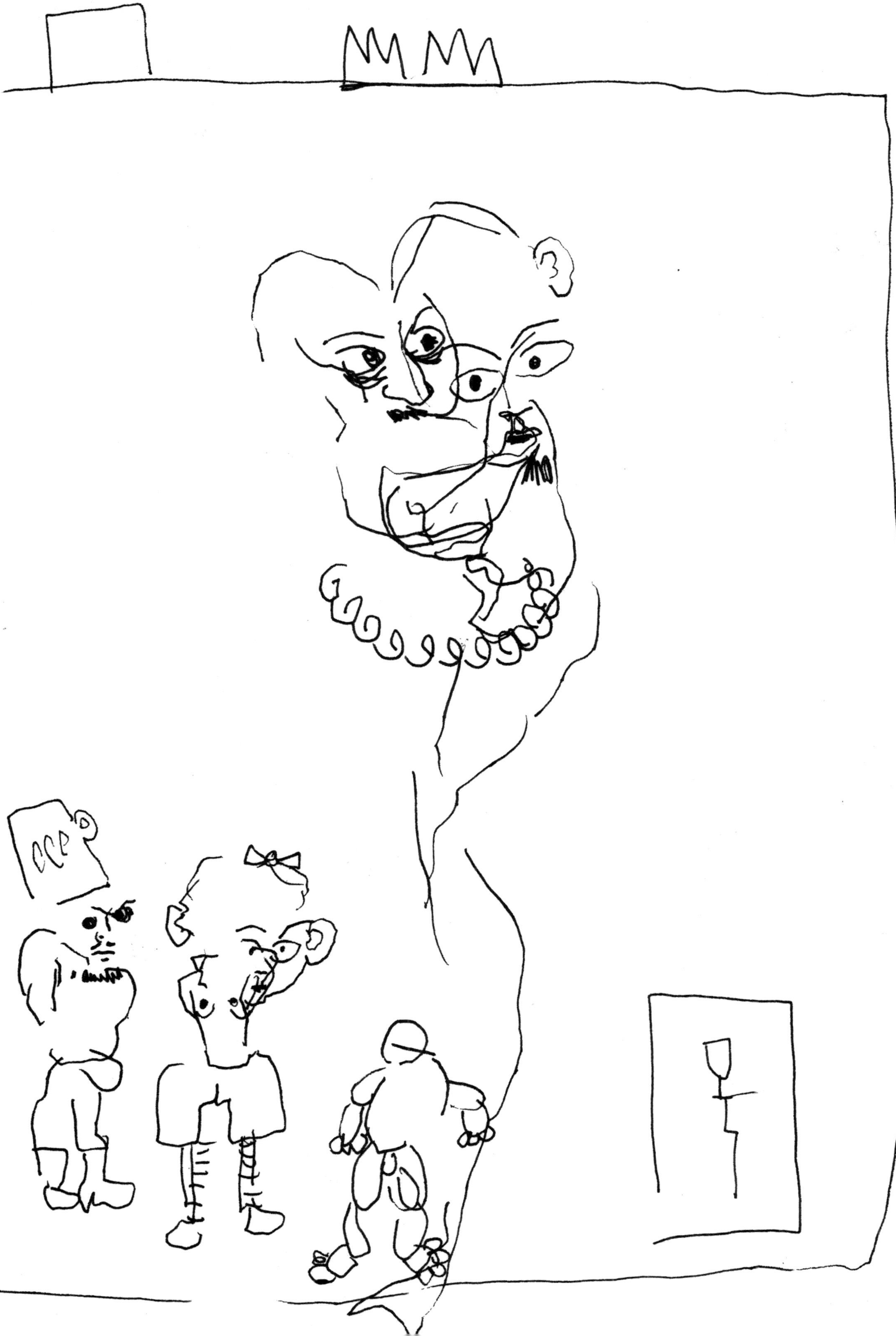

But I will go. Go you before me, sirrah;
Say I will come.

LAUNCELOT
I will go before, sir. Mistress, look out at window, for all this;
There will come a Christian by,
Will be worth a Jewess' eye.

stay with him.
The ring is a sound-proof territory, and the treacherous orchestra waits at the doorway to strike him with the new spots, the new stench, and still he does not know how far it will lead.

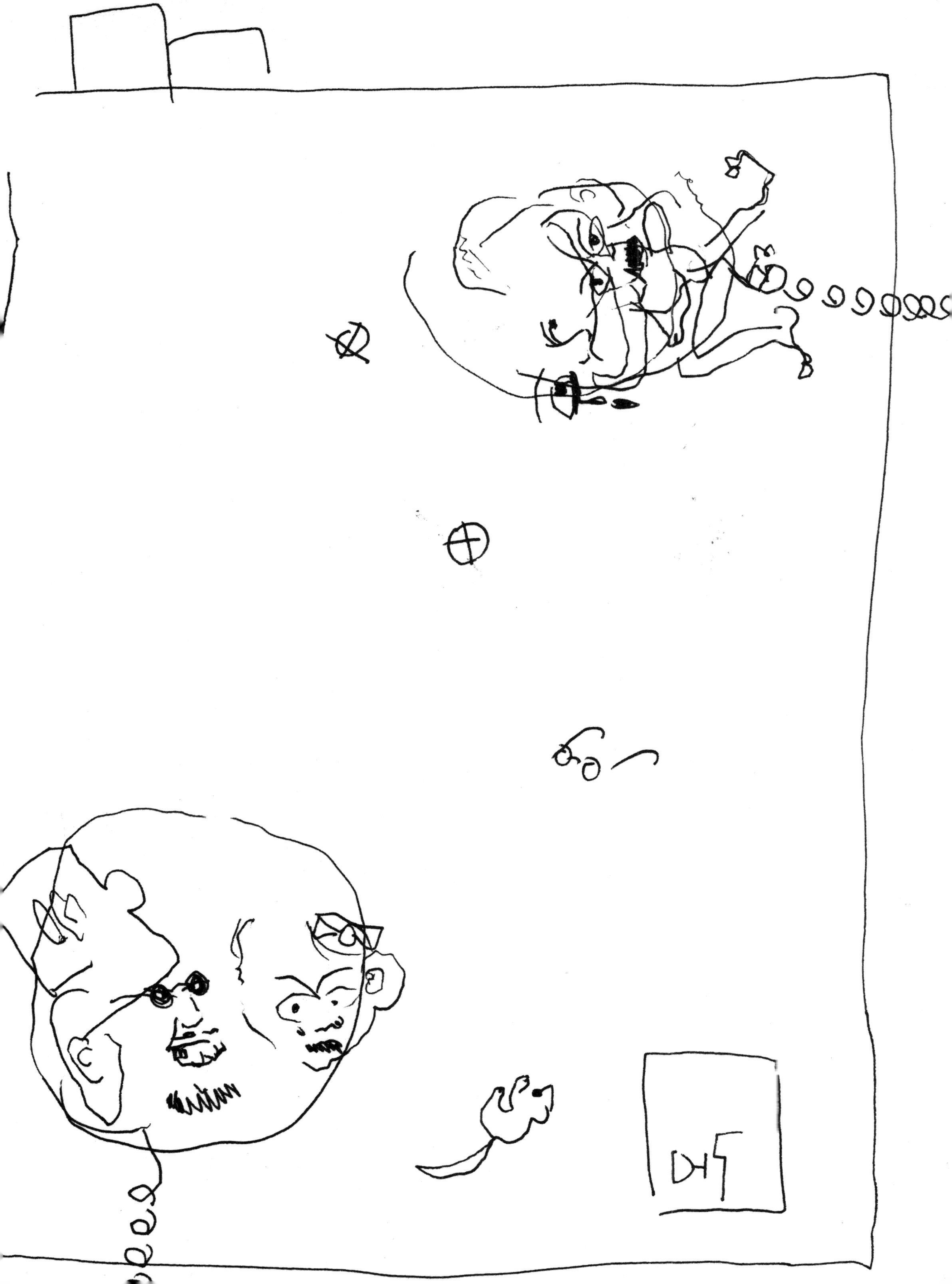

SHYLOCK
What says that fool of Hagar's offspring, ha?

JESSICA
His words were, 'Farewell, mistress;' nothing else.

SHYLOCK
The patch is kind enough, but a huge feeder;
Snail-slow in profit, and he sleeps by day
More than the wild cat: drones hive not with me;
Therefore I part with him, and part with him
To one that I would have him help to waste
His borrow'd purse. Well, Jessica, go in:
Perhaps I will return immediately:
Do as I bid you; shut doors after you:
'Fast bind, fast find,'
A proverb never stale in thrifty mind.

Exit.

And so, disheveled, he wears his armor and goes to the outer outside, attempting a fanfare, still not realizing that the front is everywhere. Everywhere and behind him, in his home.

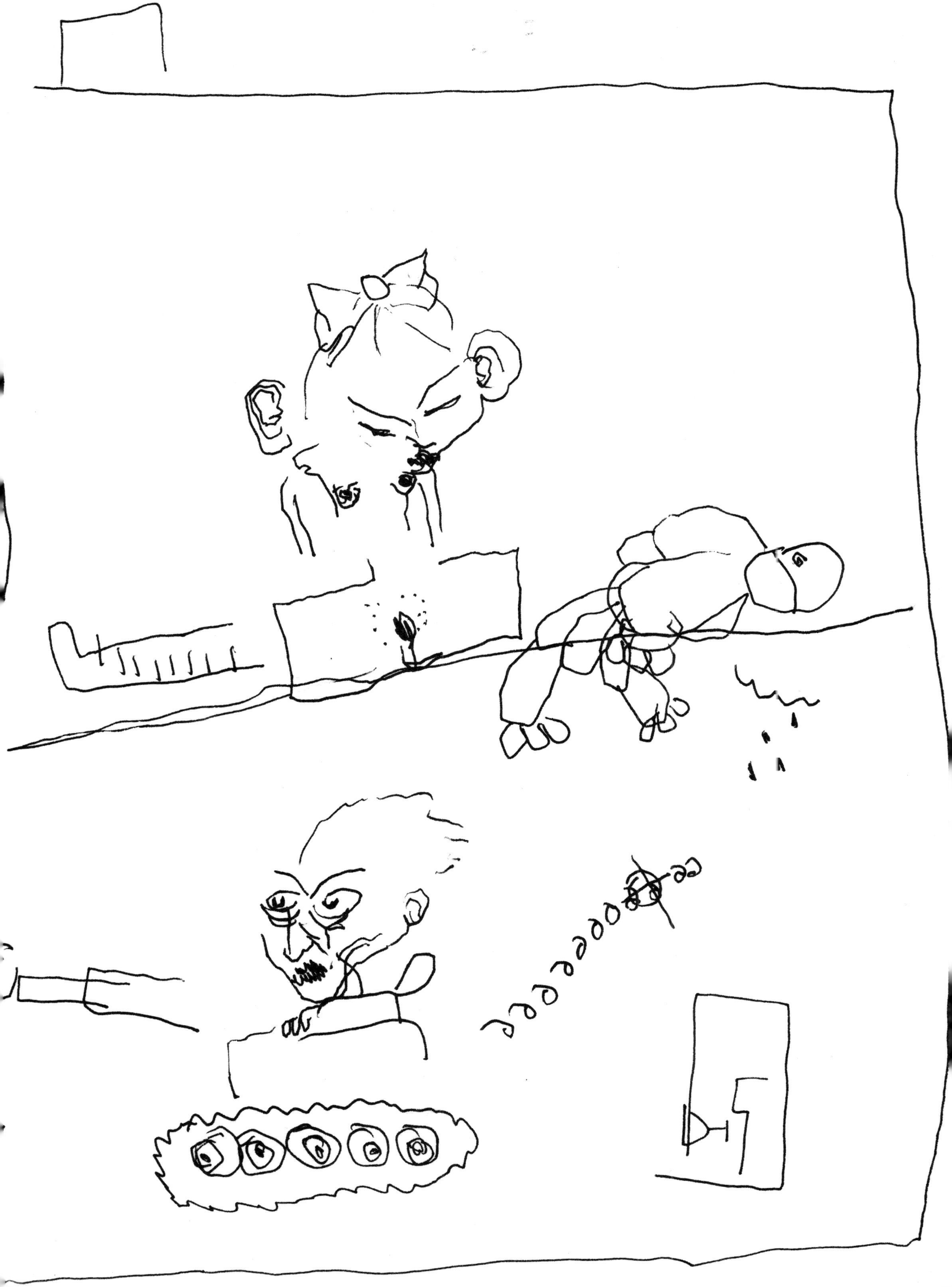

II.V.10

JESSICA
Farewell; and if my fortune be not crost,
I have a father, you a daughter, lost.

Exit.

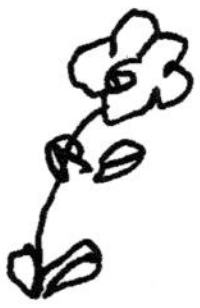

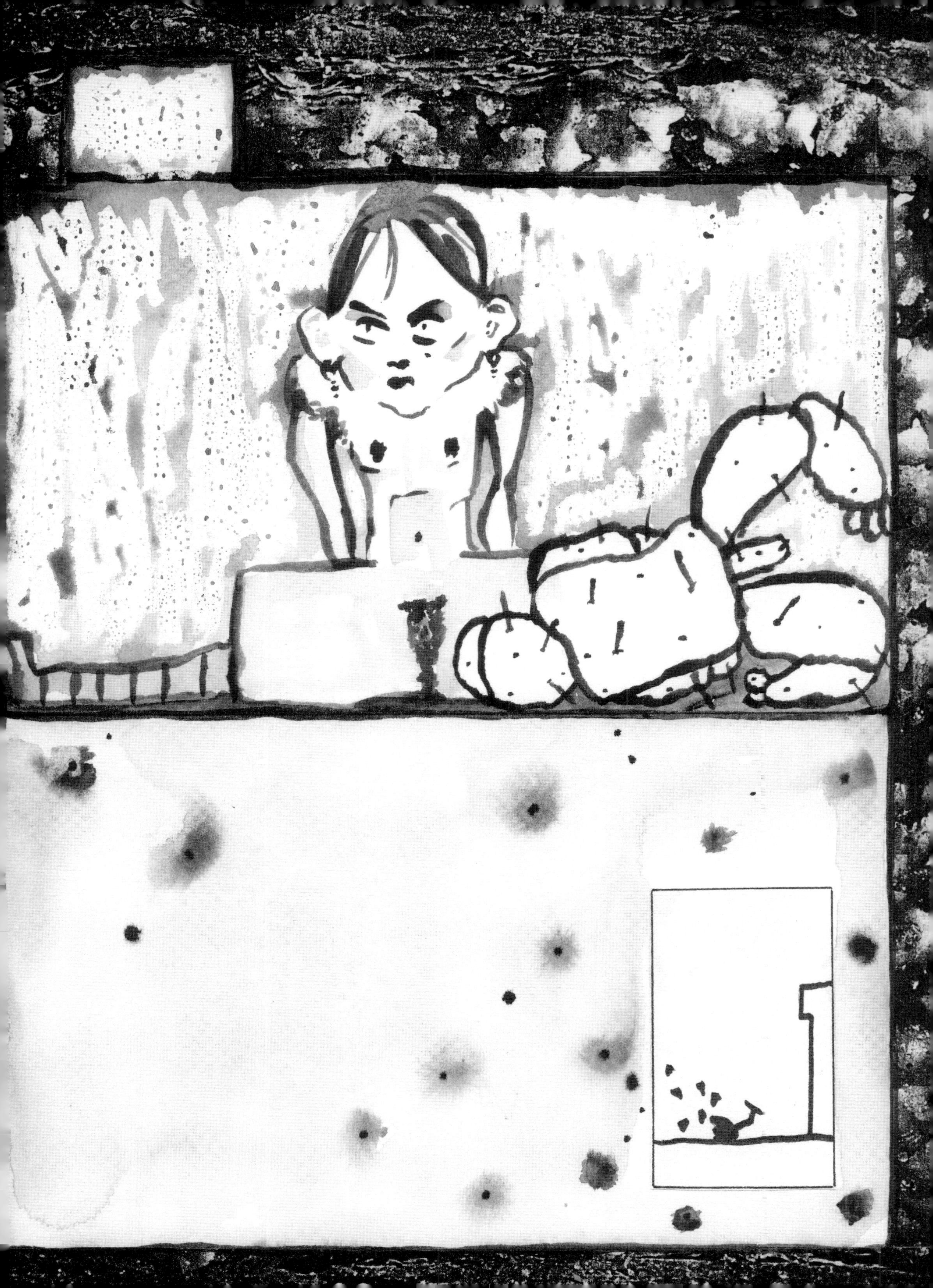

Scene VI—The Same.

Enter Gratiano and Salarino, masqued.

GRATIANO
This is the penthouse under which Lorenzo
Desir'd us to make stand.

SALARINO
His hour is almost past.

GRATIANO
And it is marvel he out-dwells his hour,
For lovers ever run before the clock.

SALARINO
O! ten times faster Venus' pigeons fly
To seal love's bonds new-made, than they are wont
To keep obliged faith unforfeited!

GRATIANO
That ever holds: who riseth from a feast
With that keen appetite that he sits down?
Where is the horse that doth untread again
His tedious measures with the unbated fire
That he did pace them first? All things that are,
Are with more spirit chased than enjoy'd.
How like a younker or a prodigal
The scarfed bark puts from her native bay,
Hugg'd and embraced by the strumpet wind!
How like the prodigal doth she return,
With over-weather'd ribs and ragged sails,
Lean, rent, and beggar'd by the strumpet wind!

SALARINO
Here comes Lorenzo: more of this hereafter.

Enter Lorenzo.

LORENZO
Sweet friends, your patience for my long abode;
Not I, but my affairs, have made you wait:
When you shall please to play the thieves for wives,
I'll watch as long for you then. Approach;
Here dwells my father Jew. Ho! who's within?

Enter Jessica above, in boy's clothes.

JESSICA
Who are you? Tell me, for more certainty,
Albeit I'll swear that I do know your tongue.

LORENZO
Lorenzo, and thy love.

JESSICA
Lorenzo, certain; and my love indeed,
For whom love I so much? And now who knows
But you, Lorenzo, whether I am yours?

LORENZO
Heaven and thy thoughts are witness that thou art.

JESSICA
Here, catch this casket; it is worth the pains.
I am glad 'tis night, you do not look on me,
For I am much asham'd of my exchange;
But love is blind, and lovers cannot see
The pretty follies that themselves commit;
For if they could, Cupid himself would blush
To see me thus transformed to a boy.

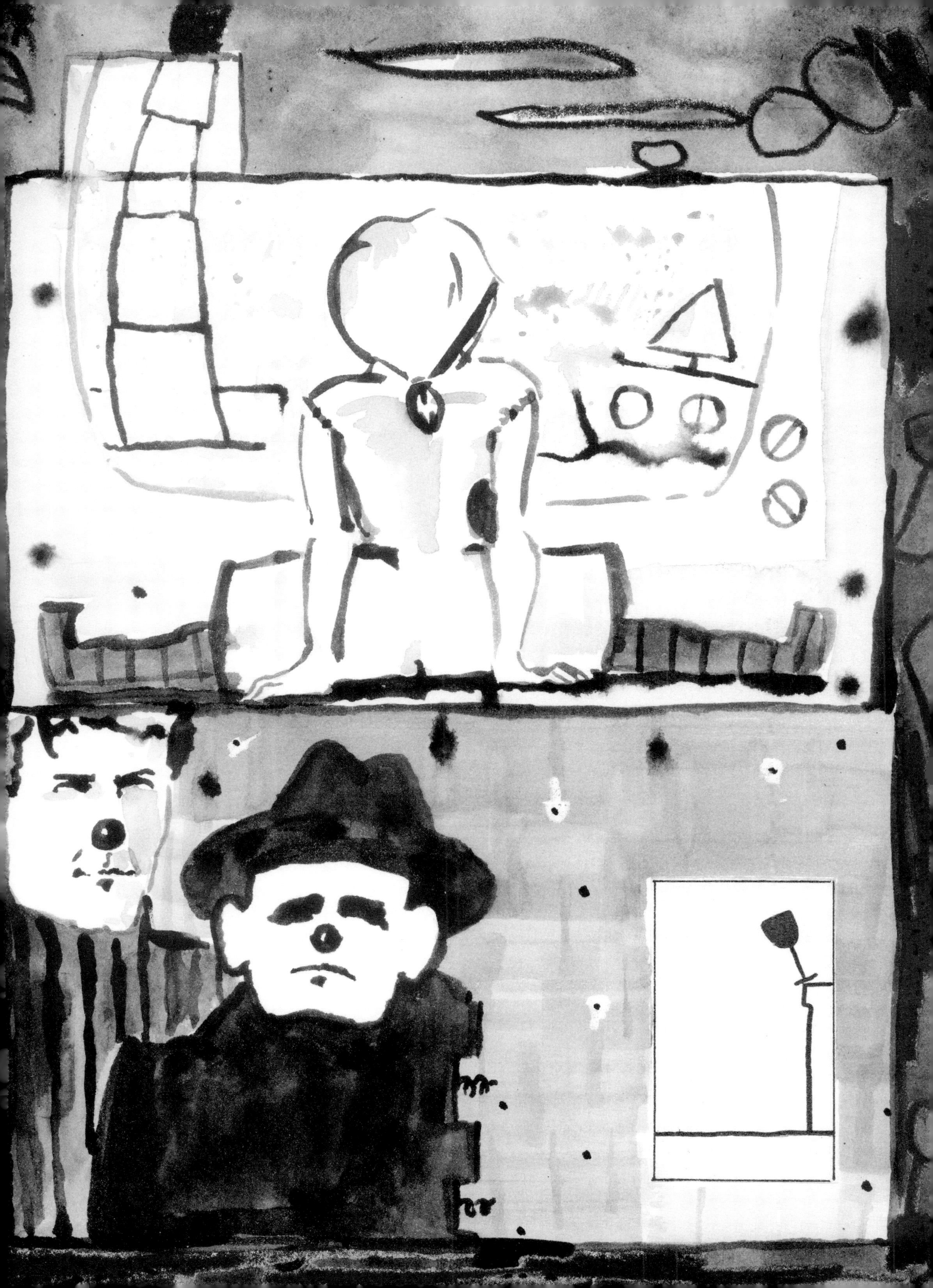

II.VI.2

LORENZO
Descend, for you must be my torch-bearer.

JESSICA
What! must I hold a candle to my shames?
They in themselves, good sooth, are too-too light.
Why, 'tis an office of discovery, love,
And I should be obscur'd.

LORENZO
So are you, sweet,
Even in the lovely garnish of a boy.
But come at once;
For the close night doth play the runaway,
And we are stay'd for at Bassanio's feast.

JESSICA
I will make fast the doors, and gild myself
With some more ducats, and be with you straight.

Exit above.

GRATIANO
Now, by my hood, a Gentile, and no Jew.

LORENZO
Beshrew me, but I love her heartily;
For she is wise, if I can judge of her,
And fair she is, if that mine eyes be true,
And true she is, as she hath prov'd herself;
And therefore, like herself, wise, fair, and true,
Shall she be placed in my constant soul.

Enter Jessica.

What, art thou come? On, gentlemen; away!
Our masquing mates by this time for us stay.

Exit with Jessica and Salarino.

Enter Antonio.

ANTONIO
Who's there?

GRATIANO
Signior Antonio!

ANTONIO
Fie, fie, Gratiano! where are all the rest?
'Tis nine o'clock; our friends all stay for you.
No masque to-night: the wind is come about;
Bassanio presently will go aboard:
I have sent twenty out to seek for you.

GRATIANO
I am glad on't: I desire no more delight
Than to be under sail and gone to-night.

Exeunt.

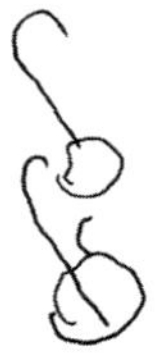

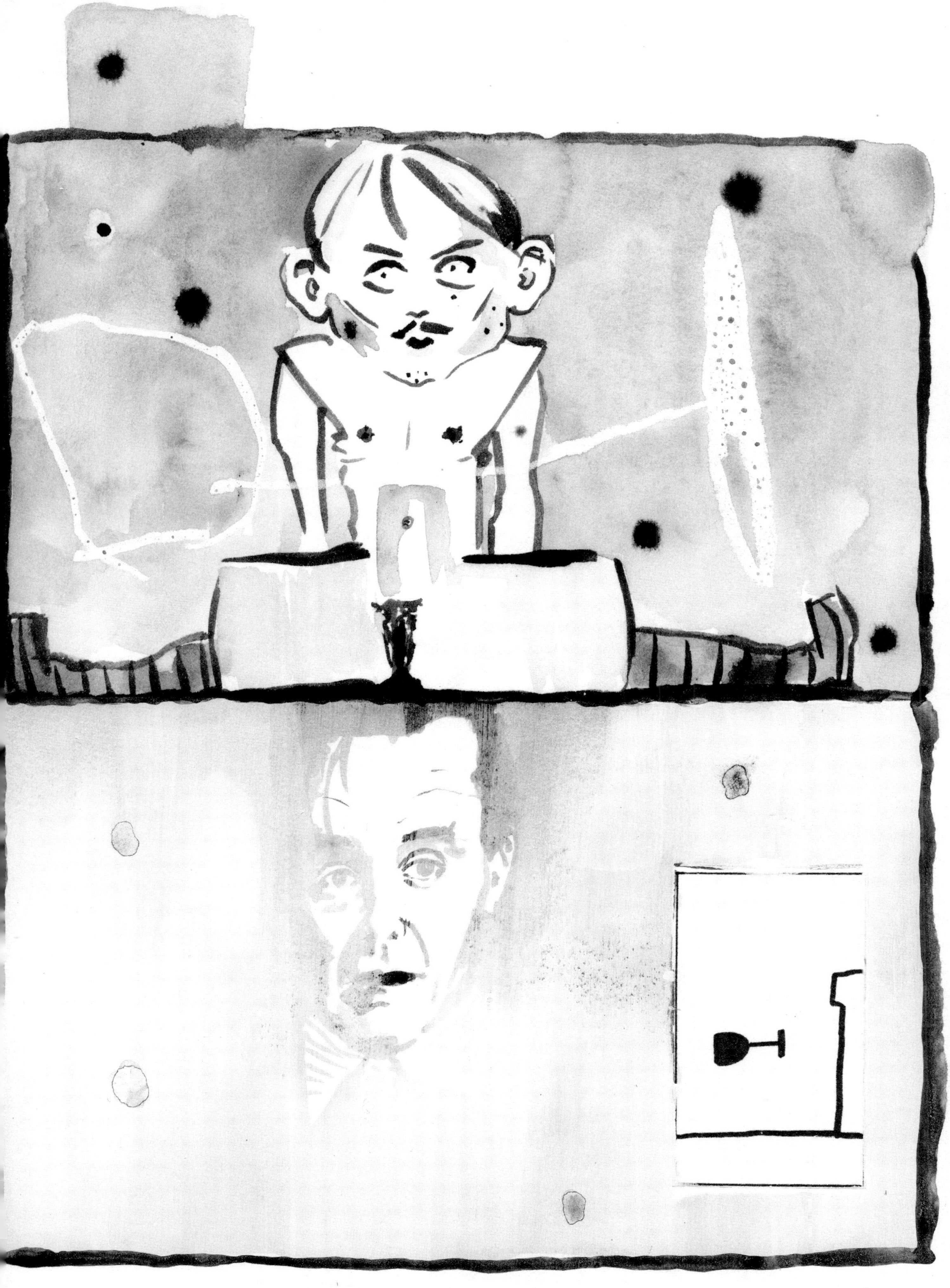

Scene VII—Belmont. A Room in Portia's House.

MORROCO PREPARES TO PERFORM

Flourish of Cornets. Enter Portia, with the Prince of Morocco, and their Trains.

PORTIA

Go, draw aside the curtains, and discover
The several caskets to this noble prince.
Now make your choice.

MOROCCO

The first, of gold, which this inscription bears:
Who chooseth me shall gain what many men desire.
The second, silver, which this promise carries:
Who chooseth me shall get as much as he deserves.
This third, dull lead, with warning all as blunt:
Who chooseth me must give and hazard all he hath.
How shall I know if I do choose the right?

PORTIA

The one of them contains my picture, prince:
If you choose that, then I am yours withal.

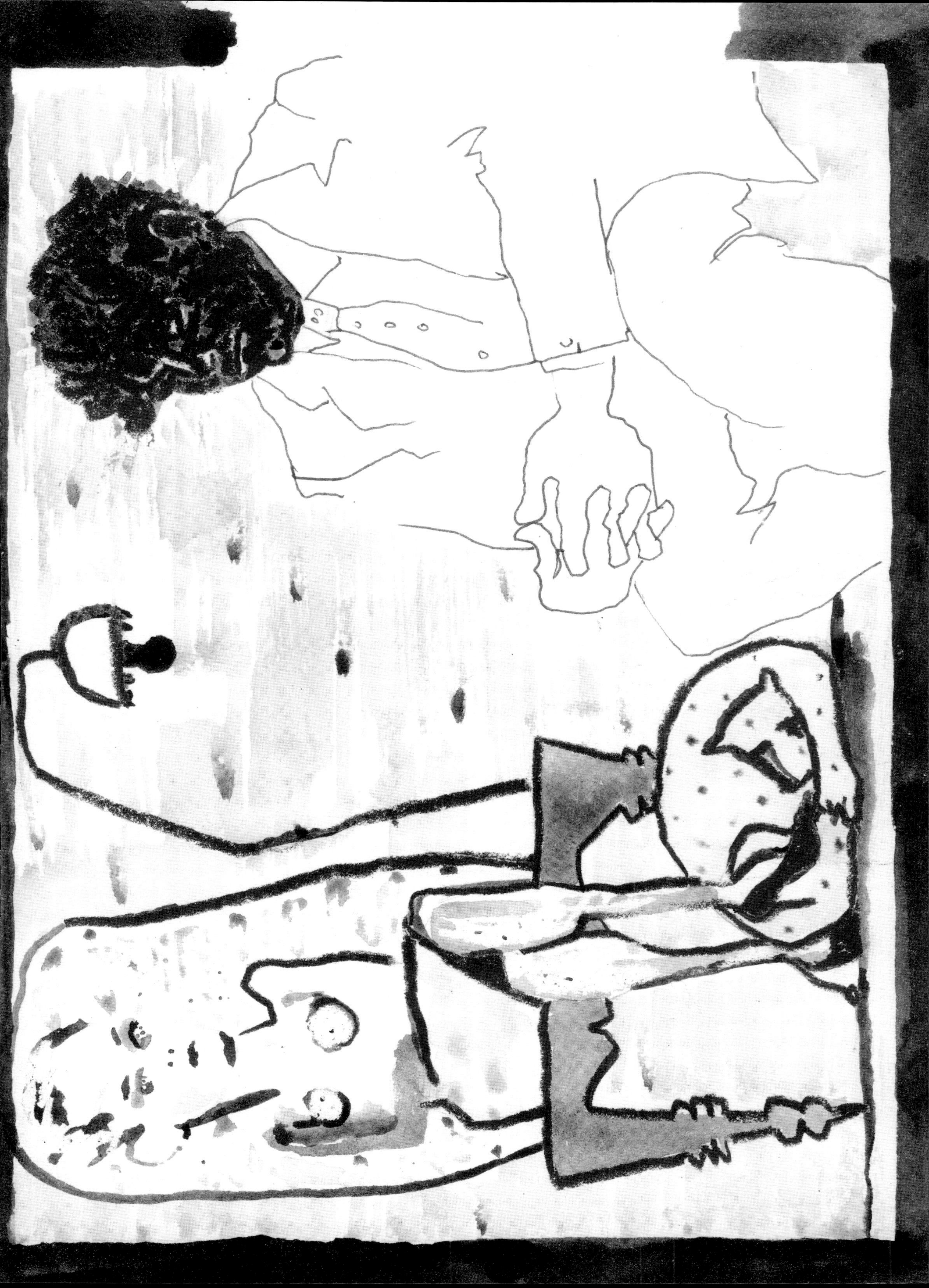

MORROCO CHOSES HIS WAY, SUPPORTED BY THE IMAGES OF HIS ROYAL PARENTS AND THEIR BLACK LIGHTS

MOROCCO
Some god direct my judgment! Let me see:
I will survey the inscriptions back again:
What says this leaden casket?
Who chooseth me must give and hazard all he hath.
Must give: For what? for lead? hazard for lead?
This casket threatens. Men that hazard all
Do it in hope of fair advantages:
A golden mind stoops not to shows of dross;
I'll then nor give nor hazard aught for lead.
What says the silver with her virgin hue?
Who chooseth me shall get as much as he deserves.
As much as he deserves! Pause there, Morocco,
And weigh thy value with an even hand.
If thou be'st rated by thy estimation,
Thou dost deserve enough; and yet enough
May not extend so far as to the lady:
And yet to be afeard of my deserving
Were but a weak disabling of myself.
As much as I deserve! Why, that's the lady:
I do in birth deserve her, and in fortunes,
In graces, and in qualities of breeding;
But more than these, in love I do deserve.
What if I stray'd no further, but chose here?
Let's see once more this saying grav'd in gold:
Who chooseth me shall gain what many men desire.
Why, that's the lady: all the world desires her;
From the four corners of the earth they come,
To kiss this shrine, this mortal-breathing saint:
The Hyrcanian deserts and the vasty wilds
Of wide Arabia are as throughfares now
For princes to come view fair Portia:
The watery kingdom, whose ambitious head
Spits in the face of heaven, is no bar
To stop the foreign spirits, but they come,
As o'er a brook, to see fair Portia.
One of these three contains her heavenly picture.
Is't like that lead contains her? 'Twere damnation
To think so base a thought: it were too gross
To rib her cerecloth in the obscure grave.
Or shall I think in silver she's immur'd,
Being ten times undervalu'd to tried gold?
O sinful thought! Never so rich a gem
Was set in worse than gold. They have in England
A coin that bears the figure of an angel
Stamped in gold, but that's insculp'd upon;
But here an angel in a golden bed
Lies all within. Deliver me the key:
Here do I choose, and thrive I as I may!

PORTIA
There, take it, prince; and if my form lie there,
Then I am yours.

He unlocks the golden casket.

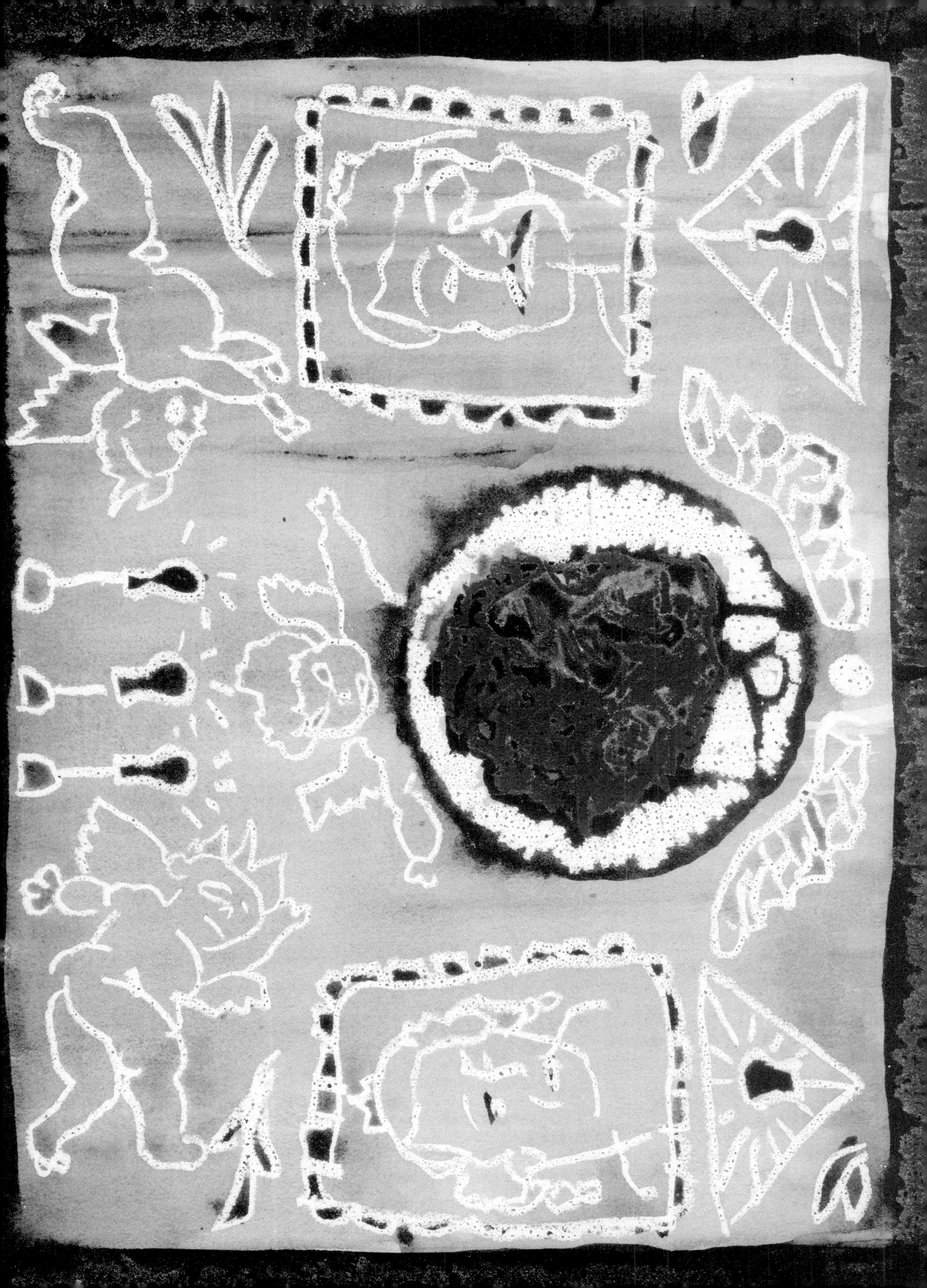

MORROCO FAILS COMPLETELY AND IS BELITTLED

MOROCCO

O hell! what have we here?
A carrion Death, within whose empty eye
There is a written scroll. I'll read the writing.

All that glisters is not gold;
Often have you heard that told:
Many a man his life hath sold
But my outside to behold:
Gilded tombs do worms infold.
Had you been as wise as bold,
Young in limbs, in judgment old,
Your answer had not been inscroll'd:
Fare you well; your suit is cold.

Cold, indeed; and labour lost:
Then, farewell, heat, and welcome, frost!
Portia, adieu. I have too griev'd a heart
To take a tedious leave: thus losers part.

Exit with his Train. Flourish of Cornets.

PORTIA

A gentle riddance. Draw the curtains: go.
Let all of his complexion choose me so.

Exeunt.

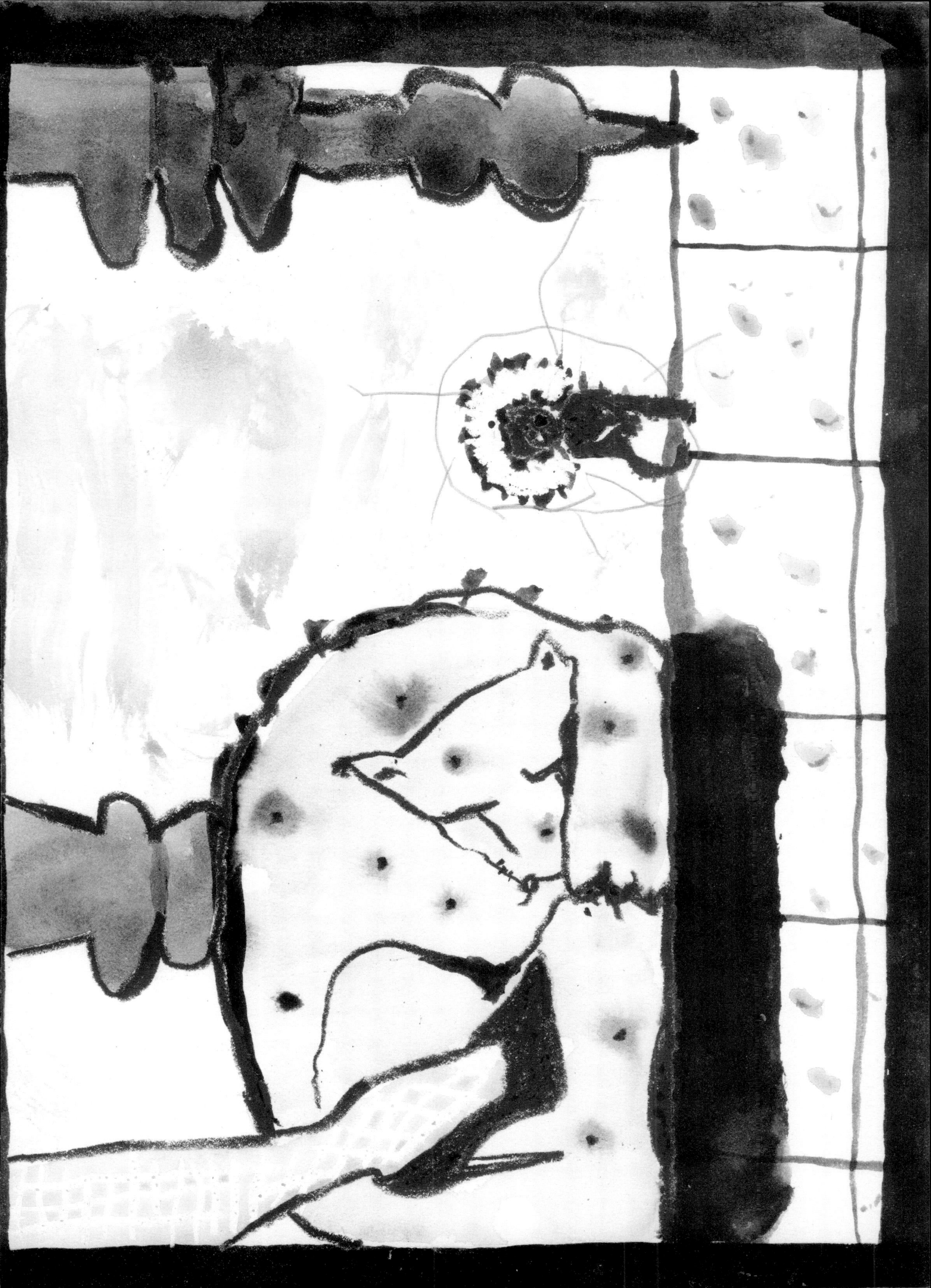

II.VII.4

THE SPEECH OF LACK-OF-PRESENCE OF THE PRINCE OF MOROCCO

I am Morocco of Morocco, and I deserve less.
They sliced it off me, because I did not deserve it.
It is gone forever, and I qualify for nothing.
So extreme is my seclusion that even my own black presence I do not deserve.
I am black Morocco of Morocco.
I cannot be valued materially.
Not gold, nor silver, nor lead. Not even dirty plastic.
What was once my royal rod for me, a tiny black joke elsewhere, is now a void.
I am prince Morocco of Morocco.
Without it, my desires are microbic, and I am very excitable.
The rustle of magazine pages is Purcell for me. I am moved to tears.
When I sense an ant, I sense, and when I sense, my nerves are terribly titillated. And I sense all the time.
Marvel suffocates me when I see something, for instance, a chair. Every something is an overdose.
I fall in love with cigarette butts.
I fall in love all the time.
Because I am revolting, nobody touches me, and for that I am grateful.
If I were to be touched by a hand, a real hand, even through a rubber glove, the extra-fine Morocco-vessel would explode from turbulence, and an end would come to the meager Morocco fluids.
But then I would also be grateful, as I am tiny Morocco from Morocco, and do not deserve even an end.

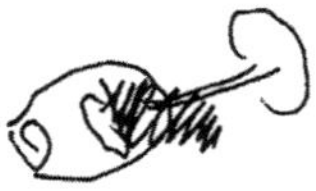

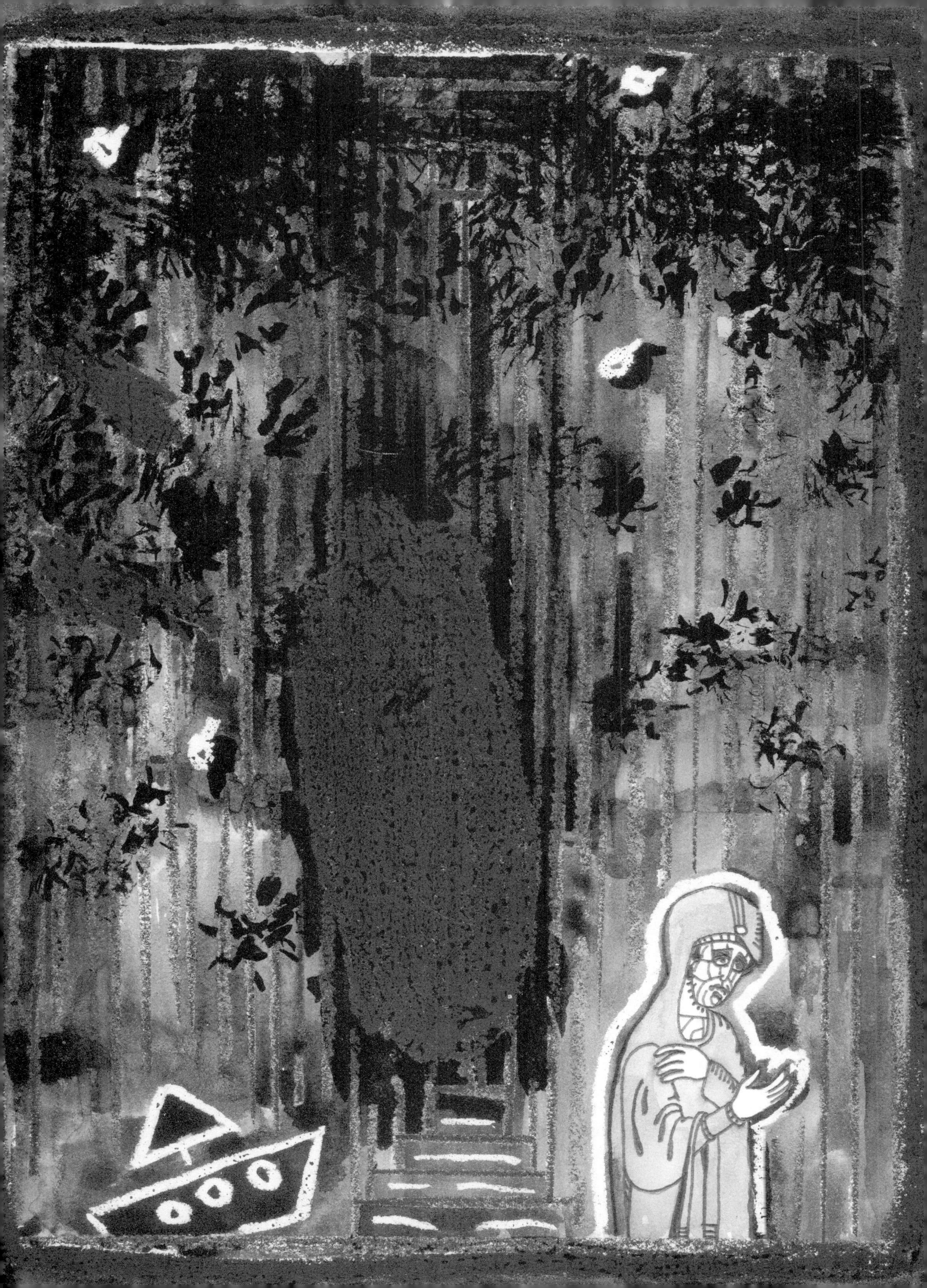

Scene VIII—Venice. A Street.

Enter Salarino and Salanio.

SALARINO
Why, man, I saw Bassanio under sail:
With him is Gratiano gone along;
And in their ship I'm sure Lorenzo is not.

SALANIO
The villain Jew with outcries rais'd the duke,
Who went with him to search Bassanio's ship.

SALARINO
He came too late, the ship was under sail:
But there the duke was given to understand
That in a gondola were seen together
Lorenzo and his amorous Jessica.
Besides, Antonio certified the duke
They were not with Bassanio in his ship.

SALANIO
I never heard a passion so confus'd,
So strange, outrageous, and so variable,
As the dog Jew did utter in the streets:
'My daughter! O my ducats! O my daughter!
Fled with a Christian! O my Christian ducats!
Justice! the law! my ducats, and my daughter!
A sealed bag, two sealed bags of ducats,
Of double ducats, stol'n from me by my daughter!
And jewels! two stones, two rich and precious stones,
Stol'n by my daughter! Justice! find the girl!
She hath the stones upon her, and the ducats.'

SALARINO
Why, all the boys in Venice follow him,
Crying, his stones, his daughter, and his ducats.

SALANIO
Let good Antonio look he keep his day,
Or he shall pay for this.

SALARINO
Marry, well remember'd.
I reason'd with a Frenchman yesterday,
Who told me,—in the narrow seas that
The French and English,—there miscarried
A vessel of our country richly fraught.
I thought upon Antonio when he told me,
And wish'd in silence that it were not his.

SALANIO
You were best to tell Antonio what you hear;
Yet do not suddenly, for it may grieve him.

Without wanting to, I am coerced to say something on Solanio and Salerio.
Of all my friends in Venice I envy them the most. Maybe it is because they are so marginal.
I am curiously drawn to their mouths.
The thin, correct lips, the teeth behind, perfect teeth, an almost unreal, glowing white. I feel like inserting a finger in between the two rows and stroking their tongue for a while.
Perhaps my fear of them is the attraction.
They are so bad!
All of us are very tired already, but not them.
They are compelled to talk, and their adherence to the humorous verges on a military discipline.
They were censored so that mostly what they discussed was Shylock, and their hatred towards him. Hence they are not opportunists: they are purposeful, and the purpose, as it has to do with something other than themselves, is, if you will, one can almost say, altruistic.
Maybe that is why I envy them.

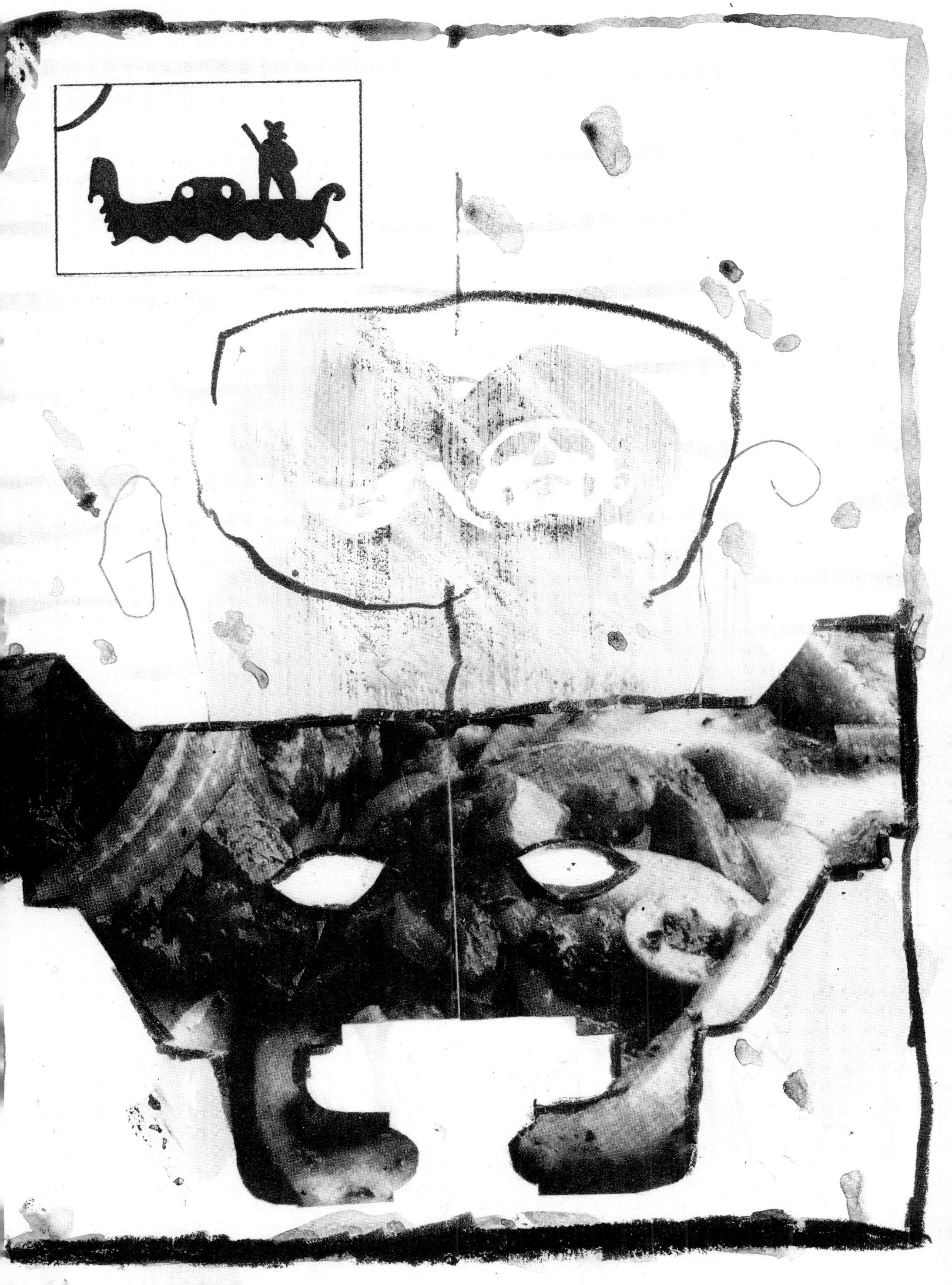

II.VIII.2

SALARINO

A kinder gentleman treads not the earth.
I saw Bassanio and Antonio part:
Bassanio told him he would make some speed
Of his return: he answer'd 'Do not so;
Slubber not business for my sake, Bassanio,
But stay the very riping of the time;
And for the Jew's bond which he hath of me,
Let it not enter in your mind of love:
Be merry, and employ your chiefest thoughts
To courtship and such fair ostents of love
As shall conveniently become you there:'
And even there, his eye being big with tears,
Turning his face, he put his hand behind him,
And with affection wondrous sensible
He wrung Bassanio's hand; and so they parted.

SALANIO

I think he only loves the world for him.
I pray thee, let us go and find him out,
And quicken his embraced heaviness
With some delight or other.

SALARINO

Do we so.

Exeunt.

Maybe it is the beautiful hats.
The unique overcoat.
This togetherness. Their togetherness is obvious, no doubt, but that should not mean it is taken for granted. It is an admirable togetherness.
Occasionally, they would appear separately in public, but they are clearly not at ease then. It is mistaken and obscene.
Besides all that—I know I think they remind me of something. Perhaps some other marginal duo, or something dirty from the past. It may be so, but I should be cautious.
Mechanically it is very ambiguous.
It calls for admittance—
I do not know.
I shall say what I can:
They, they do not ask themselves: "How can a smell be described?"
At night, in bed, they enjoy an immense pleasure, being two and one.
That is all that can be said.

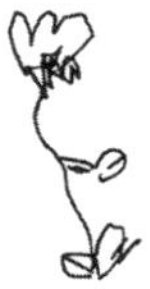

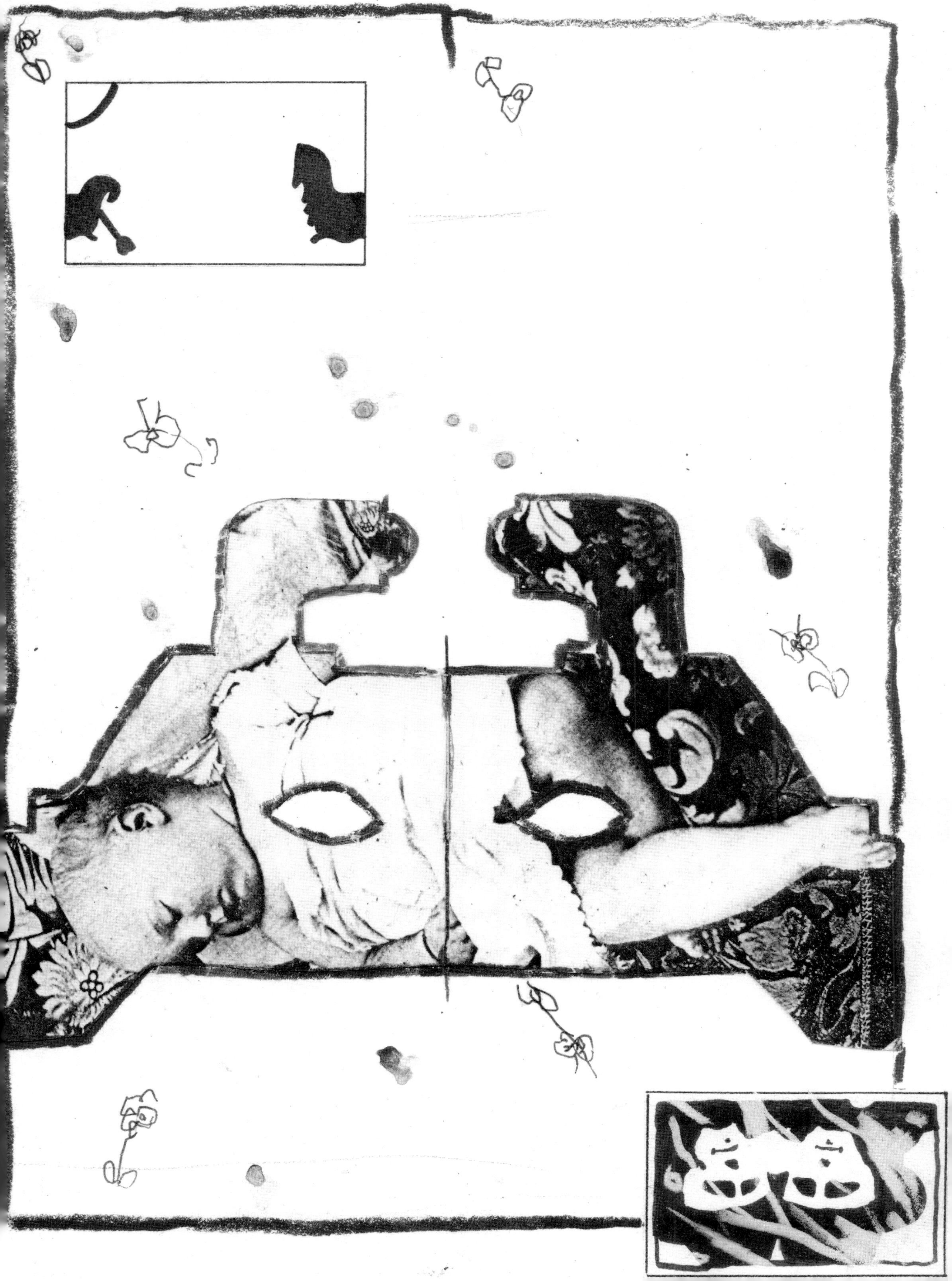

Scene IX—Belmont. A Room in Portia's House.

ARAGON PREPARES TO PERFORM

Enter Nerissa, with a Servitor.

NERISSA
Quick, quick, I pray thee; draw the curtain straight:
The Prince of Aragon hath ta'en his oath,
And comes to his election presently.

Flourish of Cornets. Enter the Prince of Aragon, Portia, and their Trains.

PORTIA
Behold, there stands the caskets, noble prince:
If you choose that wherein I am contain'd,
Straight shall our nuptial rites be solemniz'd;
But if you fail, without more speech, my lord,
You must be gone from hence immediately.

ARAGON
I am enjoin'd by oath to observe three things:
First, never to unfold to any one
Which casket 'twas I chose; next, if I fail
Of the right casket, never in my life
To woo a maid in way of marriage;
Lastly,
If I do fail in fortune of my choice,
Immediately to leave you and be gone.

PORTIA
To these injunctions every one doth swear
That comes to hazard for my worthless self.

ARAGON
And so have I address'd me. Fortune now
To my heart's hope! Gold, silver, and base lead.

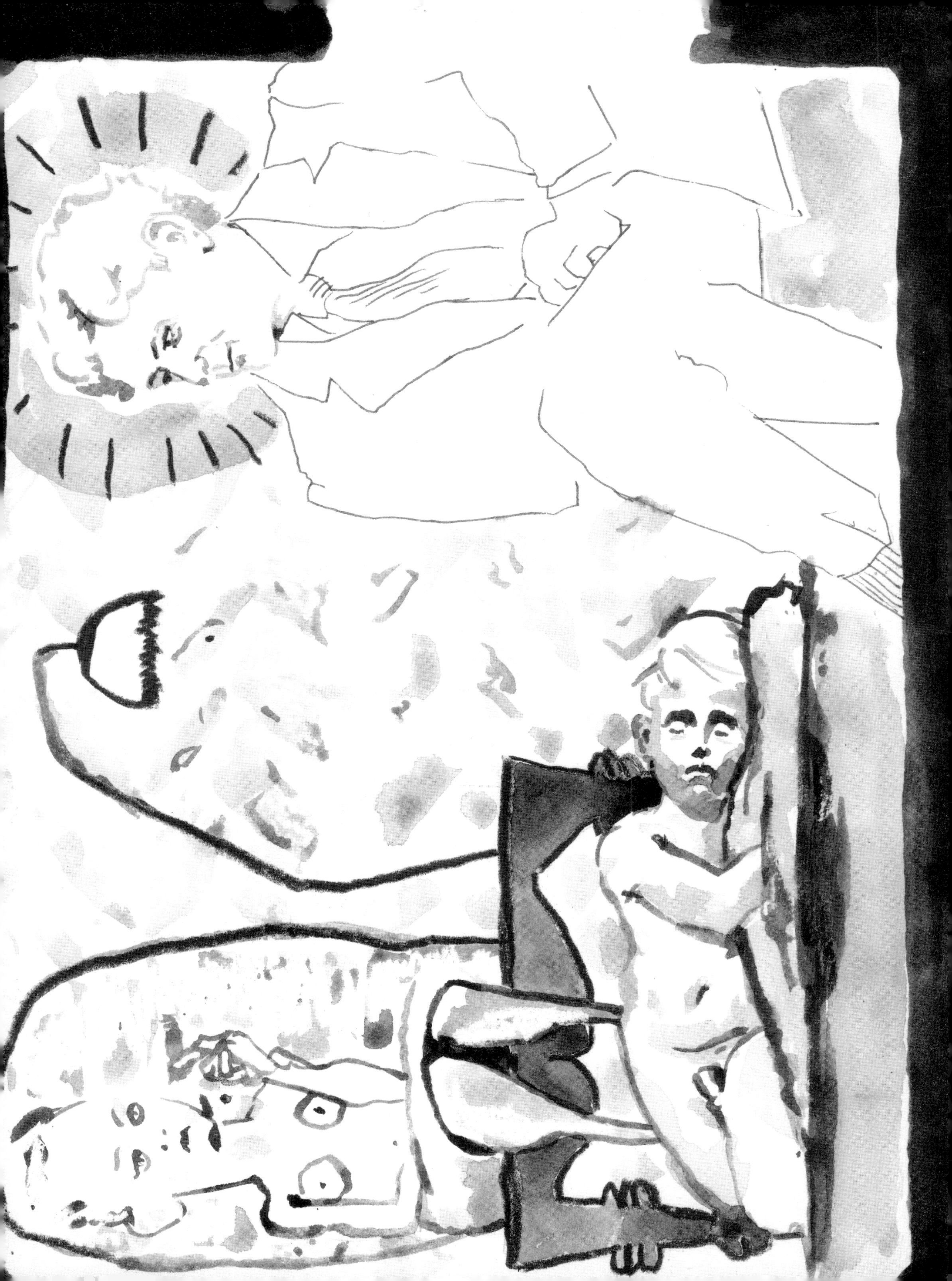

ARAGON CHOSES HIS WAY, SUPPORTED BY THE SIMILITUDE OF THE CROWN TO THE SWAMP FLOWER, HIS JEWELRY AND REFLECTIONS.

Who chooseth me must give and hazard all he hath:
You shall look fairer, ere I give or hazard.
What says the golden chest? ha! let me see:
Who chooseth me shall gain what many men desire.
What many men desire! that 'many' may be meant
By the fool multitude, that choose by show,
Not learning more than the fond eye doth teach;
Which pries not to the interior, but, like the martlet,
Builds in the weather on the outward wall,
Even in the force and road of casualty.
I will not choose what many men desire,
Because I will not jump with common spirits
And rank me with the barbarous multitude.
Why, then to thee, thou silver treasure-house;
Tell me once more what title thou dost bear:
Who chooseth me shall get as much as he deserves.
And well said too; for who shall go about
To cozen fortune and be honourable
Without the stamp of merit? Let none presume
To wear an undeserved dignity.
O! that estates, degrees, and offices
Were not deriv'd corruptly, and that clear honour
Were purchas'd by the merit of the wearer.
How many then should cover that stand bare;
How many be commanded that command;
How much low peasantry would then be glean'd
From the true seed of honour; and how much honour
Pick'd from the chaff and ruin of the times
To be new varnish'd! Well, but to my choice:
Who chooseth me shall get as much as he deserves.
I will assume desert. Give me a key for this,
And instantly unlock my fortunes here.

He opens the silver casket.

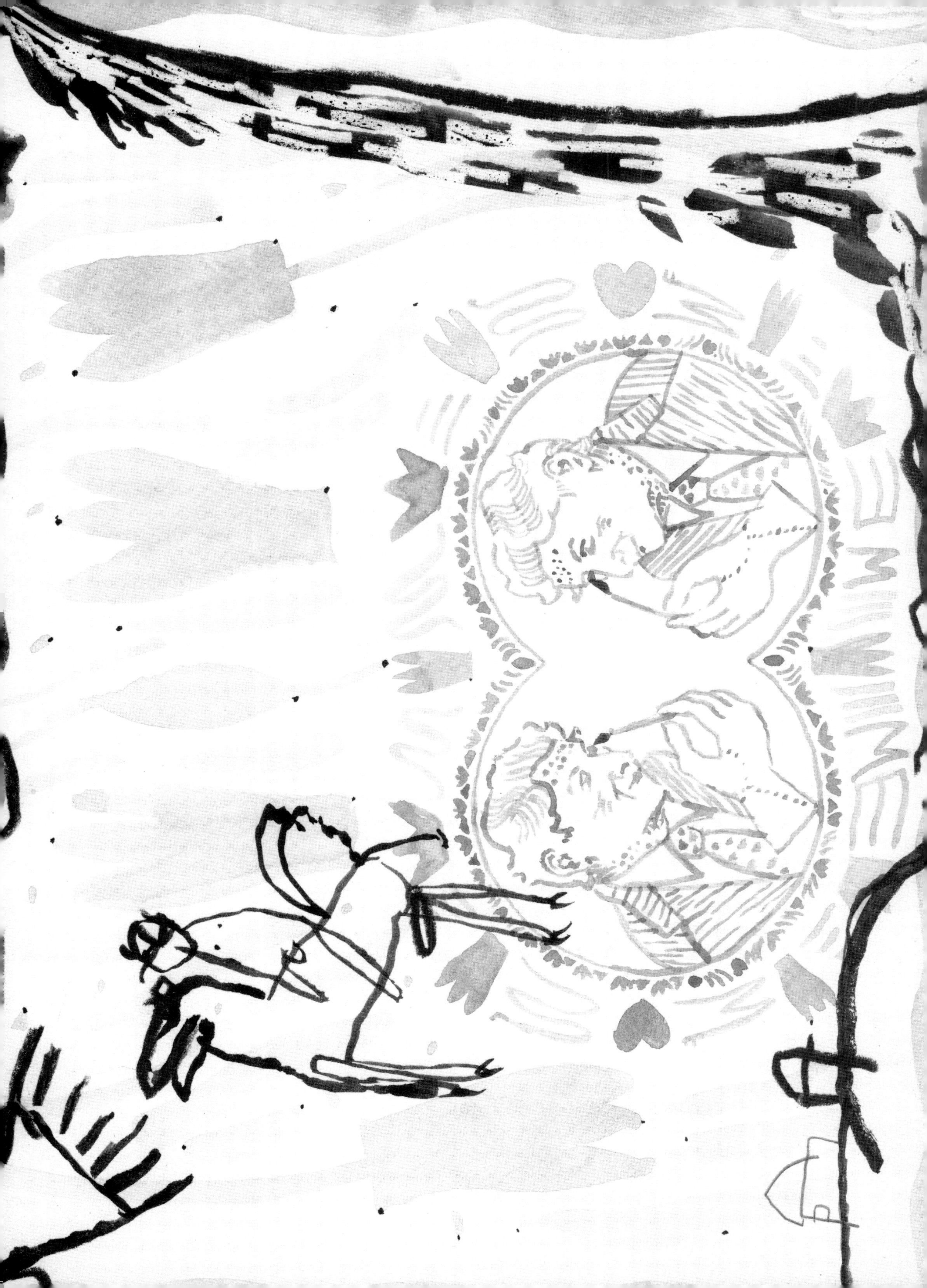

ARAGON FAILS COMPLETELY AND IS BELITTLED

PORTIA
Too long a pause for that which you find there.

ARAGON
What's here? the portrait of a blinking idiot,
Presenting me a schedule! I will read it.
How much unlike art thou to Portia!
How much unlike my hopes and my deservings!
Who chooseth me shall have as much as he deserves.
Did I deserve no more than a fool's head?
Is that my prize? are my deserts no better?

PORTIA
To offend, and judge, are distinct offices,
And of opposed natures.

ARAGON
What is here?

The fire seven times tried this:
Seven times tried that judgment is
That did never choose amiss.
Some there be that shadows kiss;
Such have but a shadow's bliss:
There be fools alive, I wis,
Silver'd o'er; and so was this.
Take what wife you will to bed,
I will ever be your head:
So be gone, sir: you are sped.

Still more fool I shall appear
By the time I linger here:
With one fool's head I came to woo,
But I go away with two.
Sweet, adieu. I'll keep my oath,
Patiently to bear my wroth.

Exit Aragon with his Train.

PORTIA
Thus hath the candle sing'd the moth.
O, these deliberate fools! when they do choose,
They have the wisdom by their wit to lose.

NERISSA
The ancient saying is no heresy:
'Hanging and wiving goes by destiny.'

PORTIA
Come, draw the curtain, Nerissa.

Enter a Servant.

SERVANT
Where is my lady?

PORTIA
Here; what would my lord?

SERVANT
Madam, there is alighted at your gate
A young Venetian, one that comes before
To signify the approaching of his lord;
From whom he bringeth sensible regreets,
To wit,—besides commends and courteous breath,—
Gifts of rich value. Yet I have not seen
So likely an embassador of love.
A day in April never came so sweet,
To show how costly summer was at hand,
As this fore-spurrer comes before his lord.

PORTIA
No more, I pray thee: I am half afeard
Thou wilt say anon he is some kin to thee,
Thou spend'st such high-day wit in praising him.
Come, come, Nerissa; for I long to see
Quick Cupid's post that comes so mannerly.

NERISSA
Bassanio, lord Love, if thy will it be!

Exeunt.

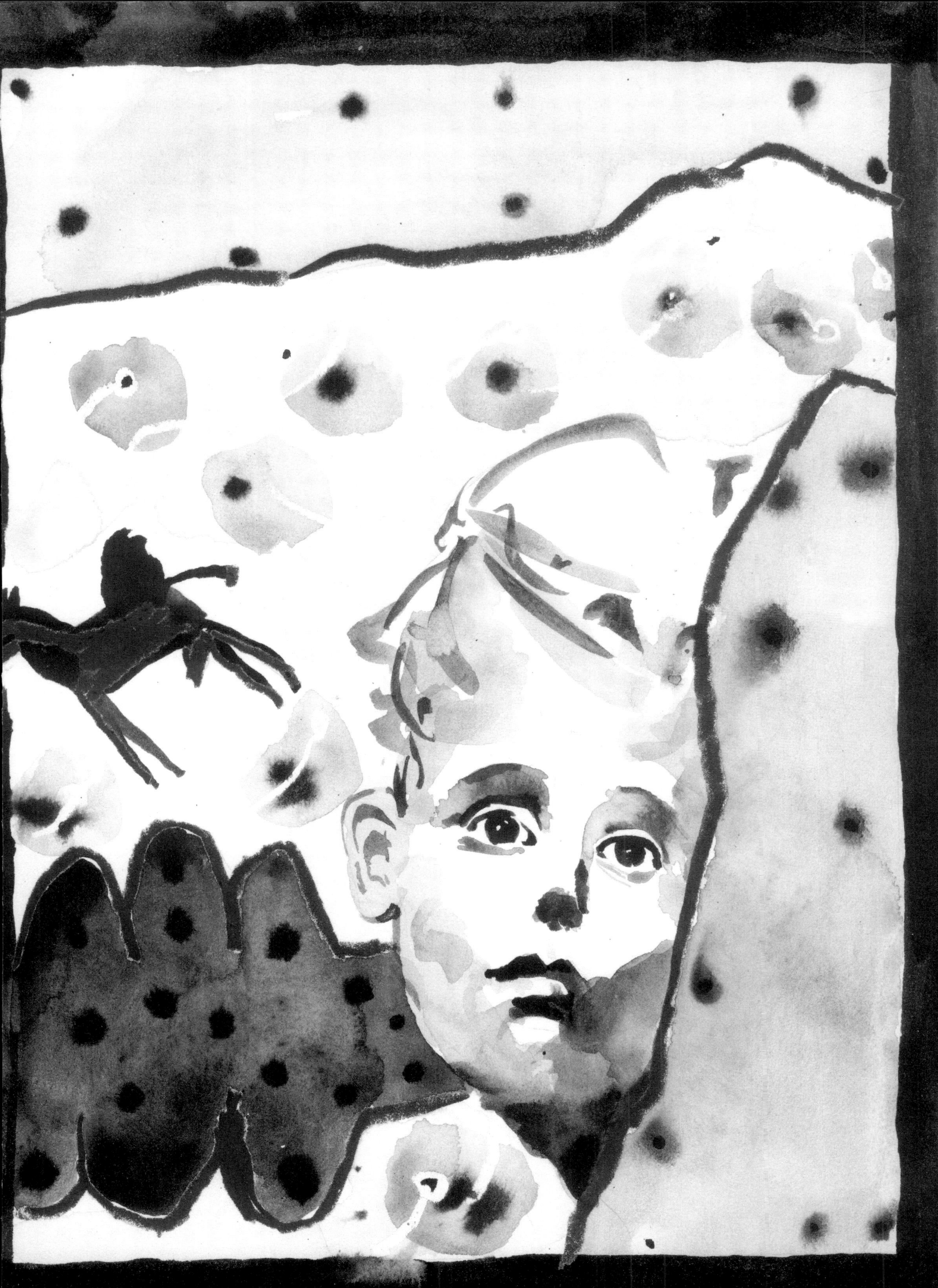

THE SPEECH OF LACK-OF-PRESENCE OF THE PRINCE OF ARAGON

I was Aragon the slick.
When I was, I contemplated myself daily.
How pale I was. How graceful. What a style.
A decent melancholic prince, even past the age of thirty-five, being self-aware, can undervalue himself in his way of obstinate scratching, thus recognizing his true value, so little and yet so much!
Adam, the first man, had no belly button.
I am the last man. The last man is all belly button.
Being aware of my self-awareness, and also aware of my self-awareness awareness, I would hence, at the count of three, reduce myself to the final speck of ash, and also fly up above.
How clever I was. Everything was a bore.
I was Aragon the slick.
With unprecedented sophistry, with earnest playfulness, I have mastered the labyrinth of masturbation made reflection. I had a schematic draft, explaining it aesthetically.
Now all taken.
Was not even worth being proved wrong.
It was not a murder. Not a suicide. Not melting. Not even common fading.
It was taken.
Once, in the palace. Listing different smiles and creams.
Now, not even no one.
Spot, no Spot.

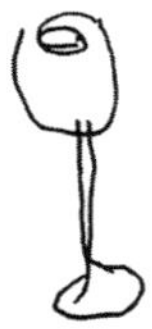

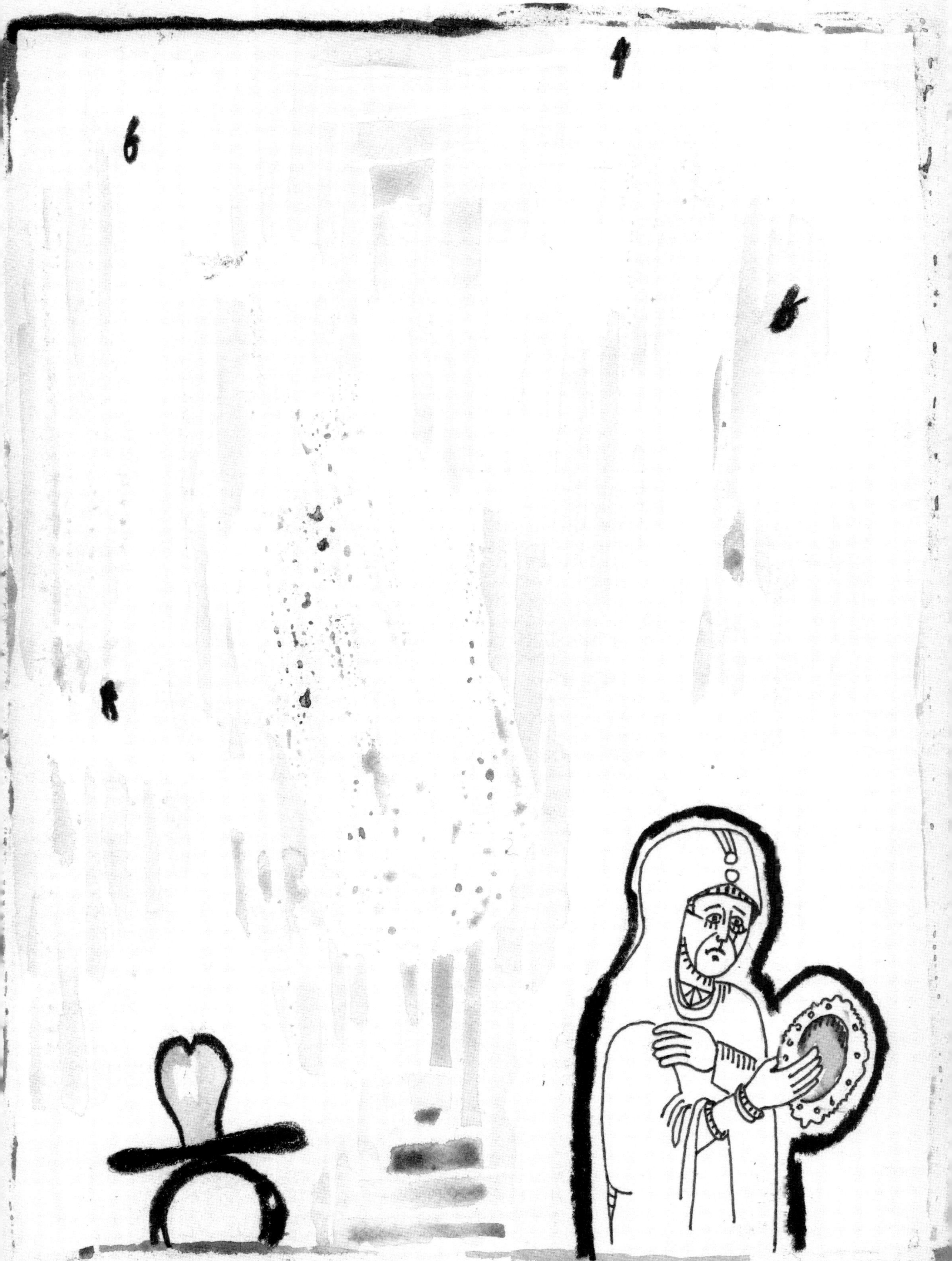

THIRD ACT

A VISIT TO THE ZOO

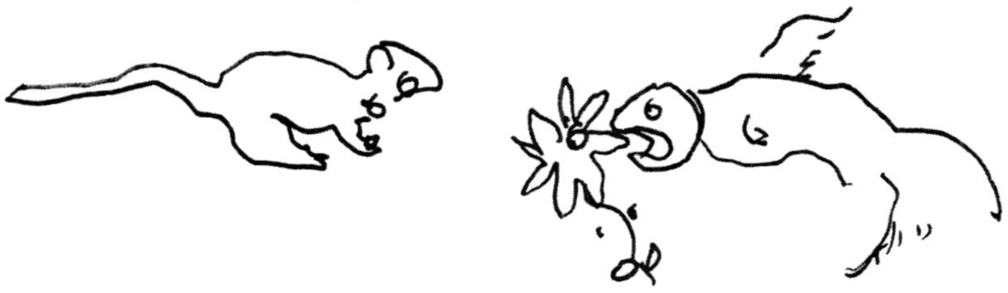

Scene I—Venice. A Street.

Enter Salanio and Salarino.

SALANIO
Now, what news on the Rialto?

SALARINO
Why, yet it lives there unchecked that Antonio hath a ship of rich lading wracked on the narrow seas; the Goodwins, I think they call the place; a very dangerous flat, and fatal, where the carcasses of many a tall ship lie buried, as they say, if my gossip Report be an honest woman of her word.

SALANIO
I would she were as lying a gossip in that as ever knapped ginger, or made her neighbours believe she wept for the death of a third husband. But it is true,—without any slips of prolixity or crossing the plain highway of talk,—that the good Antonio, the honest Antonio,—O, that I had a title good enough to keep his name company!—

SALARINO
Come, the full stop.

SALANIO
Ha! what sayst thou? Why, the end is, he hath lost a ship.

SALARINO
I would it might prove the end of his losses.

SALANIO
Let me say 'amen' betimes, lest the devil cross my prayer, for here he comes in the likeness of a Jew.

I am coerced to speak.
Doomed to affirm, to affirm.
Would have given much to be silent.
It is a proper day, I cannot deny, the light is fair, yes, but I do not want.
From without, I see the stage, the stages, two more stages in the conversion of Shylock to silence.
I see Solanio and Salerio prepare for their humble, horrible role. Yes, yes.

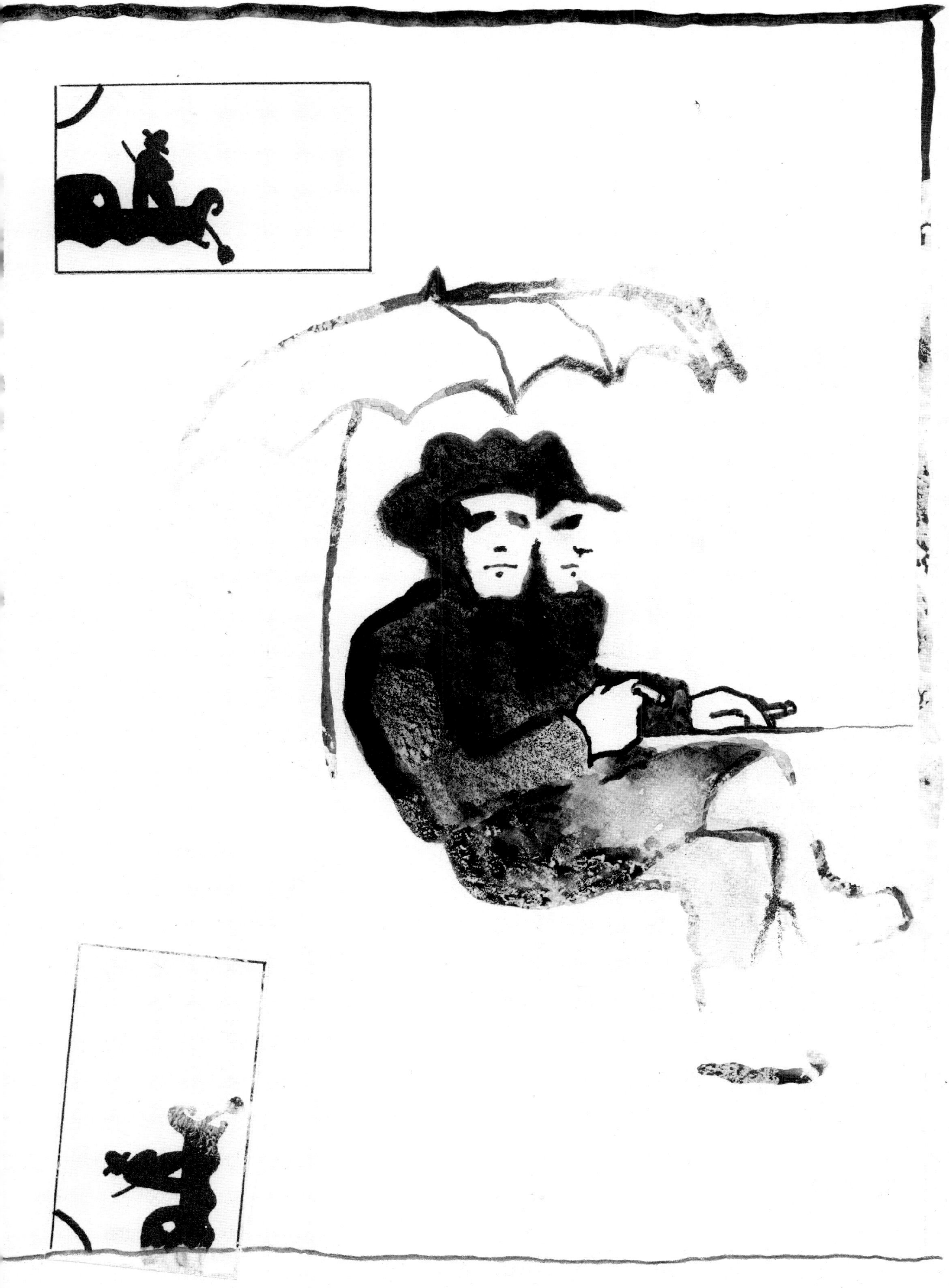

Enter Shylock.

How now, Shylock! what news among the merchants?

SHYLOCK
You knew, none so well, none so well as you, of my daughter's flight.

SALARINO
That's certain: I, for my part, knew the tailor that made the wings she flew withal.

SALANIO
And Shylock, for his own part, knew the bird was fledged; and then it is the complexion of them all to leave the dam.

SHYLOCK
She is damned for it.

SALARINO
That's certain, if the devil may be her judge.

SHYLOCK
My own flesh and blood to rebel!

So shrewd and composed are Solanio and Salerio. They handle Shylock so smartly—like surgeons, like glass merchants, they keep calm and see through him, see everything.
They are odorless.
They know their part.
They eye his new lesions and welts.
They know his rolling tongue would unfurl and strong words would leap out.
Once the words are out, Shylock will be less words. They are merely to help the words come out, and to stay composed.

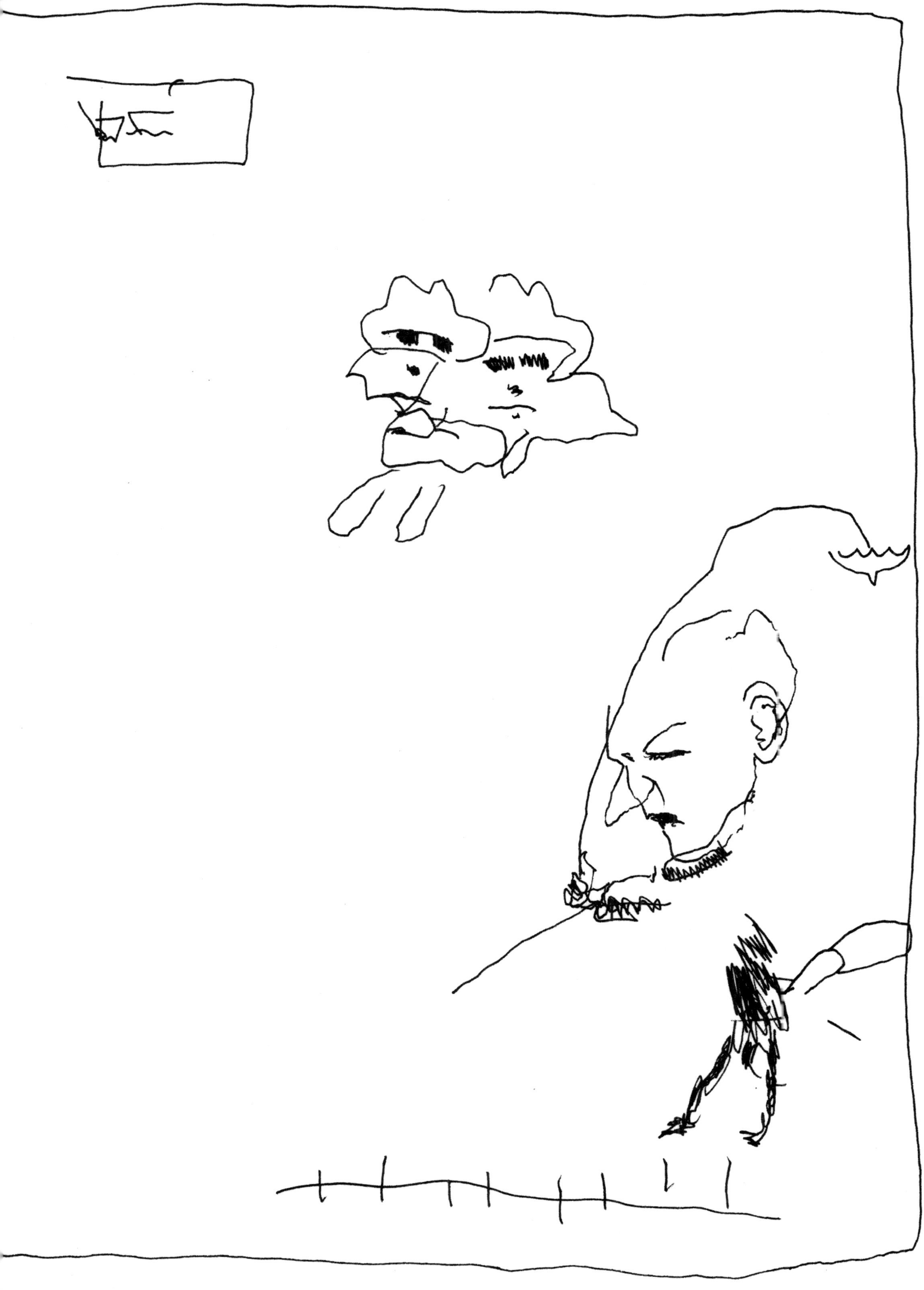

SALANIO
Out upon it, old carrion! rebels it at these years?

SHYLOCK
I say my daughter is my flesh and blood.

SALARINO
There is more difference between thy flesh and hers than between jet and ivory; more between your bloods than there is between red wine and Rhenish. But tell us, do you hear whether Antonio have had any loss at sea or no?

SHYLOCK
There I have another bad match: a bankrupt, a prodigal, who dare scarce show his head on the Rialto; a beggar, that used to come so smug upon the mart; let him look to his bond: he was wont to call me usurer; let him look to his bond: he was wont to lend money for a Christian courtesy; let him look to his bond.

SALARINO
Why, I am sure, if he forfeit thou wilt not take his flesh: what's that good for?

Pincers. Side. Attack. Little. Puss. Press.
Solanio says:
    I am a small mosquito!
Salerio says:
    I am a small cancer!
How tactful. And how clever.
They bite his heels.
Prick him, tiny tweezers.
Pinch him, frigid tongs.
They rob him with slimy jokes,
they ridicule his falling flesh,
they heat, heat up the Shylock vessel till
the strong words burst out, Here, Here:

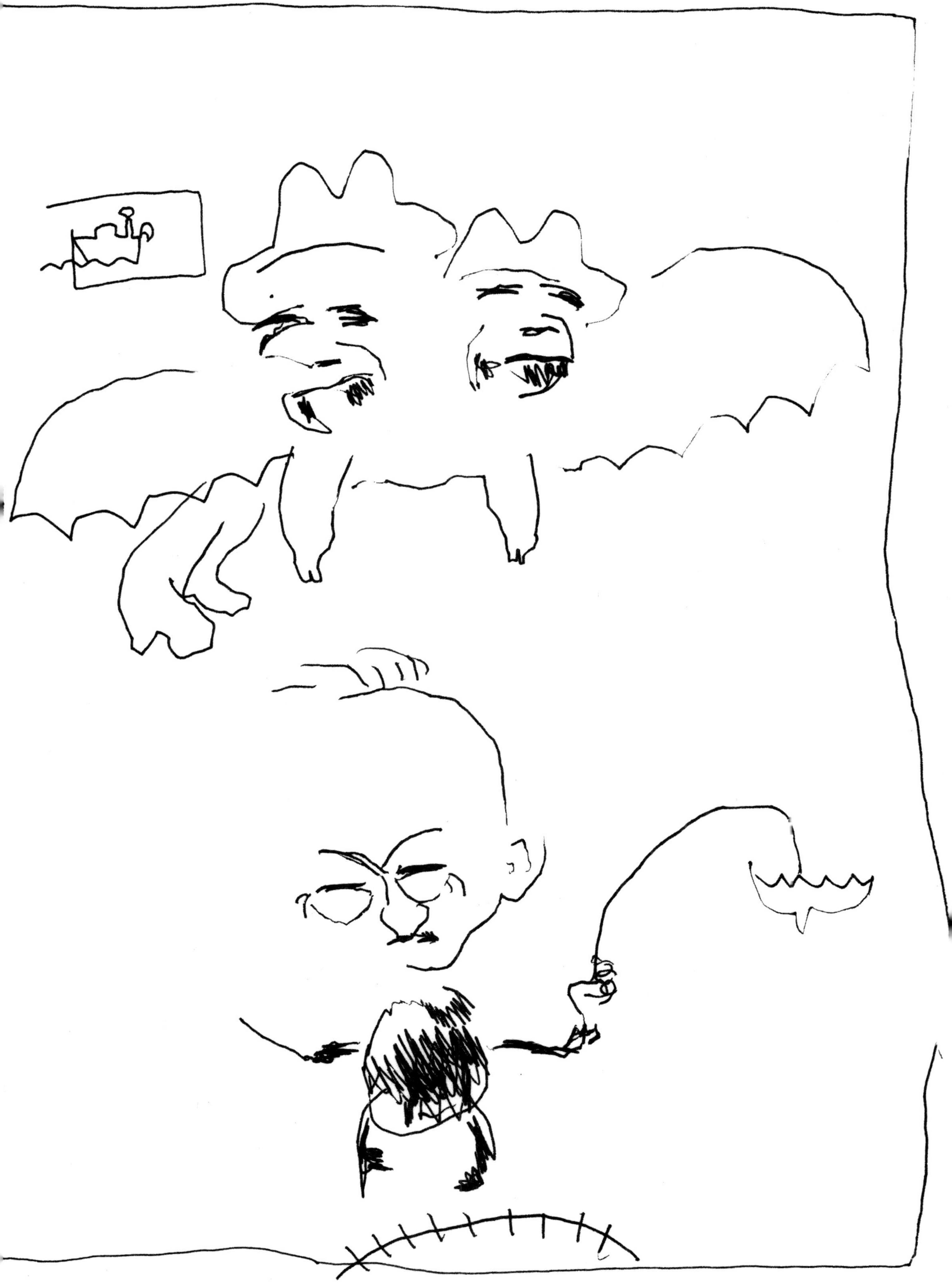

III.I.4

SHYLOCK

To bait fish withal: if it will feed nothing else, it will feed my revenge. He hath disgraced me, and hindered me half a million, laughed at my losses, mocked at my gains, scorned my nation, thwarted my bargains, cooled my friends, heated mine enemies; and what's his reason? I am a Jew.

withall.
If it will feed nothing
else, it will feed my revenge.

He hath disgraced
me, and hindered me
half a million.
Laughed
at my losses, mocked at
my gains, scorned my Nation,
thwarted my bargains,
cooled my friends, heated
mine enemies, and whats
his reason?

I am a Jew.

Hath not a Jew eyes? hath not a Jew hands, organs, dimensions, senses, affections, passions? fed with the same food, hurt with the same weapons, subject to the same diseases, healed by the same means, warmed and cooled by the same winter and summer, as a Christian is? If you prick us, do we not bleed? if you tickle us, do we not laugh? if you poison us, do we not die? and if you wrong us, shall we not revenge? If we are like you in the rest, we will resemble you in that. If a Jew wrong a Christian, what is his humility? Revenge. If a Christian wrong a Jew, what should his sufferance be by Christian example? Why, revenge. The villany you teach me I will execute, and it shall go hard but I will better the instruction.

Hath not a Jew eyes?

Now the words are out, sustained in the air, sustaining the air, overwhelming. But it is a powerless strength. All Solanio and Salerio ought to do is maintain their silence. No response. Release clamps and exit. Offstage.

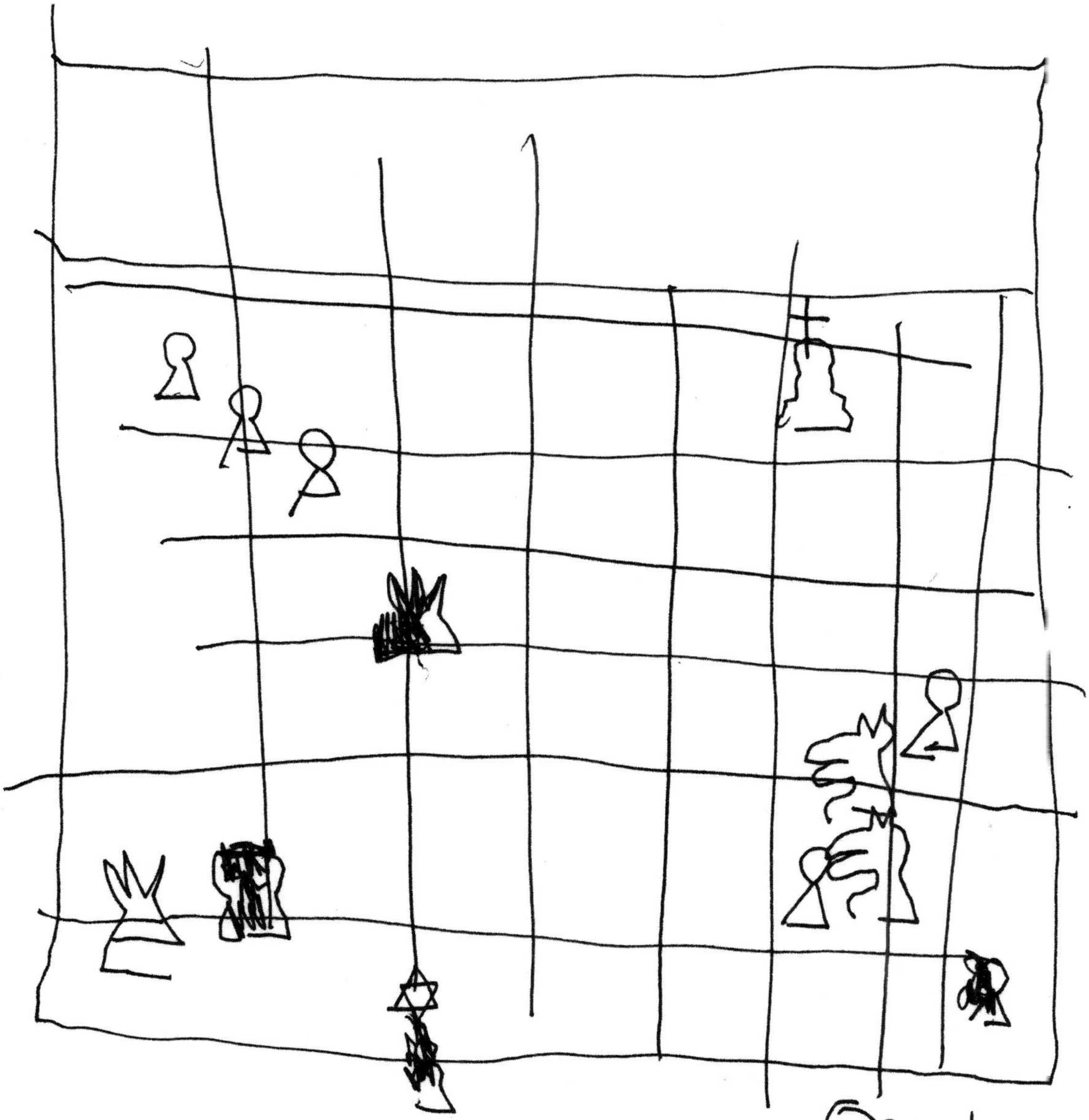

...Qe4+

white's turn

Enter a Servant.

SERVANT
Gentlemen, my master Antonio is at his house, and desires to speak with you both.

SALARINO
We have been up and down to seek him.

Enter Tubal.

SALANIO
Here comes another of the tribe: a third cannot be matched, unless the devil himself turn Jew.

Exeunt Salanio, Salarino and Servant.

Their silence says:
    we didn't hear.
It says:
    the words were spoken foreign.
Strong words and no ears mean only
another death wish—as Toozenbach said:
"Fancy being able to play so exquisitely
and yet have nobody, nobody at all to
appreciate it!"
Now, as the words are out and static,
they would dehydrate and be forgotten.
Just maintain silence, no response, exit,
let the fall proceed, enter Shylock's
only friend.

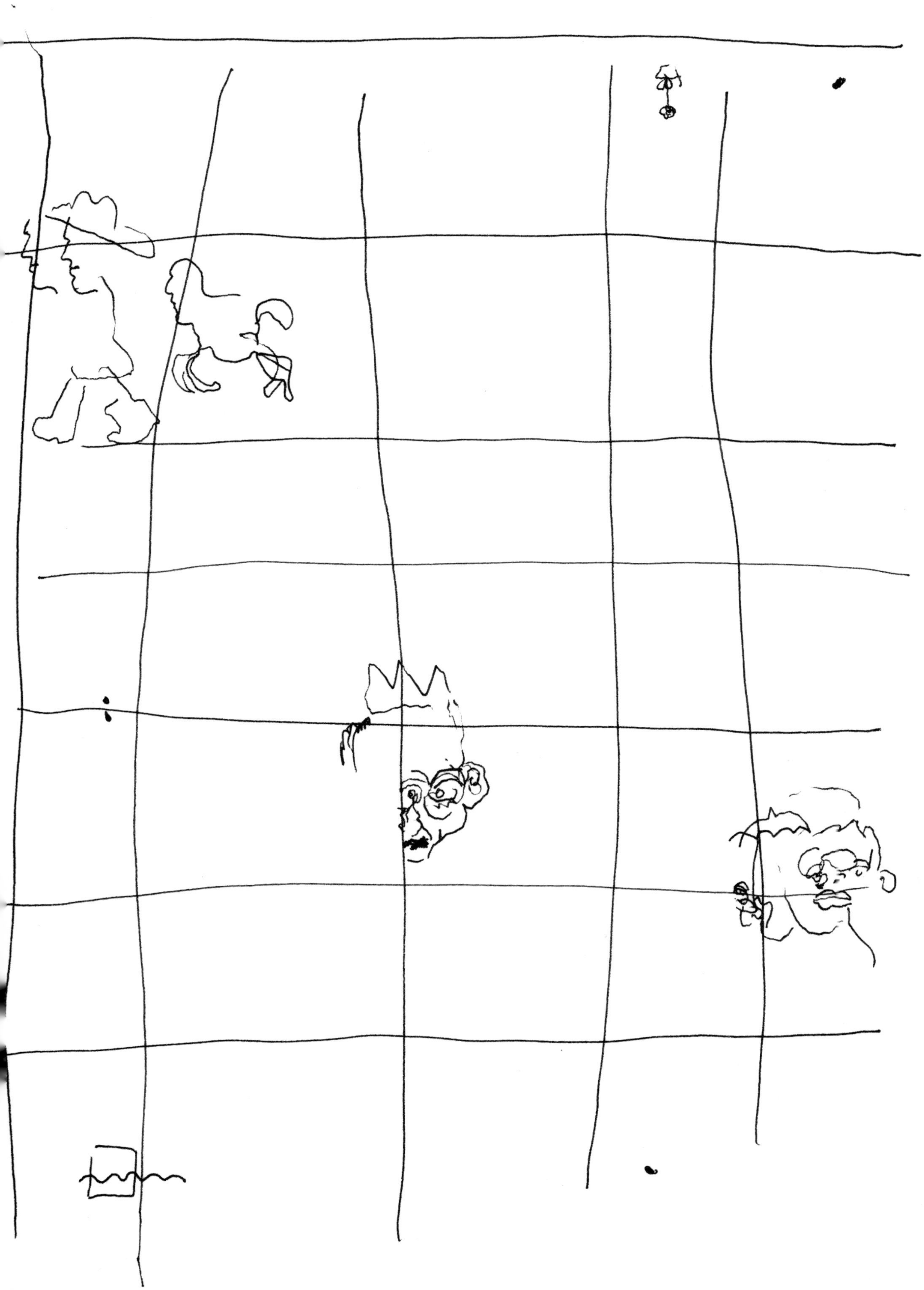

SHYLOCK

How now, Tubal! what news from Genoa? Hast thou found my daughter?

TUBAL

I often came where I did hear of her, but cannot find her.

SHYLOCK

Why there, there, there! a diamond gone, cost me two thousand ducats in Frankfort! The curse never fell upon our nation till now; I never felt it till now: two thousand ducats in that; and other precious, precious jewels. I would my daughter were dead at my foot, and the jewels in her ear! would she were hearsed at my foot, and the ducats in her coffin! No news of them? Why, so: and I know not what's spent in the search: Why thou—loss upon loss! the thief gone with so much, and so much to find the thief; and no satisfaction, no revenge: nor no ill luck stirring but what lights on my shoulders; no sighs but of my breathing; no tears but of my shedding.

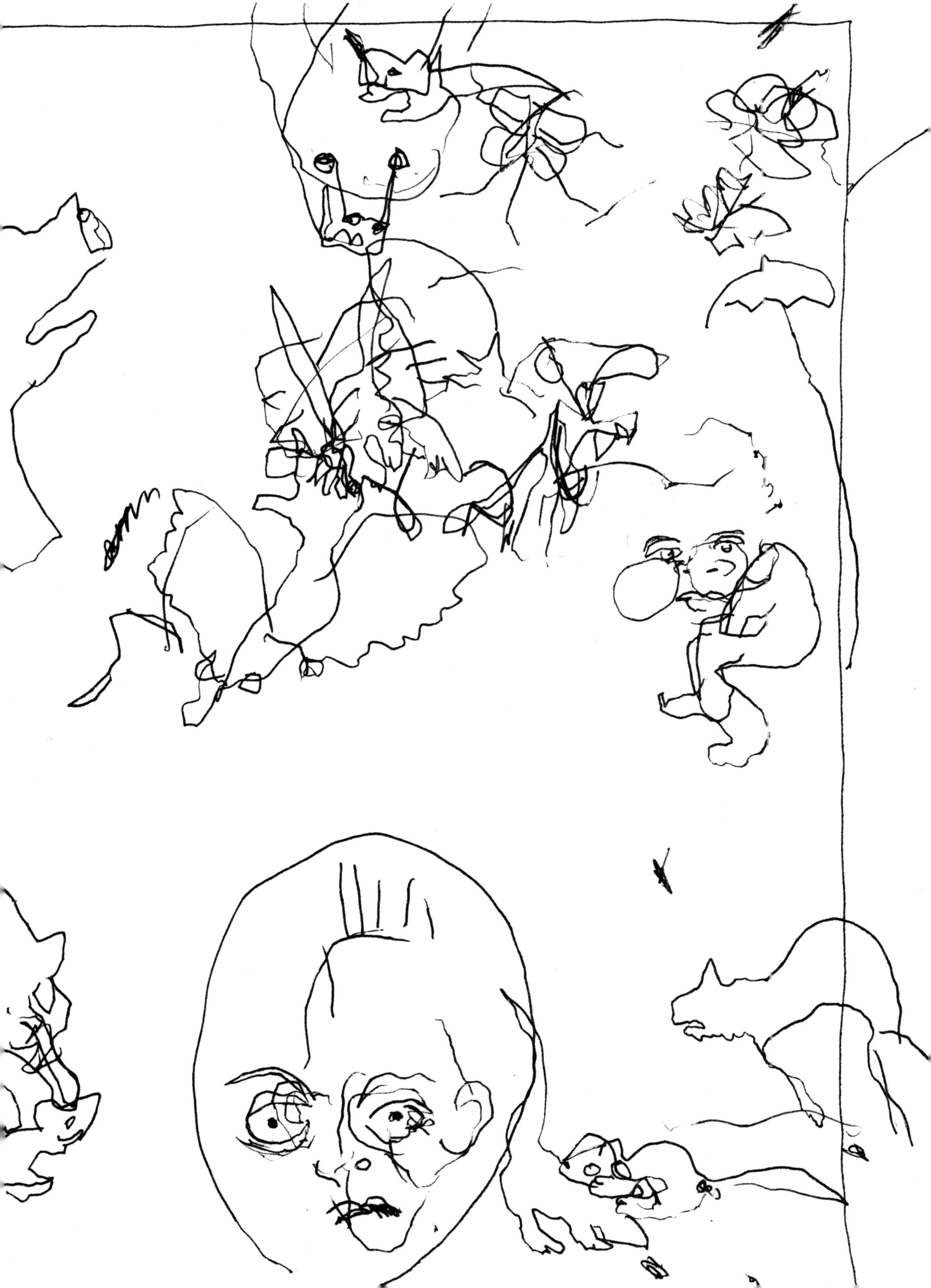

TUBAL
Yes, other men have ill luck too. Antonio, as I heard in Genoa,—

SHYLOCK
What, what, what? ill luck, ill luck?

TUBAL
—hath an argosy cast away, coming from Tripolis.

SHYLOCK
I thank God! I thank God! Is it true? is it true?

TUBAL
I spoke with some of the sailors that escaped the wrack.

SHYLOCK
I thank thee, good Tubal. Good news, good news! ha, ha! Where? in Genoa?

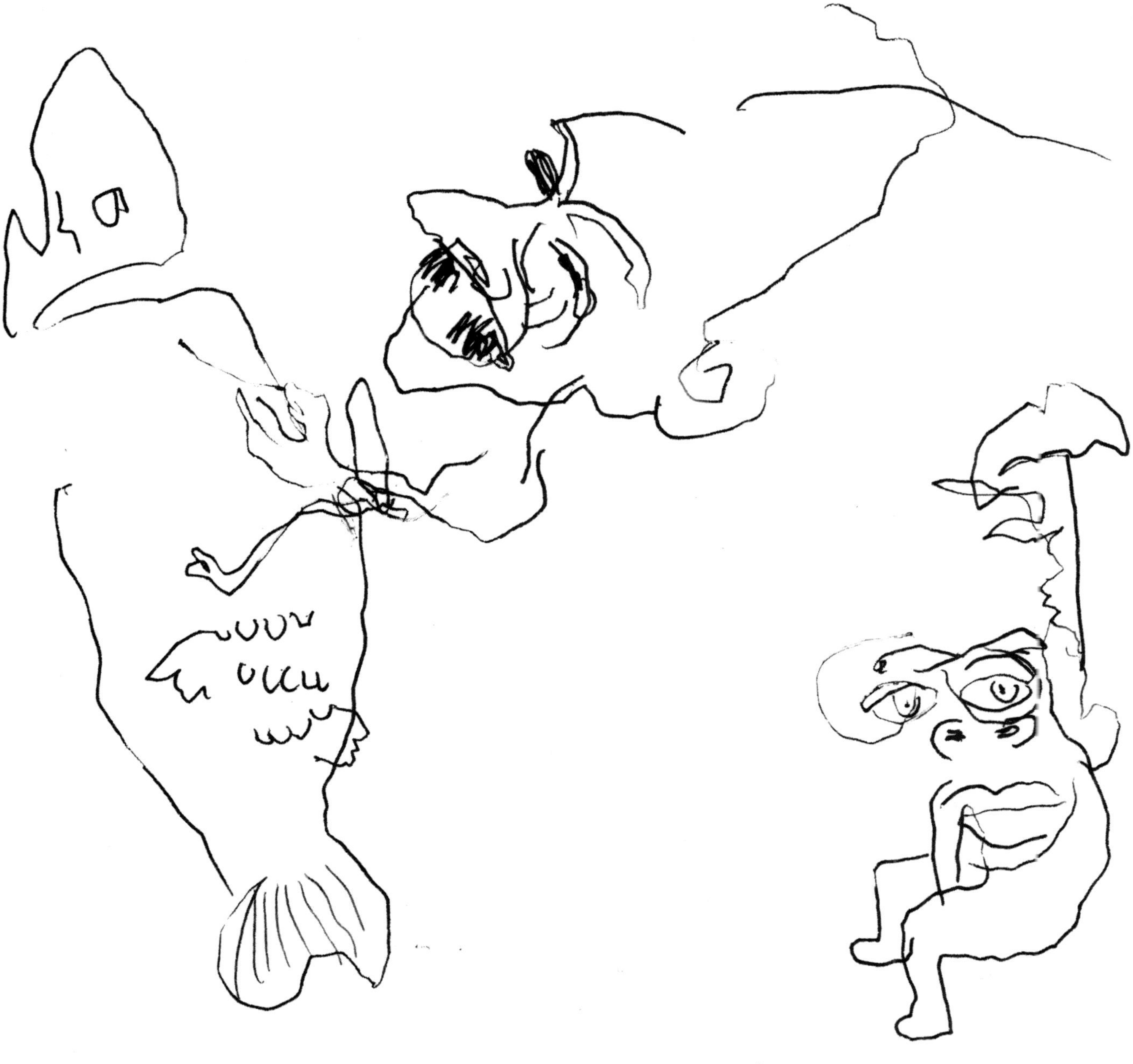

TUBAL
Your daughter spent in Genoa, as I heard, one night, fourscore ducats.

SHYLOCK
Thou stick'st a dagger in me: I shall never see my gold again: fourscore ducats at a sitting! fourscore ducats!

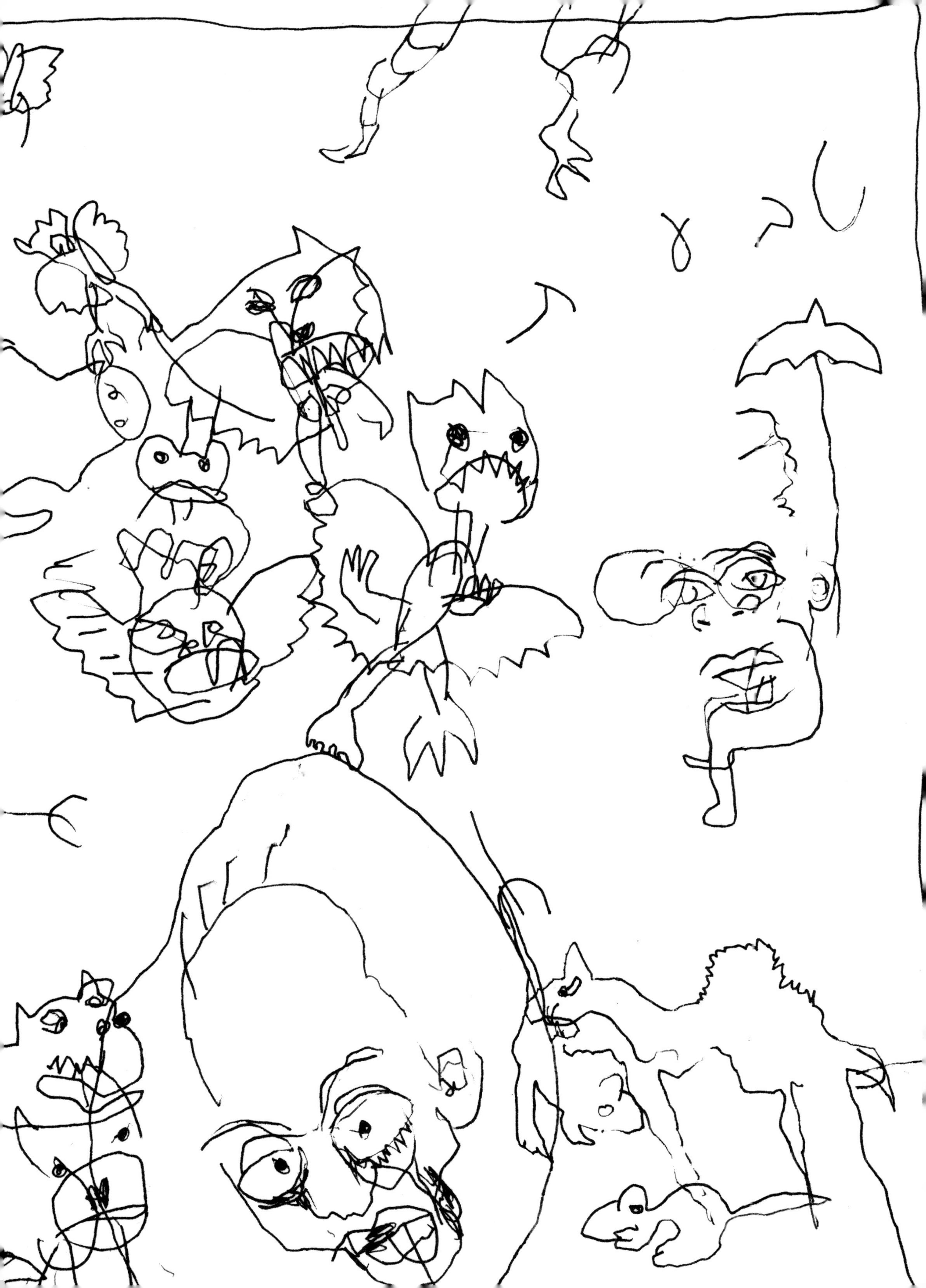

TUBAL

There came divers of Antonio's creditors in my company to Venice, that swear he cannot choose but break.

SHYLOCK

I am very glad of it: I'll plague him; I'll torture him: I am glad of it.

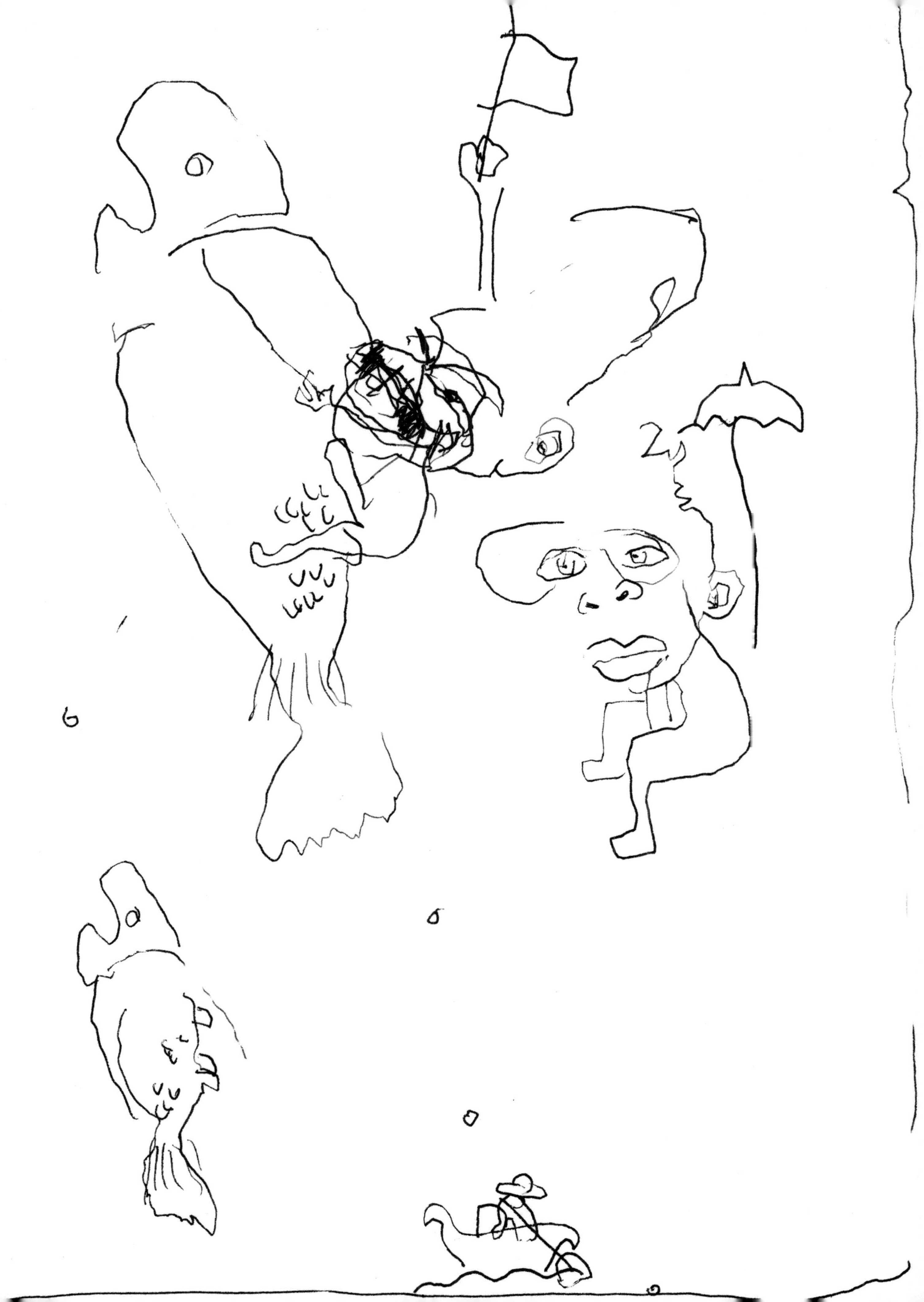

TUBAL

One of them showed me a ring that he had of your daughter for a monkey.

SHYLOCK

Out upon her! Thou torturest me, Tubal: it was my turquoise; I had it of Leah when I was a bachelor: I would not have given it for a wilderness of monkeys.

TUBAL

But Antonio is certainly undone.

SHYLOCK

Nay, that's true, that's very true. Go, Tubal, fee me an officer; bespeak him a fortnight before. I will have the heart of him, if he forfeit; for, were he out of Venice, I can make what merchandise I will. Go, go, Tubal, and meet me at our synagogue; go, good Tubal; at our synagogue, Tubal.

Exeunt.

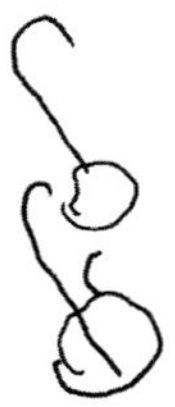

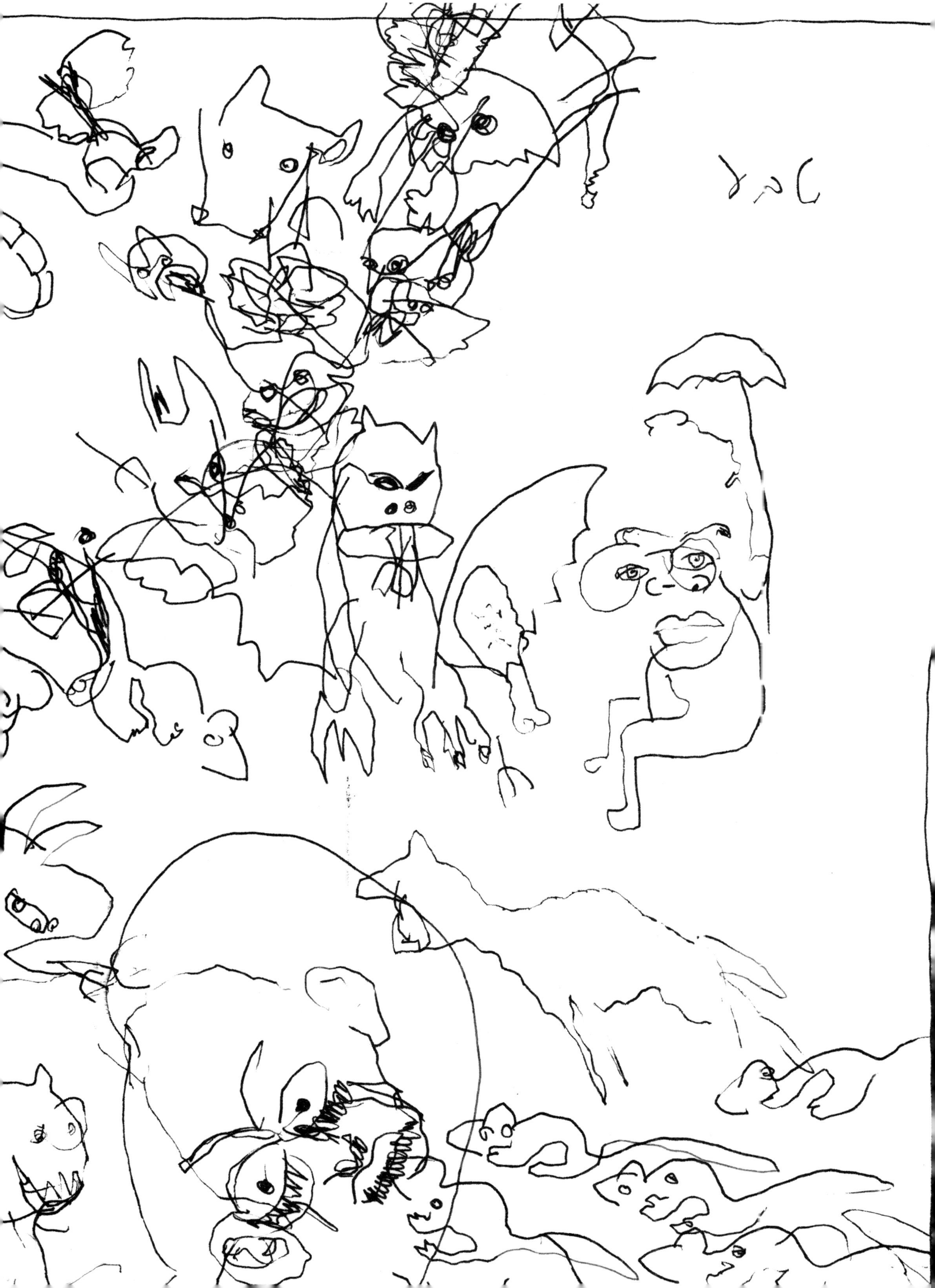

Scene I—Belmont. A Room in Portia's House.

Enter Bassanio, Portia, Gratiano, Nerissa, and Attendants.

PORTIA
I pray you, tarry: pause a day or two
Before you hazard; for, in choosing wrong,
I lose your company: therefore, forbear awhile.
There's something tells me, but it is not love,
I would not lose you; and you know yourself,
Hate counsels not in such a quality.
But lest you should not understand me well,—
And yet a maiden hath no tongue but thought,—
I would detain you here some month or two
Before you venture for me. I could teach you
How to choose right, but then I am forsworn;
So will I never be: so may you miss me;
But if you do, you'll make me wish a sin,
That I had been forsworn. Beshrew your eyes,
They have o'erlook'd me and divided me:
One half of me is yours, the other half yours,
Mine own, I would say; but if mine, then yours,
And so all yours. O! these naughty times
Put bars between the owners and their rights;
And so, though yours, not yours. Prove it so,
Let fortune go to hell for it, not I.
I speak too long; but 'tis to peise the time,
To eke it and to draw it out in length,
To stay you from election.

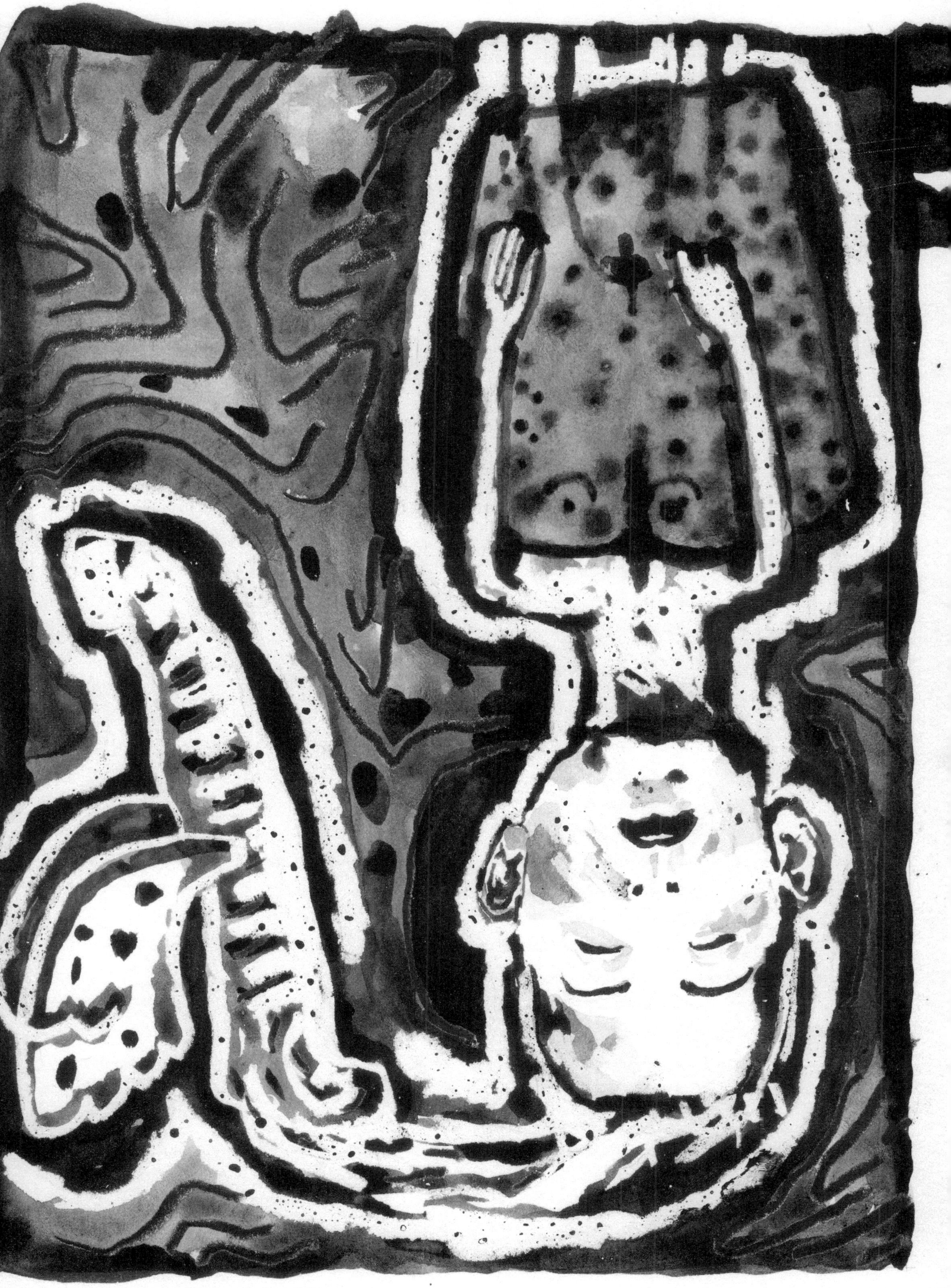

BASSANIO
Let me choose;
For as I am, I live upon the rack.

PORTIA
Upon the rack, Bassanio! then confess
What treason there is mingled with your love.

BASSANIO
None but that ugly treason of mistrust,
Which makes me fear th' enjoying of my love:
There may as well be amity and life
'Tween snow and fire, as treason and my love.

PORTIA
Ay, but I fear you speak upon the rack,
Where men enforced do speak anything.

BASSANIO
Promise me life, and I'll confess the truth.

PORTIA
Well then, confess, and live.

BASSANIO
'Confess' and 'love'
Had been the very sum of my confession:
O happy torment, when my torturer
Doth teach me answers for deliverance!
But let me to my fortune and the caskets.

PORTIA
Away then! I am lock'd in one of them:
If you do love me, you will find me out.
Nerissa and the rest, stand all aloof.
Let music sound while he doth make his choice;
Then, if he lose, he makes a swan-like end,
Fading in music: that the comparison
May stand more proper, my eye shall be the stream
And watery death-bed for him. He may win;
And what is music then? then music is
Even as the flourish when true subjects bow
To a new-crowned monarch: such it is
As are those dulcet sounds in break of day
That creep into the dreaming bridegroom's ear,
And summon him to marriage. Now he goes,
With no less presence, but with much more love,
Than young Alcides, when he did redeem
The virgin tribute paid by howling Troy
To the sea-monster: I stand for sacrifice;
The rest aloof are the Dardanian wives,
With bleared visages, come forth to view
The issue of the exploit. Go, Hercules!
Live thou, I live: with much, much more dismay
I view the fight than thou that mak'st the fray.

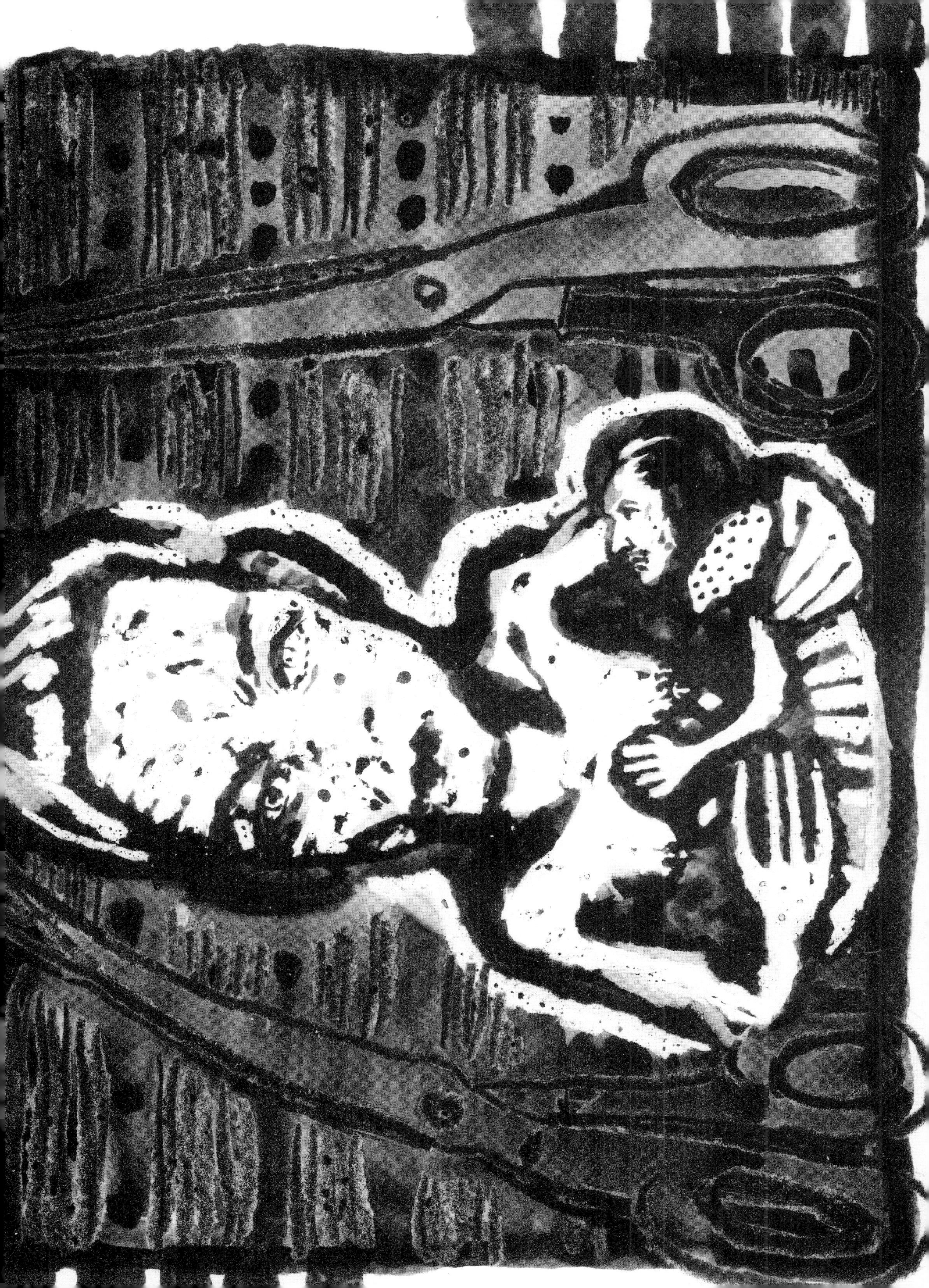

III.II.3

A Song, whilst Bassanio comments on the caskets to himself.

Tell me where is fancy bred,
Or in the heart or in the head?
How begot, how nourished?
    Reply, reply.
It is engender'd in the eyes,
With gazing fed; and fancy dies
In the cradle where it lies
    Let us all ring fancy's knell;
    I'll begin it,—Ding, dong, bell.

ALL

Ding, dong, bell.

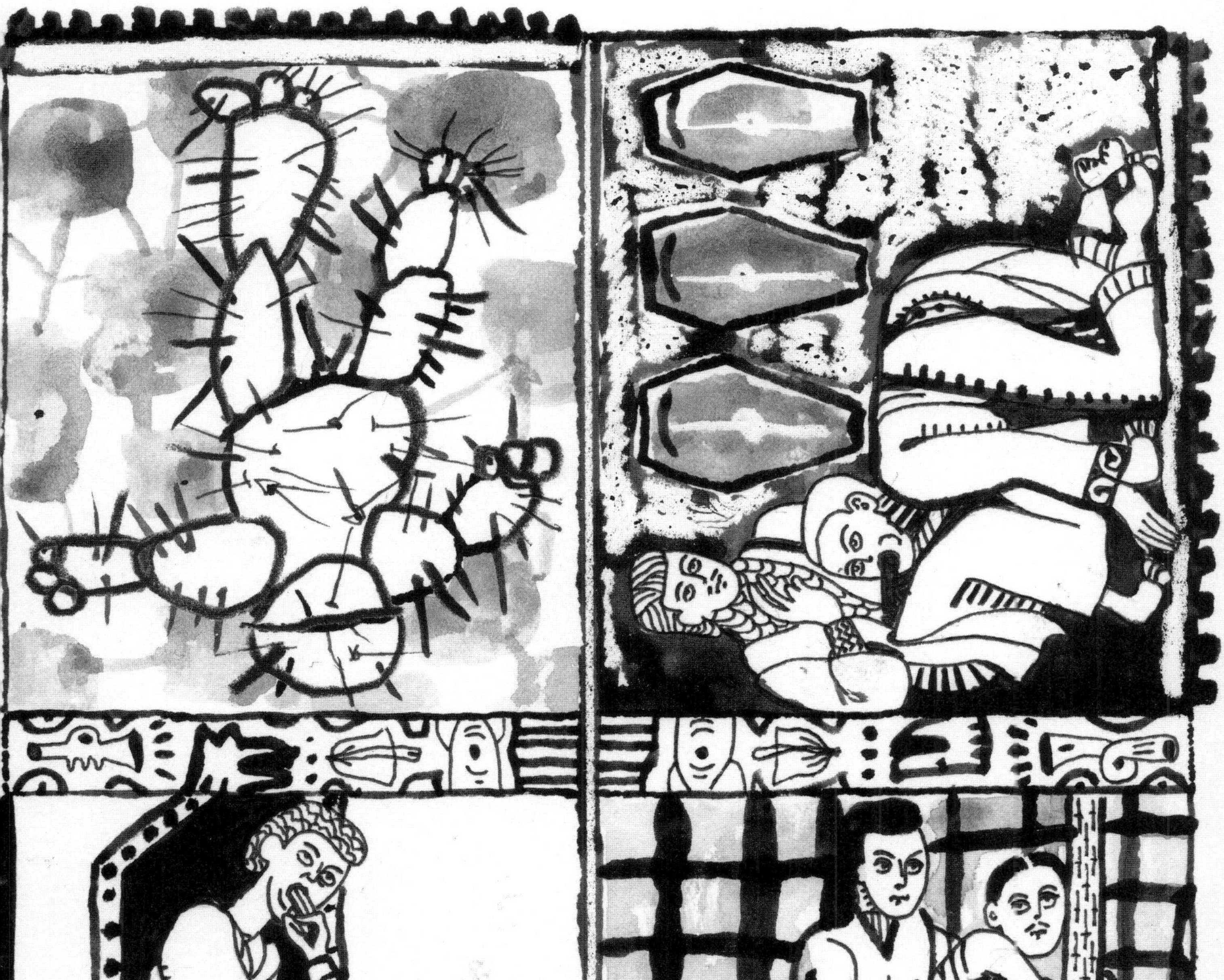

BASSANIO
So may the outward shows be least themselves:
The world is still deceiv'd with ornament.
In law, what plea so tainted and corrupt
But, being season'd with a gracious voice,
Obscures the show of evil? In religion,
What damned error, but some sober brow
Will bless it and approve it with a text,
Hiding the grossness with fair ornament?
There is no vice so simple but assumes
Some mark of virtue on his outward parts.
How many cowards, whose hearts are all as false
As stairs of sand, wear yet upon their chins
The beards of Hercules and frowning Mars,
Who, inward search'd, have livers white as milk;
And these assume but valour's excrement
To render them redoubted! Look on beauty,
And you shall see 'tis purchas'd by the weight;
Which therein works a miracle in nature,
Making them lightest that wear most of it:
So are those crisped snaky golden locks
Which make such wanton gambols with the wind,
Upon supposed fairness, often known
To be the dowry of a second head,
The skull that bred them, in the sepulchre.
Thus ornament is but the guiled shore
To a most dangerous sea; the beauteous scarf
Veiling an Indian beauty; in a word,
The seeming truth which cunning times put on
To entrap the wisest. Therefore, thou gaudy gold,
Hard food for Midas, I will none of thee;
Nor none of thee, thou pale and common drudge
'Tween man and man: but thou, thou meagre lead,
Which rather threat'nest than dost promise aught,
Thy plainness moves me more than eloquence,
And here choose I: joy be the consequence!

PORTIA
[*Aside.*] How all the other passions fleet to air,
As doubtful thoughts, and rash-embrac'd despair,
And shuddering fear, and green-ey'd jealousy.
O love! be moderate; allay thy ecstasy;
In measure rain thy joy; scant this excess;
I feel too much thy blessing; make it less,
For fear I surfeit!

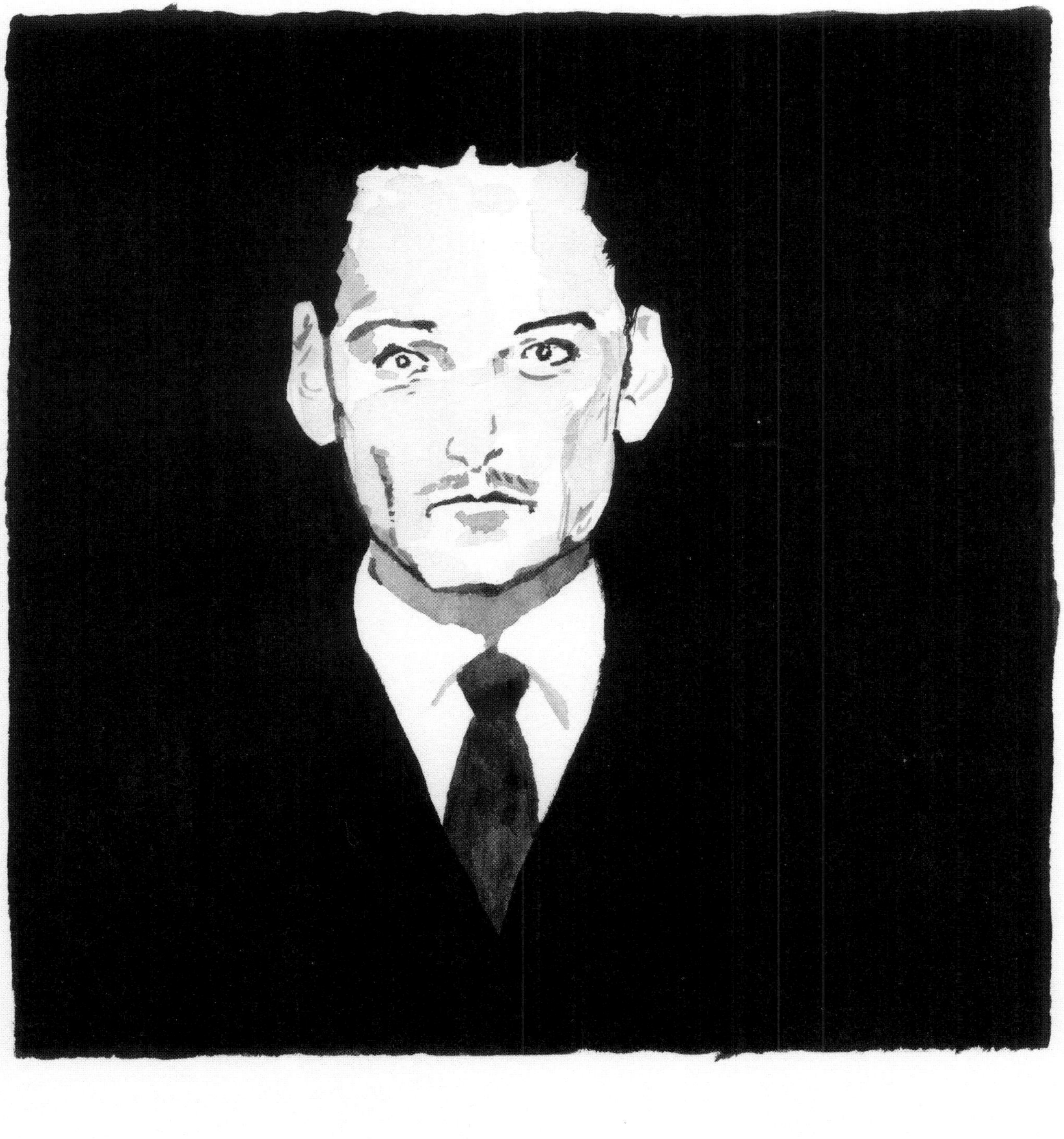

III.II.5

BASSANIO

What find I here?

Opening the leaden casket.

Fair Portia's counterfeit! What demi-god
Hath come so near creation? Move these eyes?
Or whether, riding on the balls of mine,
Seem they in motion? Here are sever'd lips,
Parted with sugar breath; so sweet a bar
Should sunder such sweet friends. Here, in her hairs
The painter plays the spider, and hath woven
A golden mesh to entrap the hearts of men
Faster than gnats in cobwebs: but her eyes!—
How could he see to do them? having made one,
Methinks it should have power to steal both his
And leave itself unfurnish'd: yet look, how far
The substance of my praise doth wrong this shadow
In underprizing it, so far this shadow
Doth limp behind the substance. Here's the scroll,
The continent and summary of my fortune.

You that choose not by the view,
Chance as fair and choose as true!
Since this fortune falls to you,
Be content and seek no new.
If you be well pleas'd with this
And hold your fortune for your bliss,
Turn you where your lady is
And claim her with a loving kiss.

A gentle scroll. Fair lady, by your leave;

Kissing her.

I come by note, to give and to receive.
Like one of two contending in a prize,
That thinks he hath done well in people's eyes,
Hearing applause and universal shout,
Giddy in spirit, still gazing in a doubt
Whether those peals of praise be his or no;
So, thrice-fair lady, stand I, even so,
As doubtful whether what I see be true,
Until confirm'd, sign'd, ratified by you.

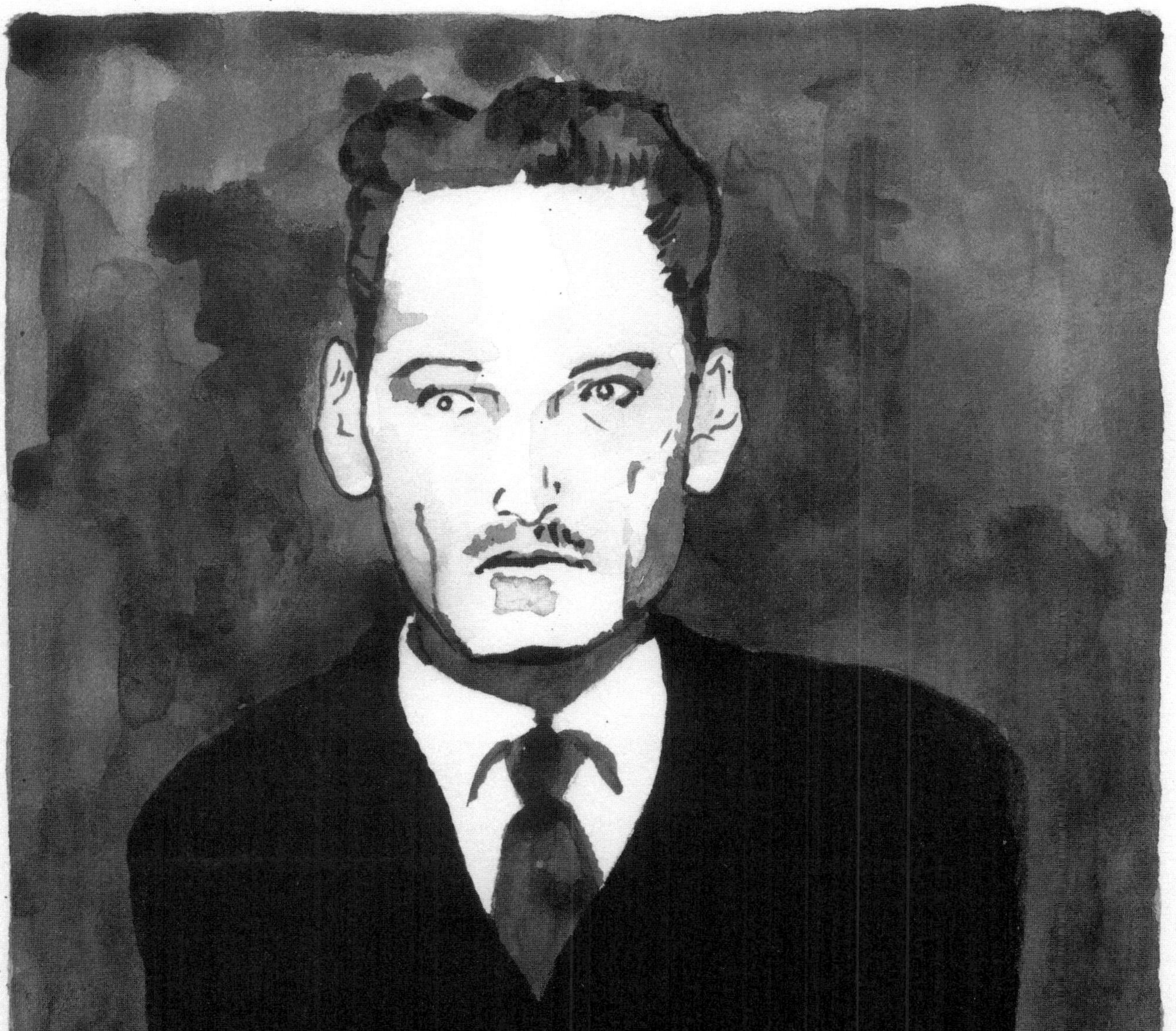

PORTIA

You see me, Lord Bassanio, where I stand,
Such as I am: though for myself alone
I would not be ambitious in my wish,
To wish myself much better; yet, for you
I would be trebled twenty times myself;
A thousand times more fair, ten thousand times
More rich;
That only to stand high in your account,
I might in virtues, beauties, livings, friends,
Exceed account: but the full sum of me
Is sum of nothing; which, to term in gross,
Is an unlesson'd girl, unschool'd, unpractis'd;
Happy in this, she is not yet so old
But she may learn; happier than this,
She is not bred so dull but she can learn;
Happiest of all is that her gentle spirit
Commits itself to yours to be directed,
As from her lord, her governor, her king.
Myself and what is mine to you and yours
Is now converted: but now I was the lord
Of this fair mansion, master of my servants,
Queen o'er myself; and even now, but now,
This house, these servants, and this same myself
Are yours, my lord. I give them with this ring;
Which when you part from, lose, or give away,
Let it presage the ruin of your love,
And be my vantage to exclaim on you.

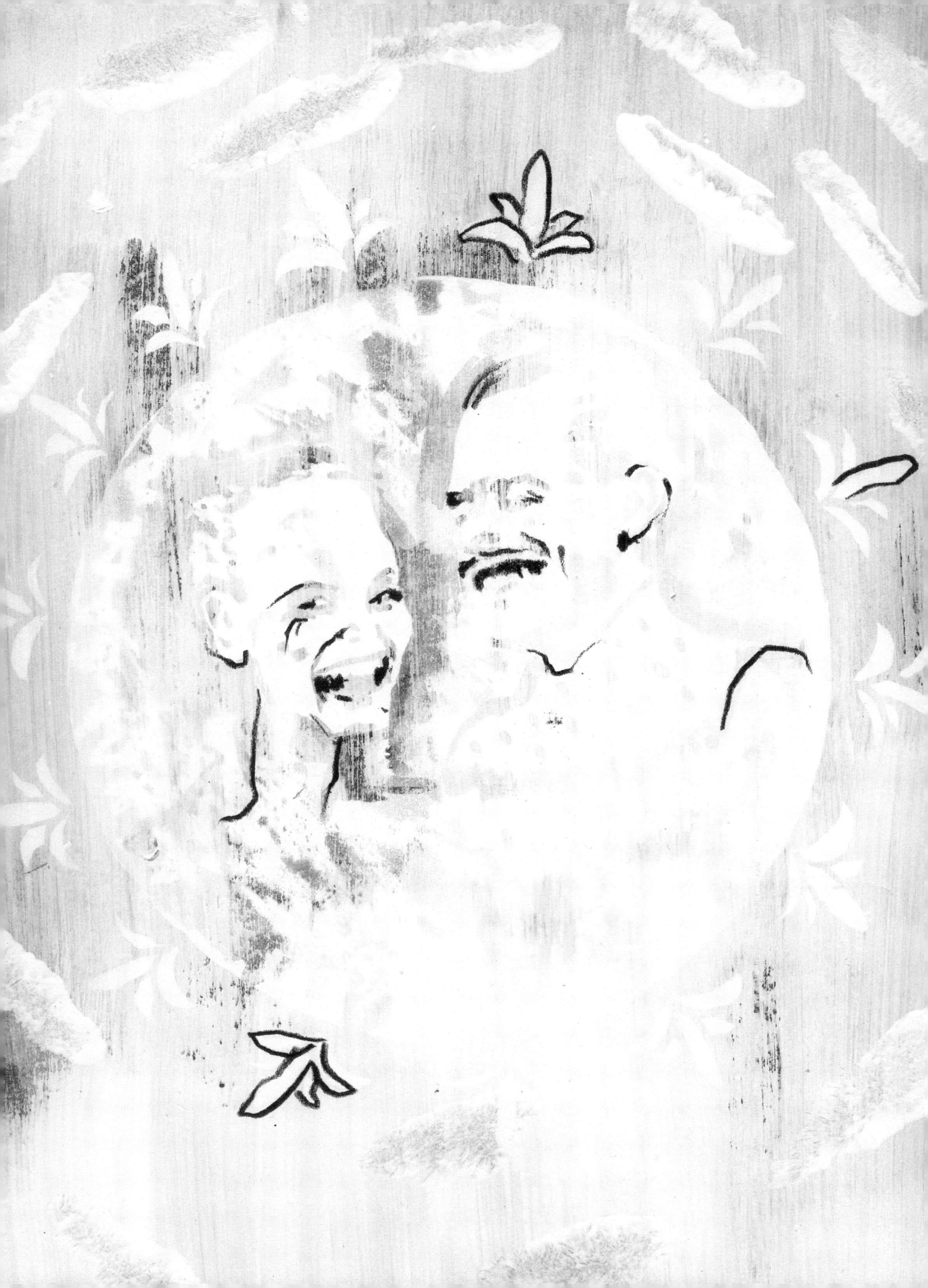

BASSANIO
Madam, you have bereft me of all words,
Only my blood speaks to you in my veins;
And there is such confusion in my powers,
As, after some oration fairly spoke
By a beloved prince, there doth appear
Among the buzzing pleased multitude;
Where every something, being blent together,
Turns to a wild of nothing, save of joy,
Express'd and not express'd. But when this ring
Parts from this finger, then parts life from hence:
O! then be bold to say Bassanio's dead.

What was that?
As Bassanio prepared to perform, as Portia spoke to him, did you notice, her voice betrayed an apprehension, a frailty, it modulated on the brink of hysteria.
One may answer simply, directly—it was her moment of love, her fear, her important rare fear. And him, his death, as he faced, as he was faced. And them now, all of them, they all cling, not only he and she, but the rest of them now, ringing themselves around each other, Portia and Bassanio, Gratiano and Nerissa, Jessica and Lorenzo. They are so wet, and I so dry.
I wish not to listen. I am not well. I ask permission. We want simple. They will go on, and we away—to the zoo. The beautiful zoo. Can you see? I feel so proud and relieved.

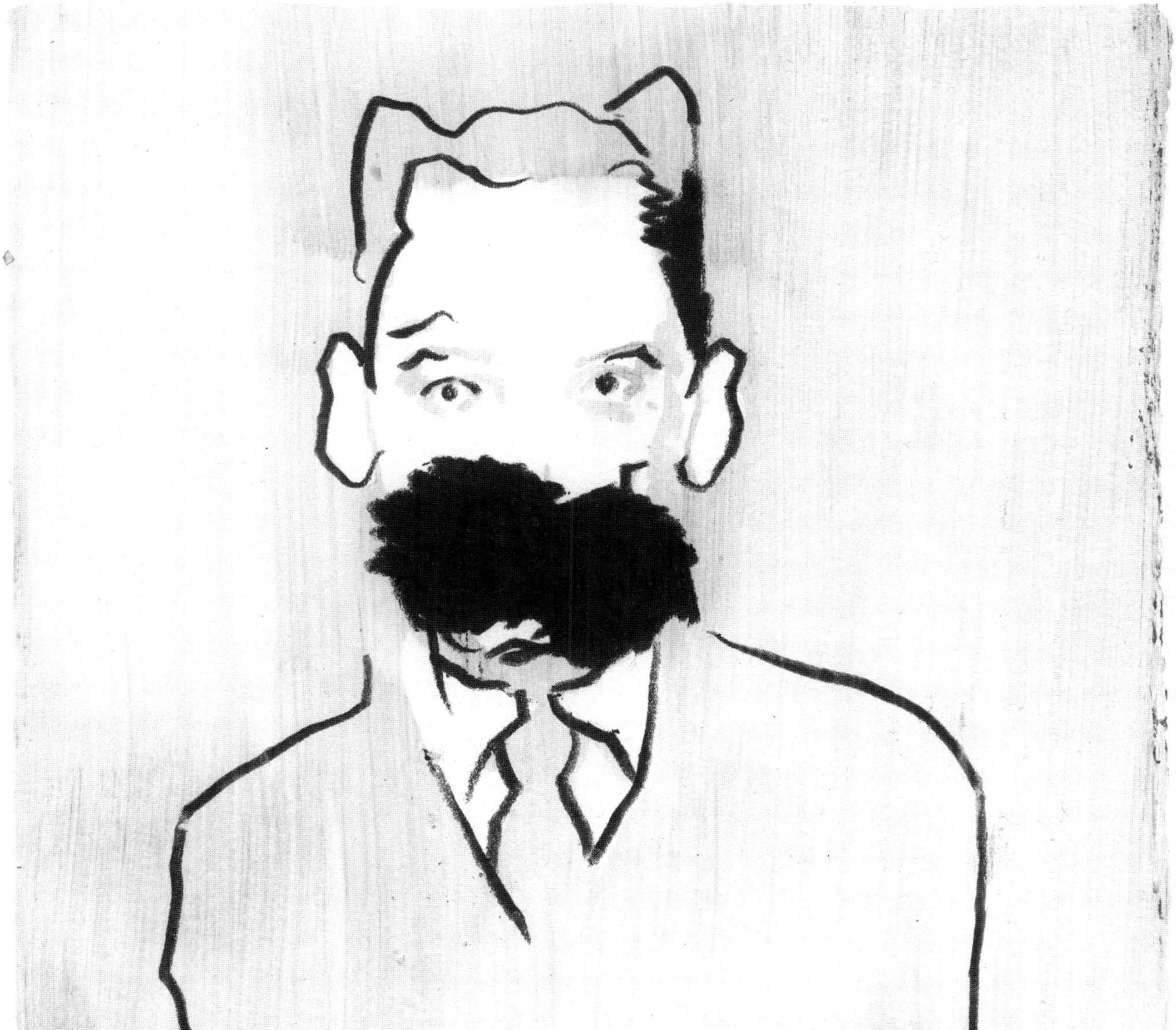

NERISSA
My lord and lady, it is now our time,
That have stood by and seen our wishes prosper,
To cry, good joy. Good joy, my lord and lady!

GRATIANO
My Lord Bassanio and my gentle lady,
I wish you all the joy that you can wish;
For I am sure you can wish none from me:
And when your honours mean to solemnize
The bargain of your faith, I do beseech you,
Even at that time I may be married too.

BASSANIO
With all my heart, so thou canst get a wife.

GRATIANO
I thank your lordship, you have got me one.
My eyes, my lord, can look as swift as yours:
You saw the mistress, I beheld the maid;
You lov'd, I lov'd for intermission.
No more pertains to me, my lord, than you.
Your fortune stood upon the caskets there,
And so did mine too, as the matter falls;
For wooing here until I sweat again,
And swearing till my very roof was dry
With oaths of love, at last, if promise last,
I got a promise of this fair one here
To have her love, provided that your fortune
Achiev'd her mistress.

PORTIA
Is this true, Nerissa?

NERISSA
Madam, it is, so you stand pleas'd withal.

BASSANIO
And do you, Gratiano, mean good faith?

GRATIANO
Yes, faith, my lord.

BASSANIO
Our feast shall be much honour'd in your marriage.

GRATIANO
We'll play with them the first boy for a thousand ducats.

NERISSA
What! and stake down?

GRATIANO
No; we shall ne'er win at that sport, and stake down.
But who comes here? Lorenzo and his infidel?
What! and my old Venetian friend, Salanio?

See the gate. Look! My beautiful animals!

Enter Lorenzo, Jessica, and Salanio.

BASSANIO
Lorenzo, and Salanio, welcome hither,
If that the youth of my new interest here
Have power to bid you welcome. By your leave,
I bid my very friends and countrymen,
Sweet Portia, welcome.

PORTIA
So do I, my lord:
They are entirely welcome.

LORENZO
I thank your honour. For my part, my lord,
My purpose was not to have seen you here;
But meeting with Salanio by the way,
He did entreat me, past all saying nay,
To come with him along.

SALANIO
I did, my lord,
And I have reason for it. Signior Antonio
Commends him to you.

Gives Bassanio a letter.

BASSANIO
Ere I ope his letter,
I pray you, tell me how my good friend doth.

SALANIO
Not sick, my lord, unless it be in mind;
Nor well, unless in mind: his letter there
Will show you his estate.

GRATIANO
Nerissa, cheer yon stranger; bid her welcome.
Your hand, Salanio. What's the news from Venice?
How doth that royal merchant, good Antonio?
I know he will be glad of our success;
We are the Jasons, we have won the fleece.

My diaphanous flying fish.

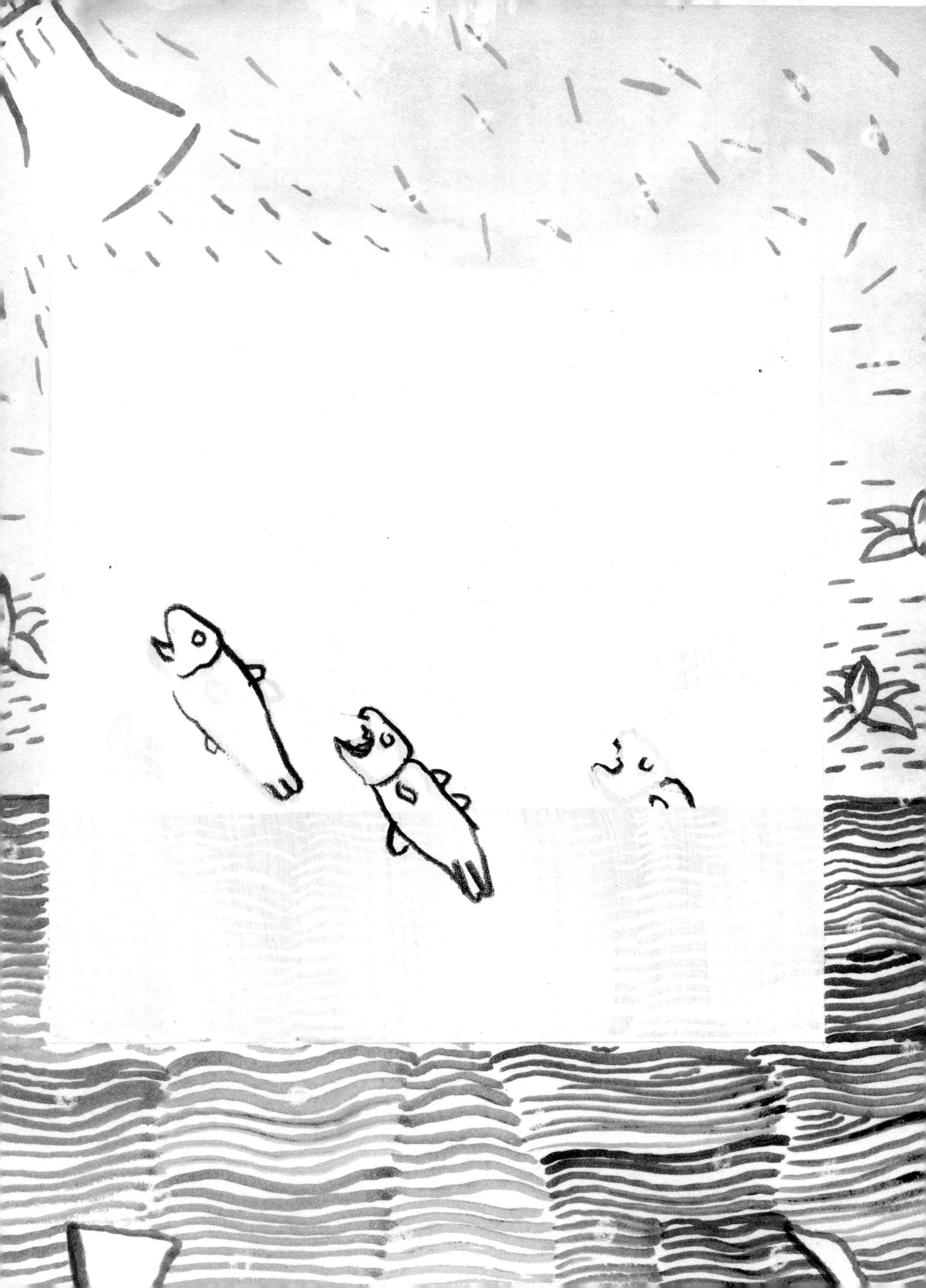

SALANIO
I would you had won the fleece that he hath lost.

PORTIA
There are some shrewd contents in yon same paper,
That steal the colour from Bassanio's cheek:
Some dear friend dead, else nothing in the world
Could turn so much the constitution
Of any constant man. What, worse and worse!
With leave, Bassanio; I am half yourself,
And I must freely have the half of anything
That this same paper brings you.

BASSANIO
O sweet Portia!
Here are a few of the unpleasant'st words
That ever blotted paper. Gentle lady,
When I did first impart my love to you,
I freely told you all the wealth I had
Ran in my veins, I was a gentleman:
And then I told you true; and yet, dear lady,
Rating myself at nothing, you shall see
How much I was a braggart. When I told you
My state was nothing, I should then have told you
That I was worse than nothing; for, indeed,
I have engag'd myself to a dear friend,
Engag'd my friend to his mere enemy,
To feed my means. Here is a letter, lady;
The paper as the body of my friend,
And every word in it a gaping wound,
Issuing life-blood. But is it true, Salanio?
Hath all his ventures fail'd? What, not one hit?
From Tripolis, from Mexico, and England,
From Lisbon, Barbary, and India?
And not one vessel 'scape the dreadful touch
Of merchant-marring rocks?

SALANIO
Not one, my lord.
Besides, it should appear, that if he had
The present money to discharge the Jew,
He would not take it. Never did I know
A creature, that did bear the shape of man,
So keen and greedy to confound a man.
He plies the duke at morning and at night,
And doth impeach the freedom of the state,
If they deny him justice: twenty merchants,
The duke himself, and the magnificoes
Of greatest port, have all persuaded with him;
But none can drive him from the envious plea
Of forfeiture, of justice, and his bond.

My house mice.

JESSICA
When I was with him, I have heard him swear
To Tubal and to Chus, his countrymen,
That he would rather have Antonio's flesh
Than twenty times the value of the sum
That he did owe him; and I know, my lord,
If law, authority, and power deny not,
It will go with poor Antonio.

My shouting trout, garnished in almonds.

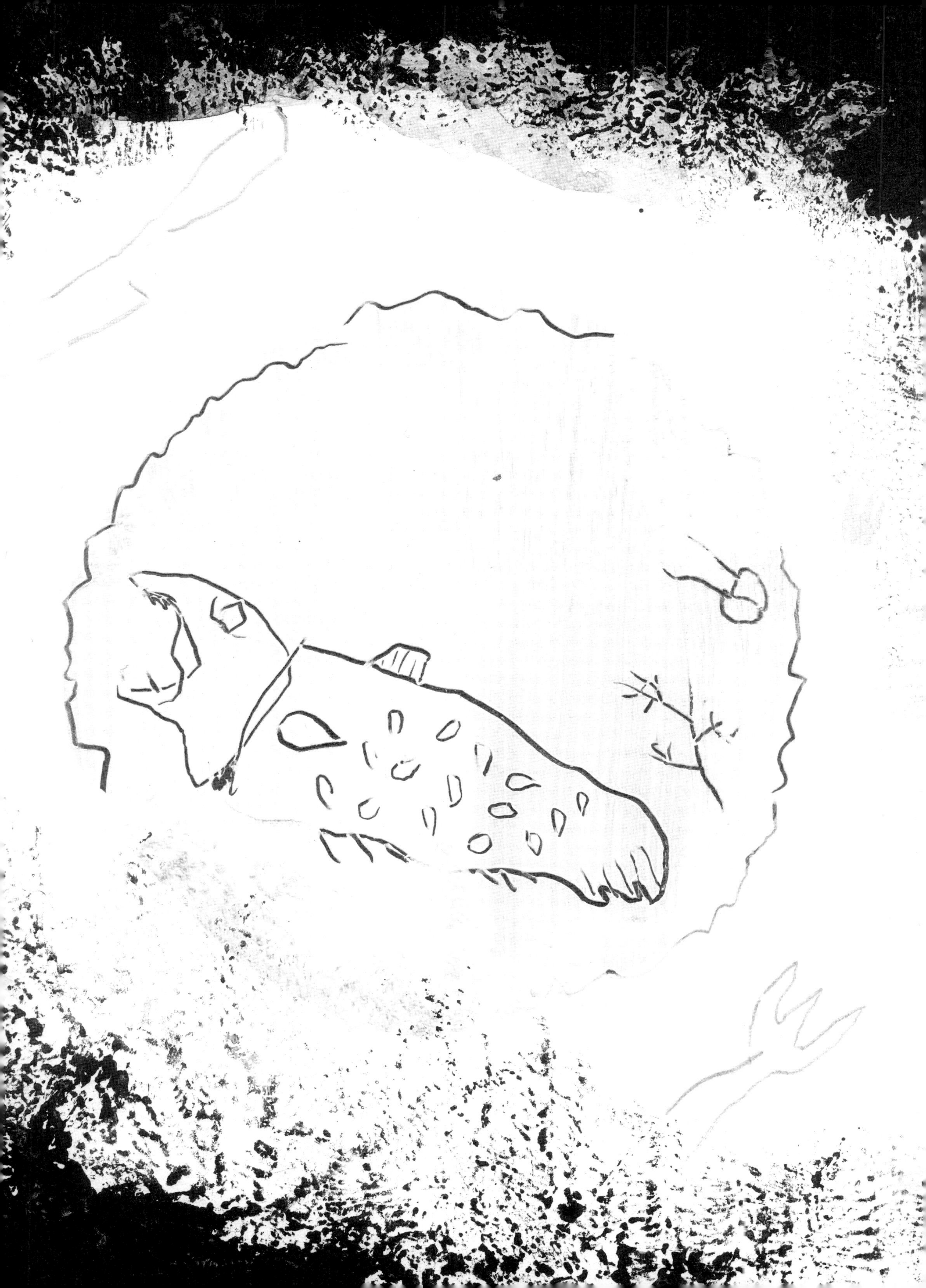

III.II.12

PORTIA
Is it your dear friend that is thus in trouble?

BASSANIO
The dearest friend to me, the kindest man,
The best-condition'd and unwearied spirit
In doing courtesies, and one in whom
The ancient Roman honour more appears
Than any that draws breath in Italy.

PORTIA
What sum owes he the Jew?

BASSANIO
For me, three thousand ducats.

PORTIA
What, no more?
Pay him six thousand, and deface the bond;
Double six thousand, and then treble that,
Before a friend of this description
Shall lose a hair thorough Bassanio's fault.
First go with me to church and call me wife,
And then away to Venice to your friend;
For never shall you lie by Portia's side
With an unquiet soul. You shall have gold
To pay the petty debt twenty times over:
When it is paid, bring your true friend along.
My maid Nerissa and myself meantime,
Will live as maids and widows. Come, away!
For you shall hence upon your wedding-day.
Bid your friends welcome, show a merry cheer;
Since you are dear bought, I will love you dear.
But let me hear the letter of your friend.

BASSANIO
'Sweet Bassanio, my ships have all miscarried, my creditors grow cruel, my estate is very low, my bond to the Jew is forfeit; and since, in paying it, it is impossible I should live, all debts are cleared between you and I, if I might but see you at my death. Notwithstanding, use your pleasure: if your love do not persuade you to come, let not my letter.'

My St. Peter amnesia cock.

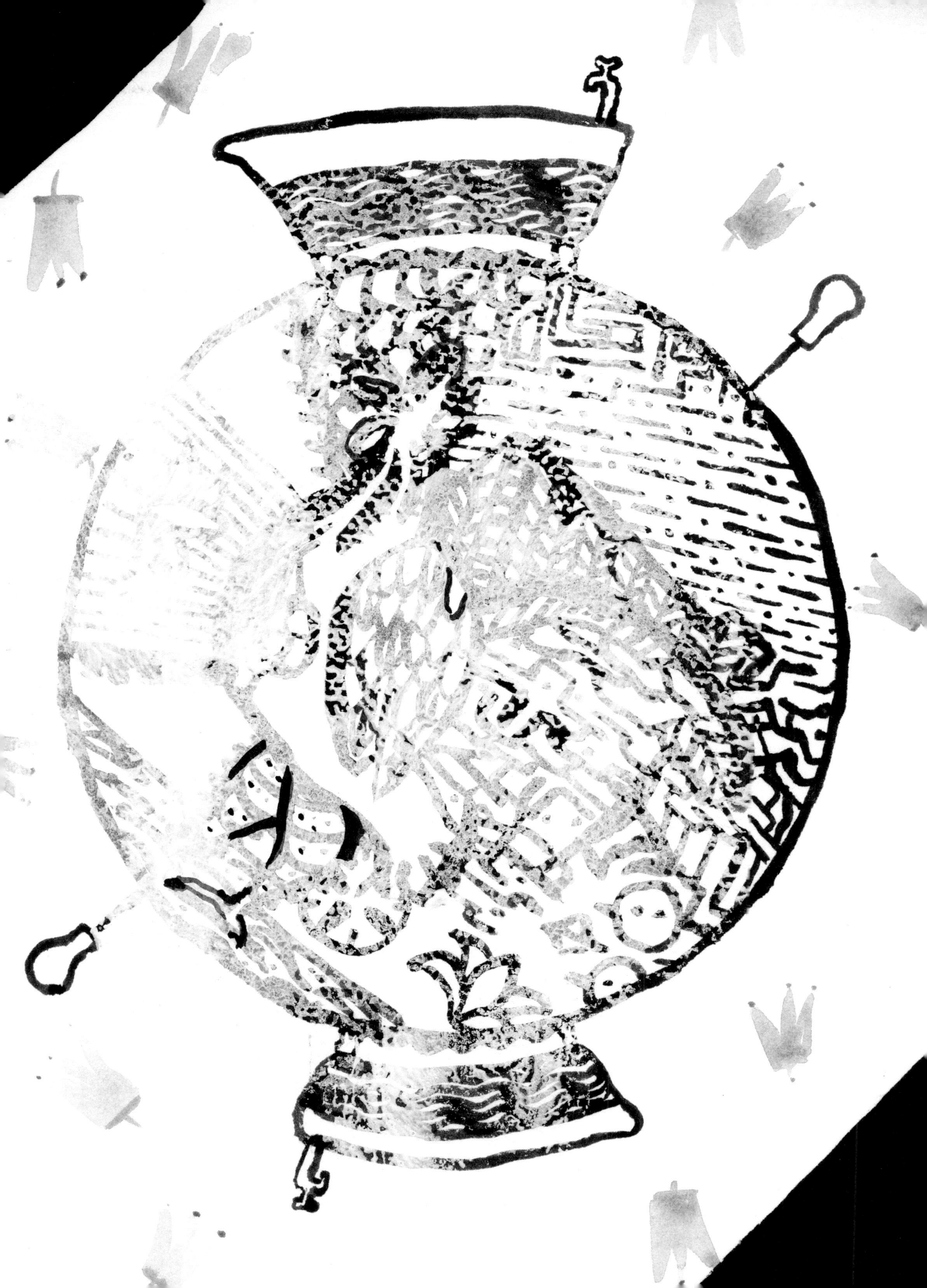

PORTIA
O love, dispatch all business, and be gone!

BASSANIO
Since I have your good leave to go away,
I will make haste; but, till I come again,
No bed shall e'er be guilty of my stay,
Nor rest be interposer 'twixt us twain.

Exeunt.

My dog. There.

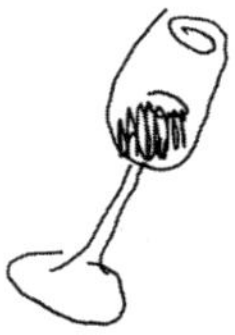

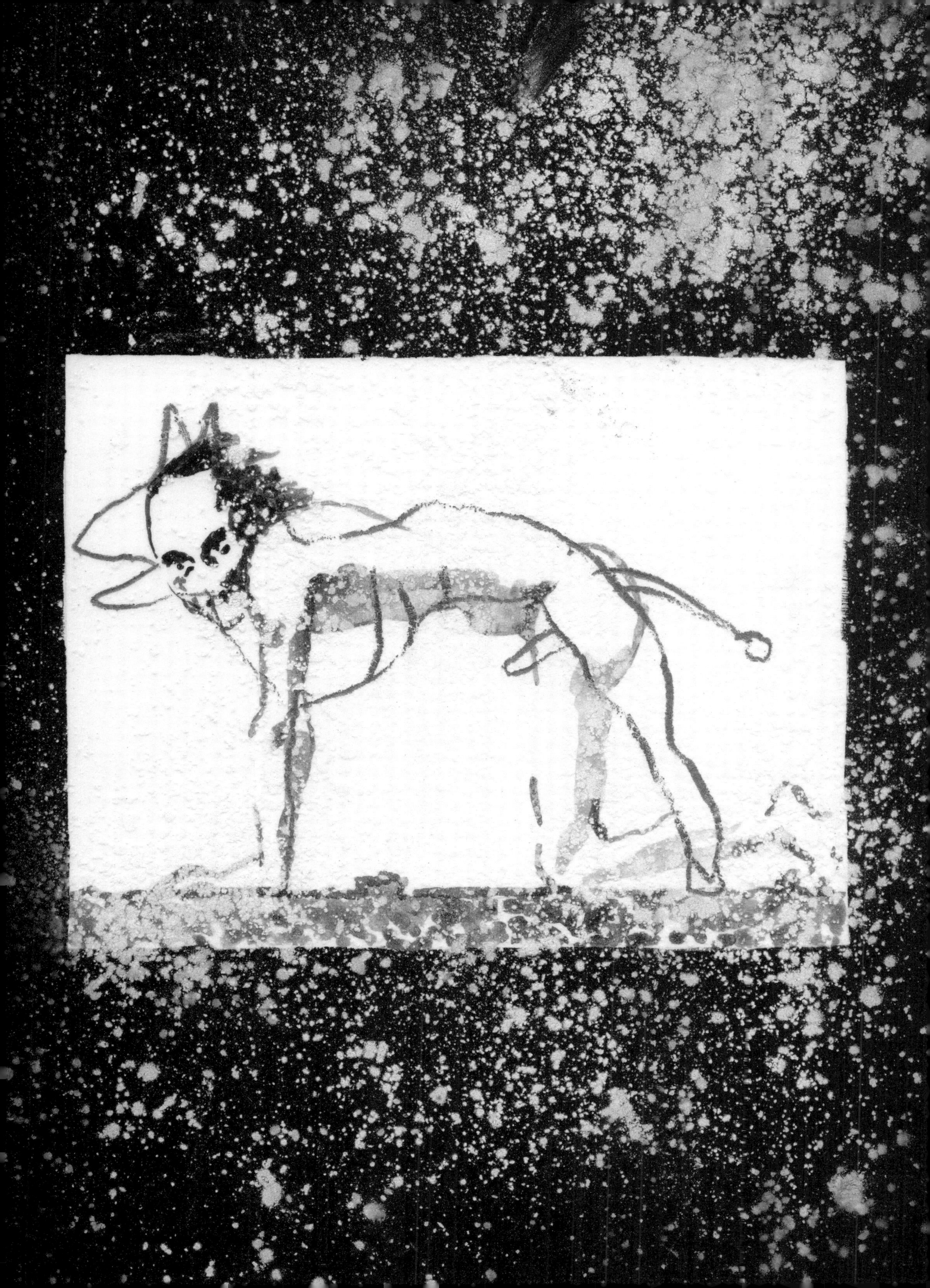

Scene III—Venice. A Street.

Enter Shylock, Salarino, Antonio, and Gaoler.

SHYLOCK
Gaoler, look to him: tell not me of mercy;
This is the fool that lent out money gratis:
Gaoler, look to him.

ANTONIO
Hear me yet, good Shylock.

So they face each other, the lost Antonio
and the won Shylock, the notarized death
bond in his pocket.
The loss of the ring released Shylock
from the burden of doubt.
The bricks are lined.
The loss of the ring released Shylock
from the burden of faith.
The little children are scared.
The loss of the ring released Shylock
from the burden of love, desire,
satisfaction.
Shylock is unleashed.
The vision stamped on his mind is total
and uniform and black, consistent now
with the uniform blackness his retina
registers.
No shades and hues and relations.
The loss of the ring balanced Shylock
and now he is balanced.
There is no house.
The house that was was not.
What will be will not.
Shylock is an act,

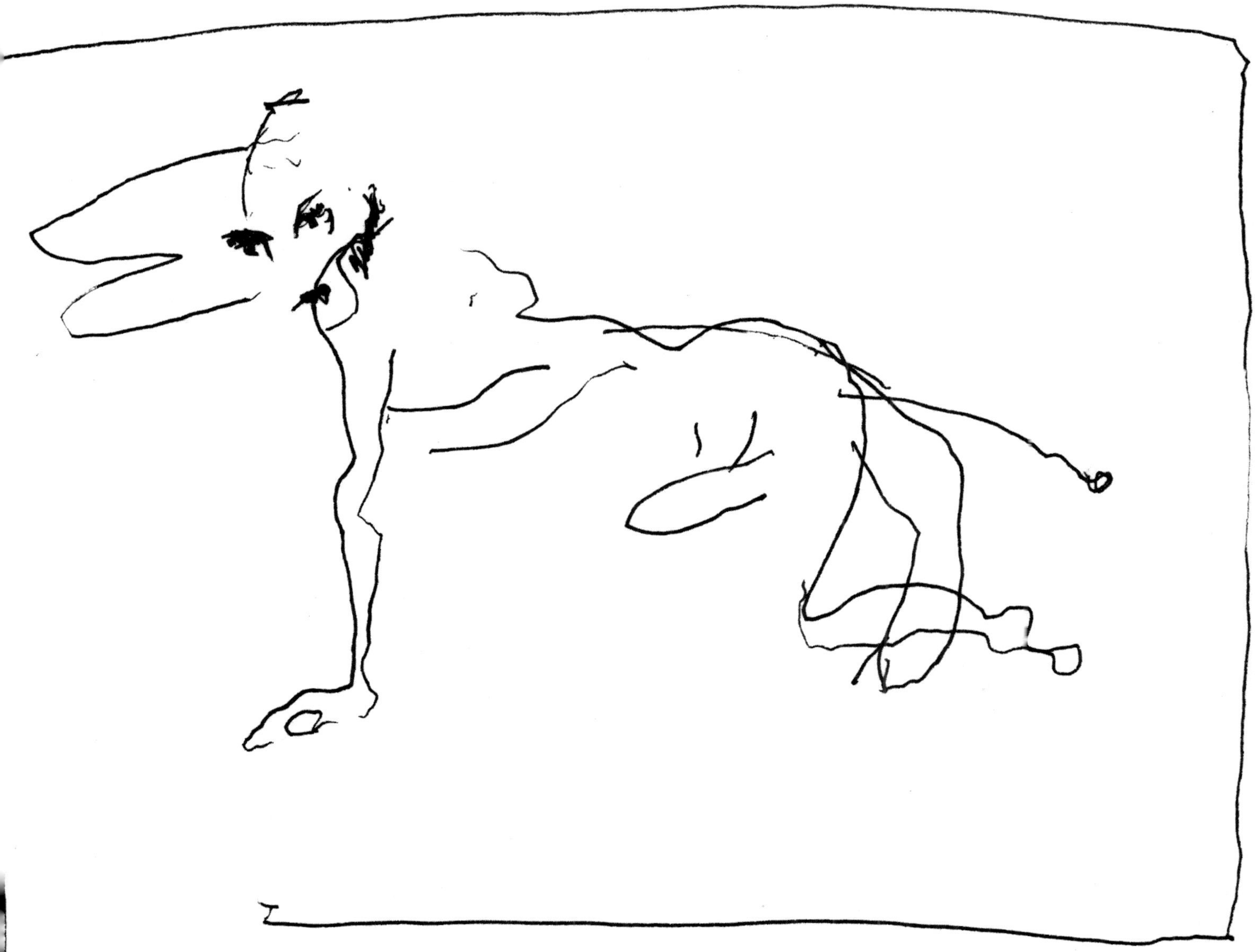

SHYLOCK
I'll have my bond; speak not against my bond
I have sworn an oath that I will have my bond.
Thou call'dst me dog before thou hadst a cause,
But, since I am a dog, beware my fangs:
The duke shall grant me justice. I do wonder,
Thou naughty gaoler, that thou art so fond
To come abroad with him at his request.

ANTONIO
I pray thee, hear me speak.

SHYLOCK
I'll have my bond; I will not hear thee speak:
I'll have my bond, and therefore speak no more.
I'll not be made a soft and dull-eyed fool,
To shake the head, relent, and sigh, and yield
To Christian intercessors. Follow not;
I'll have no speaking; I will have my bond.

Exit.

Shylock will act,
as the dead poet wrote:
"Life called; us do."
And all that is wanted now is a viewer—
the want of a viewer now, Sh- Shy-
Shylock needs a viewer, at least one
viewer to be entertained and chilled,
one, the jailer, say, the little jailer, say,
to activate the act that is Shylock, the
Jewish kamikaze in the service of loss.
The jailer, to watch with widened pupils,
to feel his testicles shrink, to exclaim:
Me bedazzled!
But this Shylock, this Shylock is
precisely Shylock!
The Jew is exactly the Jew!
A strong will was willed here!
Something was confirmed today!
I will have constipation for
three days!

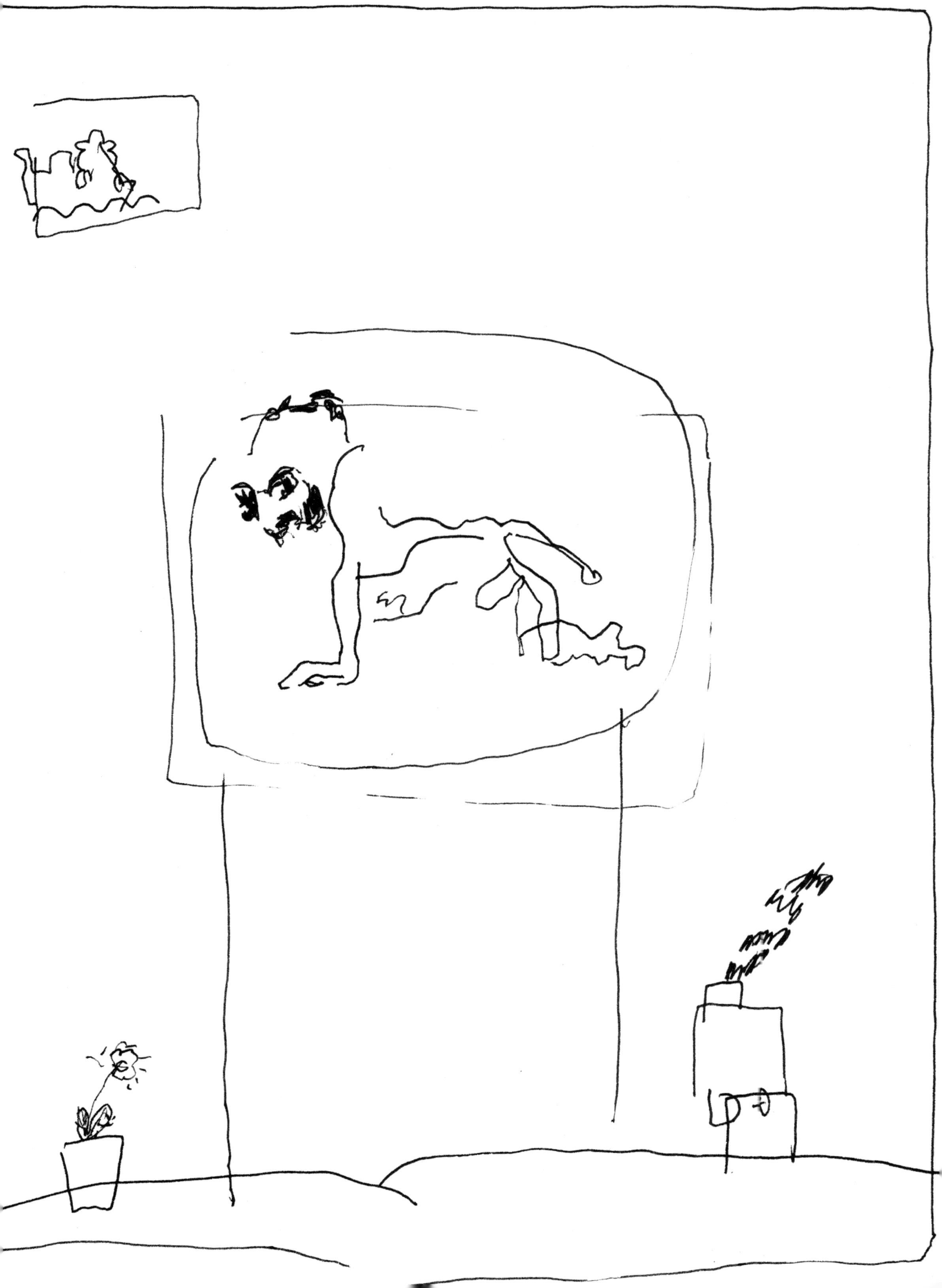

SALARINO
It is the most impenetrable cur
That ever kept with men.

ANTONIO
Let him alone:
I'll follow him no more with bootless prayers.
He seeks my life; his reason well I know.
I oft deliver'd from his forfeitures
Many that have at times made moan to me;
Therefore he hates me.

SALARINO
I am sure the duke
Will never grant this forfeiture to hold.

So they face each other, the won Shylock and the lost Antonio, in an iron cage, two small dishes in the corner, lukewarm water, a few grains, and slightly above his head, on the back wall, hangs his nothing, raised and waving like an achievement.
With an electric instrument the plumage was shaved off my body and now I am ready, vulnerable, appetizing, pink, smooth, fragile, skinny, vexing. I raise my eyes forward with pride, with contempt, with a cultural sense.
The potent nurse grabs Antonio's hands from behind and thrusts her knee into his back—thus my body is convexed, a clean arch with the breast served forward, to ease the penetration, the skin stretched and transparent, the heart beats clearly visible, a rhythmic, delicate movement within a labyrinth of ribs and veins, everything is perfectly visible and fragile, fledgling that I am.
The spectators are glued to their seats.
Bassanio has a splendid seat, fourth row center.
He glares,

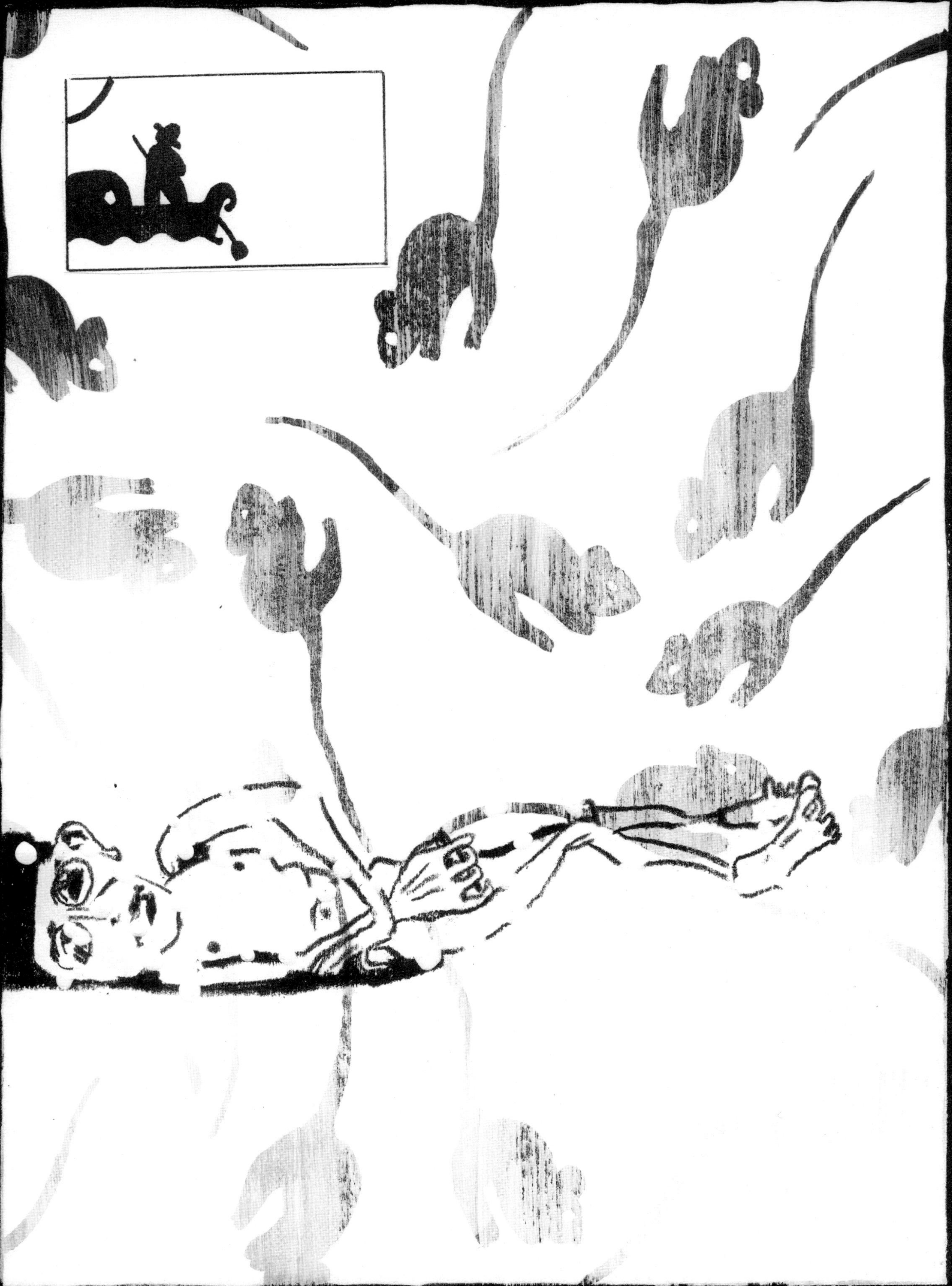

ANTONIO
The duke cannot deny the course of law:
For the commodity that strangers have
With us in Venice, if it be denied,
'Twill much impeach the justice of the state;
Since that the trade and profit of the city
Consisteth of all nations. Therefore, go:
These griefs and losses have so bated me,
That I shall hardly spare a pound of flesh
To-morrow to my bloody creditor.
Well, gaoler, on. Pray God, Bassanio come
To see me pay his debt, and then I care not!

Exeunt.

glares, as the poet wrote:

"Ghastly / with open eyes,
he attends, blind."

The signal is given.

A ticklish pen marks a blue circle with the left nipple for its center. Heads lean. The nurse's knee still stable at the back. Professional, sanitized fingers are pressed to the chest. Between them the scalpel which will be inserted. The scalpel is piercing the skin. The long knife penetrates slowly through the nipple, groping, digging. I look forward, ignoring the activity in my body, the pouring blood, the turning flesh, the busy metal. I see the Duke swooning. I smile sarcastically, lifting mostly my upper lip, like a small rodent. The knife locates the heart. I feel a stab in my heart. The stab turns demanding. The stab turns my life into my death. I sense my eyes swirling in their sockets. The pincers grab my heart and squeeze. The quiet Jew sharpens his fork. The viewers so fascinated they are chewing their peanuts without being aware at all of the taste. The heart is pulled out like a fetus, jerking, red, screaming. My heart is given to the Jew. The Jew brings it to his lips.

My Antonio body shrinks and pales. As he falls asleep, the vigilant rats leap from the corpse to poison the waters of Venice. The blood blackens on Shylock's face. Then the future, in a loop.

Bassanio and the large woman in bed. He penetrates her from the front, then the mouth, then the back, three times, three times, three times, like so. Hours, hours of hasty, hurried movement. He sweats. The silk sheets irritate his skin. Hours, hours, hours. A whole night with no memory. He looks. Get hints. See signs. The white sheet. The red spots on his skin. Her pink body. The black black. Afterwards, the cock crows. He remembers, and remembers, and bursts crying.

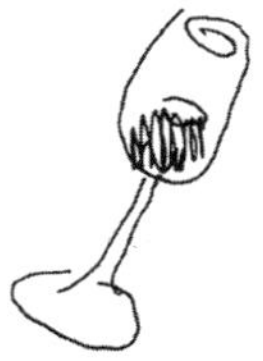

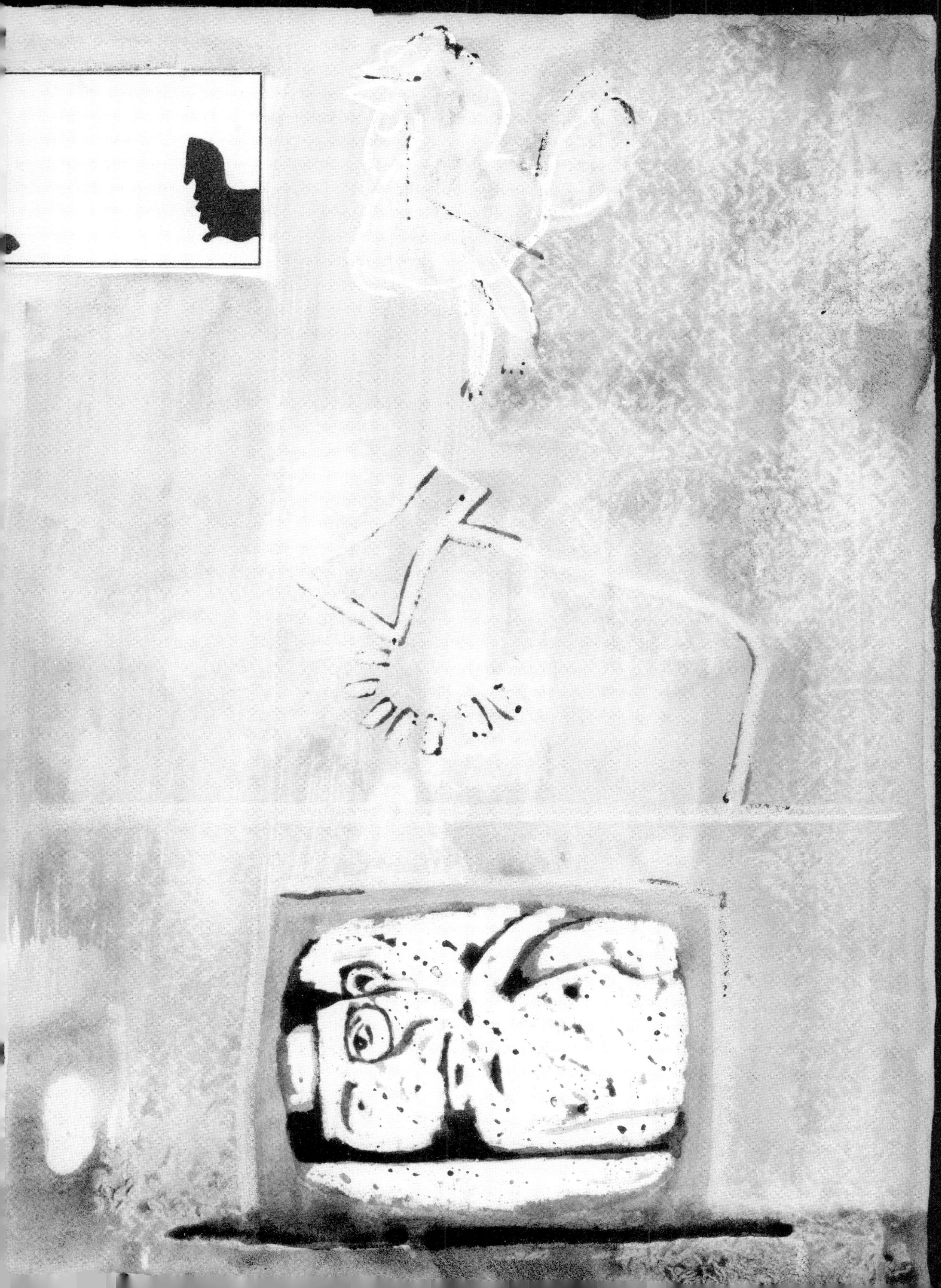

Scene IV—Belmont. A Room in Portia's House.

Enter Portia, Nerissa, Lorenzo, Jessica, and Balthazar.

LORENZO
Madam, although I speak it in your presence,
You have a noble and a true conceit
Of god-like amity; which appears most strongly
In bearing thus the absence of your lord.
But if you knew to whom you show this honour,
How true a gentleman you send relief,
How dear a lover of my lord your husband,
I know you would be prouder of the work
Than customary bounty can enforce you.

PORTIA
I never did repent for doing good,
Nor shall not now: for in companions
That do converse and waste the time together,
Whose souls do bear an equal yoke of love,
There must be needs a like proportion
Of lineaments, of manners, and of spirit;
Which makes me think that this Antonio,
Being the bosom lover of my lord,
Must needs be like my lord. If it be so,
How little is the cost I have bestow'd
In purchasing the semblance of my soul
From out the state of hellish cruelty!
This comes too near the praising of myself;
Therefore, no more of it: hear other things.
Lorenzo, I commit into your hands
The husbandry and manage of my house
Until my lord's return: for mine own part,
I have toward heaven breath'd a secret vow
To live in prayer and contemplation,
Only attended by Nerissa here,
Until her husband and my lord's return.
There is a monastery two miles off,
And there will we abide. I do desire you
Not to deny this imposition,
The which my love and some necessity
Now lays upon you.

LORENZO
Madam, with all my heart:
I shall obey you in all fair commands.

PORTIA
My people do already know my mind,
And will acknowledge you and Jessica
In place of Lord Bassanio and myself.
So fare you well till we shall meet again.

LORENZO
Fair thoughts and happy hours attend on you!

JESSICA
I wish your ladyship all heart's content.

PORTIA
I thank you for your wish, and am well pleas'd
To wish it back on you: fare you well, Jessica.

Exeunt Jessica and Lorenzo.

Portia's time had come. Longitudes and latitudes marked, screws tightened. Automaton perfection. Portia is about to leave for Venice, dressed like a doctor of law, to crush Shylock. On the selfsame occasion she will save Antonio, the pathetic cockroach, from the death he seems so eager for. She will save him and degrade him. He will be repressed out of the picture. No more of his dubious sadness. The better sadness wins the carrot. She will also set a sweating routine for Bassanio, explicating the burden of the ring. A perfect move. But the effort it entails. And Portia suffers from severe fatigue. Her eyes barely open, her knees melt. She, who erased dozens of suitors without leaving the throne, is about to glide upon a long diagonal to Venice, and employ many words, so that she may, at last, perhaps, lock herself in a small chamber and cry.

* * *

Facing Portia politely is Lorenzo, the *charmant*. Portia, who will be a judge in Venice, tells him she will be a nun in Belmont. The lie illuminates a graceful, classical contrast: male and female, marvels of the mind and afflictions of the body. Portia assumes Lorenzo would believe, as he saw her with Nerissa. Lorenzo is hawk-eyed and experienced. He observes the lie, but remains polite. Lorenzo is extremely tired, and Portia repels him, and he is so very tired, and besides, he has his own final move, smaller and concealed, one that has strictly to do with his own genitalia. The empty palace is perfect: with its acoustic insulation, the Japanese chef, the accessories collection, under his own absolute reign, the palace is preferable to any other arena. In his mind's eye Lorenzo envisions his final tableau vivant: a small, locked room. Flanked, reclined, the monkey dances jerkily to his right, to his left trembles Jessica, thumb in mouth. The little room and the bizarre scenery are his to ignore. Smeared on a wide mattress. Hooves spread. Face up. Numb. Sealed—

* * * *

so they face each other.

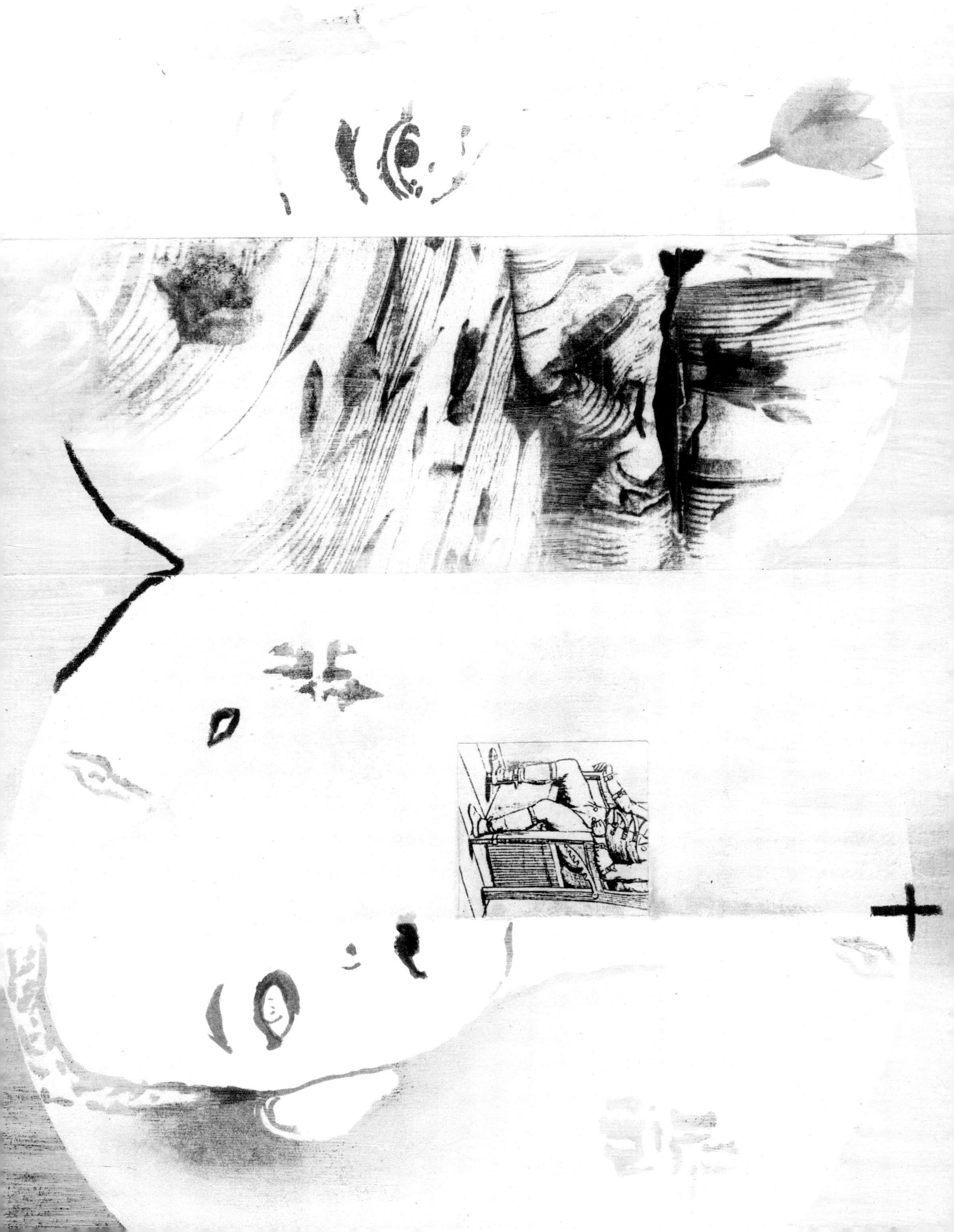

III.IV.2

Now, Balthazar,
As I have ever found thee honest-true,
So let me find thee still. Take this same letter,
And use thou all the endeavour of a man
In speed to Padua: see thou render this
Into my cousin's hand, Doctor Bellario;
And, look, what notes and garments he doth give thee,
Bring them, I pray thee, with imagin'd speed
Unto the traject, to the common ferry
Which trades to Venice. Waste no time in words,
But get thee gone: I shall be there before thee.

BALTHAZAR
Madam, I go with all convenient speed.

Exit.

PORTIA
Come on, Nerissa: I have work in hand
That you yet know not of: we'll see our husbands
Before they think of us.

NERISSA
Shall they see us?

PORTIA
They shall, Nerissa; but in such a habit
That they shall think we are accomplished
With that we lack. I'll hold thee any wager,
When we are both accoutred like young men,
I'll prove the prettier fellow of the two,
And wear my dagger with the braver grace,
And speak between the change of man and boy
With a reed voice, and turn two mincing steps
Into a manly stride, and speak of frays
Like a fine bragging youth, and tell quaint lies,
How honourable ladies sought my love,
Which I denying, they fell sick and died:
I could not do withal; then I'll repent,
And wish, for all that, that I had not kill'd them:
And twenty of these puny lies I'll tell,
That men shall swear I have discontinu'd school
Above a twelvemonth. I have within my mind
A thousand raw tricks of these bragging Jacks,
Which I will practise.

NERISSA
Why, shall we turn to men?

PORTIA
Fie, what a question's that,
If thou wert near a lewd interpreter!
But come: I'll tell thee all my whole device
When I am in my coach, which stays for us
At the park gate; and therefore haste away,
For we must measure twenty miles to-day.

Exeunt.

And dark, pretty Nerissa. We glimpse Nerissa with ease. (Nerissa's mother was a woman of outstanding intelligence who served as Portia's algebra tutor and as her masseuse (work requiring outstanding endurance, as she suffered from severe rheumatoid arthritis (her (reputedly) Jewish lover vanished once she became pregnant (but her spirit was not broken, it was broken only much later (which made her death appear victorious and cynical (and a terrible death it seemed (for which Nerissa always believed Jessica to be directly responsible))))), but) We are not obliged to hear about Nerissa's mother. We are gigantic, peeping tourists.

Nerissa has a rare moment of exultation. All days she runs around naked. Her nakedness is a uniform. It designates her as a fruit, always within Portia's reach. It marks her as exposed to whim, abuse and merriment. It signifies her as not-belonging-to-herself. It posits her passionate hatred toward Portia as a circus attraction, like a hunchback, a fakir, a mutation.

Now she wears over her nakedness a man-costume and a wedding gown. Practically a garderobe. Nerissa knows there is no real change here. She realizes that the costume is only a costume, and that the groom is an idiot, an unclean animal. But the dress, the makeup, the hair ribbons. Splendor. The combination of her charming youth and the fancy package overwhelms her. She knows this happiness is too big and too small, yet still, the moment seems holy.

She carries the clothes on her body with great care, hence the somewhat stiff posture, the too-measured, ridiculous pace, the expression of panic. The happiness makes her sweat. The sweat pours from her armpits to her hips, her legs are wet and her back itches. She blinks. We find it exquisitely funny, so funny, how the happiness culminates in a wicked migraine, and a dominant, heavy, oppressive fatigue. And thus she faces orders.

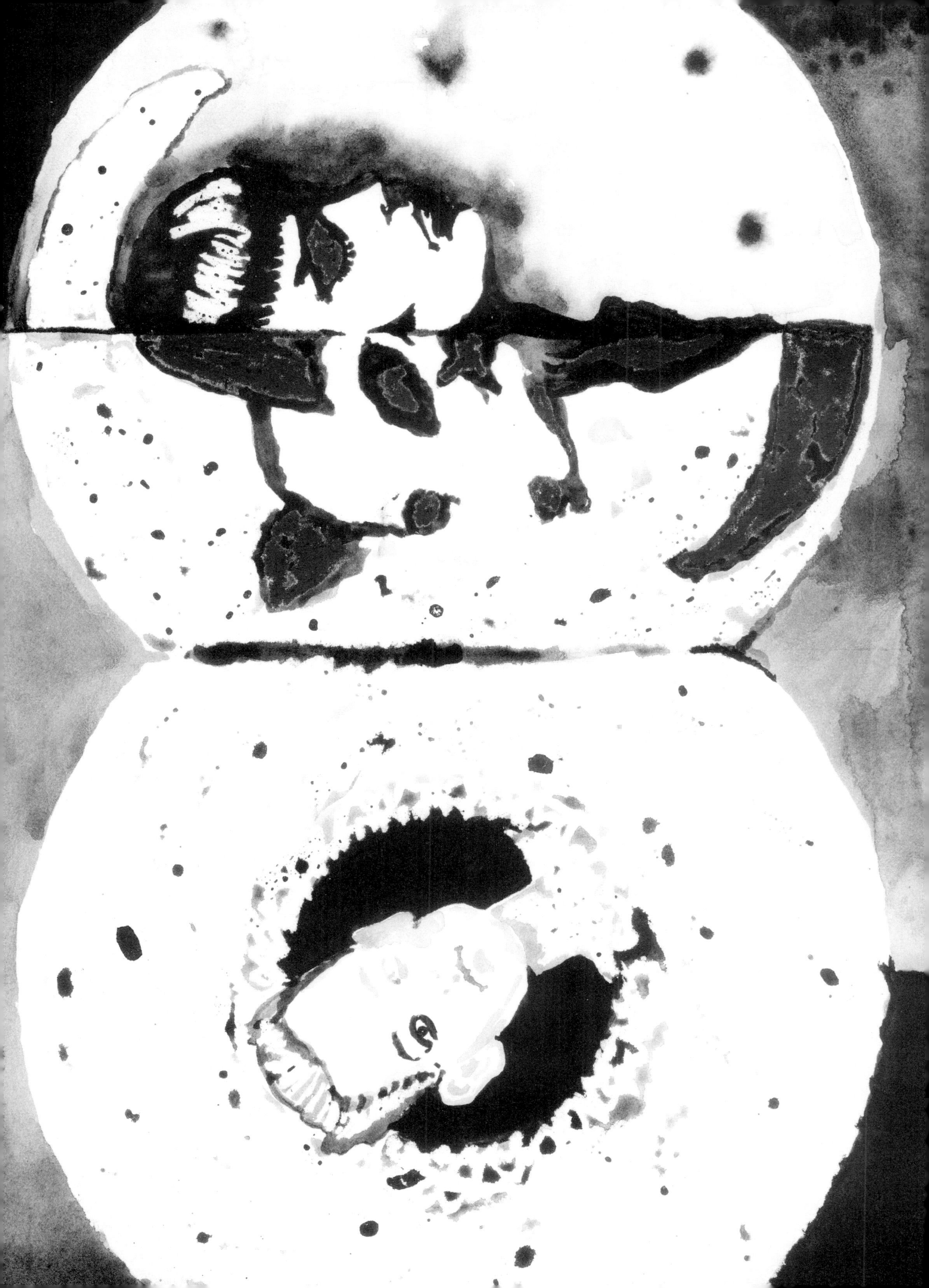

Scene V—The Same. A Garden.

Enter Launcelot and Jessica.

LAUNCELOT

Yes, truly; for, look you, the sins of the father are to be laid upon the children; therefore, I promise you, I fear you. I was always plain with you, and so now I speak my agitation of the matter: therefore be of good cheer; for, truly, I think you are damned. There is but one hope in it that can do you any good, and that is but a kind of bastard hope neither.

JESSICA

And what hope is that, I pray thee?

LAUNCELOT

Marry, you may partly hope that your father got you not, that you are not the Jew's daughter.

JESSICA

That were a kind of bastard hope, indeed: so the sins of my mother should be visited upon me.

LAUNCELOT

Truly then I fear you are damned both by father and mother: thus when I shun Scylla, your father, I fall into Charybdis, your mother: well, you are gone both ways.

JESSICA

I shall be saved by my husband; he hath made me a Christian.

LAUNCELOT

Truly the more to blame he: we were Christians enow before; e'en as many as could well live one by another. This making of Christians will raise the price of hogs: if we grow all to be pork-eaters, we shall not shortly have a rasher on the coals for money.

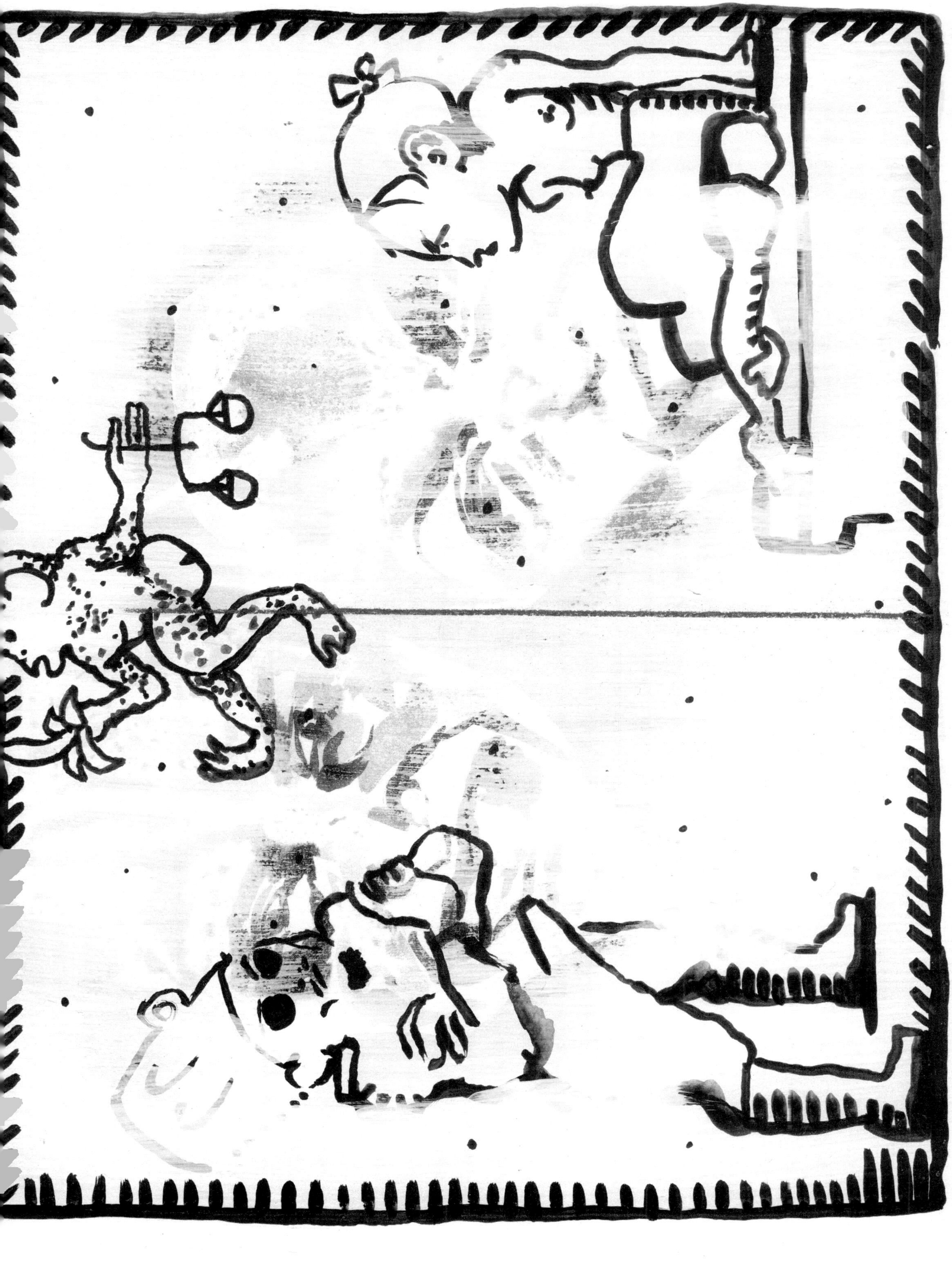

JESSICA
I'll tell my husband, Launcelot, what you say: here he comes.

Enter Lorenzo.

LORENZO
I shall grow jealous of you shortly, Launcelot, if you thus get my wife into corners.

JESSICA
Nay, you need not fear us, Lorenzo: Launcelot and I are out. He tells me flatly, there is no mercy for me in heaven, because I am a Jew's daughter: and he says you are no good member of the commonwealth, for, in converting Jews to Christians, you raise the price of pork.

LORENZO
I shall answer that better to the commonwealth than you can the getting up of the negro's belly: the Moor is with child by you, Launcelot.

LAUNCELOT
It is much that the Moor should be more than reason; but if she be less than an honest woman, she is indeed more than I took her for.

LORENZO
How every fool can play upon the word! I think the best grace of wit will shortly turn into silence, and discourse grow commendable in none only but parrots. Go in, sirrah: bid them prepare for dinner.

LAUNCELOT
That is done, sir; they have all stomachs.

LORENZO
Goodly Lord, what a wit-snapper are you! then bid them prepare dinner.

LAUNCELOT
That is done too, sir; only, 'cover' is the word.

LORENZO
Will you cover, then, sir?

LAUNCELOT
Not so, sir, neither; I know my duty.

LORENZO
Yet more quarrelling with occasion! Wilt thou show the whole wealth of thy wit in an instant? I pray thee, understand a plain man in his plain meaning: go to thy fellows; bid them cover the table, serve in the meat, and we will come in to dinner.

LAUNCELOT
For the table, sir, it shall be served in; for the meat, sir, it shall be covered; for your coming in to dinner, sir, why, let it be as humours and conceits shall govern.

Exit.

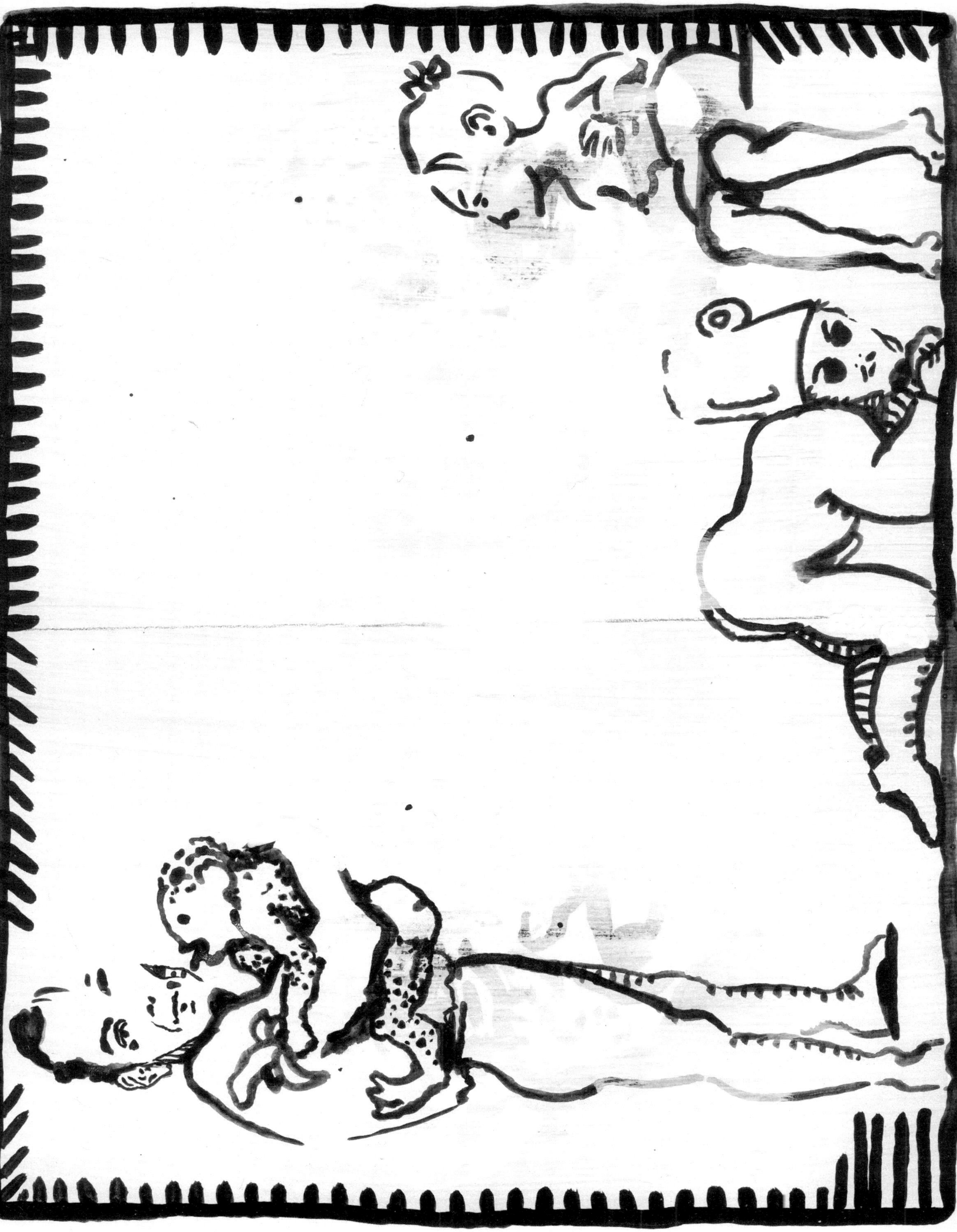

LORENZO

O dear discretion, how his words are suited!
The fool hath planted in his memory
An army of good words: and I do know
A many fools, that stand in better place,
Garnish'd like him, that for a tricksy word
Defy the matter. How cheer'st thou, Jessica?
And now, good sweet, say thy opinion;
How dost thou like the Lord Bassanio's wife?

JESSICA

Past all expressing. It is very meet,
The Lord Bassanio live an upright life,
For, having such a blessing in his lady,
He finds the joys of heaven here on earth;
And if on earth he do not mean it, then
In reason he should never come to heaven.
Why, if two gods should play some heavenly match,
And on the wager lay two earthly women,
And Portia one, there must be something else
Pawn'd with the other, for the poor rude world
Hath not her fellow.

LORENZO

Even such a husband
Hast thou of me as she is for a wife.

JESSICA

Nay, but ask my opinion too of that.

LORENZO

I will anon; first, let us go to dinner.

JESSICA

Nay, let me praise you while I have a stomach.

LORENZO

No, pray thee, let it serve for table-talk;
Then howsoe'er thou speak'st, 'mong other things
I shall digest it.

JESSICA

Well, I'll set you forth.

Exeunt.

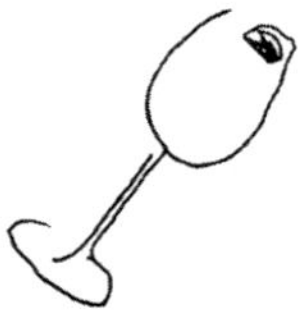

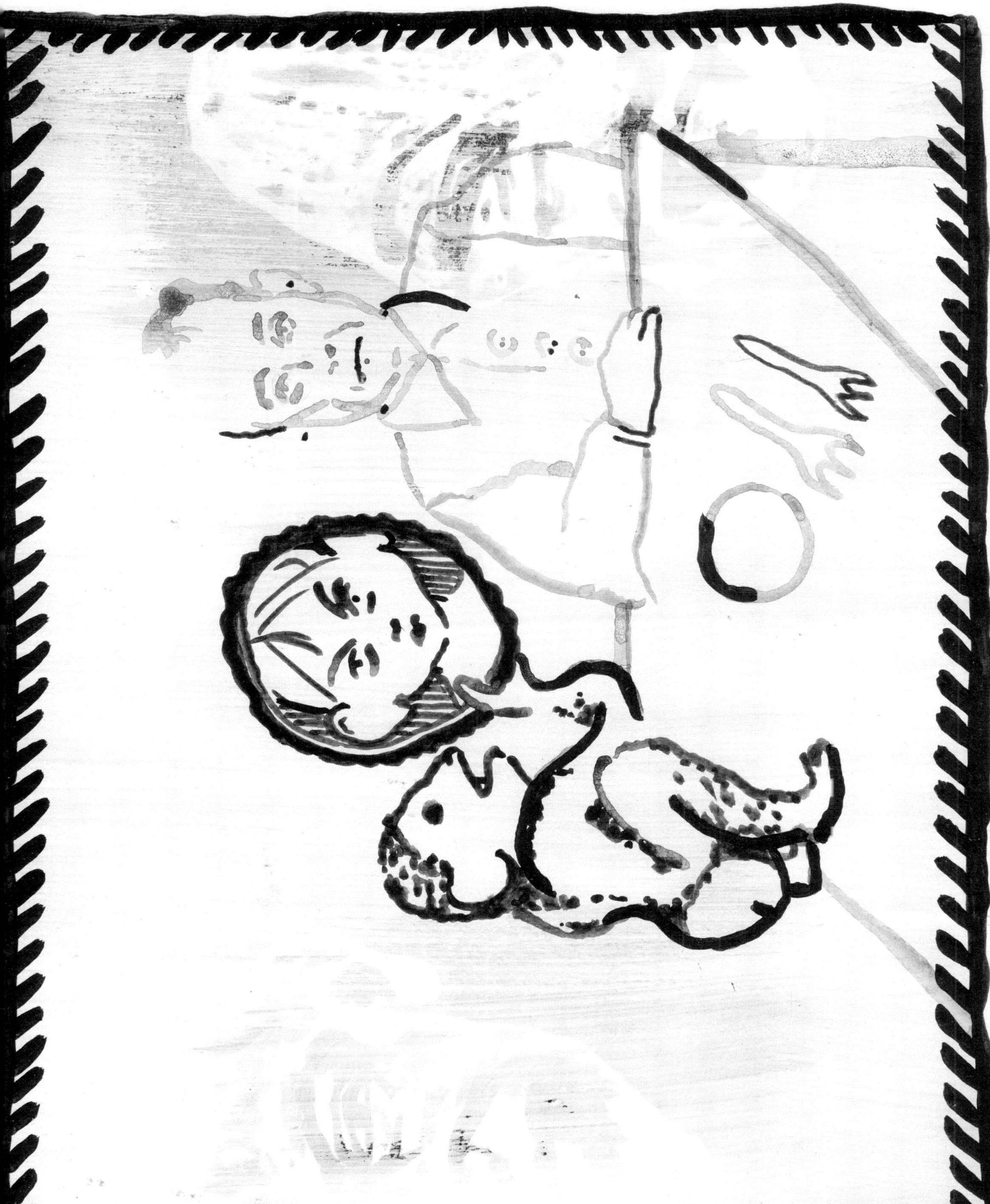

FOURTH ACT

A TRICK

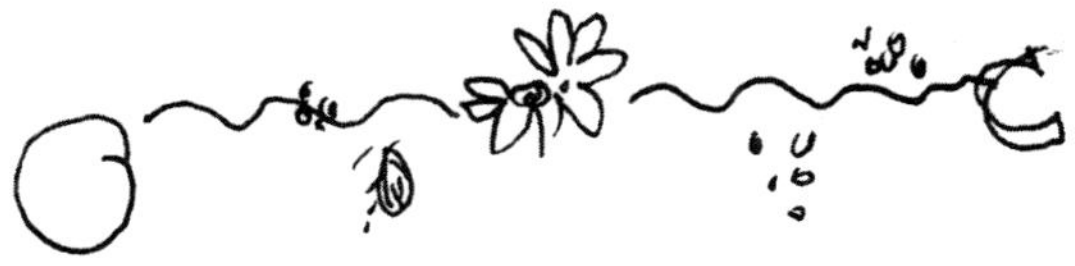

Scene I—Venice. A Court of Justice.

Enter the Duke: the Magnificoes; Antonio, Bassanio, Gratiano, Salarino, Salanio, and Others.

DUKE
What, is Antonio here?

ANTONIO
Ready, so please your Grace.

DUKE
I am sorry for thee: thou art come to answer
A stony adversary, an inhuman wretch
Uncapable of pity, void and empty
From any dram of mercy.

ANTONIO
I have heard
Your Grace hath ta'en great pains to qualify
His rigorous course; but since he stands obdurate,
And that no lawful means can carry me
Out of his envy's reach, I do oppose
My patience to his fury, and am arm'd
To suffer with a quietness of spirit
The very tyranny and rage of his.

DUKE
Go one, and call the Jew into the court.

SALARINO
He's ready at the door: he comes, my lord.

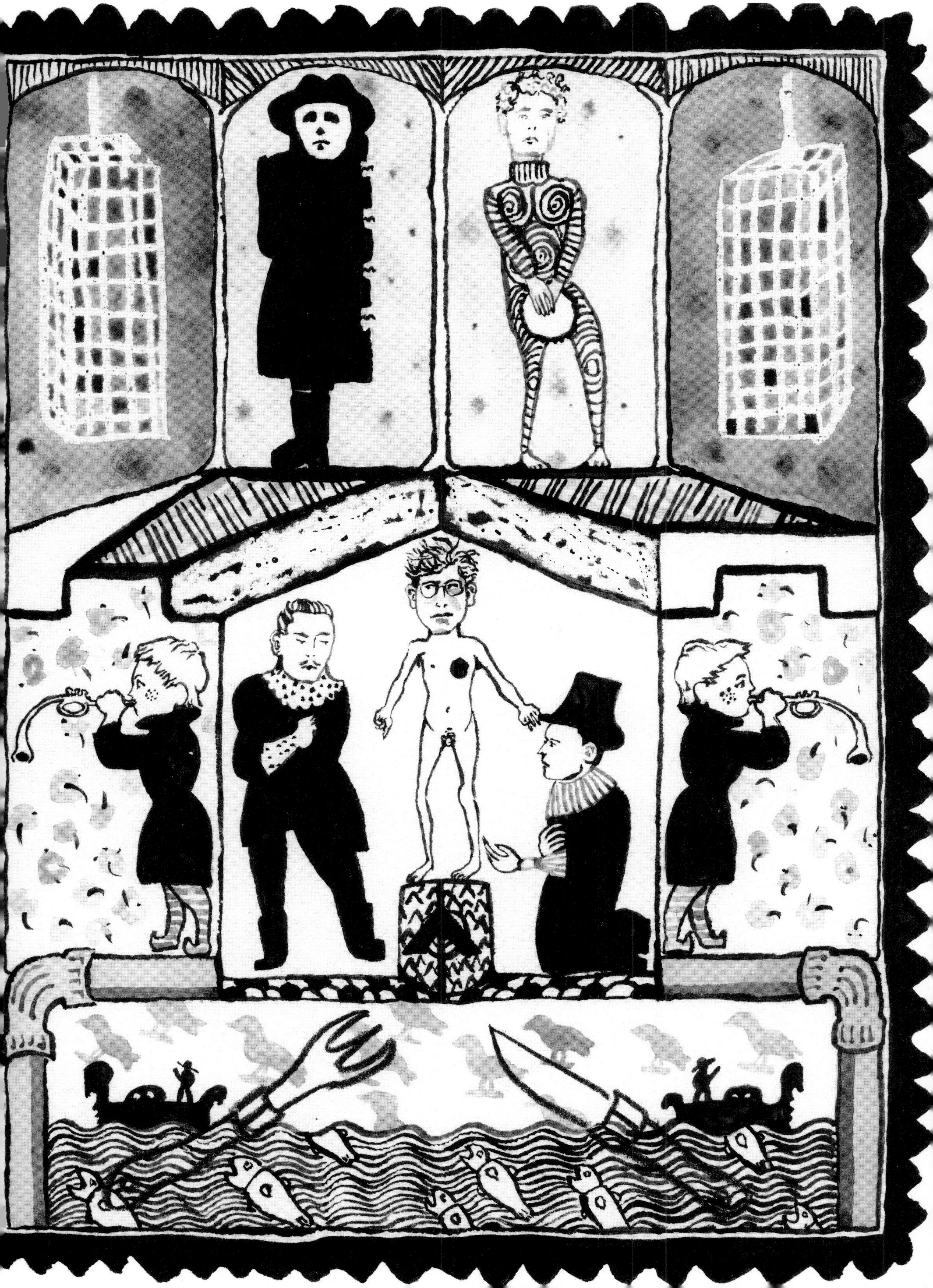

Enter Shylock.

DUKE
Make room, and let him stand before our face.
Shylock, the world thinks, and I think so too,
That thou but lead'st this fashion of thy malice
To the last hour of act; and then 'tis thought
Thou'lt show thy mercy and remorse more strange
Than is thy strange-apparent cruelty;
And where thou now exact'st the penalty,—
Which is a pound of this poor merchant's flesh,—
Thou wilt not only loose the forfeiture,
But, touch'd with human gentleness and love,
Forgive a moiety of the principal;
Glancing an eye of pity on his losses,
That have of late so huddled on his back,
Enow to press a royal merchant down,
And pluck commiseration of his state
From brassy bosoms and rough hearts of flint,
From stubborn Turks and Tartars, never train'd
To offices of tender courtesy.
We all expect a gentle answer, Jew.

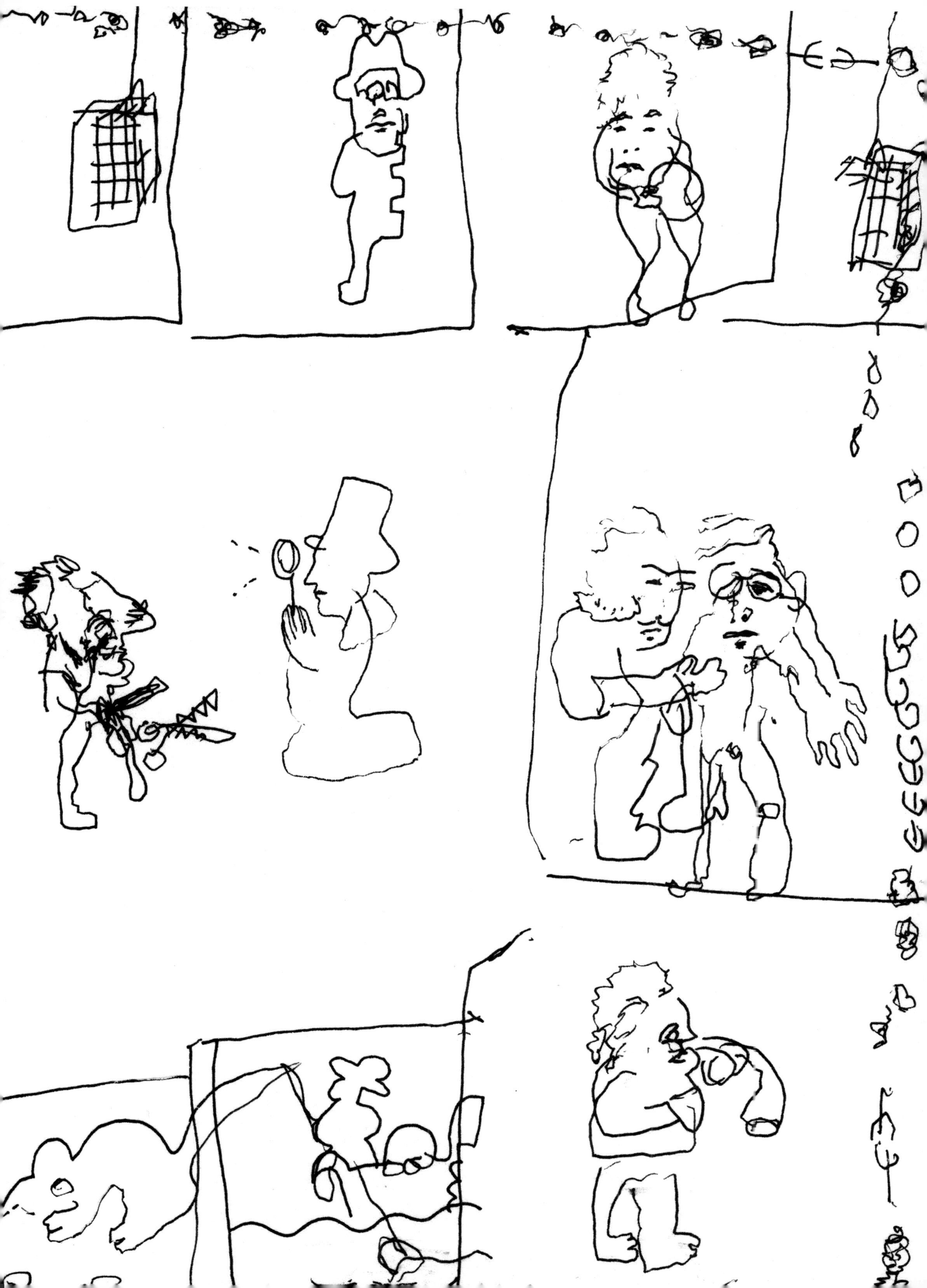

IV.I.3

SHYLOCK

I have possess'd your Grace of what I purpose;
And by our holy Sabbath have I sworn
To have the due and forfeit of my bond:
If you deny it, let the danger light
Upon your charter and your city's freedom.
You'll ask me, why I rather choose to have
A weight of carrion flesh than to receive
Three thousand ducats: I'll not answer that:
But say it is my humour: is it answer'd?
What if my house be troubled with a rat,
And I be pleas'd to give ten thousand ducats
To have it ban'd? What, are you answer'd yet?
Some men there are love not a gaping pig;
Some, that are mad if they behold a cat;
And others, when the bagpipe sings i' the nose,
Cannot contain their urine: for affection,
Mistress of passion, sways it to the mood
Of what it likes, or loathes. Now, for your answer:
As there is no firm reason to be render'd,
Why he cannot abide a gaping pig;
Why he, a harmless necessary cat;
Why he, a wauling bagpipe; but of force
Must yield to such inevitable shame
As to offend, himself being offended;
So can I give no reason, nor I will not,
More than a lodg'd hate and a certain loathing
I bear Antonio, that I follow thus
A losing suit against him. Are you answer'd?

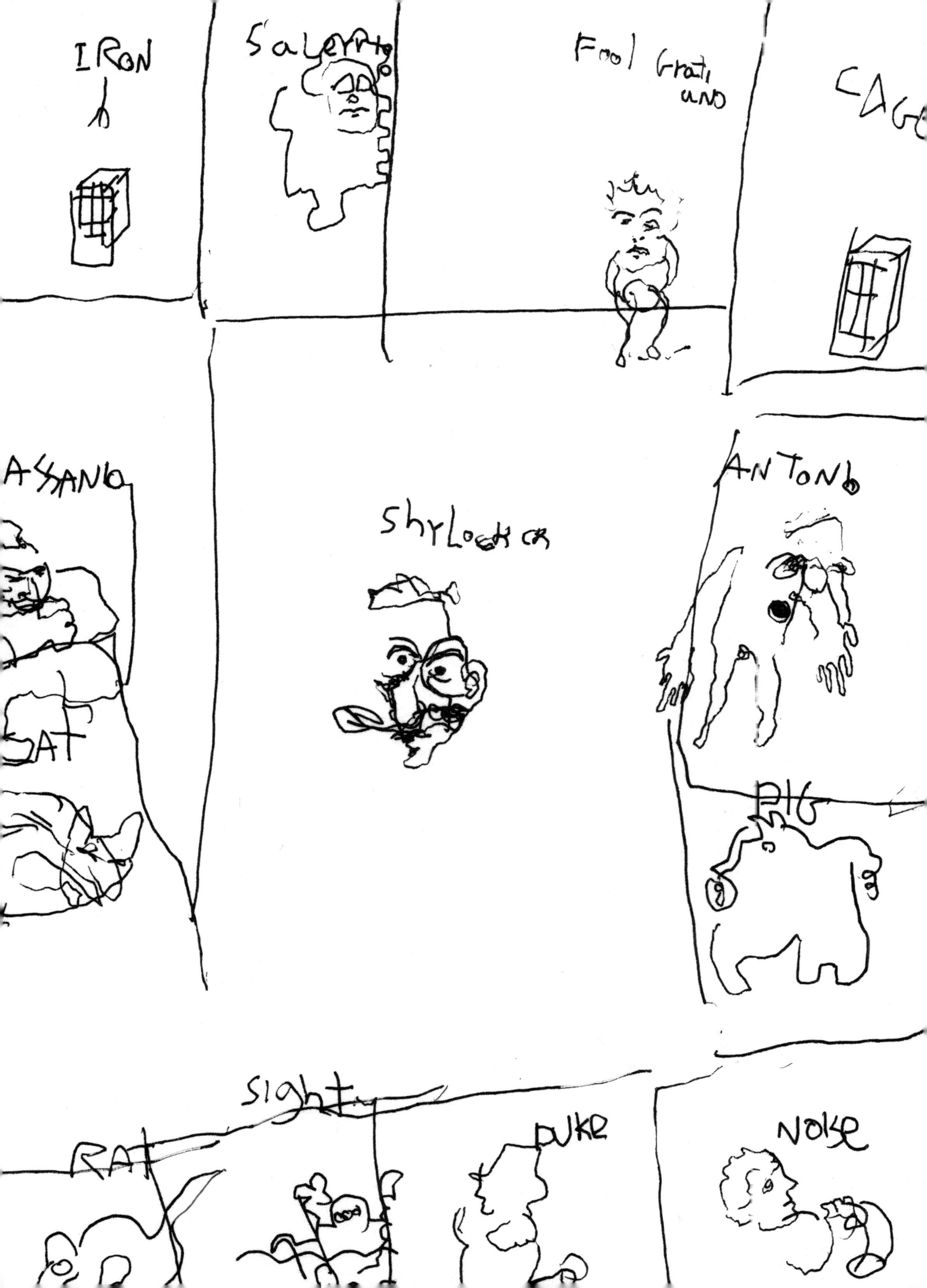
IRON
Salerrio
Fool Grati ano
CAGE
ASSANIO
Shylocker
ANTONIO
CAT
PIG
Sight
RAT
DUKE
NOISE

BASSANIO
This is no answer, thou unfeeling man,
To excuse the current of thy cruelty.

SHYLOCK
I am not bound to please thee with my answer.

BASSANIO
Do all men kill the things they do not love?

SHYLOCK
Hates any man the thing he would not kill?

BASSANIO
Every offence is not a hate at first.

SHYLOCK
What! wouldst thou have a serpent sting thee twice?

ANTONIO
I pray you, think you question with the Jew:
You may as well go stand upon the beach,
And bid the main flood bate his usual height;
You may as well use question with the wolf,
Why he hath made the ewe bleat for the lamb;
You may as well forbid the mountain pines
To wag their high tops, and to make no noise
When they are fretted with the gusts of heaven;
You may as well do anything most hard,
As seek to soften that—than which what's harder?—
His Jewish heart: therefore, I do beseech you,
Make no more offers, use no further means;
But with all brief and plain conveniency,
Let me have judgment, and the Jew his will.

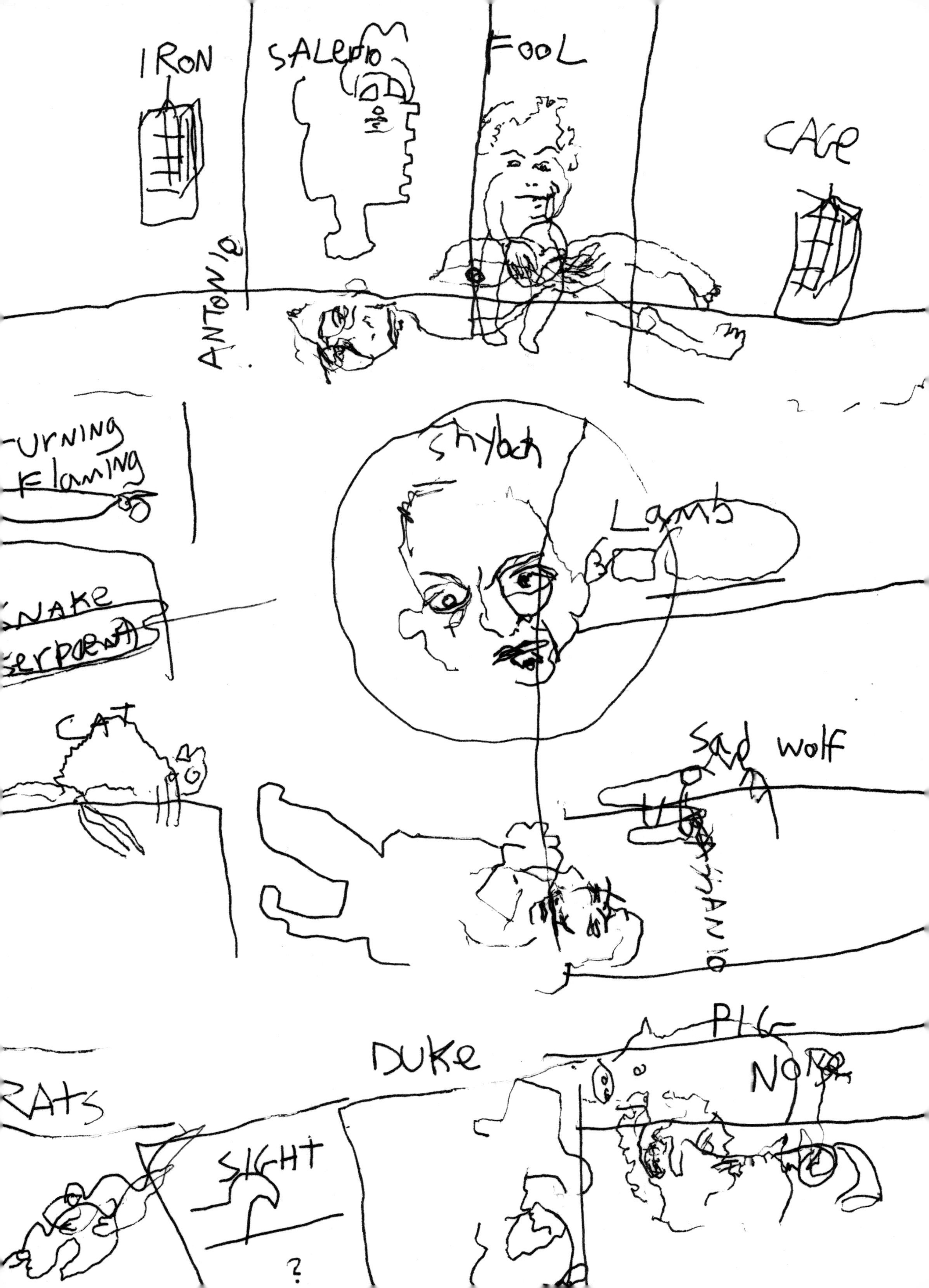
IRON
SALERIO
FOOL
CAGE
ANTONIO
URNING
Flaming
shylock
Lamb
NAKE
erpents
CAT
Sad wolf
DUKE
PIG
RATS
SIGHT
?

BASSANIO
For thy three thousand ducats here is six.

SHYLOCK
If every ducat in six thousand ducats
Were in six parts and every part a ducat,
I would not draw them; I would have my bond.

DUKE
How shalt thou hope for mercy, rendering none?

SHYLOCK
What judgment shall I dread, doing no wrong?
You have among you many a purchas'd slave,
Which, like your asses and your dogs and mules,
You use in abject and in slavish parts,
Because you bought them: shall I say to you,
Let them be free, marry them to your heirs?
Why sweat they under burdens? let their beds
Be made as soft as yours, and let their palates
Be season'd with such viands? You will answer:
'The slaves are ours:' so do I answer you:
The pound of flesh which I demand of him,
Is dearly bought; 'tis mine and I will have it.
If you deny me, fie upon your law!
There is no force in the decrees of Venice.
I stand for judgment: answer; shall I have it?

DUKE
Upon my power I may dismiss this court,
Unless Bellario, a learned doctor,
Whom I have sent for to determine this,
Come here to-day.

SALARINO
My lord, here stays without
A messenger with letters from the doctor,
New come from Padua.

DUKE
Bring us the letters: call the messenger.

BASSANIO
Good cheer, Antonio! What, man, courage yet!
The Jew shall have my flesh, blood, bones, and all,
Ere thou shalt lose for me one drop of blood.

ANTONIO
I am a tainted wether of the flock,
Meetest for death: the weakest kind of fruit
Drops earliest to the ground; and so let me:
You cannot better be employ'd, Bassanio,
Than to live still, and write mine epitaph.

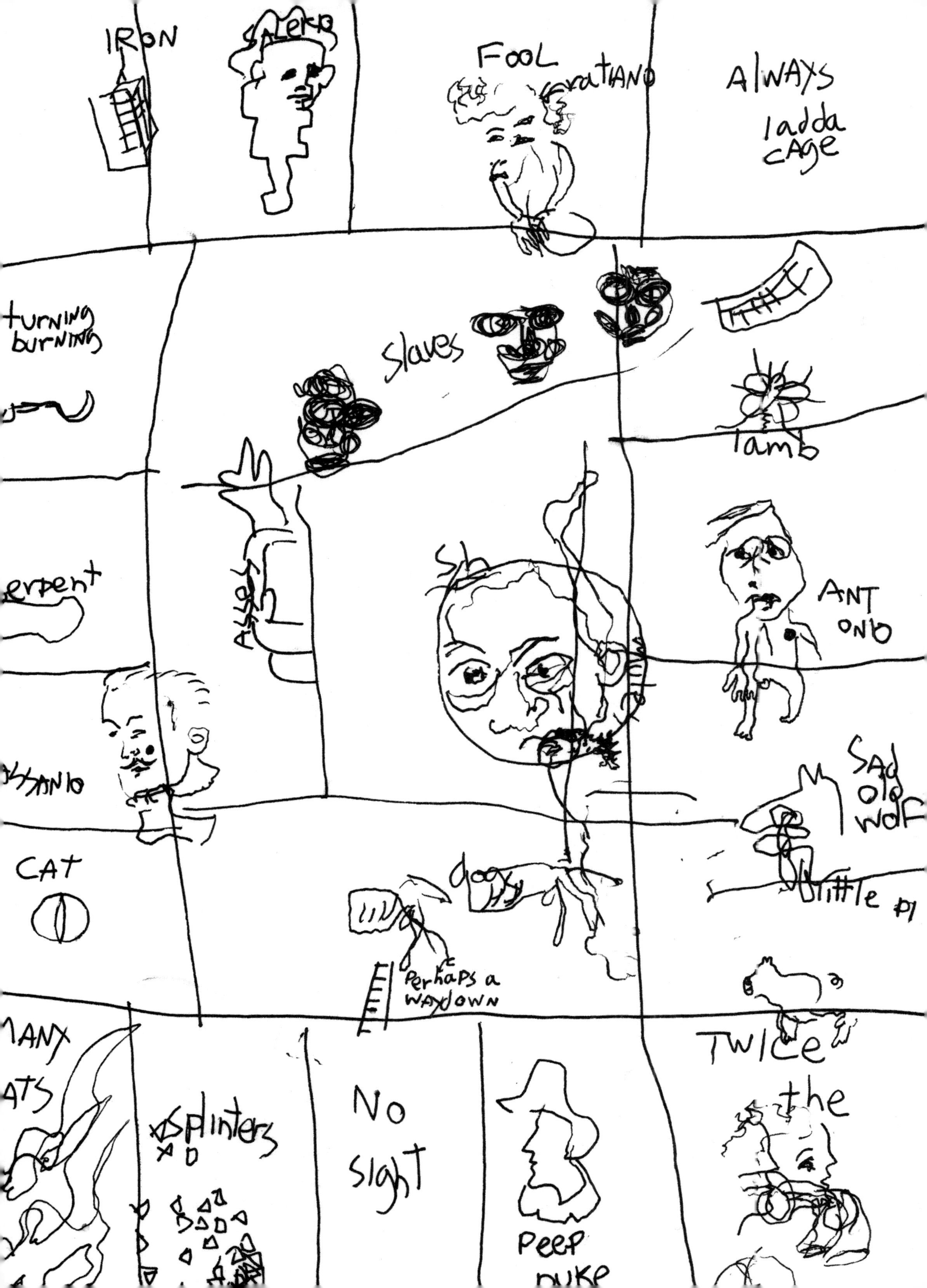
IRON
FOOL
ALWAYS
ladda
cage
turning
burning
slaves
lamb
ANT
ONIO
Sad
old
wolf
CAT
Perhaps a
waydown
splinters
No
sight
TWICE
the

Enter Nerissa, dressed like a lawyer's clerk.

DUKE
Came you from Padua, from Bellario?

NERISSA
From both, my lord. Bellario greets your Grace.

Presents a letter.

BASSANIO
Why dost thou whet thy knife so earnestly?

SHYLOCK
To cut the forfeiture from that bankrupt there.

GRATIANO
Not on thy sole, but on thy soul, harsh Jew,
Thou mak'st thy knife keen; but no metal can,
No, not the hangman's axe, bear half the keenness
Of thy sharp envy. Can no prayers pierce thee?

SHYLOCK
No, none that thou hast wit enough to make.

GRATIANO
O, be thou damn'd, inexecrable dog!
And for thy life let justice be accus'd.
Thou almost mak'st me waver in my faith
To hold opinion with Pythagoras,
That souls of animals infuse themselves
Into the trunks of men: thy currish spirit
Govern'd a wolf, who, hang'd for human slaughter,
Even from the gallows did his fell soul fleet,
And whilst thou lay'st in thy unhallow'd dam,
Infus'd itself in thee; for thy desires
Are wolfish, bloody, starv'd, and ravenous.

SHYLOCK
Till thou canst rail the seal from off my bond,
Thou but offend'st thy lungs to speak so loud:
Repair thy wit, good youth, or it will fall
To cureless ruin. I stand here for law.

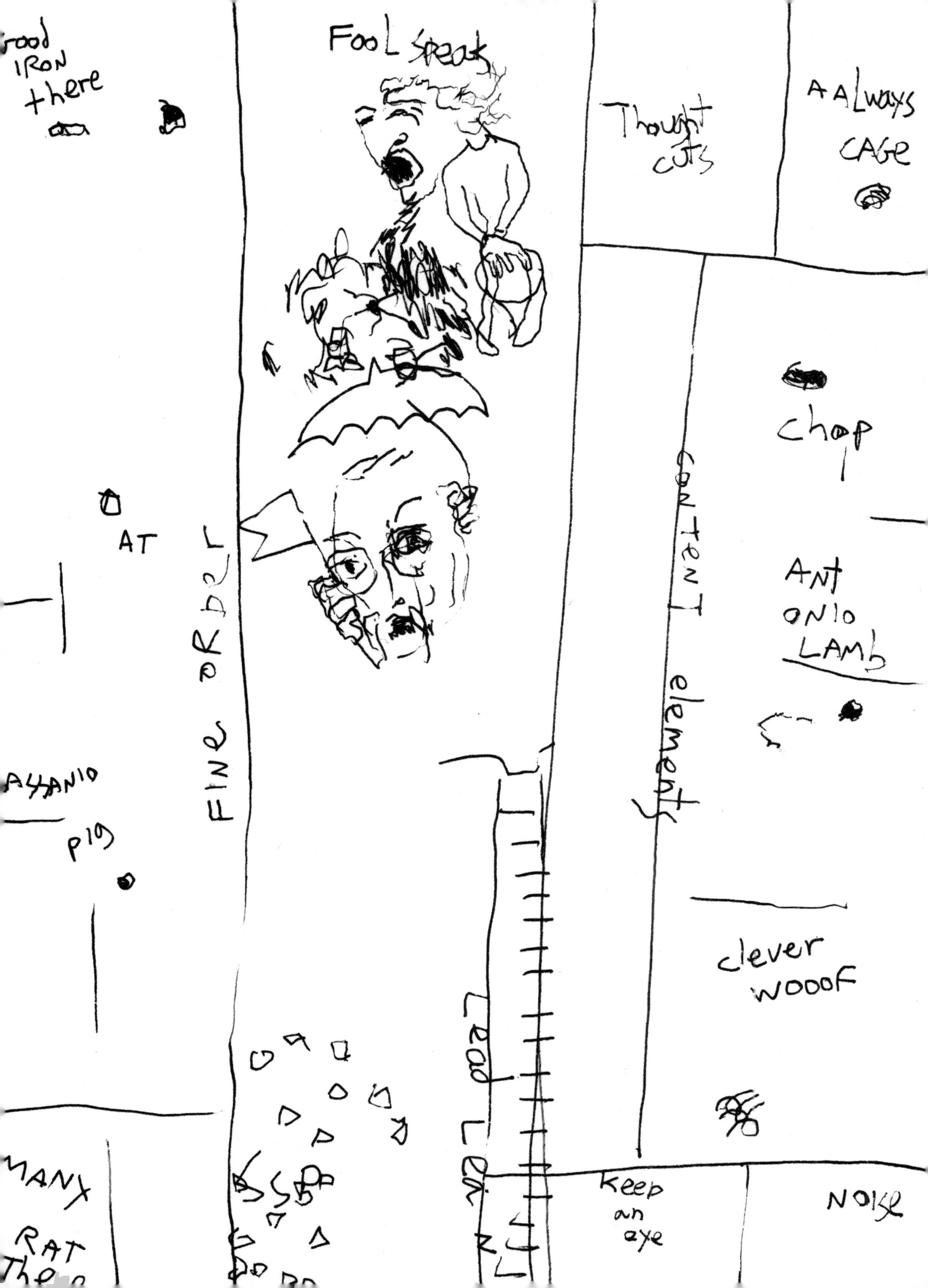

IRON
there
Fool speak
Thought cuts
A ALways CAGE
chop
CONTENT
elements
ANT ONIO LAMB
clever WOOOF
keep an eye
NOISE
FINE ORDER
AT
pig
MANY
RAT

DUKE
This letter from Bellario doth commend
A young and learned doctor to our court.
Where is he?

NERISSA
He attendeth here hard by,
To know your answer, whether you'll admit him.

DUKE
With all my heart: some three or four of you
Go give him courteous conduct to this place.
Meantime, the court shall hear Bellario's letter.

CLERK
'Your Grace shall understand that at the receipt of your letter I am very sick; but in the instant that your messenger came, in loving visitation was with me a young doctor of Rome; his name is Balthazar. I acquainted him with the cause in controversy between the Jew and Antonio the merchant: we turned o'er many books together: he is furnished with my opinion; which, bettered with his own learning,—the greatness whereof I cannot enough commend,—comes with him, at my importunity, to fill up your Grace's request in my stead I beseech you, let his lack of years be no impediment to let him lack a reverend estimation, for I never knew so young a body with so old a head. I leave him to your gracious acceptance, whose trial shall better publish his commendation.'

DUKE
You hear the learn'd Bellario, what he writes:
And here, I take it, is the doctor come.

Enter Portia, dressed like a doctor of laws.

Give me your hand. Came you from old Bellario?

PORTIA
I did, my lord.

DUKE
You are welcome: take your place.
Are you acquainted with the difference
That holds this present question in the court?

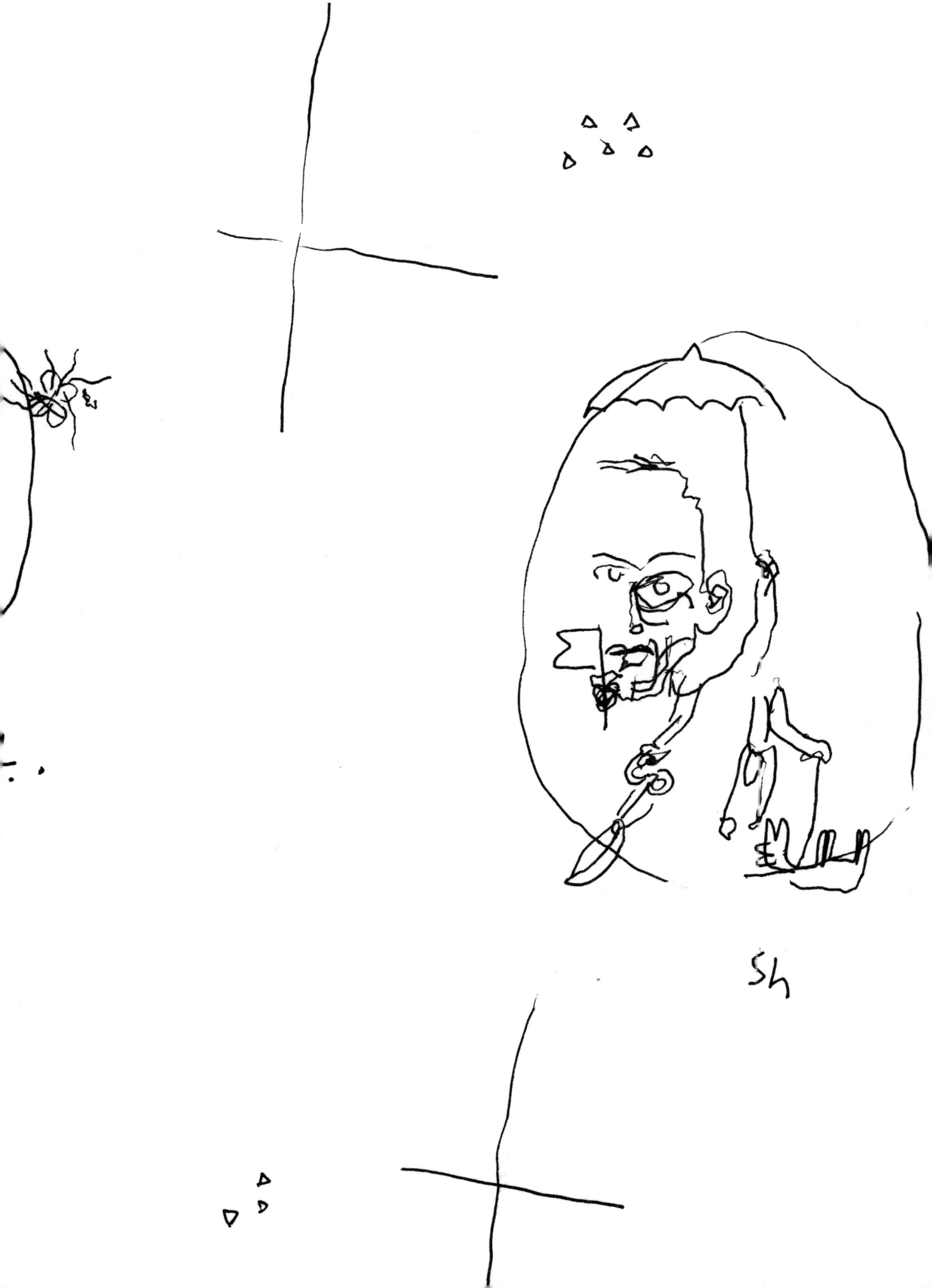
Sh

PORTIA
I am informed throughly of the cause.
Which is the merchant here, and which the Jew?

DUKE
Antonio and old Shylock, both stand forth.

PORTIA
Is your name Shylock?

SHYLOCK
Shylock is my name.

PORTIA
Of a strange nature is the suit you follow;
Yet in such rule that the Venetian law
Cannot impugn you as you do proceed.
[*To Antonio.*] You stand within his danger, do you not?

ANTONIO
Ay, so he says.

PORTIA
Do you confess the bond?

ANTONIO
I do.

PORTIA
Then must the Jew be merciful.

SHYLOCK
On what compulsion must I? tell me that.

**Hear a new voice without a sex.
As for me—not interested and not uninterested.**

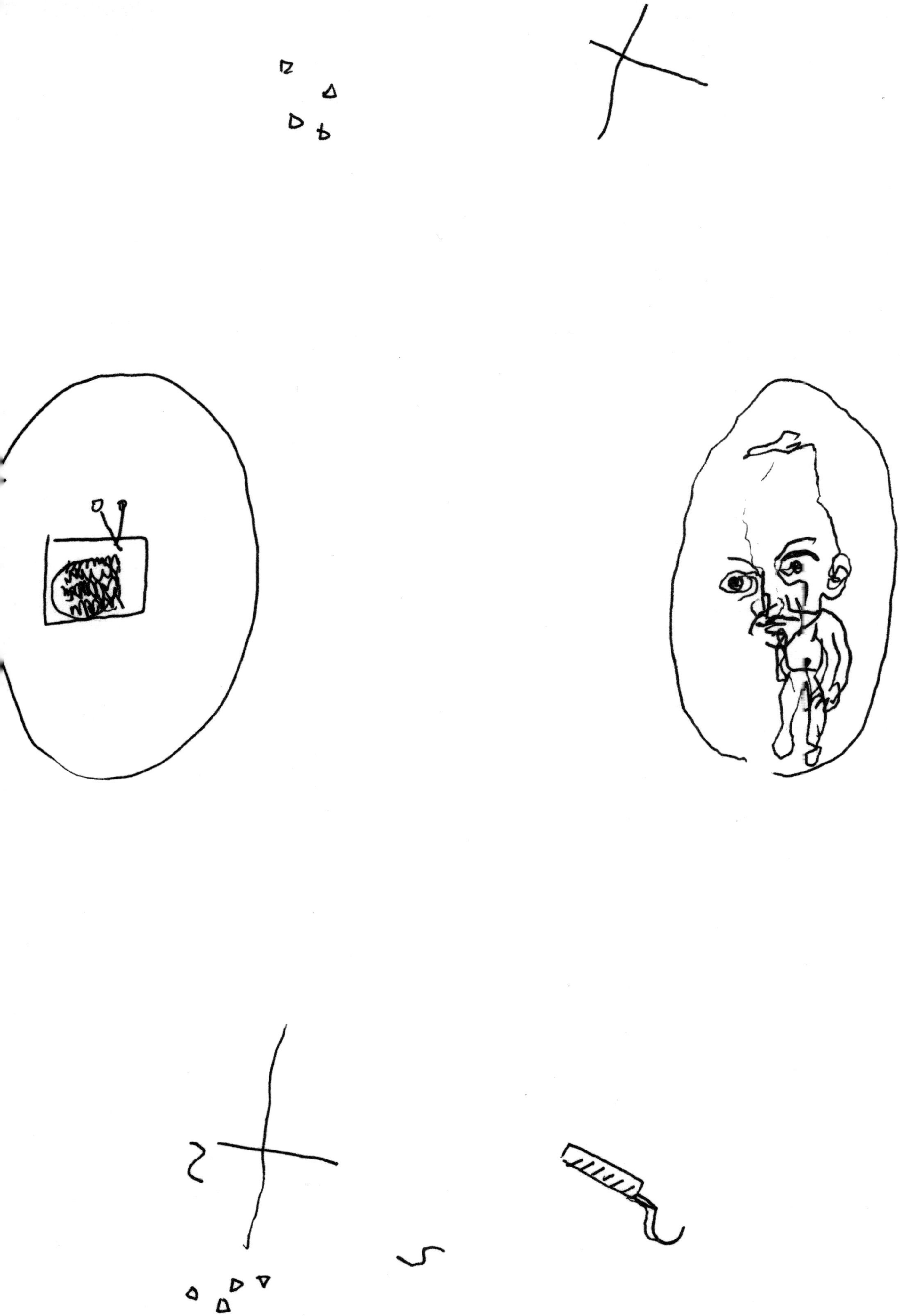

PORTIA
The quality of mercy is not strain'd,
It droppeth as the gentle rain from heaven
Upon the place beneath: it is twice bless'd;
It blesseth him that gives and him that takes:
'Tis mightiest in the mightiest; it becomes
The throned monarch better than his crown;
His sceptre shows the force of temporal power,
The attribute to awe and majesty,
Wherein doth sit the dread and fear of kings;
But mercy is above this sceptred sway,
It is enthroned in the hearts of kings,
It is an attribute to God himself,
And earthly power doth then show likest God's
When mercy seasons justice. Therefore, Jew,
Though justice be thy plea, consider this,
That in the course of justice none of us
Should see salvation: we do pray for mercy,
And that same prayer doth teach us all to render
The deeds of mercy. I have spoke thus much
To mitigate the justice of thy plea,
Which if thou follow, this strict court of Venice
Must needs give sentence 'gainst the merchant there.

SHYLOCK
My deeds upon my head! I crave the law,
The penalty and forfeit of my bond.

PORTIA
Is he not able to discharge the money?

BASSANIO
Yes, here I tender it for him in the court;
Yea, twice the sum: if that will not suffice,
I will be bound to pay it ten times o'er,
On forfeit of my hands, my head, my heart.
If this will not suffice, it must appear
That malice bears down truth. And, I beseech you,
Wrest once the law to your authority:
To do a great right, do a little wrong,
And curb this cruel devil of his will.

Voice has no shape and no sex.
All enemies are known but the voice unknown.
Hence, the voice is not an enemy—and yet it is an enemy, as all is enemy.
Hear a voice.
Caution. Show no interest.
Slowly. Slowly.

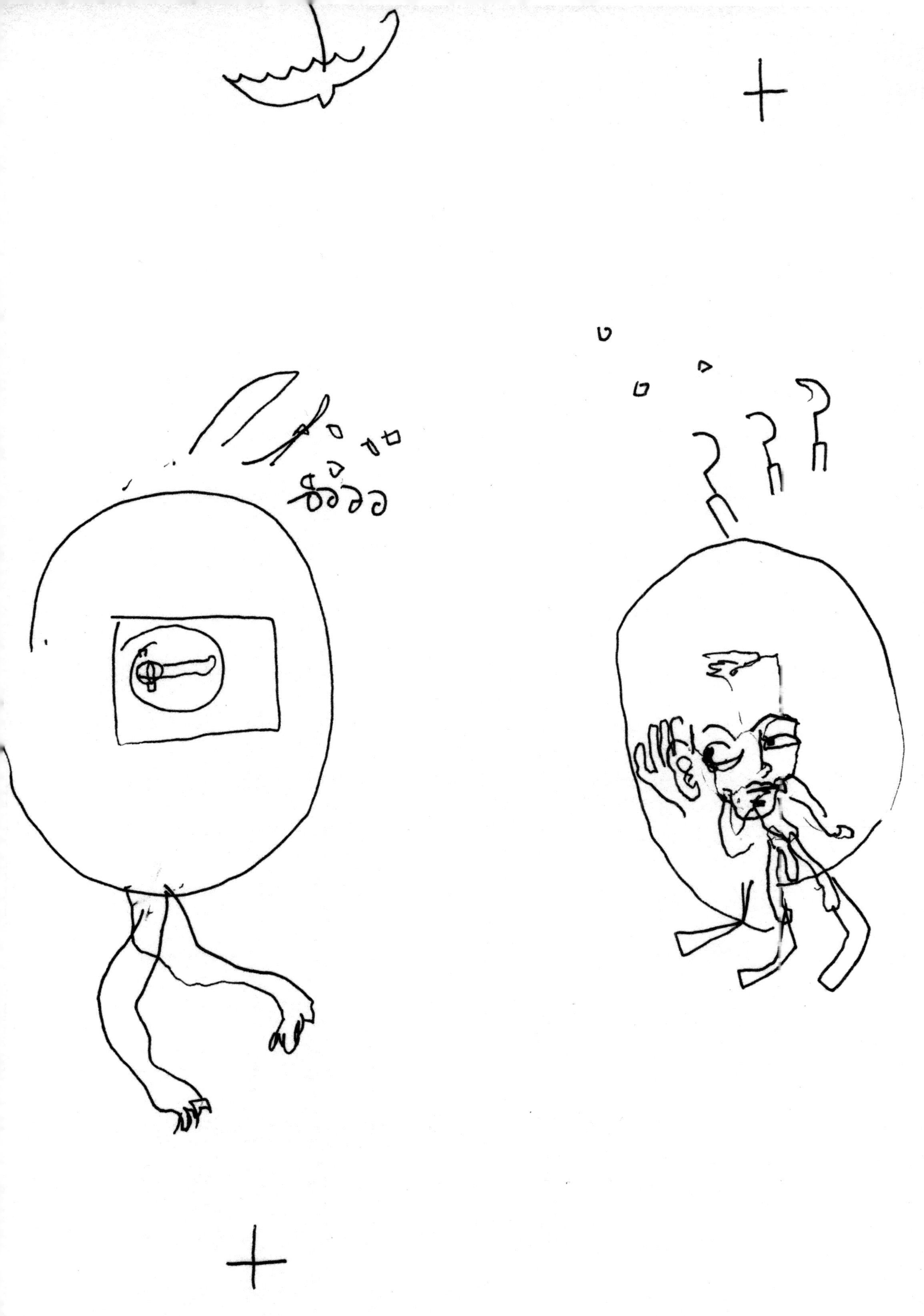

PORTIA
It must not be. There is no power in Venice
Can alter a decree established:
'Twill be recorded for a precedent,
And many an error by the same example
Will rush into the state. It cannot be.

SHYLOCK
A Daniel come to judgment! yea, a Daniel!
O wise young judge, how I do honour thee!

PORTIA
I pray you, let me look upon the bond.

SHYLOCK
Here 'tis, most reverend doctor; here it is.

PORTIA
Shylock, there's thrice thy money offer'd thee.

SHYLOCK
An oath, an oath, I have an oath in heaven:
Shall I lay perjury upon my soul?
No, not for Venice.

PORTIA
Why, this bond is forfeit;
And lawfully by this the Jew may claim
A pound of flesh, to be by him cut off
Nearest the merchant's heart. Be merciful:
Take thrice thy money; bid me tear the bond.

SHYLOCK
When it is paid according to the tenour.
It doth appear you are a worthy judge;
You know the law, your exposition
Hath been most sound: I charge you by the law,
Whereof you are a well-deserving pillar,
Proceed to judgment: by my soul I swear
There is no power in the tongue of man
To alter me. I stay here on my bond.

ANTONIO
Most heartily I do beseech the court
To give the judgment.

Voice is sexless and shapeless.
It is unheard of.
There is a place for thought,
but not for me.
I am only act, act at the most,
and have no place.
Voice is sexless and shapeless,
hence placeless.
Hence voice is also only act.
Caution, careful, slowly slowly, grope.

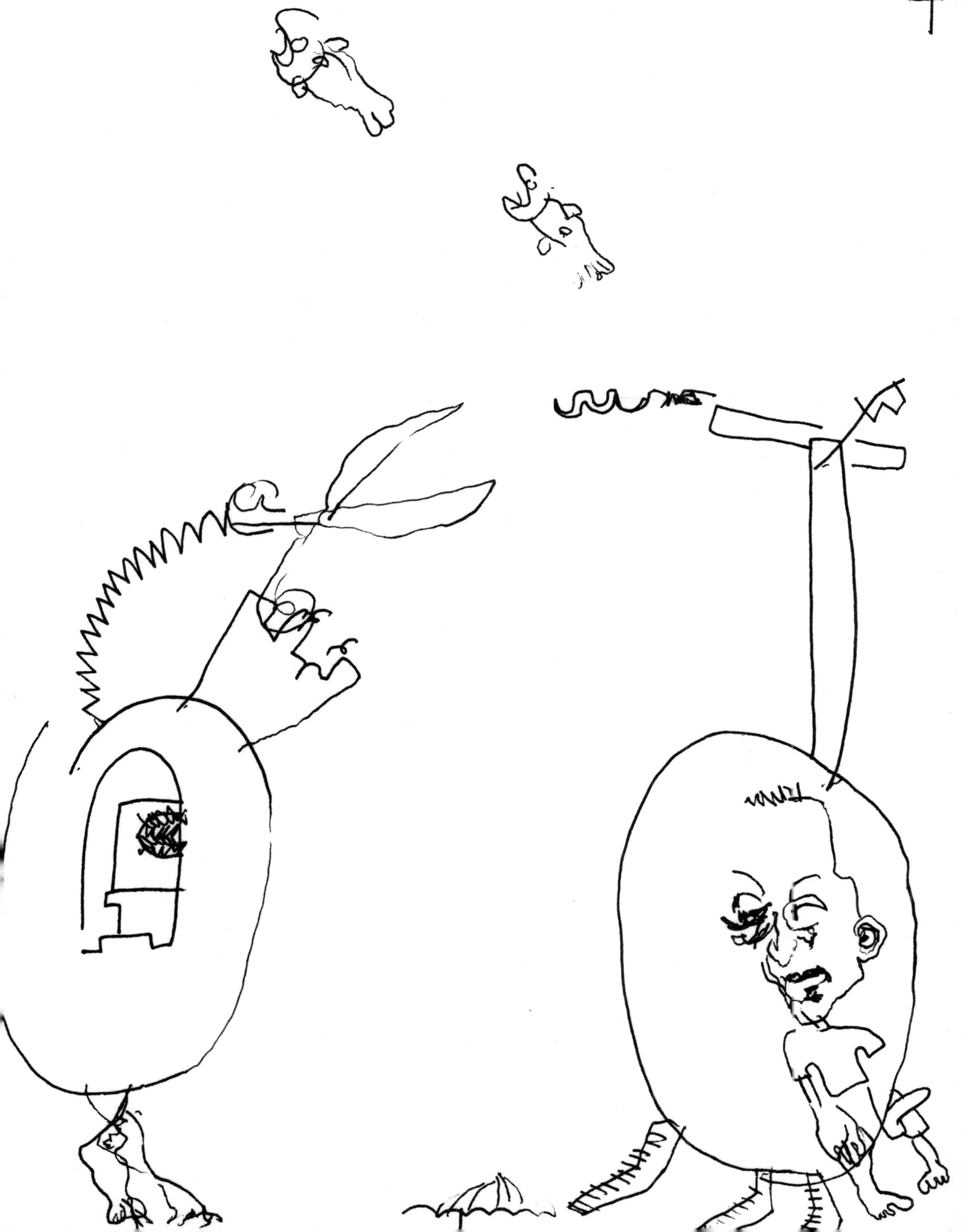

PORTIA
Why then, thus it is:
You must prepare your bosom for his knife.

SHYLOCK
O noble judge! O excellent young man!

PORTIA
For, the intent and purpose of the law
Hath full relation to the penalty,
Which here appeareth due upon the bond.

SHYLOCK
'Tis very true! O wise and upright judge!
How much more elder art thou than thy looks!

PORTIA
Therefore lay bare your bosom.

SHYLOCK
Ay, 'his breast:'
So says the bond:—doth it not, noble judge?—
'Nearest his heart:' those are the very words.

PORTIA
It is so. Are there balance here to weigh
The flesh?

SHYLOCK
I have them ready.

Gentlemen!
Me and Voice Us!
Me and Voice Act!
We pro Us, Machine con Them!
Would cut meat!
Would slice parts!
Me and Voice revenge!
Place where We no matter is!
Hence no place is!
Gentlemen! We done you were!
Voice and Me done you were!

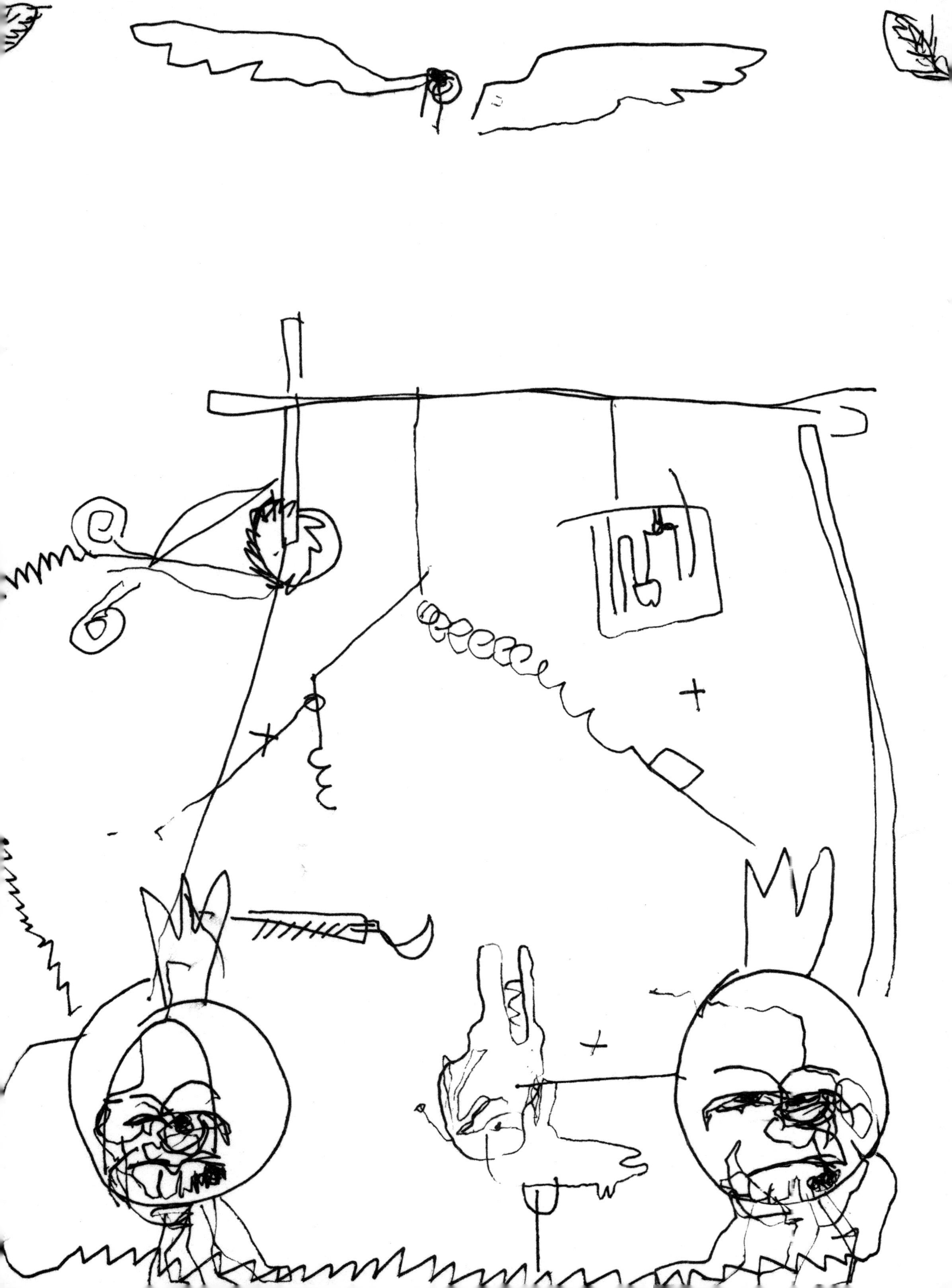

PORTIA
Have by some surgeon, Shylock, on your charge,
To stop his wounds, lest he do bleed to death.

SHYLOCK
Is it so nominated in the bond?

PORTIA
It is not so express'd; but what of that?
'Twere good you do so much for charity.

SHYLOCK
I cannot find it: 'tis not in the bond.

PORTIA
You, merchant, have you anything to say?

ANTONIO
But little: I am arm'd and well prepar'd.
Give me your hand, Bassanio: fare you well!
Grieve not that I am fallen to this for you;
For herein Fortune shows herself more kind
Than is her custom: it is still her use
To let the wretched man outlive his wealth,
To view with hollow eye and wrinkled brow
An age of poverty; from which lingering penance
Of such a misery doth she cut me off.
Commend me to your honourable wife:
Tell her the process of Antonio's end;
Say how I lov'd you, speak me fair in death;
And, when the tale is told, bid her be judge
Whether Bassanio had not once a love.
Repent not you that you shall lose your friend,
And he repents not that he pays your debt;
For if the Jew do cut but deep enough,
I'll pay it instantly with all my heart.

BASSANIO
Antonio, I am married to a wife
Which is as dear to me as life itself;
But life itself, my wife, and all the world,
Are not with me esteem'd above thy life:
I would lose all, ay, sacrifice them all,
Here to this devil, to deliver you.

PORTIA
Your wife would give you little thanks for that,
If she were by to hear you make the offer.

GRATIANO
I have a wife, whom, I protest, I love:
I would she were in heaven, so she could
Entreat some power to change this currish Jew.

NERISSA
'Tis well you offer it behind her back;
The wish would make else an unquiet house.

SHYLOCK
These be the Christian husbands! I have a daughter;
Would any of the stock of Barabbas
Had been her husband rather than a Christian!
We trifle time; I pray thee, pursue sentence.

PORTIA
A pound of that same merchant's flesh is thine:
The court awards it, and the law doth give it.

SHYLOCK
Most rightful judge!

PORTIA
And you must cut this flesh from off his breast:
The law allows it, and the court awards it.

SHYLOCK
Most learned judge! A sentence! come, prepare!

PORTIA
Tarry a little: there is something else.

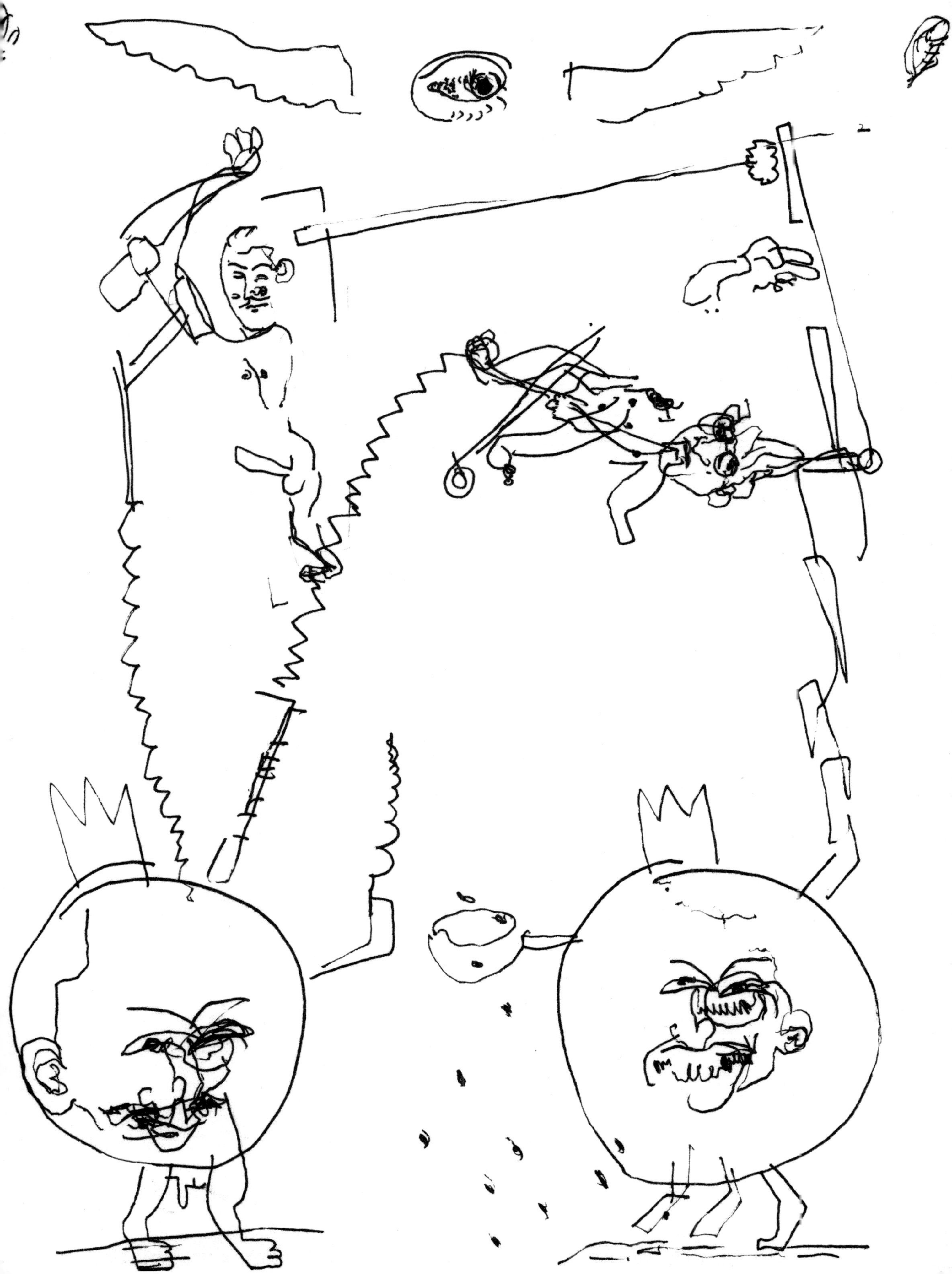

This bond doth give thee here no jot of blood;
The words expressly are 'a pound of flesh:'
Then take thy bond, take thou thy pound of flesh;
But, in the cutting it, if thou dost shed
One drop of Christian blood, thy lands and goods
Are, by the laws of Venice, confiscate
Unto the state of Venice.

GRATIANO
O upright judge! Mark, Jew: O learned judge!

SHYLOCK
Is that the law?

PORTIA
Thyself shalt see the act;
For, as thou urgest justice, be assur'd
Thou shalt have justice, more than thou desir'st.

GRATIANO
O learned judge! Mark, Jew: a learned judge!

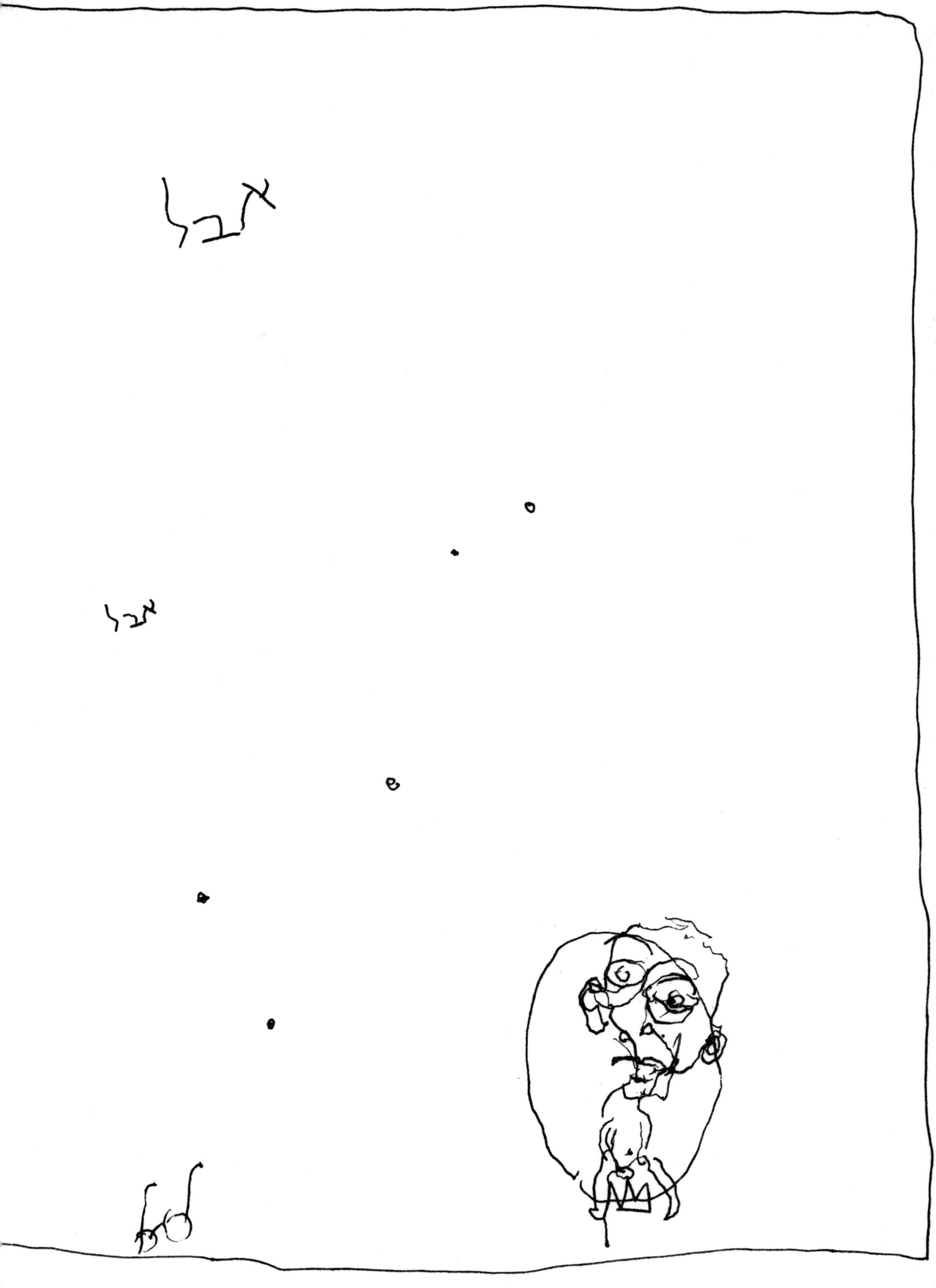
אבל
אבל

IV.I.14

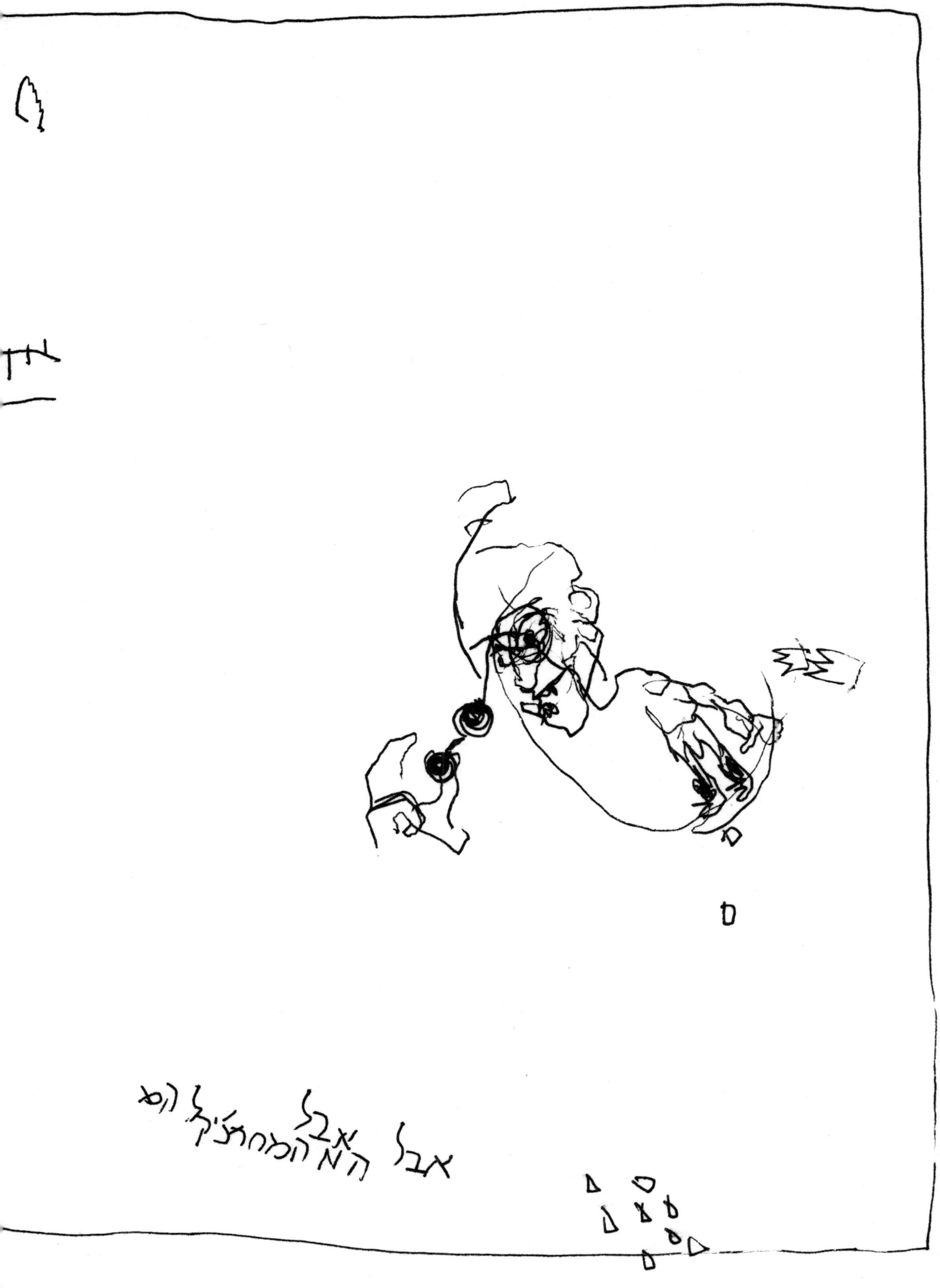
אבל
אבל

SHYLOCK
I take this offer then: pay the bond thrice,
And let the Christian go.

BASSANIO
Here is the money.

PORTIA
Soft!
The Jew shall have all justice; soft! no haste:—
He shall have nothing but the penalty.

GRATIANO
O Jew! an upright judge, a learned judge!

PORTIA
Therefore prepare thee to cut off the flesh.
Shed thou no blood; nor cut thou less, nor more,
But just a pound of flesh: if thou tak'st more,
Or less, than a just pound, be it but so
As makes it light or heavy in the substance,
Or the division of the twentieth part
Of one poor scruple, nay, if the scale do turn
But in the estimation of a hair,
Thou diest and all thy goods are confiscate.

GRATIANO
A second Daniel, a Daniel, Jew!
Now, infidel, I have thee on the hip.

PORTIA
Why doth the Jew pause? take thy forfeiture.

SHYLOCK
Give me my principal, and let me go.

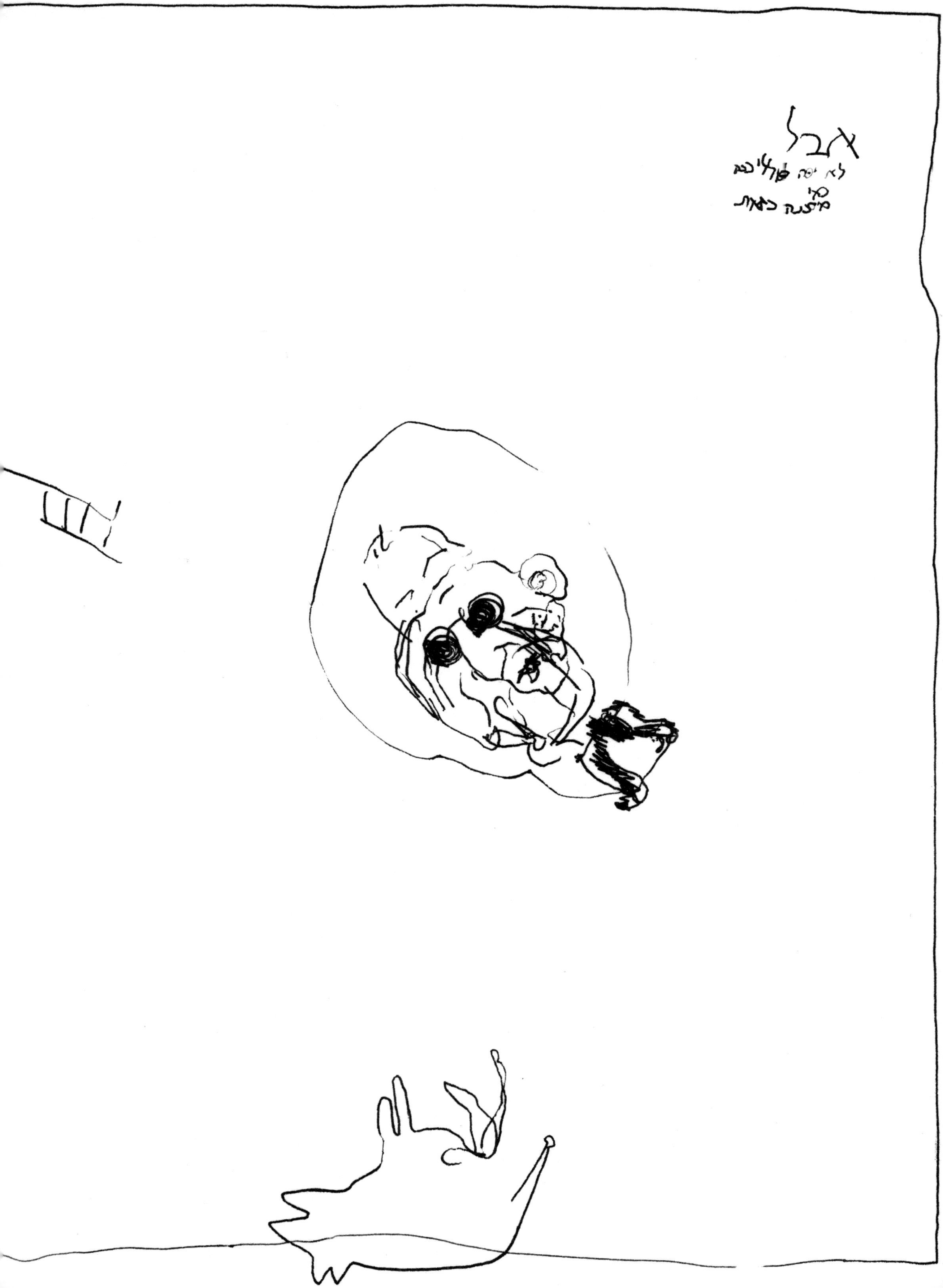
אבל
לא יפה שלכם
סבי
מיטה כזאת

BASSANIO
I have it ready for thee; here it is.

PORTIA
He hath refus'd it in the open court:
He shall have merely justice, and his bond.

GRATIANO
A Daniel, still say I; a second Daniel!
I thank thee, Jew, for teaching me that word.

SHYLOCK
Shall I not have barely my principal?

PORTIA
Thou shalt have nothing but the forfeiture,
To be so taken at thy peril, Jew.

SHYLOCK
Why, then the devil give him good of it!
I'll stay no longer question.

PORTIA
Tarry, Jew:
The law hath yet another hold on you.
It is enacted in the laws of Venice,
If it be prov'd against an alien
That by direct or indirect attempts
He seek the life of any citizen,
The party 'gainst the which he doth contrive
Shall seize one half his goods; the other half
Comes to the privy coffer of the state;
And the offender's life lies in the mercy
Of the duke only, 'gainst all other voice.
In which predicament, I say, thou stand'st;
For it appears by manifest proceeding,
That indirectly and directly too
Thou hast contriv'd against the very life
Of the defendant; and thou hast incurr'd
The danger formerly by me rehears'd.
Down therefore and beg mercy of the duke.

GRATIANO
Beg that thou mayst have leave to hang thyself:
And yet, thy wealth being forfeit to the state,
Thou hast not left the value of a cord;
Therefore thou must be hang'd at the state's charge.

DUKE
That thou shalt see the difference of our spirits,
I pardon thee thy life before thou ask it.
For half thy wealth, it is Antonio's;
The other half comes to the general state,
Which humbleness may drive into a fine.

PORTIA
Ay, for the state; not for Antonio.

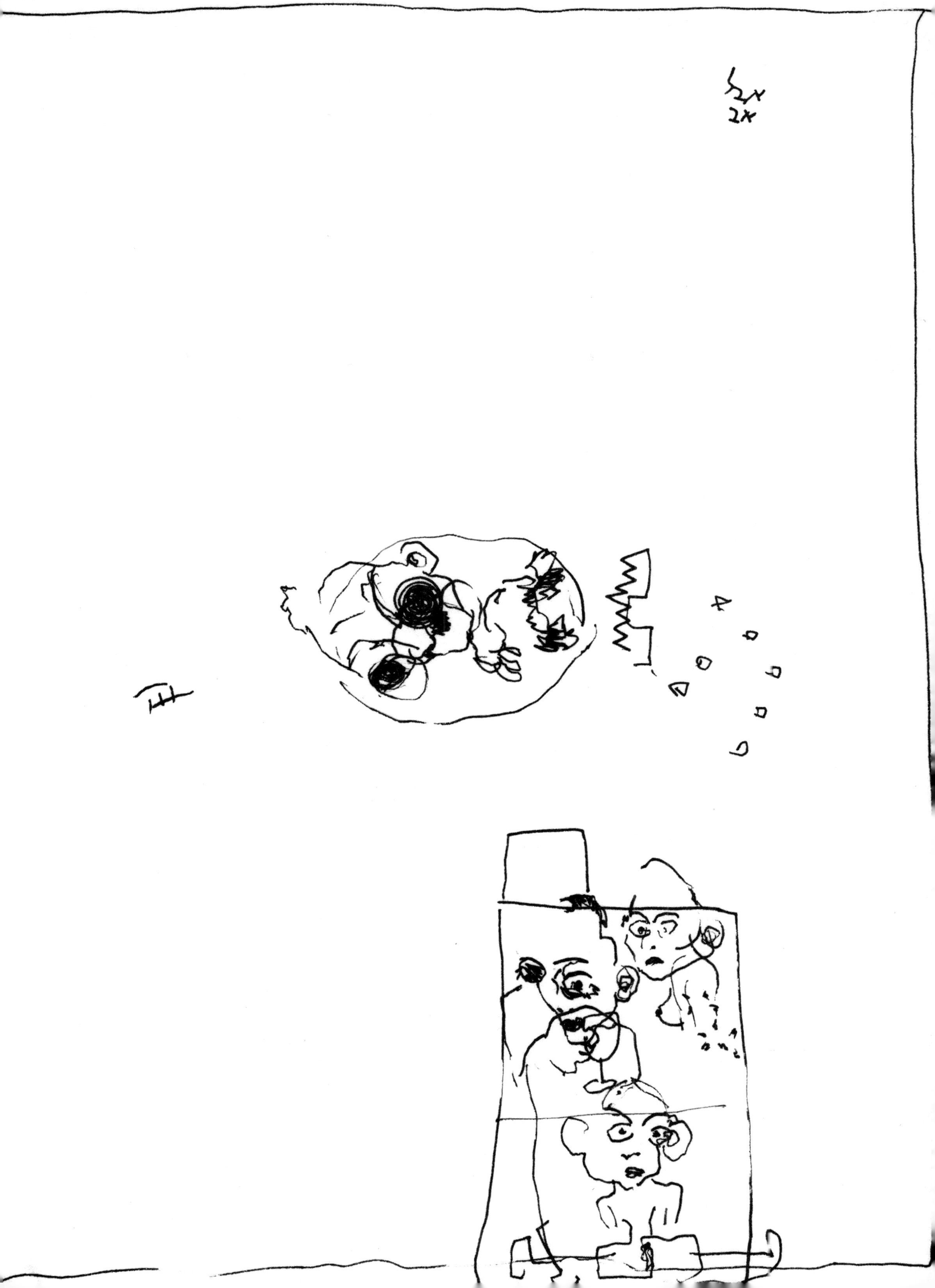

SHYLOCK
Nay, take my life and all; pardon not that:
You take my house when you do take the prop
That doth sustain my house; you take my life
When you do take the means whereby I live.

PORTIA
What mercy can you render him, Antonio?

GRATIANO
A halter gratis; nothing else, for God's sake!

ANTONIO
So please my lord the duke, and all the court,
To quit the fine for one half of his goods,
I am content; so he will let me have
The other half in use, to render it,
Upon his death, unto the gentleman
That lately stole his daughter:
Two things provided more, that, for this favour,
He presently become a Christian;
The other, that he do record a gift,
Here in the court, of all he dies possess'd,
Unto his son Lorenzo, and his daughter.

DUKE
He shall do this, or else I do recant
The pardon that I late pronounced here.

PORTIA
Art thou contented, Jew? what dost thou say?

SHYLOCK
I am content.

PORTIA
Clerk, draw a deed of gift.

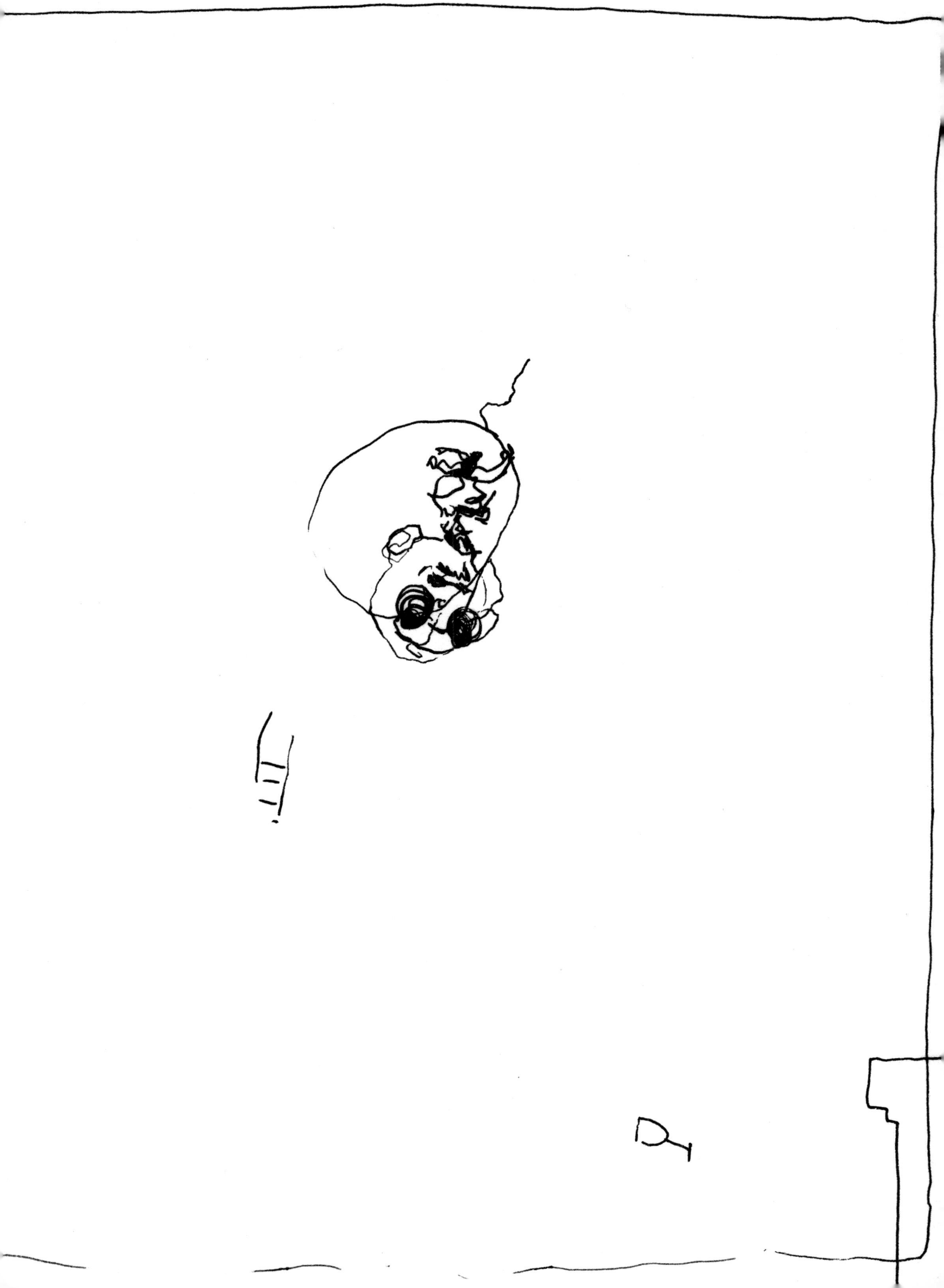

SHYLOCK
I pray you give me leave to go from hence:
I am not well. Send the deed after me,
And I will sign it.

DUKE
Get thee gone, but do it.

GRATIANO
In christening thou shalt have two godfathers;
Had I been judge, thou shouldst have had ten more,
To bring thee to the gallows, not the font.

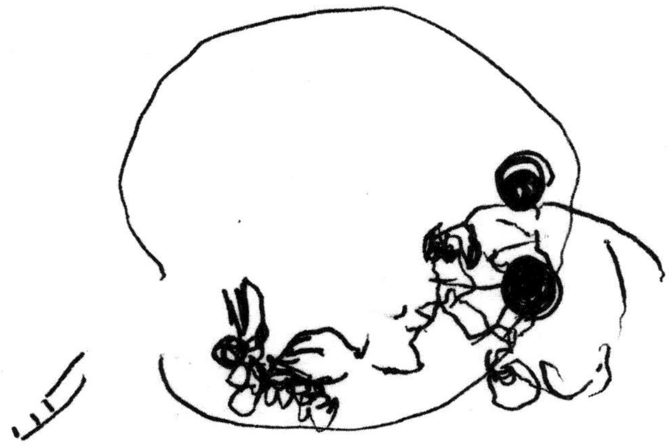

Exit Shylock.

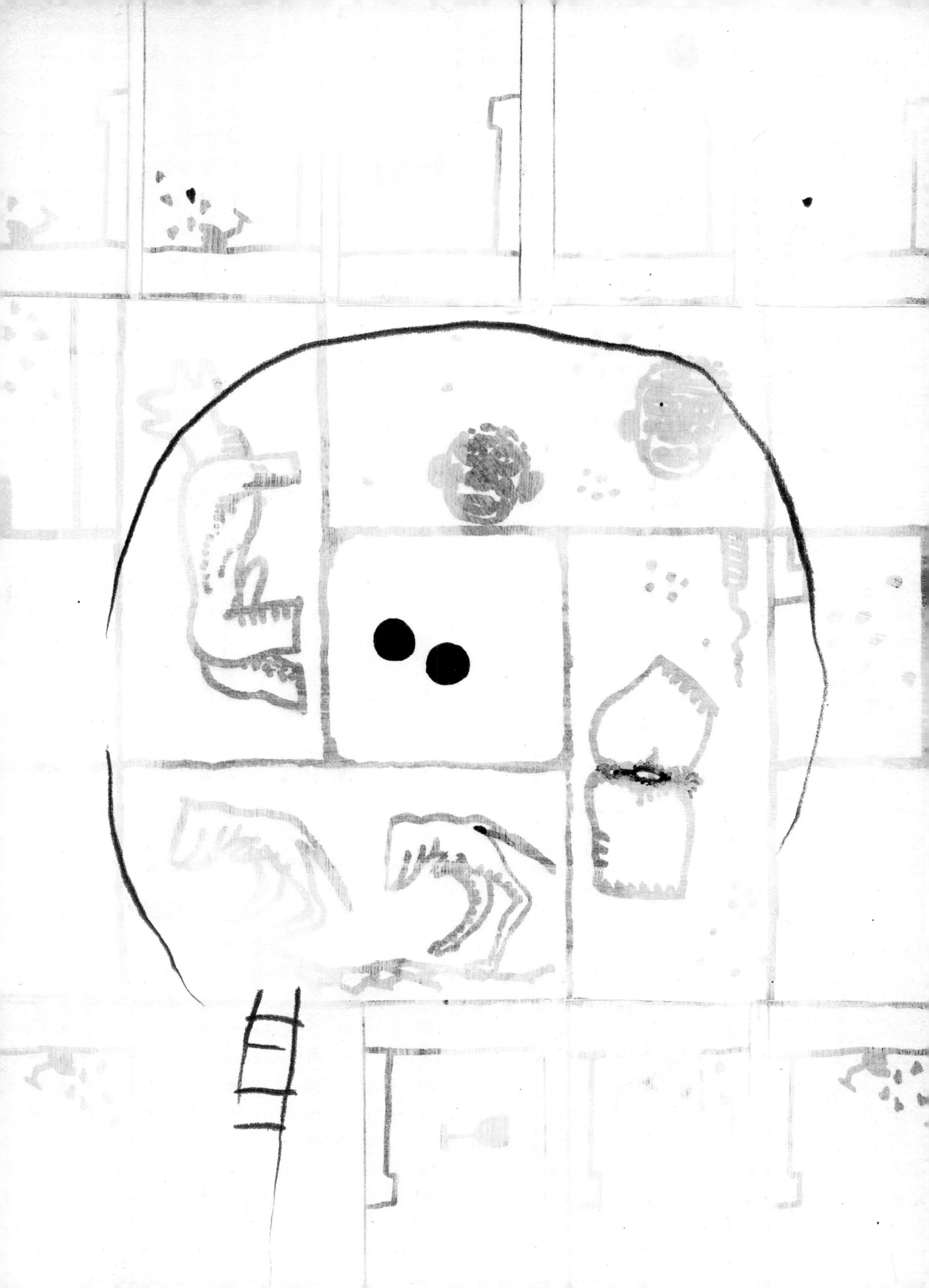

DUKE
Sir, I entreat you home with me to dinner.

PORTIA
I humbly do desire your Grace of pardon:
I must away this night toward Padua,
And it is meet I presently set forth.

DUKE
I am sorry that your leisure serves you not.
Antonio, gratify this gentleman,
For, in my mind, you are much bound to him.

Exeunt Duke, Magnificoes, and Train.

BASSANIO
Most worthy gentleman, I and my friend
Have by your wisdom been this day acquitted
Of grievous penalties; in lieu whereof,
Three thousand ducats, due unto the Jew,
We freely cope your courteous pains withal.

ANTONIO
And stand indebted, over and above,
In love and service to you evermore.

PORTIA
He is well paid that is well satisfied;
And I, delivering you, am satisfied,
And therein do account myself well paid:
My mind was never yet more mercenary.
I pray you, know me when we meet again:
I wish you well, and so I take my leave.

BASSANIO
Dear sir, of force I must attempt you further:
Take some remembrance of us, as a tribute,
Not as a fee. Grant me two things, I pray you,
Not to deny me, and to pardon me.

PORTIA
You press me far, and therefore I will yield.
[*To Antonio.*] Give me your gloves, I'll wear them for your sake;
[*To Bassanio.*] And, for your love, I'll take this ring from you.
Do not draw back your hand; I'll take no more;
And you in love shall not deny me this.

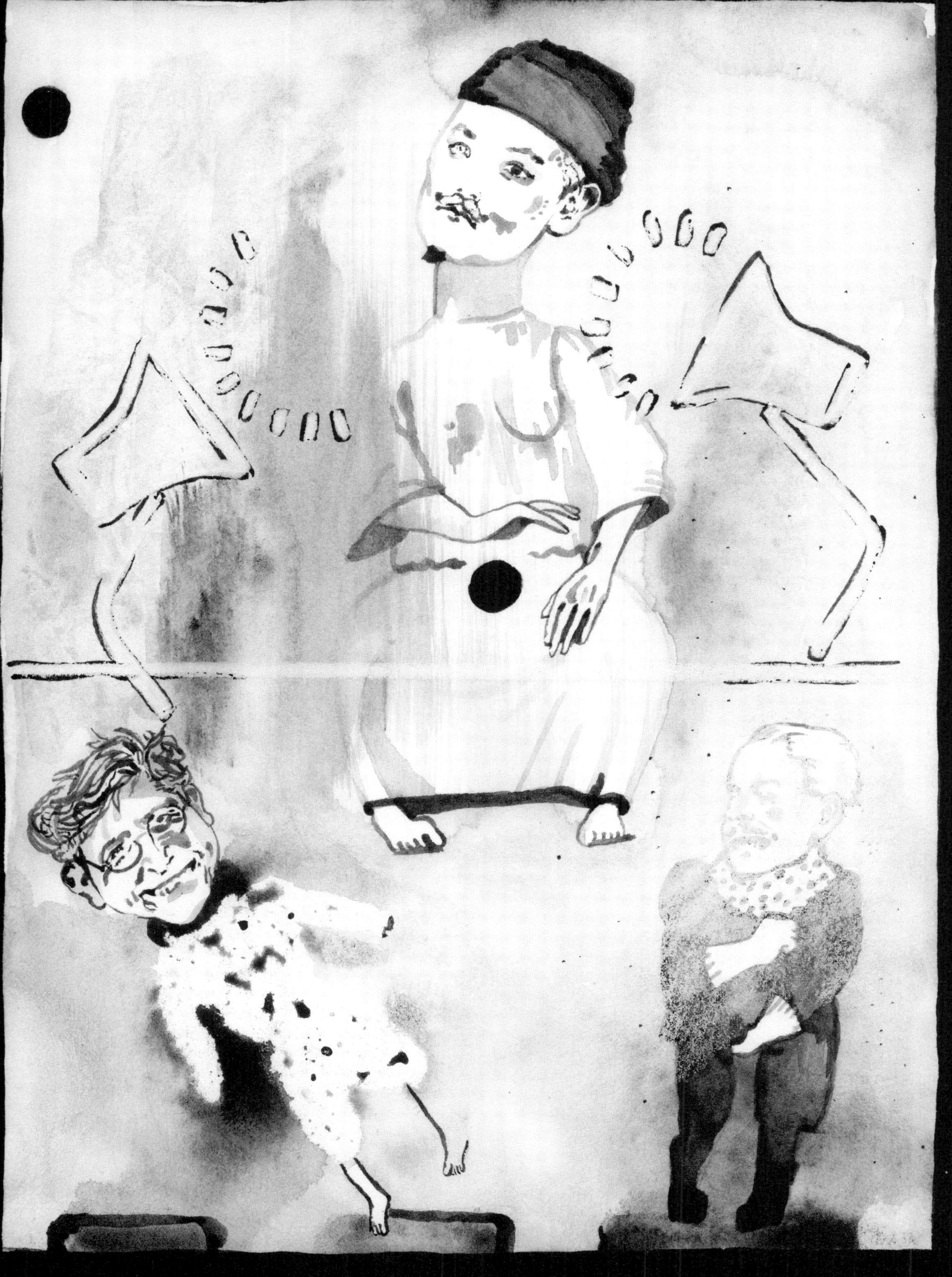

IV.I.21

BASSANIO
This ring, good sir? alas! it is a trifle;
I will not shame myself to give you this.

PORTIA
I will have nothing else but only this;
And now methinks I have a mind to it.

BASSANIO
There's more depends on this than on the value.
The dearest ring in Venice will I give you,
And find it out by proclamation:
Only for this, I pray you, pardon me.

PORTIA
I see, sir, you are liberal in offers:
You taught me first to beg, and now methinks
You teach me how a beggar should be answer'd.

BASSANIO
Good sir, this ring was given me by my wife;
And, when she put it on, she made me vow
That I should never sell nor give nor lose it.

PORTIA
That 'scuse serves many men to save their gifts.
An if your wife be not a mad-woman,
And know how well I have deserv'd the ring,
She would not hold out enemy for ever,
For giving it to me. Well, peace be with you.

Exeunt Portia and Nerissa.

ANTONIO
My Lord Bassanio, let him have the ring:
Let his deservings and my love withal
Be valu'd 'gainst your wife's commandment.

BASSANIO
Go, Gratiano; run and overtake him;
Give him the ring, and bring him, if thou canst,
Unto Antonio's house. Away! make haste.

Exit Gratiano.

Come, you and I will thither presently,
And in the morning early will we both
Fly toward Belmont. Come, Antonio.

Exeunt.

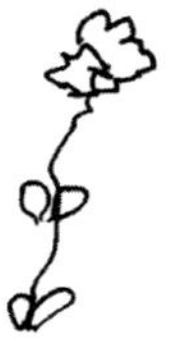

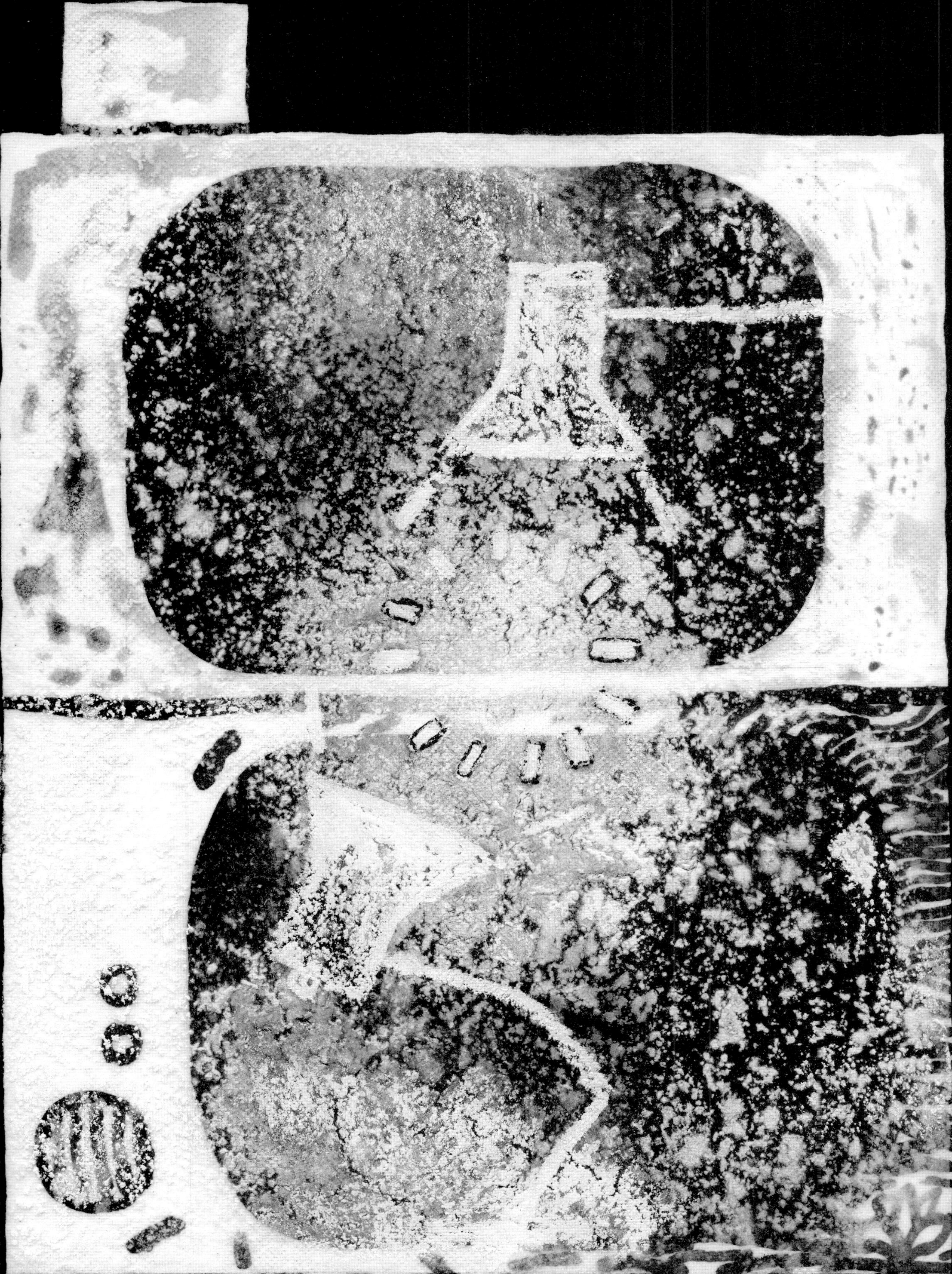

IV.II.1

Scene II—The Same. A Street.

Enter Portia and Nerissa.

PORTIA
Inquire the Jew's house out, give him this deed,
And let him sign it. We'll away to-night,
And be a day before our husbands home:
This deed will be well welcome to Lorenzo.

Enter Gratiano.

GRATIANO
Fair sir, you are well o'erta'en.
My Lord Bassanio upon more advice
Hath sent you here this ring, and doth entreat
Your company at dinner.

PORTIA
That cannot be:
His ring I do accept most thankfully;
And so, I pray you, tell him: furthermore,
I pray you, show my youth old Shylock's house.

GRATIANO
That will I do.

NERISSA
Sir, I would speak with you.
[*Aside to Portia.*] I'll see if I can get my husband's ring,
Which I did make him swear to keep for ever.

PORTIA
Thou mayst, I warrant. We shall have old swearing
That they did give the rings away to men;
But we'll outface them, and outswear them too.
Away! make haste: thou know'st where I will tarry.

NERISSA
Come, good sir, will you show me to this house?

Exeunt.

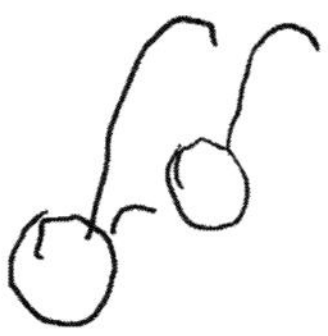

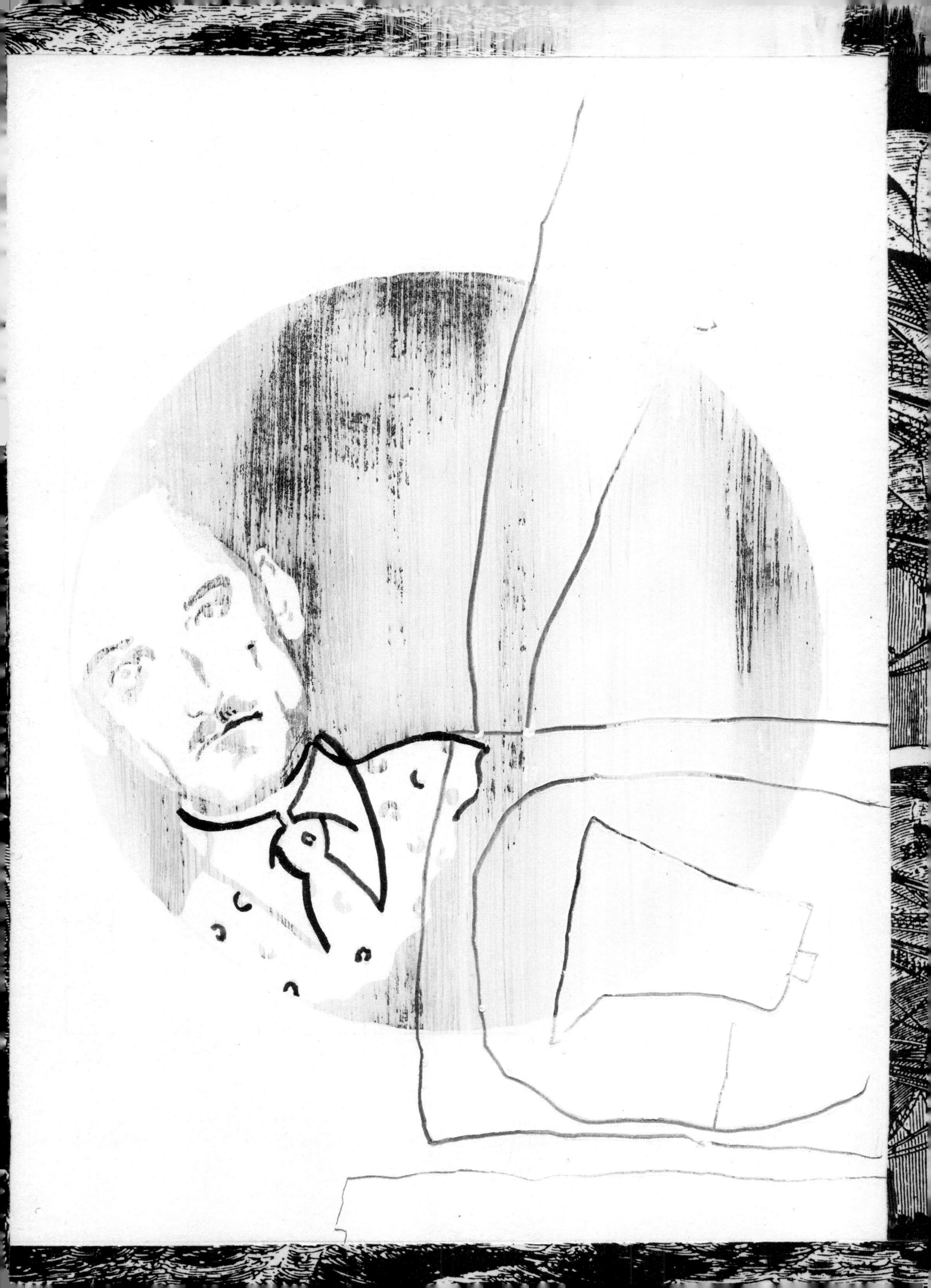

FIFTH ACT

HAPPY

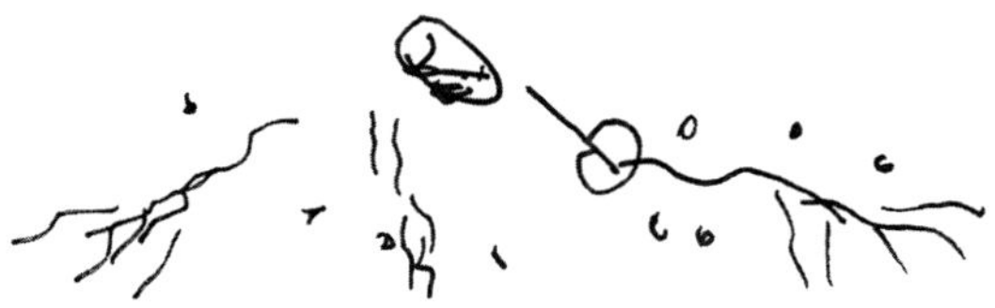

Scene I—Belmont. The Avenue to Portia's House.

Enter Lorenzo and Jessica.

LORENZO
The moon shines bright: in such a night as this,
When the sweet wind did gently kiss the trees
And they did make no noise, in such a night
Troilus methinks mounted the Troyan walls,
And sigh'd his soul toward the Grecian tents,
Where Cressid lay that night.

JESSICA
In such a night
Did Thisbe fearfully o'ertrip the dew,
And saw the lion's shadow ere himself,
And ran dismay'd away.

LORENZO
In such a night
Stood Dido with a willow in her hand
Upon the wild sea-banks, and waft her love
To come again to Carthage.

JESSICA
In such a night
Medea gather'd the enchanted herbs
That did renew old Æson.

LORENZO
In such a night
Did Jessica steal from the wealthy Jew,
And with an unthrift love did run from Venice,
As far as Belmont.

JESSICA
In such a night
Did young Lorenzo swear he lov'd her well,
Stealing her soul with many vows of faith,
And ne'er a true one.

LORENZO
In such a night
Did pretty Jessica, like a little shrew,
Slander her love, and he forgave it her.

JESSICA
I would out-night you, did no body come;
But, hark! I hear the footing of a man.

Enter Stephano.

LORENZO
Who comes so fast in silence of the night?

STEPHANO
A friend.

LORENZO
A friend! what friend? your name, I pray you, friend.

STEPHANO
Stephano is my name; and I bring word
My mistress will before the break of day
Be here at Belmont: she doth stray about
By holy crosses, where she kneels and prays
For happy wedlock hours.

LORENZO
Who comes with her?

STEPHANO
None, but a holy hermit and her maid.
I pray you, is my master yet return'd?

LORENZO
He is not, nor we have not heard from him.
But go we in, I pray thee, Jessica,
And ceremoniously let us prepare
Some welcome for the mistress of the house.

All came and brought presents.
Many pretty presents, neatly wrapped.
Elegant cellophane. Verily shapes.
All the acquaintances wait.
But I am not present.
I am busy with
an International Congress,
have a suitcase and clearly speak.
People say: Mr. Sh., Mr. Sh.
I say: not now.

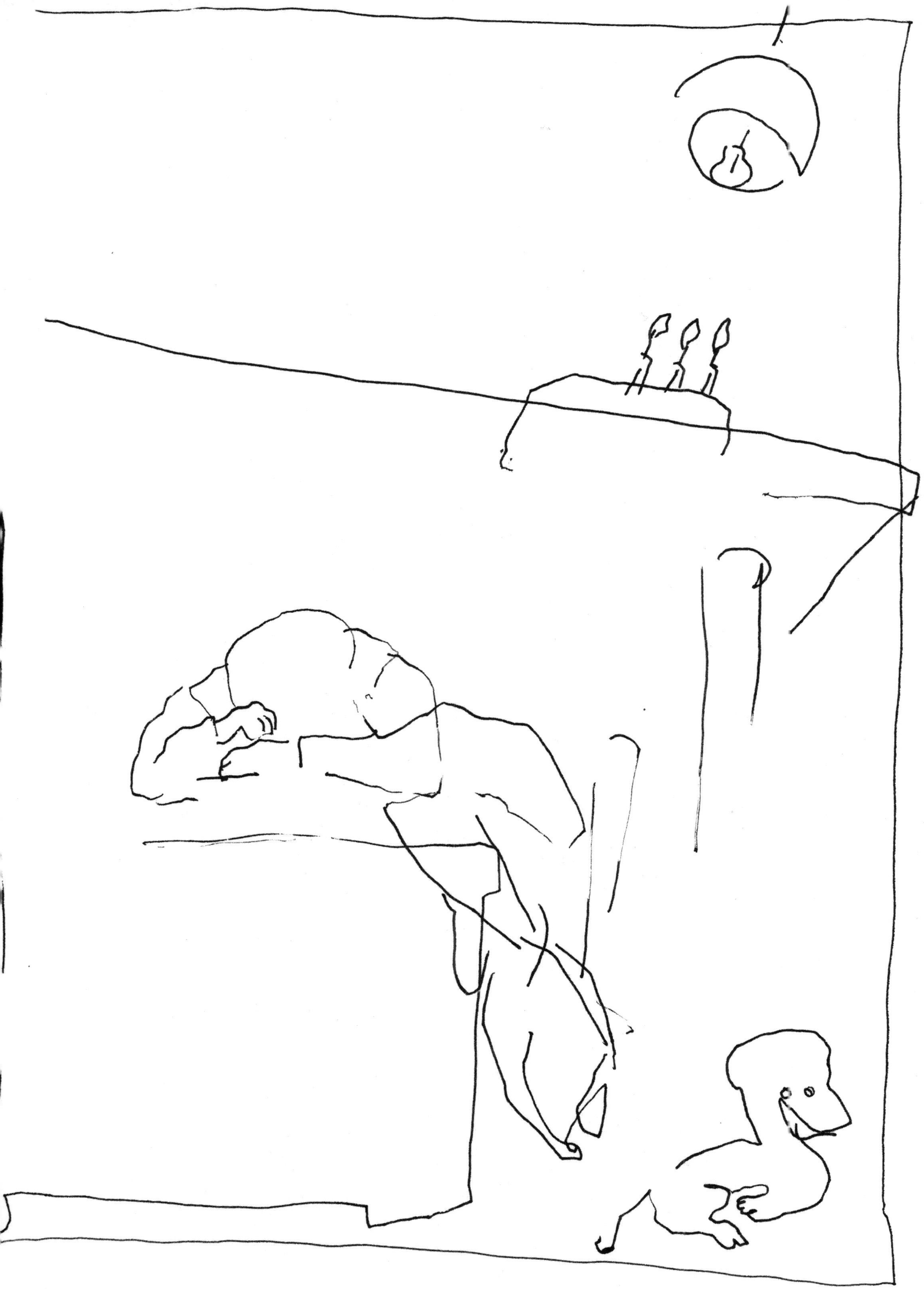

Enter Launcelot.

LAUNCELOT
Sola, sola! wo ha, ho! sola, sola!

LORENZO
Who calls?

LAUNCELOT
Sola! did you see Master Lorenzo?
Master Lorenzo! sola, sola!

LORENZO
Leave hollaing, man; here.

LAUNCELOT
Sola! where? where?

LORENZO
Here.

LAUNCELOT
Tell him there's a post come from my master, with his horn full of good news: my master will be here ere morning.

Exit.

LORENZO
Sweet soul, let's in, and there expect their coming.
And yet no matter; why should we go in?
My friend Stephano, signify, I pray you,
Within the house, your mistress is at hand;
And bring your music forth into the air.

Exit Stephano.

How sweet the moonlight sleeps upon this bank!
Here will we sit, and let the sounds of music
Creep in our ears: soft stillness and the night
Become the touches of sweet harmony.
Sit, Jessica: look, how the floor of heaven
Is thick inlaid with patines of bright gold:
There's not the smallest orb which thou behold'st
But in his motion like an angel sings,
Still quiring to the young-eyed cherubins;
Such harmony is in immortal souls;
But, whilst this muddy vesture of decay
Doth grossly close it in, we cannot hear it.

Enter Musicians.

Come, ho! and wake Diana with a hymn:
With sweetest touches pierce your mistress' ear,
And draw her home with music.

Music.

JESSICA
I am never merry when I hear sweet music.

LORENZO
The reason is, your spirits are attentive:
For do but note a wild and wanton herd,
Or race of youthful and unhandled colts,
Fetching mad bounds, bellowing and neighing loud,
Which is the hot condition of their blood;
If they but hear perchance a trumpet sound,
Or any air of music touch their ears,
You shall perceive them make a mutual stand,
Their savage eyes turn'd to a modest gaze
By the sweet power of music: therefore the poet
Did feign that Orpheus drew trees, stones, and floods;
Since nought so stockish, hard, and full of rage,
But music for the time doth change his nature.
The man that hath no music in himself,
Nor is not mov'd with concord of sweet sounds,
Is fit for treasons, stratagems, and spoils;
The motions of his spirit are dull as night,
And his affections dark as Erebus:
Let no such man be trusted. Mark the music.

All the acquaintances wait in the kitchen.
Outside the sun sinks,
Prussian blue light, and inside yolk yellow, but dimmed, not too much, getting dimmer still, almost no light, very dark, just right, and music also, but very quiet, a distinguished musician, so refined you can hardly hear.
The acquaintances are pacified, almost cheerful (in a tentative, subdued way).
They cannot really smile because of the serious disease.

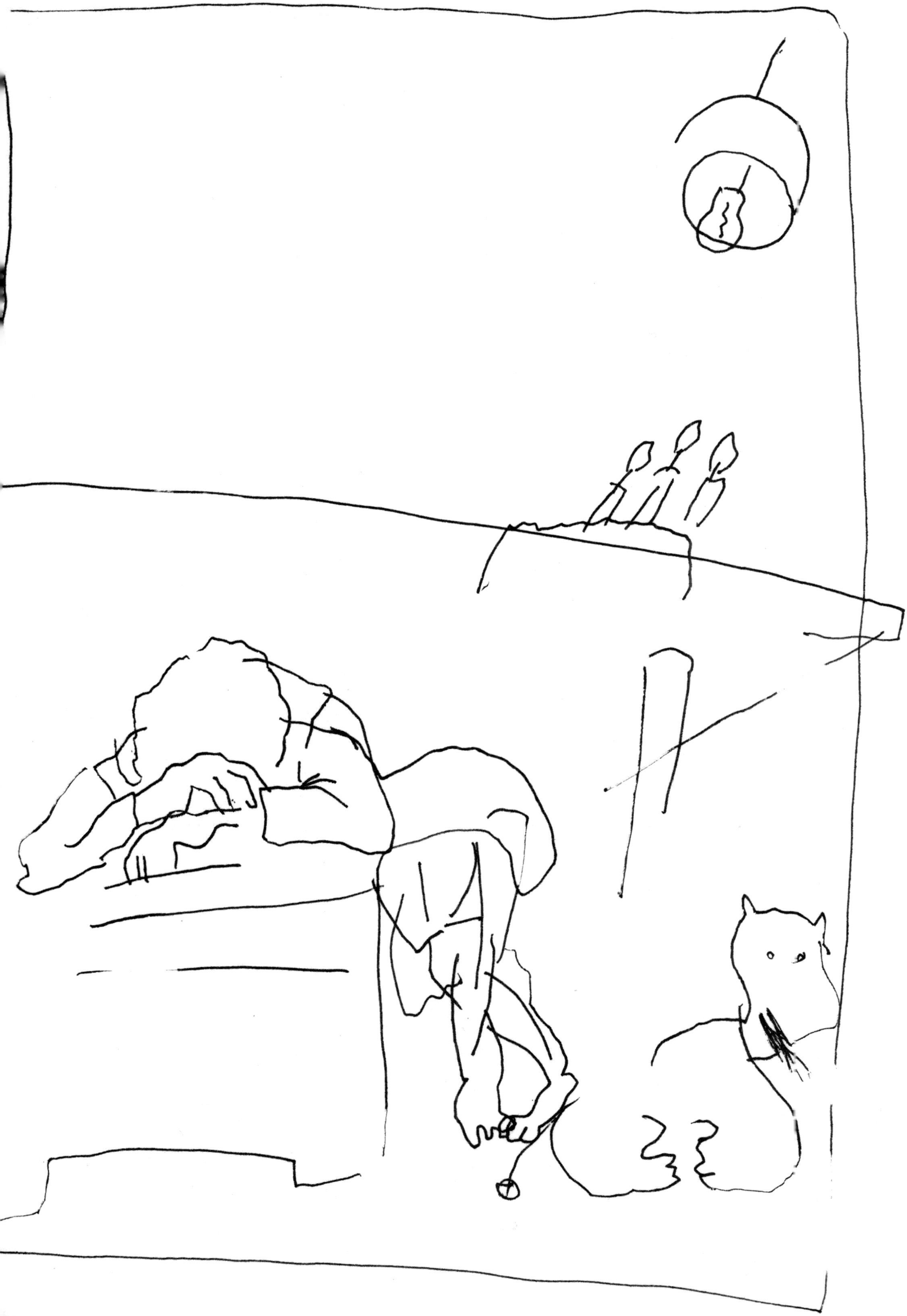

Enter Portia and Nerissa, at a distance.

PORTIA
That light we see is burning in my hall.
How far that little candle throws his beams!
So shines a good deed in a naughty world.

NERISSA
When the moon shone, we did not see the candle.

PORTIA
So doth the greater glory dim the less:
A substitute shines brightly as a king
Until a king be by, and then his state
Empties itself, as doth an inland brook
Into the main of waters. Music! hark!

NERISSA
It is your music, madam, of the house.

PORTIA
Nothing is good, I see, without respect:
Methinks it sounds much sweeter than by day.

NERISSA
Silence bestows that virtue on it, madam.

PORTIA
The crow doth sing as sweetly as the lark
When neither is attended, and I think
The nightingale, if she should sing by day,
When every goose is cackling, would be thought
No better a musician than the wren.
How many things by season season'd are
To their right praise and true perfection!
Peace, ho! the moon sleeps with Endymion,
And would not be awak'd!

Music ceases.

LORENZO
That is the voice,
Or I am much deceiv'd, of Portia.

PORTIA
He knows me, as the blind man knows the cuckoo,
By the bad voice.

LORENZO
Dear lady, welcome home.

PORTIA
We have been praying for our husbands' welfare,
Which speed, we hope, the better for our words.
Are they return'd?

LORENZO
Madam, they are not yet;
But there is come a messenger before,
To signify their coming.

PORTIA
Go in, Nerissa:
Give order to my servants that they take
No note at all of our being absent hence;
Nor you, Lorenzo; Jessica, nor you.

A tucket sounds.

LORENZO
Your husband is at hand; I hear his trumpet:
We are no tell-tales, madam; fear you not.

PORTIA
This night methinks is but the daylight sick;
It looks a little paler: 'tis a day,
Such as the day is when the sun is hid.

When I come into the kitchen, they all clap hands, carefully, for fear of breaking the glassware.
The other child is dumb.
The disease makes him move slowly, hardly move. As he moves, his skin breaks. His body shines with lubricants.
Still he claps.
They all clap.
I forgive and they leave.

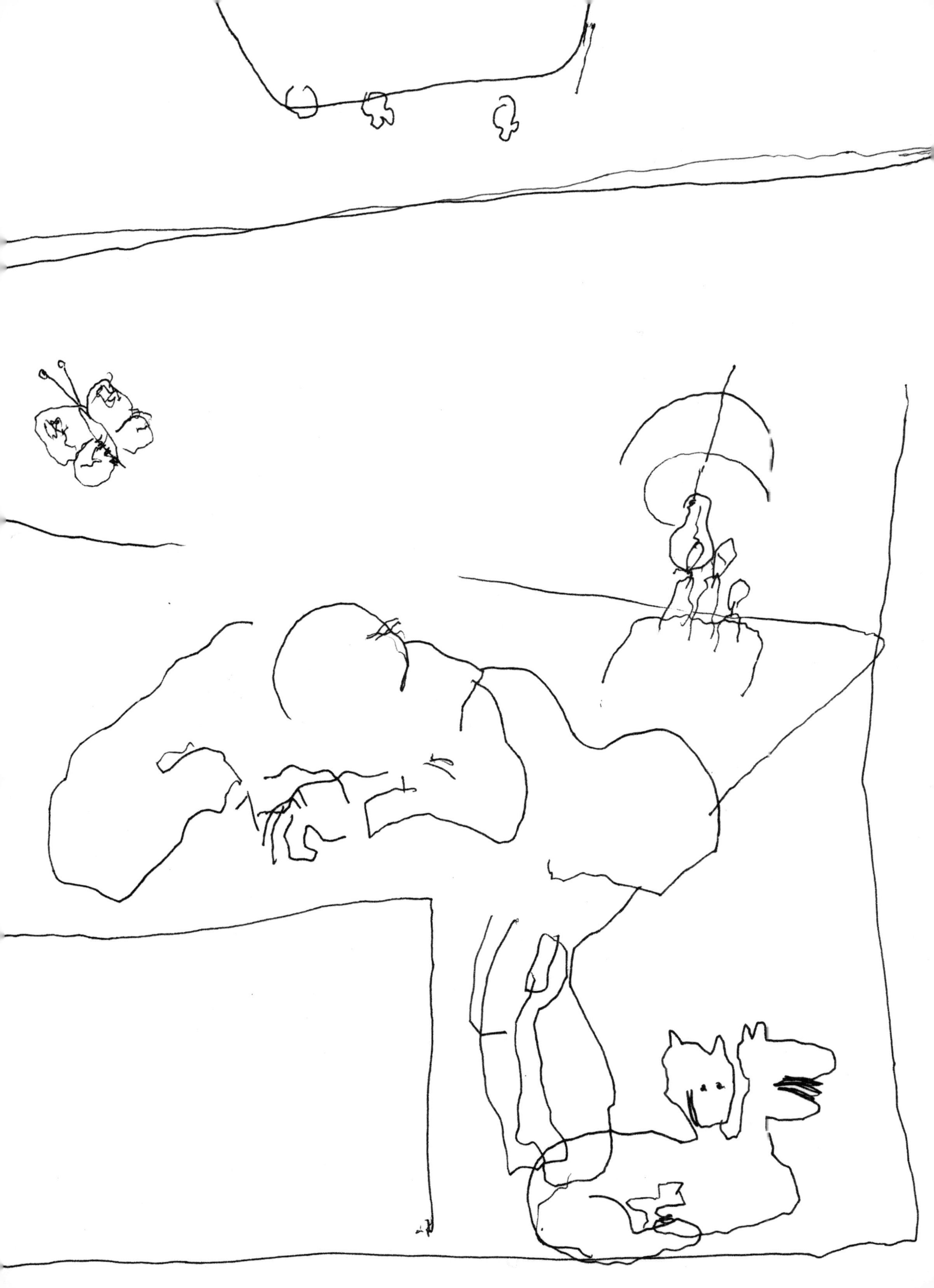

Enter Bassanio, Antonio, Gratiano, and their Followers.

BASSANIO
We should hold day with the Antipodes,
If you would walk in absence of the sun.

PORTIA
Let me give light, but let me not be light;
For a light wife doth make a heavy husband,
And never be Bassanio so for me:
But God sort all! You are welcome home, my lord.

BASSANIO
I thank you, madam. Give welcome to my friend:
This is the man, this is Antonio,
To whom I am so infinitely bound.

PORTIA
You should in all sense be much bound to him,
For, as I hear, he was much bound for you.

ANTONIO
No more than I am well acquitted of.

PORTIA
Sir, you are very welcome to our house:
It must appear in other ways than words,
Therefore I scant this breathing courtesy.

GRATIANO
[*To Nerissa.*] By yonder moon I swear you do me wrong;
In faith, I gave it to the judge's clerk:
Would he were gelt that had it, for my part,
Since you do take it, love, so much at heart.

PORTIA
A quarrel, ho, already! what's the matter?

GRATIANO
About a hoop of gold, a paltry ring
That she did give me, whose poesy was
For all the world like cutlers' poetry
Upon a knife, 'Love me, and leave me not.'

NERISSA
What talk you of the posy, or the value?
You swore to me, when I did give it you,
That you would wear it till your hour of death,
And that it should lie with you in your grave:
Though not for me, yet for your vehement oaths,
You should have been respective and have kept it.
Gave it a judge's clerk! no, God's my judge,
The clerk will ne'er wear hair on's face that had it.

GRATIANO
He will, an if he live to be a man.

NERISSA
Ay, if a woman live to be a man.

GRATIANO
Now, by this hand, I gave it to a youth,
A kind of boy, a little scrubbed boy,
No higher than thyself, the judge's clerk.
A prating boy, that begg'd it as a fee:
I could not for my heart deny it him.

Then my friend hugs me.
It gives me a pleasant sensation in the knees.
My arms feel supported.
I cling to him for a while.
Then he leaves. My friend will wait for me in the garden.
Then my wife is there.
She gives me a kiss. It tickles.
My wife will be in the other room.
We promised.
I am left with mother and father, the kitchen, warm, the cake, warm, the music, unheard.

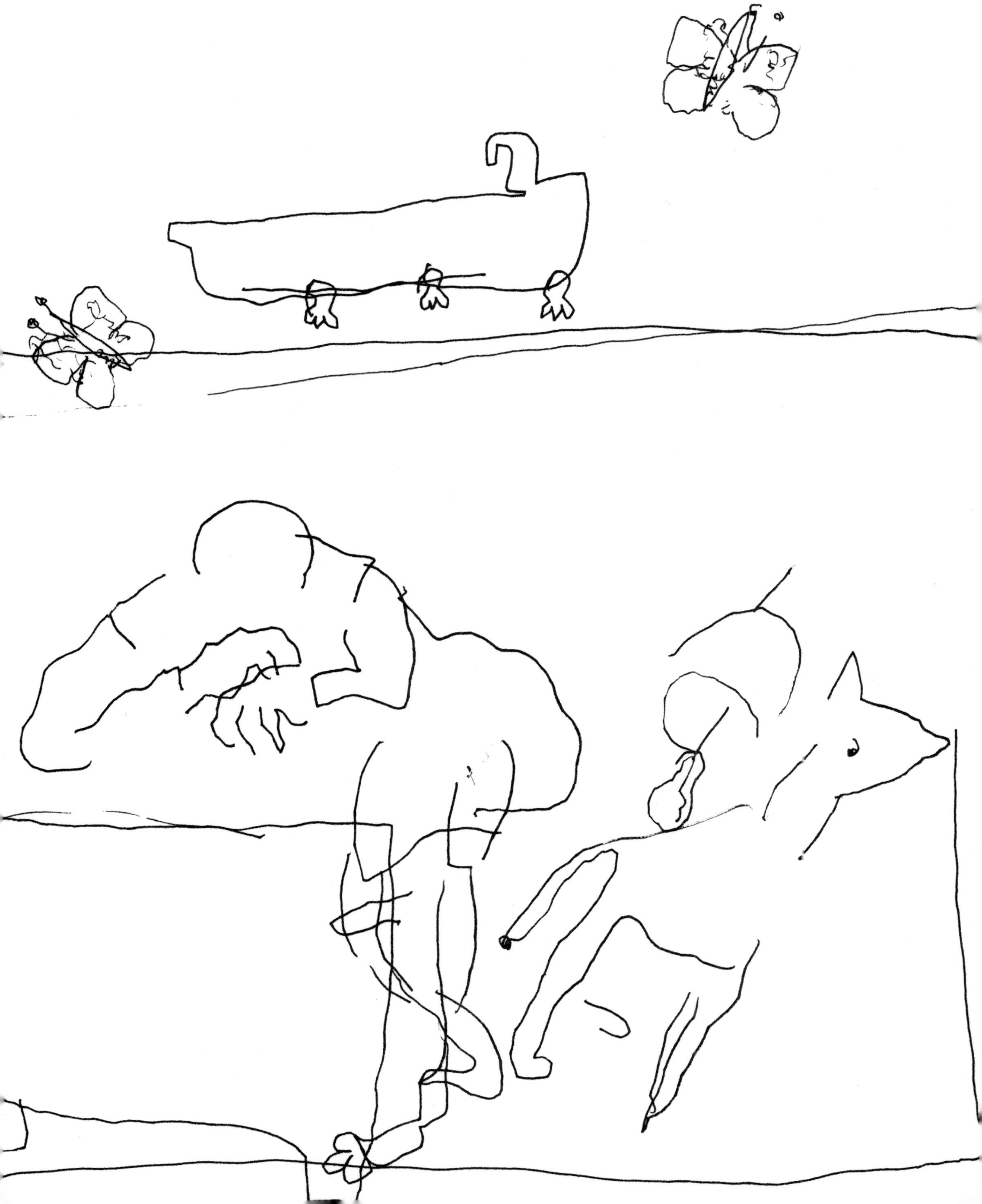

PORTIA
You were to blame,—I must be plain with you,—
To part so slightly with your wife's first gift;
A thing stuck on with oaths upon your finger,
And riveted so with faith unto your flesh.
I gave my love a ring and made him swear
Never to part with it; and here he stands,
I dare be sworn for him he would not leave it
Nor pluck it from his finger for the wealth
That the world masters. Now, in faith, Gratiano,
You give your wife too unkind a cause of grief:
An 'twere to me, I should be mad at it.

BASSANIO
[*Aside.*] Why, I were best to cut my left hand off,
And swear I lost the ring defending it.

GRATIANO
My Lord Bassanio gave his ring away
Unto the judge that begg'd it, and indeed
Deserv'd it too; and then the boy, his clerk,
That took some pains in writing, he begg'd mine;
And neither man nor master would take aught
But the two rings.

PORTIA
What ring gave you, my lord?
Not that, I hope, that you receiv'd of me.

BASSANIO
If I could add a lie unto a fault,
I would deny it; but you see my finger
Hath not the ring upon it; it is gone.

PORTIA
Even so void is your false heart of truth.
By heaven, I will ne'er come in your bed
Until I see the ring.

NERISSA
Nor I in yours,
Till I again see mine.

BASSANIO
Sweet Portia,
If you did know to whom I gave the ring,
If you did know for whom I gave the ring,
And would conceive for what I gave the ring,
And how unwillingly I left the ring,
When naught would be accepted but the ring,
You would abate the strength of your displeasure.

PORTIA
If you had known the virtue of the ring,
Or half her worthiness that gave the ring,
Or your own honour to contain the ring,
You would not then have parted with the ring.
What man is there so much unreasonable,
If you had pleas'd to have defended it
With any terms of zeal, wanted the modesty
To urge the thing held as a ceremony?
Nerissa teaches me what to believe:
I'll die for't but some woman had the ring.

BASSANIO
No, by my honour, madam, by my soul,
No woman had it; but a civil doctor,
Which did refuse three thousand ducats of me,
And begg'd the ring, the which I did deny him,
And suffer'd him to go displeas'd away;
Even he that did uphold the very life
Of my dear friend. What should I say, sweet lady?
I was enforc'd to send it after him;
I was beset with shame and courtesy;
My honour would not let ingratitude
So much besmear it. Pardon me, good lady,
For, by these blessed candles of the night,
Had you been there, I think you would have begg'd
The ring of me to give the worthy doctor.

I look up, at the table.
I can see the cake, like a ship, shiny, impeccable, patient.
Their smiles make me glow.
I know I glow.
Everything has a color.
Color this and color that. The colors are precise.

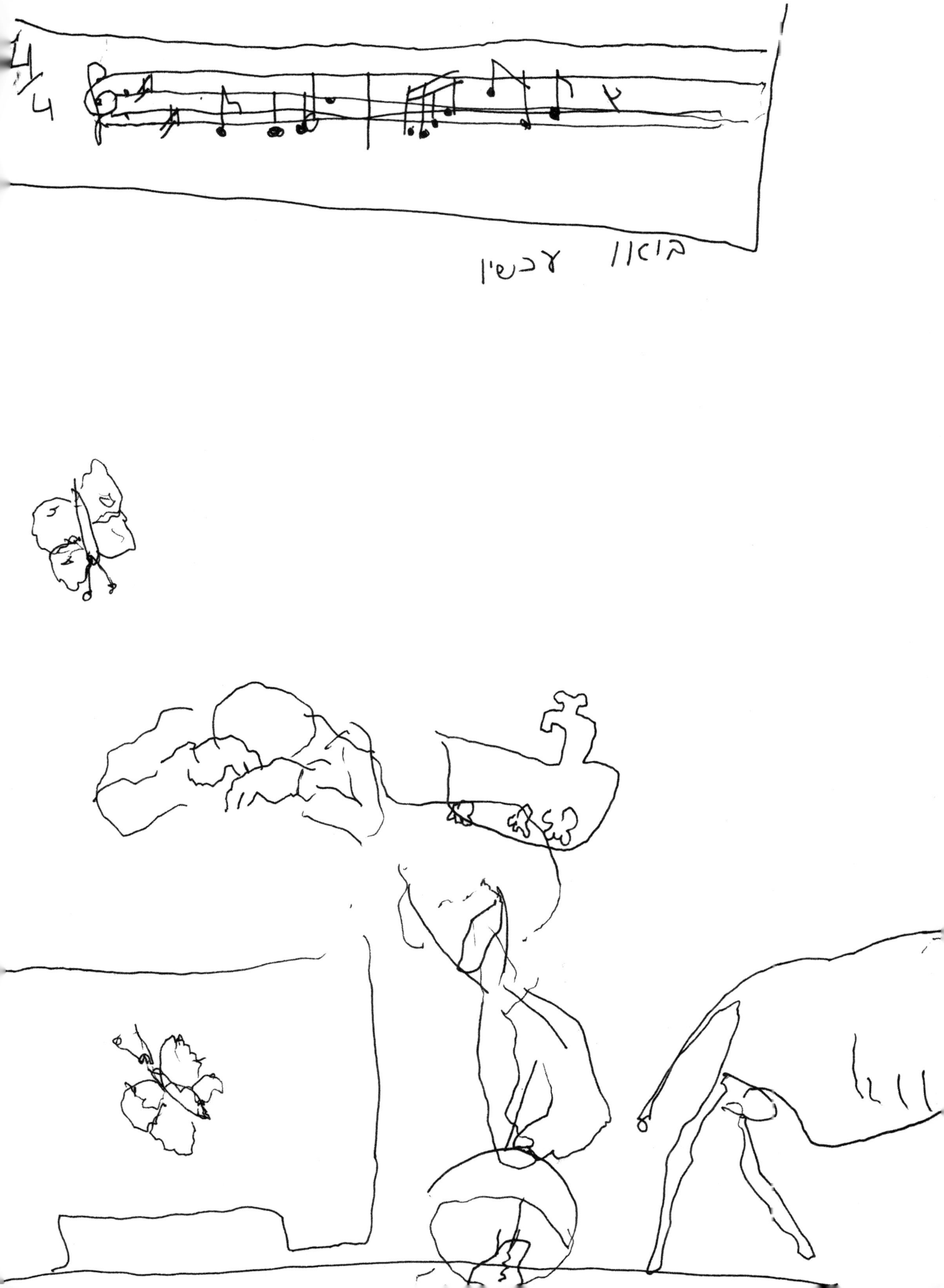
4/4
בואו עכשיו

PORTIA
Let not that doctor e'er come near my house.
Since he hath got the jewel that I lov'd,
And that which you did swear to keep for me,
I will become as liberal as you;
I'll not deny him anything I have;
No, not my body, nor my husband's bed.
Know him I shall, I am well sure of it:
Lie not a night from home; watch me like Argus:
If you do not, if I be left alone,
Now by mine honour, which is yet mine own,
I'll have that doctor for my bedfellow.

NERISSA
And I his clerk; therefore be well advis'd
How you do leave me to mine own protection.

GRATIANO
Well, do you so: let me not take him, then;
For if I do, I'll mar the young clerk's pen.

ANTONIO
I am the unhappy subject of these quarrels.

PORTIA
Sir, grieve not you; you are welcome notwithstanding.

BASSANIO
Portia, forgive me this enforced wrong;
And in the hearing of these many friends,
I swear to thee, even by thine own fair eyes,
Wherein I see myself,—

PORTIA
Mark you but that!
In both my eyes he doubly sees himself;
In each eye, one: swear by your double self,
And there's an oath of credit.

BASSANIO
Nay, but hear me:
Pardon this fault, and by my soul I swear
I never more will break an oath with thee.

ANTONIO
I once did lend my body for his wealth,
Which, but for him that had your husband's ring,
Had quite miscarried: I dare be bound again,
My soul upon the forfeit, that your lord
Will never more break faith advisedly.

PORTIA
Then you shall be his surety. Give him this,
And bid him keep it better than the other.

ANTONIO
Here, Lord Bassanio; swear to keep this ring.

BASSANIO
By heaven! it is the same I gave the doctor!

PORTIA
I had it of him: pardon me, Bassanio,
For, by this ring, the doctor lay with me.

NERISSA
And pardon me, my gentle Gratiano;
For that same scrubbed boy, the doctor's clerk,
In lieu of this last night did lie with me.

Then they sing for me.
I know the words.
Happy something something.
Something something dear something.
Happy something la la.
This is how I know safe.
I have no doubles.

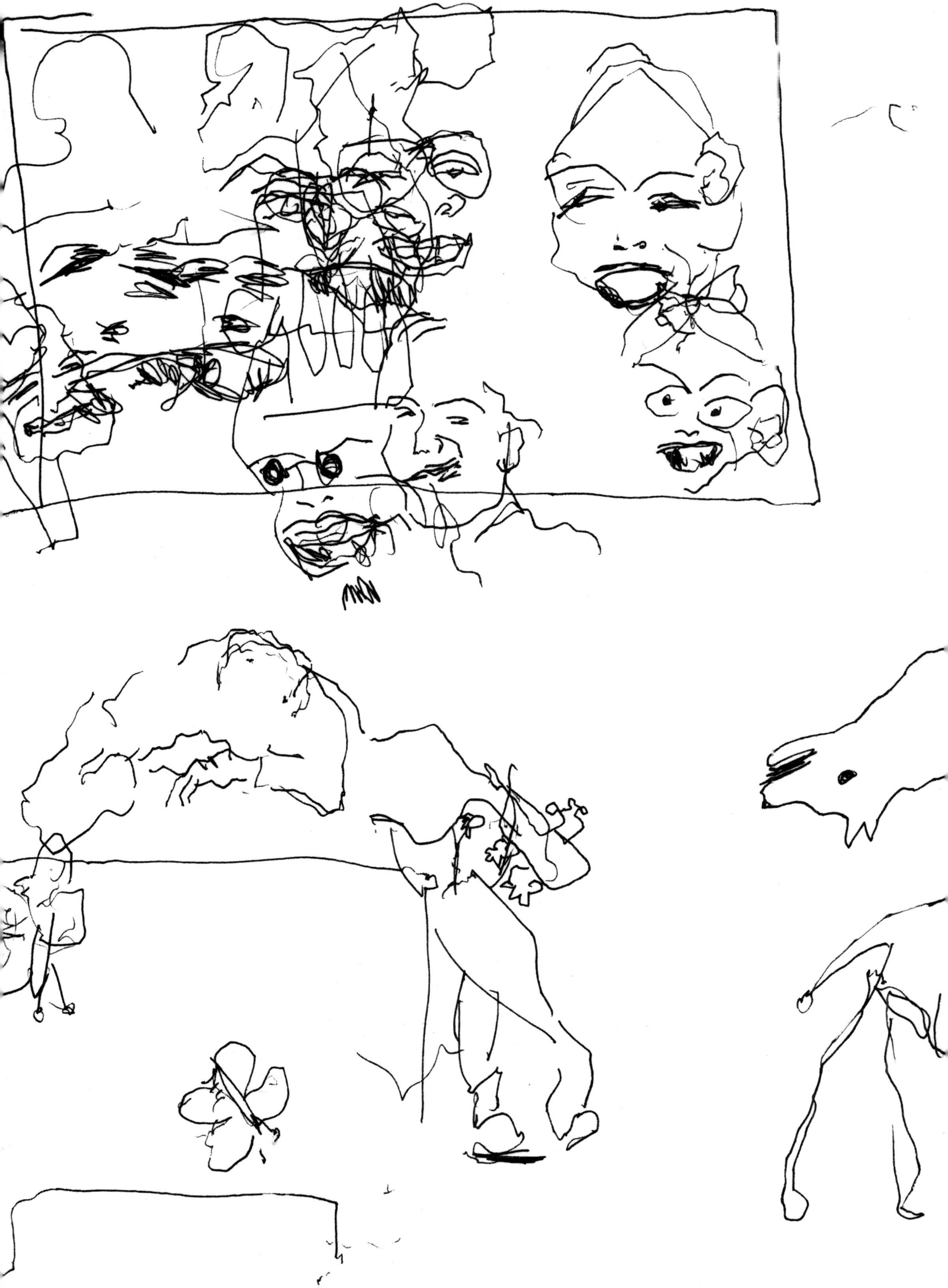

GRATIANO
Why, this is like the mending of highways
In summer, where the ways are fair enough.
What! are we cuckolds ere we have deserv'd it?

PORTIA
Speak not so grossly. You are all amaz'd:
Here is a letter; read it at your leisure;
It comes from Padua, from Bellario:
There you shall find that Portia was the doctor,
Nerissa, there, her clerk: Lorenzo here
Shall witness I set forth as soon as you
And even but now return'd; I have not yet
Enter'd my house. Antonio, you are welcome;
And I have better news in store for you
Than you expect: unseal this letter soon;
There you shall find three of your argosies
Are richly come to harbour suddenly.
You shall not know by what strange accident
I chanced on this letter.

ANTONIO
I am dumb.

BASSANIO
Were you the doctor and I knew you not?

GRATIANO
Were you the clerk that is to make me cuckold?

NERISSA
Ay; but the clerk that never means to do it,
Unless he live until he be a man.

BASSANIO
Sweet doctor, you shall be my bedfellow:
When I am absent, then, lie with my wife.

ANTONIO
Sweet lady, you have given me life and living;
For here I read for certain that my ships
Are safely come to road.

PORTIA
How now, Lorenzo!
My clerk hath some good comforts too for you.

NERISSA
Ay, and I'll give them him without a fee.
There do I give to you and Jessica,
From the rich Jew, a special deed of gift,
After his death, of all he dies possess'd of.

LORENZO
Fair ladies, you drop manna in the way
Of starved people.

PORTIA
It is almost morning,
And yet I am sure you are not satisfied
Of these events at full. Let us go in;
And charge us there upon inter'gatories,
And we will answer all things faithfully.

GRATIANO
Let it be so: the first inter'gatory
That my Nerissa shall be sworn on is,
Whe'r till the next night she had rather stay,
Or go to bed now, being two hours to day:
But were the day come, I should wish it dark,
That I were couching with the doctor's clerk.
Well, while I live I'll fear no other thing
So sore as keeping safe Nerissa's ring.

Exeunt.

How easy breathing is.
Air comes in and out,
almost unnoticed.
The same with details: almost
unnoticed, they were there, abundant,
unconstrained details.
Minute particulars.
All balanced.
One detail, just for example—
Leah's hair: brushed back, held back,
black, smooth.
There.
Or her eyes.
There is no dispute as to her details.

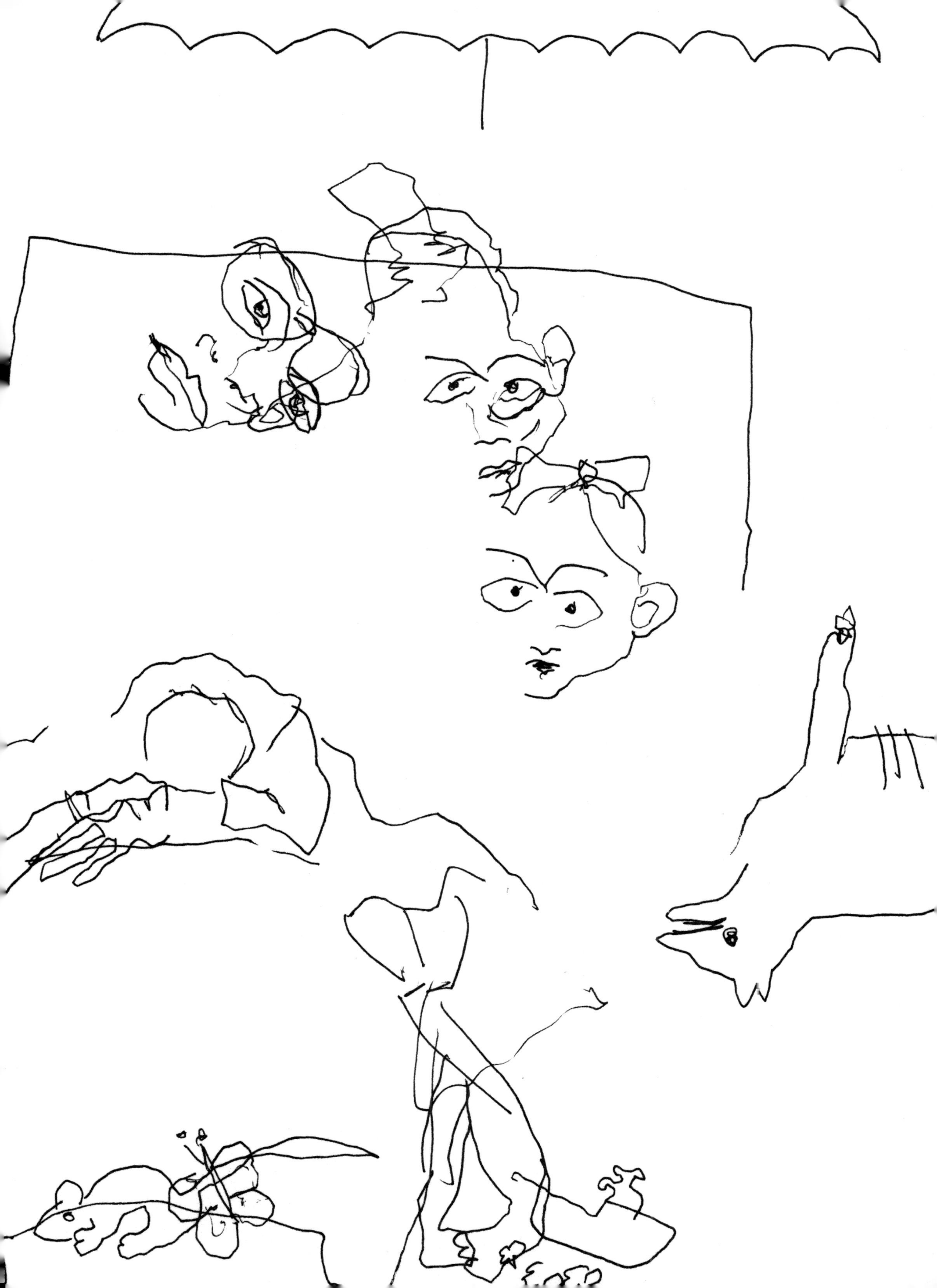

Or my shirt. White. White shirt with
short sleeves.
Short sleeved, blue shirt.
And my self-made glass,
which I made.
Now I give it now.
Happy something something.
Something something dear something
Happy something la la.
I know safe.
I know right. Don't go.

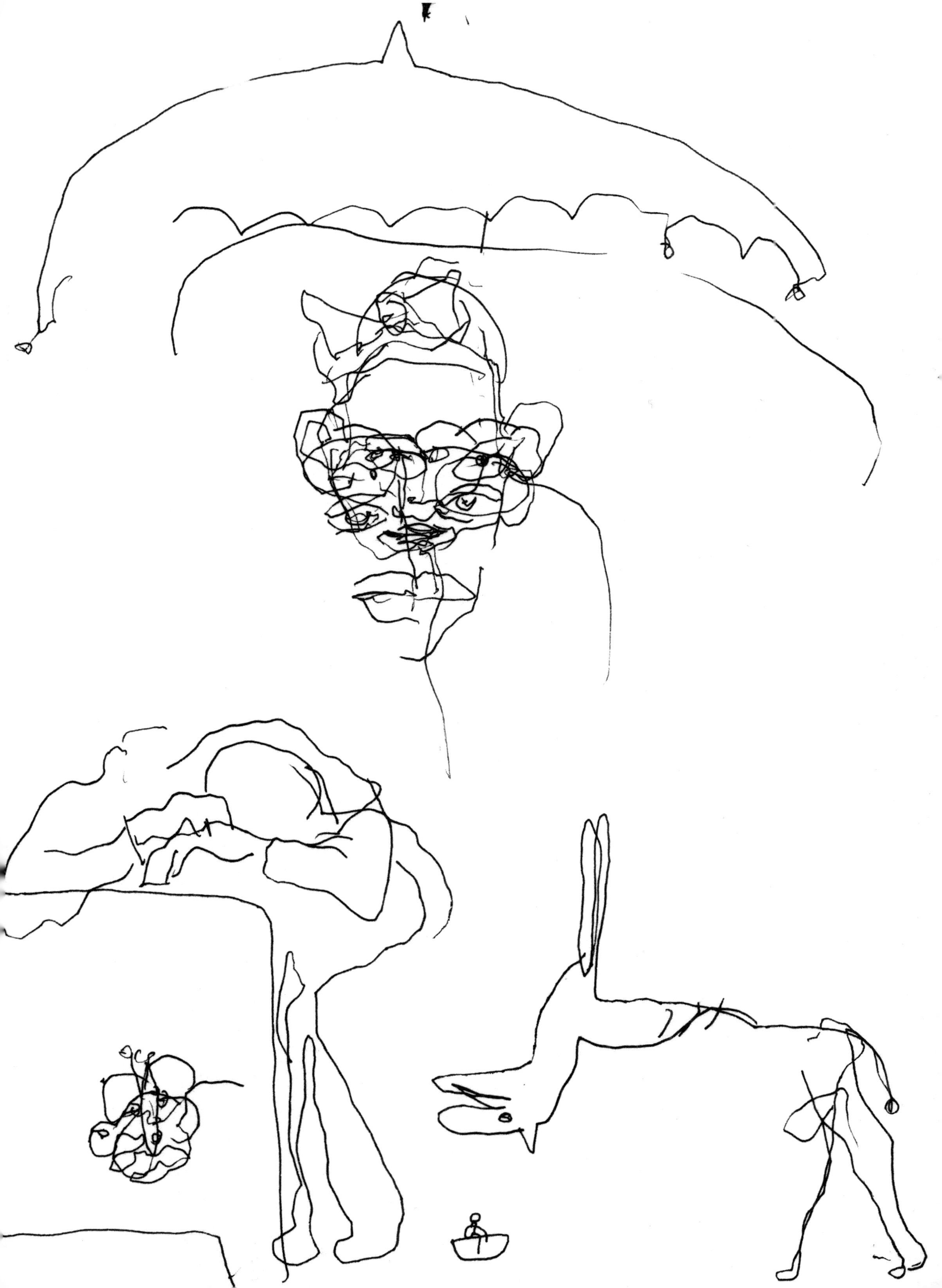

V.I.9

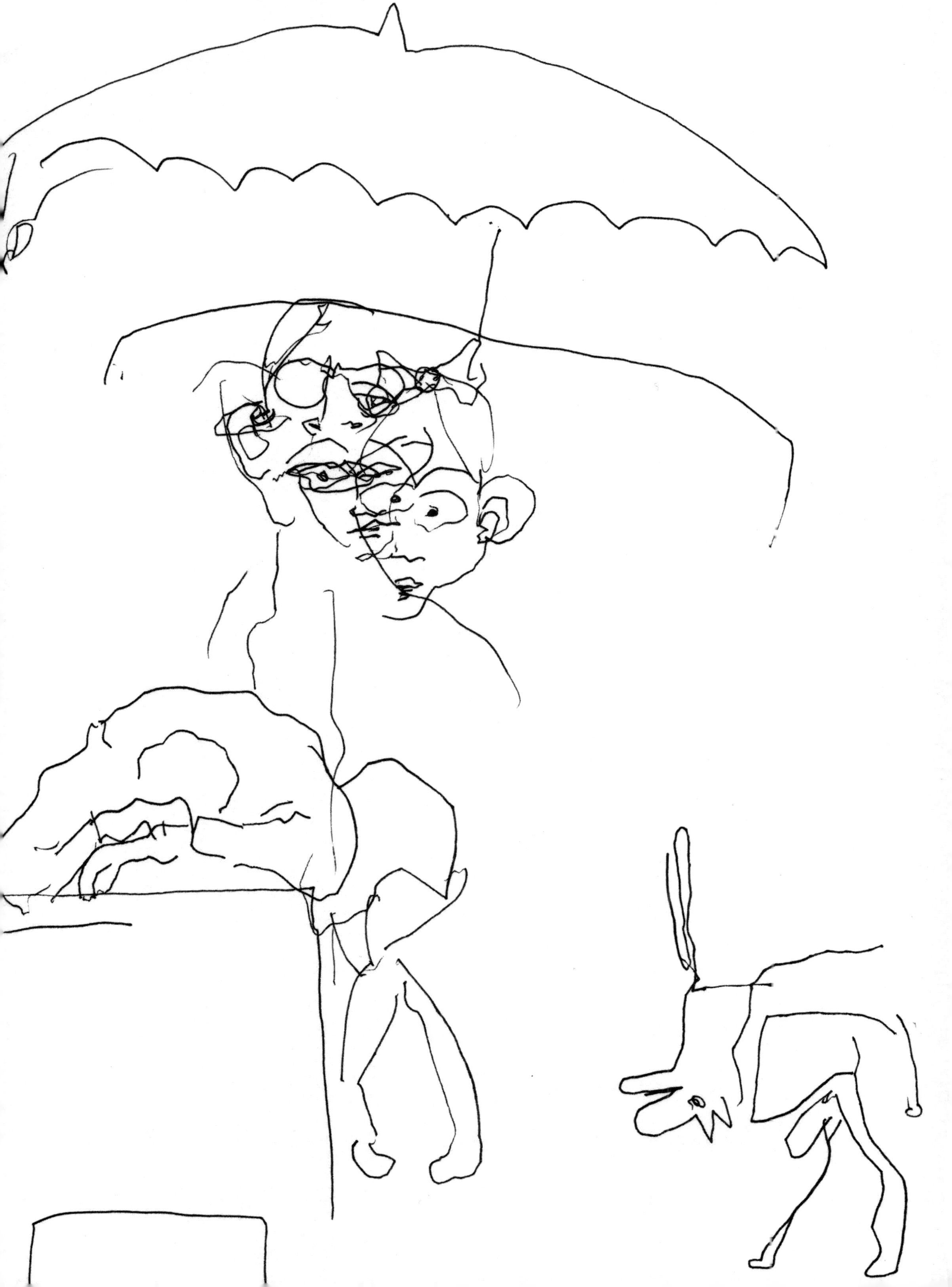

V.I.10

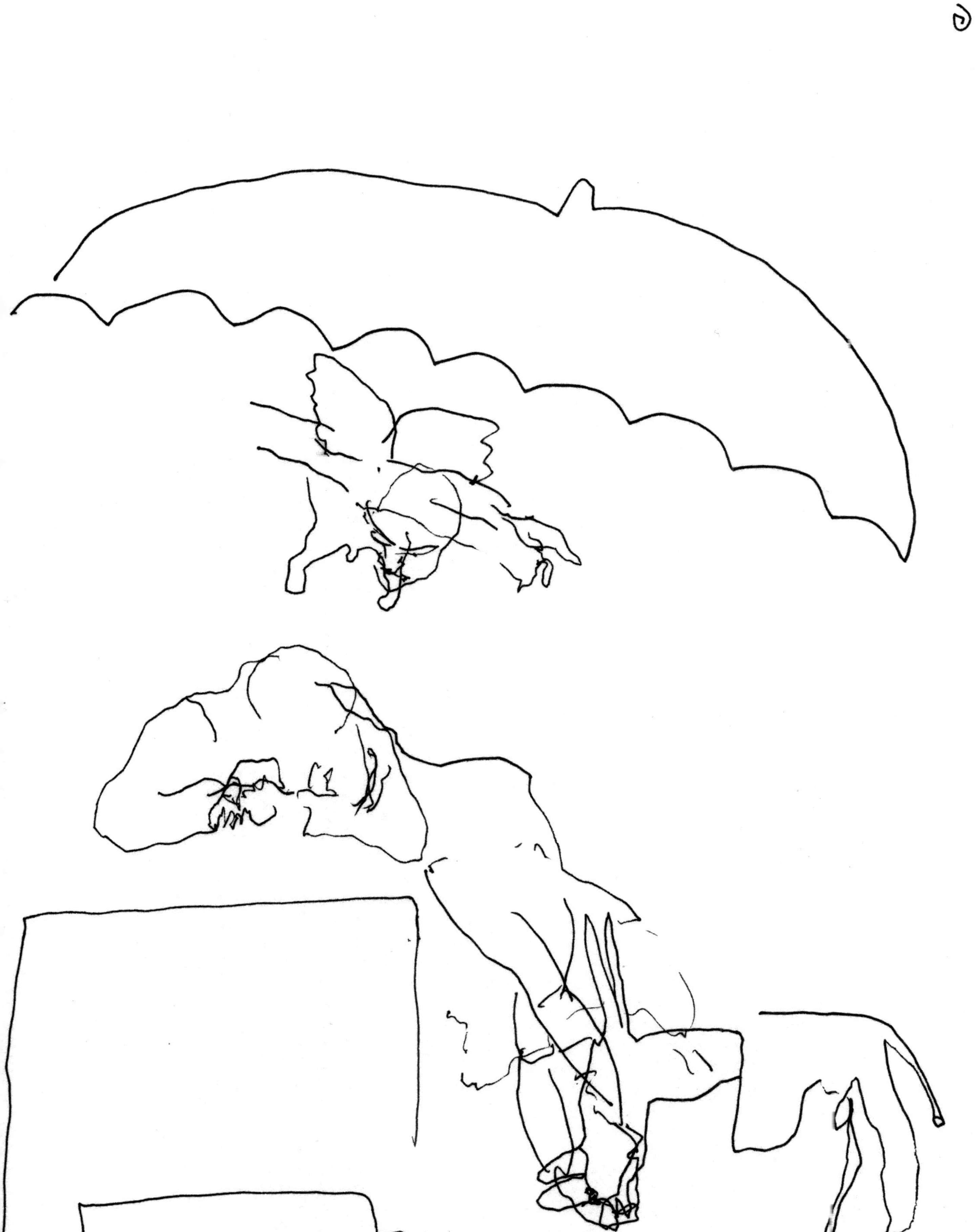

V.I.11

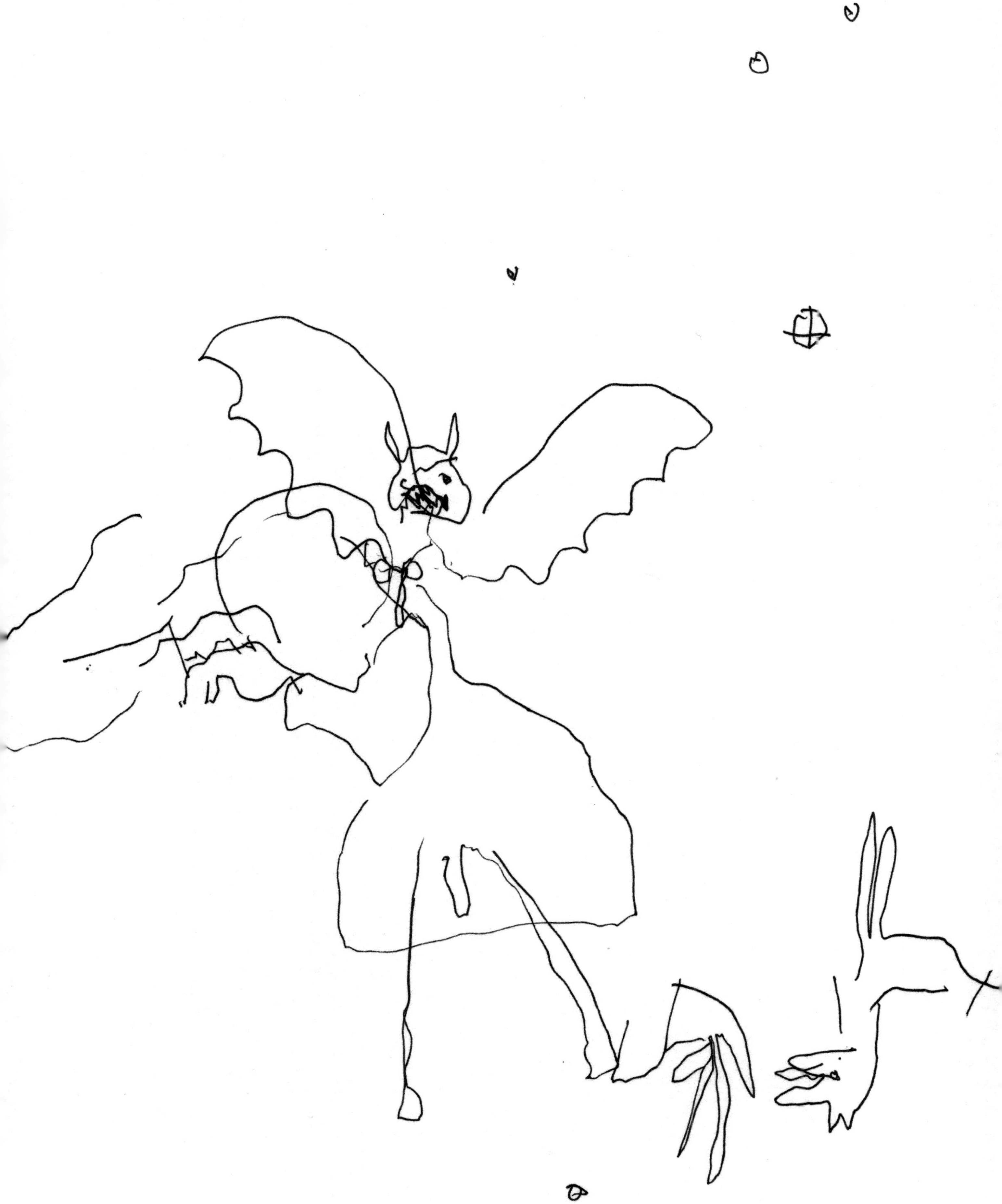

V.I.12

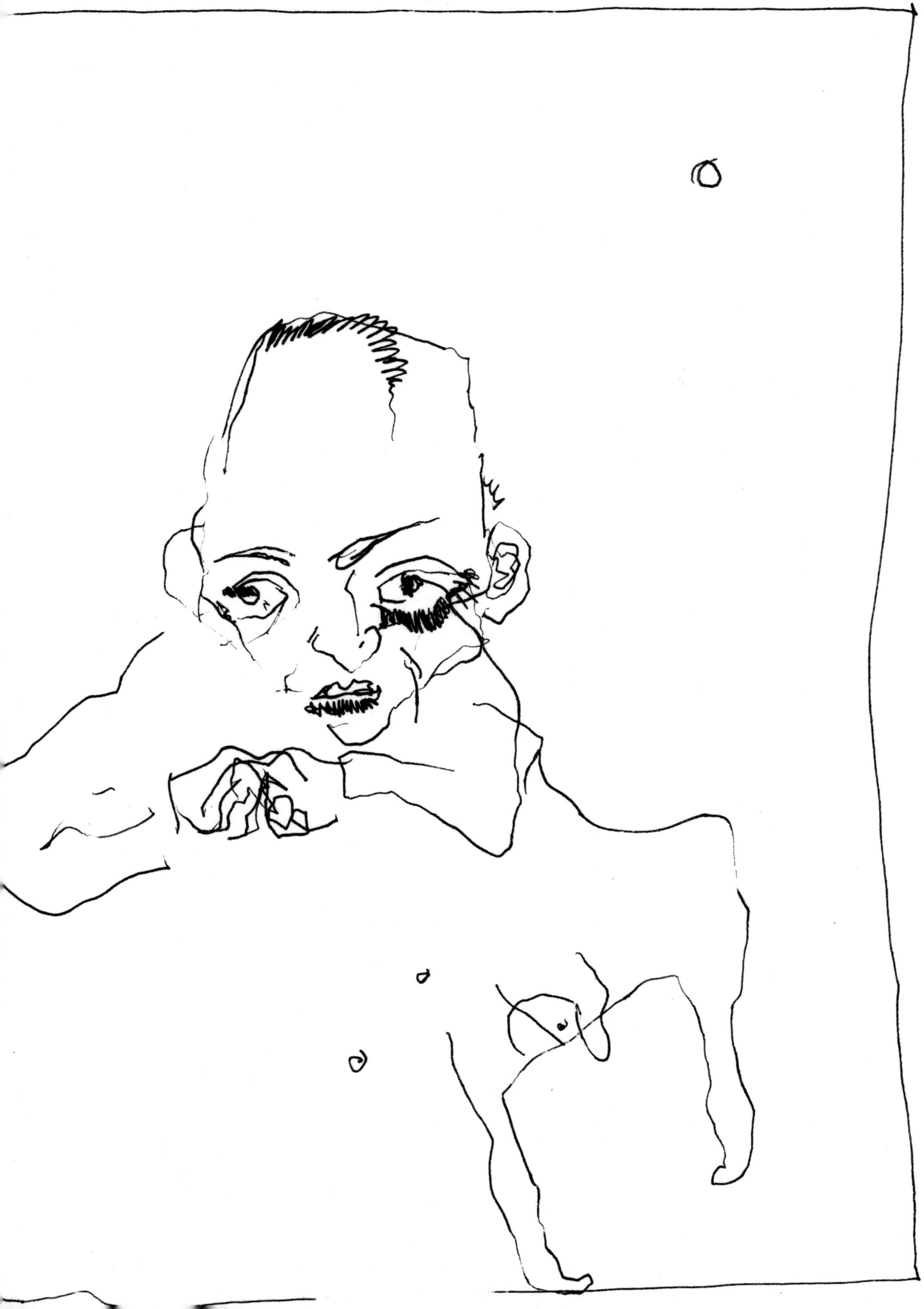

Roee Rosen
The Blind Merchant

Published by Sternberg Press

Graphic design: Rachel Kinrot
Print production: Ronny Rausnitz / Neo Production

ISBN 978-3-95679-186-4

Sternberg Press
Caroline Schneider
Karl-Marx-Allee 78
D-10243 Berlin
www.sternberg-press.com